A New Language for Psychoanalysis

A New Language for Psychoanalysis

Roy Schafer

New Haven and London, Yale University Press

1976

Published with assistance from the foundation
established in memory of Henry Weldon Barnes
of the Class of 1882, Yale College.

Designed by John O.C. McCrillis
and set in Baskerville type.
Printed in the United States of America by
The Murray Printing Co., Forge Village, Mass.

Published in Great Britain, Europe, and Africa by
Yale University Press, Ltd., London.
Distributed in Latin America by Kaiman & Polon,
Inc., New York City; in Australasia by Book &
Film Services, Artarmon. N.S.W., Australia;
in India by UBS Publishers' Distributors Pvt.,
Ltd., Delhi; in Japan by John Weatherhill,
Inc., Tokyo.

Contents

Acknowledgements

Above all I thank Dr. Robert L. Arnstein, Psychiatrist-in-Chief of the Division of Mental Hygiene, Yale University Health Services, for his making available to me the precious working time to devote to the preparation of this book; in this he drew generously on the financial resources granted to his Division by the Old Dominion Fund. I also acknowledge my great debt to the Foundation for Research in Psychoanalysis for providing the supplementary support I urgently needed to carry through this project.

I owe much to Drs. Merton M. Gill, Ernst Prelinger, and Jay Katz for the supportive interest and critical advice they provided along the way. Several philosophers—Edward S. Casey and Thomas H. Morawetz of Yale and Fay H. Sawyier of the Illinois Institute of Technology—did me the great favor of reading the work-in-progress and encouraging me to go on with it while freely making available their own expertise through stimulating questions and incisive criticisms; I learned a good deal from them and took their suggestions into account as best I could.

My thanks go also to the editors and publishers of *The International Journal of Psycho-Analysis, The Psychoanalytic Quarterly, The Psychoanalytic Study of the Child,* and *The Annual of Psychoanalysis* for their permission to reprint material that first appeared in these publications.

Mrs. Mary M. Petrini deserves a special expression of gratitude for the care and patience she showed in typing and retyping the manuscript of this book so many times; Mrs. Marie T. Meneely and Mrs. Anna M. Bishop pitched in ably to help get the job done.

Preface

This book comprises the bulk of what I wrote on psychoanalytic theory and interpretation during the years 1970-75. Although much of this material has already been published in psychoanalytic journals, the individual chapters do present a progression of thought that can be grasped and justly assessed only as a whole. This is to say that I have been engaged in only one project throughout this time—a reconceptualization of psychoanalysis in the terms of an action language. Viewed from the vantage point of the present, my previous book, *Aspects of Internalization,* now appears as a first step in this direction.

A reconceptualization is a new language in the sense of a new set of language rules; consequently, the nature of my enterprise has been as much philosophic as psychoanalytic. That this is the case became clearer and clearer to me as I continued my deliberations. My trepidation could not but increase as a result; for I am by training and experience a clinical psychologist and psychoanalyst and not a philosopher. My attempts to remedy this shortcoming in my preparation for, and execution of, this task have not, could not, make me a philosopher as well. I believe, however, that these attempts have helped me avoid serious errors in developing a systematic alternative to the established language of psychoanalysis, its metapsychology so-called. And I am confident that they have helped me overcome some of the serious philosophical problems embodied in this metapsychology.

In this connection, it is necessary to emphasize that in large part metapsychology itself is a philosophical enterprise; it, too, is a set of language rules, even though it has not usually been recognized as such. More specifically, metapsychological language presupposes a certain philosophy of science and a theory of knowledge. Freud's frequently expressed scorn of philosophy notwithstanding, in constructing his metapsychological theory of the mind he was engaged in a project in philosophical psychology. This much should become evident in the pages to follow. In like fashion it should become evident that the writings of Heinz Hartmann and other notable psychoanalytic theoreticians are instances of the same sort of project. The particular content with which Freud and the others were and are concerned is constituted by the methods and the observations of psychoanalytic work; this is the same content with which I remain steadily concerned throughout this book. What is in question is not the findings of psychoanalysis; it is the best language in which to render them and systematize them.

I have good reason to say, therefore, that my project of devising an action language to serve as a new language for psychoanalysis falls within the great and arduous tradition of systematic and clinically oriented psychoanalytic thinking, and that it is not, as would be suggested by the automatic conservative responses I have encountered on the part of some analytic colleagues, a retreat from "the body" and "the inner world," one that amounts to a virtual defection from Freudian psychoanalysis. I have been sustained in this belief by the interest and enthusiasm with which other psychoanalytic colleagues have greeted my ideas when I have presented them in publications, at meetings and workshops organized by various psychoanalytic societies and institutes, and at panel discussions held at national meetings of the American Psychoanalytic Association. Also, I have been encouraged to go on by the appearance in recent years of certain compatible and instructive writings by fellow psychoanalysts; I shall refer to these in appropriate places in the text. Additionally, there now exist a number of philosophical treatises on psychoanalysis that are generally, if not quite specifically, compatible with my views and from which I have gathered many useful ideas; these, too, I shall cite as I develop my argument. Finally, several philosophers familiar with my work have both encouraged me to go on with it and have made helpful suggestions.

In these different ways I have been reinforced in my belief that far from being a solitary undertaking, my revisionary work is part of a new critical movement concerned with the logic, language, implications, and applications of Freudian psychoanalysis. This movement is one that points not only toward a more unified psychoanalytic theory and a better understood, more consistent and effective clinical work: it points as well toward a new and fruitful interaction between psychoanalysis and all those intellectual disciplines concerned with the study of human beings as persons.

It is a large claim to make to say that I am developing a clinically useful and systematic alternative to metapsychology. But that is the only kind of claim that warrants my assembling these essays, more or less revising them, combining them with much new material, and representing the resulting book as unified and worthy of a reader's attention. It remains, as always, for the reader to judge whether, or to what extent, this claim is justified.

* * * * *

I plan to develop my argument in the following fashion. In part I, I shall set forth the primary rule of action language and some of its principal corollaries. This exposition should serve to orient the reader to the general nature of this new language. However, before going further with a direct and more detailed discussion of this language, I shall present several essays that constitute a preparation for the remainder of the book. This will be part II of the book. There I shall discuss first, under the general heading of the psychoanalytic vision of reality, different aspects of the view of existence, experience and personal change that has always been inherent in psychoanalytic interpretation. Secondly, in relation to the theoretical writings of Heinz Hartmann particularly, I shall conduct a critical examination of the presuppositions, lines of development, and inescapable problems of the traditional metapsychological language of psychoanalytic theory. Thirdly, I shall identify the mechanistic and anthropomorphic modes of thought that are essential and correlative aspects of metapsychological conceptualizations; in this connection I shall also attempt to examine the appeal of, and the problems associated with, newer concepts such as ego autonomy, identity, and self that some psychoanalysts have introduced and elaborated as contributions to this tradition.

In part III we shall again be concerned directly with action language. After first surveying the general theoretical and clinical aspects of action language, I shall go on to a series of studies of the strategically significant concepts of internalization, self and identity, psychodynamic explanation, and resistance. Then, in part IV, I shall present an extended critical discussion and revision, in terms of action and its modes, of the language of emotion. Because the emotions ("affects") have typically been discussed in terms of simplistic and unworkable assumptions about stimulus-response relations and body-mind relations, and because so many aspects of psychoanalytic theory have been tied to these assumptions, this crucial subject matter of psychoanalysis stands in need of a full-scale theoretical review and reformulation. In this connection I shall attempt to develop a logically consistent, integrated understanding of the correlative ideas of situation, action, emotion, and subjective experience in general; for in the course of discussing the emotions, it will become obvious that before one may use this new action language securely one must appreciate how these ideas logically depend on one another.

In part V, finally, I shall summarize the rules of action language that I have been concerned with throughout the book. I shall also offer some concluding remarks on the work that remains to be done in order to realize fully my objective of developing an alternative to metapsychology that is superior to it both logically and in its relation to the procedures and observations that make up our primary point of reference—clinical psychoanalysis.

A New Language for Psychoanalysis

Part I

Introduction

1 Metapsychology and Action Language

1. THE PROBLEM*

Freudian psychoanalysts can no longer afford to maintain unchallenged the conviction that psychoanalytic propositions must be formulated in the terms of Freud's metapsychology or in terms compatible with it. Indeed, it is high time we stopped using this mixed physicochemical and evolutionary biological language altogether. I am referring to the eclectic language of, on the one hand, force, energy, cathexis, mechanism, and sublimation or neutralization and, on the other hand, function, structure, drive, object, and adaptation.

We shall, however, be disappointed if, when we stop using this language, we trust that some fortunate combination of clear thinking, common sense, clinical experience, humanistic sentiments, and judicious selection of key concepts, such as self or intentionality or relationship, will constitute a sound basis for new and better theoretical developments. We shall be on much firmer ground if, before we abandon metapsychology, we have at least a rudimentary version of another language to replace it. More than omission, we require new elements and a new ordering of them.

Up to the present time, we have lacked this alternative. Melanie Klein and her so-called English School have not provided it, having instead carried the reifications of metapsychology to a grotesque extreme. In contrast, Sullivan, Horney, and other neo-Freudians have, in attempting to make do with a fundamentally commonsensical and humanistic type of discourse, never been conceptually rigorous and systematic; that is to say, they have not imposed on themselves the creative discipline of adhering firmly to definite language rules. The writings of the existential analysts suffer from this same defect;

*This section is a modified version of one portion of my article, "Psychoanalysis without Psychodynamics" which first appeared in the *International Journal of Psycho-Analysis*, 56 (1975): 41-55 (see also chapter 10).

for in these we typically encounter quasi-literary tours de force urged on us as both a better kind of theory and a superior form of humanity. Triumphant style, the apt phrase, the problematic non-clinical example, however suggestive they may be, do not make a system. I should add, however, that I am referring to the systematic *defects* of these alternative approaches; for Freudian psychoanalysts have been steadily, if not always graciously, assimilating what is *best* in them, such as their insights into preoedipal fantasy life and object relations, the constitutive influence of the social environment, and the importance of discovering each person's experiential-representational life themes and then working out the right "language" for his or her representative situations and projects. These assimilations make up a large part of the current concerns of Freudian ego psychology.

In referring to metapsychology as a language, I am following Wittgenstein's conception of language as a set of rules for saying things of the sort that constitute or communicate a version of reality or a world. Here, I shall note two important points only in passing: one is that the words *constitute* and *communicate* have the same meaning in this context (Pears 1969), and the other is that, for psychoanalytic purposes, the idea of reality must be understood to include psychic reality, too.

It is only by means of sets of language rules that we are ever able to achieve a systematic approach to knowing anything, including knowing anything psychoanalytically. By adopting these rules, we establish what shall count as facts, factual coherence, and ascriptive limits; thereby we also establish the criteria of consistency and relevance in our psychological discussions. The great appeal and the considerable, though rapidly diminishing, value of Freud's mixture of the physico-chemical and biological languages of his time have stemmed largely from its being a language in this sense. As psychoanalysts, we have known how to talk about our observations in its terms. We have acquired competence in developing the implications of these terms and in extending their applications. Consequently, the psychoanalytic knowledge we claim to possess has always existed in these very terms. So much is this so that this knowledge has seemed to us *pre*conceptual; that is, it has seemed to be a body of facts about which we have theorized only *after* having discovered and studied them. But the truth is that these "facts" have always been as much created as found. As I understand them, modern theorists of knowledge, unlike the positivistic ones of Freud's formative era, would generally accept some version of this argument. Thus, to give only one instance, the contemporary historian, Carr, agrees with one of Pirandello's characters: "A fact is like a sack—it won't stand up till you've put something in it" (1961, p. 9).

That Freud had a partial grasp of the idea of a metalanguage as a set of rules (though he still regarded the phenomena as simply given) is evident in the following unequivocal and succinct statement he made about his theorizing (it is from his "Introductory Lectures on Psycho-Analysis"):

> I need ask you to bear in mind as a model the manner in which we have treated these phenomena. From this example you can learn the aims of our psychology. We seek not merely to describe and to clarify phenomena, but to understand them as signs of an interplay of forces in the mind, as a manifestation of purposeful intentions working concurrently or in mutual opposition. We are concerned with a *dynamic view* of mental phenomena. On our view the phenomena that are perceived must yield in importance to trends which are only hypothetical (1916b, p. 67, Freud's italics).

The appeal of metapsychology stems not only from its being a formalized language, but also from its being congruent with the archaic bodily language of infancy. That language has long pervaded the live and dead metaphors of everyday speech. For example, "She spoke from the heart," "Those thoughts keep crowding in on me," and, "He is an empty person." This bodily language is concretistic; that is to say, it is organized around substantive designations of immaterial phenomena and processes, and around such corollaries of these substantive designations as location, movement, impulsion, quantity, impact, and mass. It is also relatively deficient in terms that define the child as the agent of its actions. In the first years of life, ideas about oneself and others are inconsistant, diffuse, and unstably, if at all, differentiated. Freud showed how the child perpetuates its concretistic, poorly differentiated, archaic bodily orientation to the world by repressing much of it and then carrying it forward into what is called variously the *Un-*

conscious, the *Id,* and the *primary process thinking* of the adult. Our notions of internal, external, boundaries, thresholds, damming up, and discharging—all these and many others—may be viewed as a psychosexual bodily language inappropriately elevated to the status of theoretical terms. (I shall develop this point further in chapter 8, especially.)

Thus it is that to stop using Freud's theoretical language is to alter radically our relations with this most intricate, intimate, pervasive, and consequential set of mental categories and operations as well as with language traditions that long antedate the tradition of Newtonian, Cartesian, and Darwinian models of mind within which Freud fashioned his eclectic mode of conceptualization.

What is to be done? It seems that to succeed in replacing the established metapsychology with another language, we shall have to devise one by which we can continue to render that sense of being of the people of our civilization that is based on both their personal and their communal history. Further, we shall have to compose this alternative language out of words which, through common use, we have already endowed, even though not always as richly, with significant and extensive personal connotations. I do not quite mean that it is to be a language *within* our everyday language; nor do I quite mean that it is to be an altogether *new way* of using our language; and certainly I do not mean that we are to begin coining *new words.* To put what I mean affirmatively: for purposes of psychological describing and explaining, we shall have to codify certain usages that are familiar, direct, evocative, and plastic; additionally, the language must be personal and must provide a basis for some kind of eloquence. Only this achievement will give it a reasonable chance of being accepted and used. And we shall have to develop and apply this codification tirelessly and unflinchingly; for, if we do not obey the rules, we shall not really know or speak the language, and in the end we shall not have a single, coherent world to be psychoanalytic about. In the long run, it is one's fidelity to the rules that makes all the difference in systematic thinking. Here, one cannot be too faithful or fastidious. That this is so is evident from the painstaking work of Hartmann, Rapaport, and their coworkers and students; for it is they who produced the ultimate refinement of Freud's metapsychology (see, e.g., Hartmann 1964, and Rapaport 1967). It must, of course, be a fidelity and fastidiousness based not on authority but on understanding and on the intellectual currents of the present era.

It is a tall order. Far more than Freud's metapsychology, we shall be setting aside age-old modes of thought that so inform personal development and social communication as to seem to us the very material of human existence. But what are the alternatives? We might stay with the established language, despite some dissatisfaction with it, on the argument that it has been useful in the past, that we have organized a considerable amount of experience in its terms, and that it is therefore better than newly improvised systems with doubtful futures. But this alternative entails continuing eclectically to subordinate new ideas and fresh alternatives to old solutions. Many psychoanalysts have chosen this alternative. Another alternative is to abandon all interest in systematization—privately, if not explicitly. But this course of action merely opens one up to haphazard and ultimately confused discourse.

A choice in this matter is not, as some would argue, simply a question of taste, style, or so-called character make-up. It is a response to serious challenges directed against the adequacy, the inevitability, the logical consistency, and the heuristic value of all Freudian propositions. The necessity to make a choice thus exists impersonally. Consequently, we may evaluate the choice made in a like manner. Each of us does choose, and it is best to acknowledge that we do so. As in clinical psychoanalysis, by acknowledging one's choices, however poor they may be, one makes a significant advance beyond insisting defensively, perhaps depressively, that there is no choice, that presuppositions about unalterable reality or fixed necessity must remain unquestioned, and that personal transformation is out of the question. In his statement that I quoted earlier, Freud showed his awareness that there is a choice to be made in this regard.

For my part, I have chosen to attempt to develop an alternative to the eclectic language of mechanism, force, structure, etc. It is an action language that I shall describe shortly. I believe that this alternative satisfies the criteria I mentioned earlier, such as developmental, historical, and cultural relevance together with actual and potential communicative richness. It will be obvious that, in developing it, I have used, as best I could, certain ideas culled from modern philosophical writings on existentialism, phenomenology, mind, and action; e.g., by Binswanger (1936, 1946), Sartre (1943), Wittgenstein (1934-35), Ryle (1949), and others. These writings have all been, in effect if not by design, contributions to the development of some alternative to the premodern language of mind used by Freud. (See now also Edelson's [1972] employment of modern linguistics in relation to the psychology of dreams.)

I have devised my alternative specifically for us human beings. We show properties of mental functioning that cannot be attributed to any other creature. We are unique in existing culturally and intellectually through a language that embraces self, other, time, metaphor, hypotheticals, mortality, and so forth. Therefore, we must build our discontinuity with respect to all other species into any psychological theory we attempt.

My alternative allows us to continue taking into account the significance of bodily processes, both reactive and maturational. Now, however, we shall do so from the vantage point of personal actions, and we shall neither work in terms of presuppositions about psychoeconomics of a Newtonian cast nor burden ourselves with biological commitments of a Darwinian cast to explain and guarantee the continuity of the species. That people are creatures cannot be overemphasized; but it is only human symbol-using intelligence that can take that creaturehood into account. Many of Freud's monumental developmental propositions are in the form I am recommending; that is, they express those phase-specific, pervasive, and enduring human conceptions of body, body parts, other bodies, persons ("objects"), pleasure, pain, and other such variables, as these are constituted by human intelligence from the time of early childhood on.

In devising my alternative, I have also attempted to clarify and enhance that feature of psychoanalytic interpretation from which its transformative significance stems. As I shall argue especially in chapters 3 and 7, interpretation brings home to the analysand the extent to which, and the terms in which, the analysand has been the author of his or her own life, unconsciously and preconsciously as well as consciously; at the same time, it brings home the extent to which, and the terms in which, the analysand has been disclaiming this activity. And what is more distinctively human than psychoanalytic inter-pretation?

At this point I shall set forth the fundamental rule of this action language and discuss some of its consequences. In parts III and IV, I shall develop in some detail the application of this rule to such strategically significant theoretical terms and their clinical referents as conflict, mind, internalization, resistance, psychodynamics, and affects. The full sense of my enterprise will emerge only in the course of these discussions. Additional language rules will be developed in the appropriate contexts. Finally, in part V, I shall present and discuss the set of rules of action language that I shall have developed up to that point. It is more than likely that these rules will require some revision and supplementation in the future. For the time being, how-ever, the immediately following discussion should provide an adequate orientation to the reconceptualizations of psycho-analytic terms and propositions that follow.

2. THE FUNDAMENTAL RULE OF ACTION LANGUAGE

(1) We shall regard each psychological process, event, ex-perience, or behavior as some kind of activity, henceforth to be called action, and shall designate each action by an active verb stating its nature and by an adverb (or adverbial locution), when applicable, stating the mode of this action.

Adopting this rule entails that, insofar as it is possible to do so sensibly, we shall not use nouns and adjectives to refer to psychological processes, events, etc. In this, we should avoid substantive designations of actions as well as adjectival or traitlike designations of modes of action. Thus, we should not use such phrases as "a strong ego," "the dynamic uncon-scious," "the inner world," "libidinal energy," "rigid defense," "an intense emotion," "autonomous ego function," and "in-stinctual drive." This radical departure from accustomed desig-nations is what it takes really to discontinue physicochemical and biological modes of psychological thinking. The essential referents of these designations will, however, be preserved in other terms.

We must understand the word action to include all private psychological activity that can be made public through gesture and speech, such as dreaming and the unspoken thinking of everyday life, as well as all initially public activity, such as ordinary speech and motoric behavior, that has some goal-directed or symbolic properties. Whether initially private or public, the activity may be pursued unconsciously. What we must exclude as psychologically inaccessible is only what is altogether unutterable or on the level of biological reflex; no doubt, there will remain some difficult borderline cases.

On this basis it can be claimed that this action language is not a behavioristic language in any usual sense of that designation; for it includes everything that psychoanalytic propositions have included from the beginning. Rather, the difference lies in this, that in certain respects we shall speak about people more plainly, and, while continuing to emphasize action in the unconscious mode, we shall neither engage in speculation about what is ultimately unutterable in any form nor build elaborate theories on the basis of unfalsifiable propositions concerning mental activity at the very beginning of infancy. Attributions of meaning and thus of action reach a vanishing point as one moves back toward that period of life (see in this regard Escalona 1968).

Simply to illustrate the type of verb-adverb formulation I mean, I offer the following statements: "She resolutely strives to perceive her situation objectively;" "He makes sure never to think of how sensuously he engages in competition;" "Unfailingly, though still apprehensively, she avoids remembering those events of her childhood to which she reacted in a traumatized fashion;" "He carries out his sadistic practices unconsciously;" and "Preconsciously, she defers to those in authority sullenly."

It is necessary, next, to state and discuss four consequences of adopting the rule of using verbs and adverbs in place of substantives and adjectives. Each of these consequences or corollaries is another rule of action language.

(1a) When speaking of any aspect of psychological activity or action, we shall no longer refer to location, movement, direction, sheer quantity, and the like, for these terms are suitable only for things and thinglike entities. Thus, we shall not speak of internalization except in the sense of a person's imagining his or her incorporating something; for, as there is no other conceivable inside than the imaginary one, there can be no other conceivable movement to this inside (see chapter 8). Similarly, we shall not speak of psychological depth, impulses that underlie actions, discharge or depletion of pent-up or displaced energy or cathexis, and the like.

(1b) So far as possible, we shall not use the verb *to have* in relation to psychological activity, for, in using it, we should be implying that things and thinglike entities are the referents of psychological propositions. Thus, it will no longer do to say that one *has* a feeling or an impulse or even a disposition; nor shall it be acceptable to speak of anyone's *having* habits, symptoms or sublimations.

In this connection, we ought to use the linking verbs *to be* and *to become* cautiously. This is so because, by using them, we might be inadvertently reestablishing the disallowed substantive properties or changes. Upon thinking it through, one can usually substitute for *be* and *become* a more precise statement of the desired meaning that is built around some active verb and modifying adverb. One might, for example, translate "She is lethargic" into "She behaves lethargically" and "He became more friendly" into "He worked (or talked or played) with others in a more friendly manner than before."

(1c) In order to state observations in a form suitable for systematic general propositions as well as to state these general propositions properly, we shall use only the active voice and constructions that clarify activity and modes of activity. For whenever we use the passive voice or equivalent passive or indefinite constructions, we obscure the fact that we are speaking about actions performed by persons, and, unobtrusively, we establish a basis for introducing even more substantives into our propositions; at the least—and it is no little thing—we duck the issue of how to designate the source or maker of the action in question, thereby perpetuating our theoretical difficulties. This we must avoid. For example, instead of saying, "A change was occurring in his attitude from friendliness to belligerence," we might now say, "He changed from acting friendly to acting belligerently." Instead of saying, "No hope was held that things could get better," we might now say, "No one hoped any longer to be able to improve his or her situation." "The goal of perfection was emphasized" might become "He (or she) emphasized the goal of perfection." Similarly, we might translate, "It makes me feel happy" into "I think of it happily"—and, in mentioning this last translation, I anticipate those fundamental modifications of the way in which we shall henceforth conceive of affects or emotions that I shall discuss at length in part IV. In all that follows, I shall not neglect the place of necessity or happenings in people's lives.

We use implicit equivalents of the passive voice also in connection with the linking verbs *seem* and *appear*. Consequently, in the interest of developing and sustaining an action language, we should, for example, translate "That man appears to be odd" or "It seems that that man is odd" into "I think that that man behaves oddly" or "I believe that that man acts in an odd fashion." By devising these translations, we actually amplify the desired note of tentativeness while we refrain from ascribing the impression solely to that man as stimulus.

The examples of translation I have offered thus far might easily be described as stilted, fussy, or pallid compared to the formulations they would replace, and in some instances I would, if not agree, at least find that description understandable. I attribute this seeming loss of ease and eloquence to our unfamiliarity with the mode of translation. One consequence of this unfamiliarity is that in many instances we shall have to devise new ways of using action language that are graceful, forceful, and evocative. Another consequence of the unfamiliarity is that, in many instances, we must expect to find ourselves unprepared *as yet* to attach to these action alternatives the very wide range of familiar connotations that we attach as a matter of course to the older type of statement. It remains true, however, that a considerable number of action locutions are to be found among our older or well-established ways of talking about people, clinically and otherwise. These we are not likely to judge unsatisfactory. Indeed, sometimes we find it tactless or threatening to speak as plainly and directly as we can in familiar action terms; especially is this so in such intimate circumstances as the analytic situation. People often use substantive metaphors and the passive voice in order to *protect* the listener-recipient, and perhaps themselves as well, against minor and major "shocks." For example, to say, "It's time for me to be leaving" might make a leave-taking more tolerable or less offensive than simply to say, "I'm going now." Of the various forms of eloquence, some of the most powerful are monosyllabic, unadorned, and brief. Less can be more.

In any case, the desirability of developing an alternative language for psychoanalysis must be assessed on the basis of many other considerations than the response to first and rough translations.

(1d) We shall give up the idea that there are special classes of processes that prepare or propel mental activity, that is to say, classes that are qualitatively different from the mental activity they prepare or propel; for now everything is an action. Consequently, if we discern prestages of a specific action in which we are interested, we shall regard them as being merely preliminary actions that make possible the final action in question. Thus, to make an omelette (which is an action) it is necessary to break eggs (which is also an action, one that we shall view as a prestage of the omelette action). Alternatively and, I think, more exactly, we might regard the preliminary actions rather as constitutive actions, that is, as specific actions that are subsumed by a more general or abstract action term, much as the idea of curriculum, let us say, is constituted by the ideas of specific courses and so subsumes them. In this way, breaking eggs is like getting eggs, getting a pan, starting a fire, and so on, in being one of the actions that constitutes what we call making an omelette. But whether we view it as preliminary or constitutive, it is action itself that we take as our subject and not some force or agency that impels action or makes action possible.

Also, once we regard thinking consciously as an instance of action—and, as I argue in chapter 11 especially, we should do so, for thinking consciously is just one of those things that people do—we can no longer say that, in order to occur at all, this thinking requires preparation by a qualitatively different type of event such as preconscious or unconscious mental processes. For what could that preparation be but other thinking that is, in our new terms, other action, though action in another mode. If thinking consciously requires preparation, then thinking preconsciously or unconsciously must require preparation, too, and so on ad infinitum. Thinking would never get started, and it would always be only getting started. But we cannot work with theoretical assumptions that entail an infinite regress or eternally frozen moments. Consequently, we must take all thinking as simply a certain kind of action, and, especially as psychoanalysts, we must pay close attention to its modes and its changes or sequences of mode, such as the changes from thinking unconsciously to thinking consciously and vice versa.

It follows as well that we shall not invoke propulsive entities as the initiators and sustainers of action. Traditionally, we have invoked such entities, calling them drives, principles, regulatory structures operating through specific functions, and so on. According to the physicochemical and biological rules of language that Freud followed, understanding depends upon our invoking hypothetical substantive entities that create, initiate, regulate, or modify other and qualitatively different entities. Thus, as traditional psychoanalytic conceptualizers, we might say that the energy of instinctual drives prompts fantasies and motoric acts of love and hate. In the same manner, we might say that a mechanism of defense wards off the demands or pressures of a repressed impulse. But, be it noted, we have never developed a satisfactory account of how entities of one kind can have anything whatever to do with entities of another kind. What, for example, can a hypothetical and mindless instinctual drive have to do with a phenomenal thought? Does it make any sense to assume mindless drives? In attributing aims to drives, do we not impute cognition to them, too, thereby manifestly contradicting our formal definition of them while latently—and correctly—making our variables homogeneous in nature?

In place of answers to these questions, we Freudian analysts have customarily offered up personified versions of all these substantive ideas, and we have used these personifications to give our variables the semblance of homogeneity, spontaneity, and mutual interaction. Through these traditional personifications or anthropomorphic modes of thought, we have had all the entities interact as people do—the ego with the id, the defense with the drive, the cathexis with the representation, the function with the situation. In this implicit fashion, we have been relying all along on a psychology of people engaged in actions in different modes. (See in this regard Grossman and Simon 1969; Simon 1973; and especially chapter 7, below.) In switching to action language, we must think of each of these as sets of actions in various modes and not as entities of some other kind, and we must avoid entangling ourselves with prompters that require prompting and so on forever.

The idea of wishes—better, wish*ing*—poses no problem here.

People do, of course, wish for what they do not have or have not done. But, in the new terms, to wish is to engage in a certain kind of action; wishing is not a process of another kind that initiates action. And it is people, not wishes, who (or that) are frustrated. Certainly, people do not perform publicly, in speech or other motoric action, all that they might perform under sufficiently propitious circumstances (which may never be realized). But these would-be actions are not to be viewed as sources or applications of force that set substantive entities in motion in the manner of "the ghost in the machine" (Ryle 1949) or, as I call it in chapter 7, "the mover of the mental apparatus." They, too, are actions. We may designate them actions in another mode (conditional), preliminary or constitutive actions, or combinations of wishing and refraining actions. I shall return to this question of propulsion in chapter 10, especially.

In this light, it can be seen that all I am proposing is that we make this action language explicit, and codify and develop it, while sloughing off the remainder, which is rampant anthropomorphism, however austerely we may express it. The rationale of my theoretical program is no different from the familiar clinical rationale of interpreting the infantile unconscious, so-called: in both cases one's objective is to facilitate acts of discovery and revision through explicit confrontation, consternation, and reconsideration.

Part II

Preparatory Studies

2 The Preparatory Studies

In the preceding chapter I took a strong stand against the established view that Freud's metapsychology must remain *the* language of psychoanalytic theory, and I began my argument in favor of action language as an alternative, setting forth the basic rule of this alternative and some of its main consequences. Before going further with the exposition of action language, however, I am obliged to develop in more detail the case against metapsychology, which means also the case for an alternative. In the following chapters, therefore, I shall present three preparatory studies in which I attempt this task. It is a task that requires me to present, criticize, and begin to rework the formal conceptualization of metapsychology and the theory of the psychoanalytic process.

These three studies provide a necessary background for a full understanding of parts III, IV, and V of this book. But they do not provide a complete background in this regard. For that background in my own thinking, the reader will have to turn to my book, *Aspects of Internalization* (1968b), especially to its third and seventh chapters, and to two earlier papers on the mechanisms of defense (1968a) and activity and passivity (1968c). For the critical and innovative ideas of other psychoanalysts who have been engaged in similar projects, each in his own way, the reader should consult the work of Apfelbaum (1966), Basch (1973), Erikson (1950, 1956), Gedo and Goldberg (1973), Grossman and Simon (1969), Guntrip (1967, 1968), Holt (1965, 1967, 1972), Home (1966), G.S. Klein (1967, 1969), Loewald (1960, 1962) and Rycroft (1966, 1968), among others to whose contributions I shall refer throughout this book. Additionally, for the towering expositions of the most advanced and systematized versions of Freud's metapsychology, the reader not already familiar with them will have to consult especially the works of Hartmann and Rapaport.

As to what follows in Part II here, a few further introductory remarks are in order. Chapter 3, "The Psychoanalytic Vision of Reality," deals in a transitional way with the theory of the psychoanalytic process; a systematic discussion of this theory in the terms of action language remains a project that I hope to undertake in the not too distant future. But already in this study it becomes evident that there is a large gap between the metapsychological language and the assumptions about people, their problems, and their transformations that guide and inform the work of clinical psychoanalysis. In it I demonstrate not only the possibility of taking multiple views of the lives of people and the changes wrought through analysis; I show as well that alternative views or "visions" are part and parcel of psychoanalytic work. I also argue that clinical psychoanalysis is a certain kind of historical discipline, one that requires concepts suitable to it rather than to a laboratory science. If nothing else, this chapter should establish the clinical relevance of my enterprise.

Chapter 4, "An Overview of Heinz Hartmann's Contributions to Psychoanalysis," is another matter. It is highly theoretical. In it I review critically the chief modes of thought and assumptions that have shaped the work of the greatest modern Freudian metapsychologist. I intend to show that at its very best this metapsychology does not stand up to close scrutiny; for only by reaching this goal, and not by pointing out the shortcomings of lesser or derivative or more problematic efforts, may one justifiably take the stand that what we have been used to working with is not good enough and that alternatives must be developed.

In chapter 5, "The Mover of the Mental Apparatus," I take up especially the anthropomorphic modes of thought with which the mechanistic-organismic metapsychology is imbued, and I try to show how these modes have been inevitable in efforts to give metapsychology the appearance of viability. I also argue that recent attempts to combine self-language, identity-language, and autonomy-language with Freud's metapsychological language cannot succeed; especially in question here are the important contributions of Hartmann (again), Rapaport, Erikson, Kohut, and Guntrip. While these attempts do import into theoretical discussion some aspects of the language I consider more appropriate to the clinical analytic situation, in the end they yield propositions that are redundant, inconsistent, and sometimes self-contradictory. But they are also, as I believe, of special interest as *transitional* theoretical programs; for they are responsive to the shortcomings of the established language, and they amount to searches for, and the partial achievement of, something better and yet something Freudian in nature.

3 The Psychoanalytic Vision
of Reality*

1. INTRODUCTION

We psychoanalysts would all agree, I think, that among the aims of psychoanalysis as a therapy that of increasing the reliability of the analysand's reality-testing occupies a central position. Following Hartmann (1947, 1956), we would include under reality-testing the testing of inner reality, too, and we would emphasize the fantastic and fascinating complexity of the relations between the internal and external worlds.[1] In our writings, however, we have been adhering to a narrow conception of reality and its testing. Largely owing to our interest in the origins and early development of reality relations and reality-testing, we have been concerned mainly with what is immediate, that is to say, with whether in specific instances a perception is accurate or not, or with the respects in which it is and is not accurate. Is the breast or mother-figure really there? If so, is it seen in a distorted or overly selective way owing to the child's present state of need, interest, organization, conflict, or mood? What is that state, how did it come about, what is its effect on object relations?

Even our discussions of reality-testing in the clinical situation have tended to be narrow—no doubt narrower than what would be needed to do justice to typical analytic work. Thus, the issues raised are likely to be whether the analysand's perception of mutual feeling and influence is accurate; and, if inaccurate, with the dynamic and structural factors in his or her immediate inner reality that must be taken into account before arriving at an accurate understanding of the total situation, including the inaccurate perception of it. This engagement with reality at close quarters is essential to the day-to-day, or mo-

*This is a modified version of a paper that first appeared in the *International Journal of Psycho-Analysis*, 51 (1970): 279-97.

1. See now, however, especially chapter 8, below, for a critique of spatial metaphors in systematic propositions.

ment-to-moment, work of clinical analysts—of Freudian clinical analysts anyway. For them generalities are unanalyzable.

Reality and reality-testing may, however, be considered at a greater distance than this. For example, Hartmann's (1939b) concept of the average expectable environment implies a look at reality from a great distance. So does Erikson's (1950) concept of the life cycle. These types of conceptualization are not metaphysical; they are not addressed to the question of the ultimate nature of reality. They attempt to say something about the kind of world, broadly viewed, one lives in. What can one expect in this world? Are people and relationships with them different from, and perhaps more than, one has been ready to realize? What can one expect of oneself as a person of a specific sort in this world? What are the costs and dangers of gratification; the consequences of error and protest; the prospects for success and failure, reward and punishment, pleasure and pain; and so forth? We know that people ask and answer these questions in individually characteristic and influential ways; in analytic work, directly or indirectly, and preferably in specific instances, we analyze some of the determinants of these questions and answers, as a result of which both may change in accuracy, content, ambitiousness, and influence. Thus, while metapsychology and clinical practice have been concerned, implicitly if not explicitly, with reality in this larger sense, the clinical literature has lagged behind or skirted the issues.

Once we have extended our notion of reality, the criterion of a simple, if difficult to attain, objectivity, of being realistic or rational, of perceiving that which is true irrespective of its painfulness or our needfulness, fails us. On broad notions of reality rational people may disagree in all sorts of ways, and in many instances who is to say who is the more objective? Clearly, at this distance we are in the realm of visions of reality. The term vision implies judgments partly rooted in subjectivity, that is, in acts of imagination and articles of faith, which, however illuminating and complex they may be, necessarily involve looking at reality from certain angles and not others. As visions influence the determination of facts and their interrelations and implications, clashes between visions cannot be settled by simple appeals to "the evidence." It would not be correct to regard these clashes merely as matters of opinion.

In this chapter I explore the vision of reality inherent in psychoanalytic thought and practice. I believe there to be such a vision, a complex one that includes comic, romantic, tragic, and ironic features. I focus on the psychoanalytic process, that special reality about which we know the most, and from which we extrapolate to reality at large, for better or worse. And I try to show that it is worthwhile to attempt to define the psychoanalytic vision of this reality for the light it sheds on certain crucial aspects of the methods, goals, and results of clinical psychoanalysis.

It should seem odd to you to find an analyst asserting the existence of comic, romantic, tragic, and ironic aspects of the psychoanalytic outlook, and declaring them worthy of discussion.[2] We have all grown accustomed to, if not unreflectively dependent upon, a view of the psychoanalytic process as scientific and therapeutic; that is to say, we tend to take for granted that it is simply a rational method of investigation which uses emotionally intensified enlightenment to eliminate, so far as possible, the intrapsychic conditions that spawn symptoms and suffering and stunt the growth of the personality. Perhaps only the words tragic and ironic stirred some feeling of familiarity in you, reminding you of your having sensed a kinship between the stuff of tragedy and irony and the stuff of analysis. Indeed, the tragic and ironic aspects of analysis will occupy the center of the considerations to follow, as I believe them to be especially characteristic of the thrust of analytic work. But comic and romantic! The words suggest making a laughing matter of serious business or substituting a dreamy analysis for the analysis of dreams. Or else my introduction of these terms, together with tragic and ironic, suggests that it is my subversive intention to undercut the hard-won scientific gains and status of

---

2. These aspects correspond to the four mythic forms described by Frye (1957). Although I have transposed a number of the major reference points of this paper from Frye's discussions, I have not attempted to follow Frye exactly; nor have I attempted to render fully his views on these mythic forms. I have taken from him what seemed useful for my purposes and have merged this selection with others from the relevant literature. Among the other major sources I have drawn on are Aristotle's *Poetics* (Butcher 1907), Nietzsche's (1870) *The Birth of Tragedy;* Bradley (1904) and Bradley (1909) on Hegel; the books by Sewall (1959), Krieger (1960), and Kaufman (1968) on tragedy and the tragic vision; the collections of essays on tragedy and the tragic edited by Brooks (1955), Michel & Sewall (1963), and Abel (1967); and Lauter's (1964) collection of essays on comedy and the comic.

psychoanalysis by an insidious switch to visionary philosophy and literary device.

I cannot altogether refute the allegation of subversiveness in that I believe every investigation to be potentially subversive. In this sense, for example, the investigation that is clinical analysis is potentially subversive of the analysand's way of life—hence, the analysand's resistance to it. I can assure you, however, that I shall be advocating no changes in psycho-analytic technique, no *Weltanschauung* for analysts, and no substitution of poetic posturing for sound practice. My topic is the guiding vision of psychoanalysis, not the revision of psychoanalysis. For my descriptive and expository purposes I shall be adapting and applying certain terms that have found favor with certain literary critics and philosophers. These terms —comic, romantic, tragic, ironic—refer to certain general visions or imaginative modes of comprehending the form and content of human situations and the changes they undergo. These modes are not so much products of the ingenuity of liter-ary critics and philosophers as they are typical workings of the human mind that scholars have discerned in the mythic and artistic products of this imaginative mind confronting the world. Consequently they may help extend our understanding of psychoanalysis.

I do, however, want to point out that, in its broad implica-tions, my investigation of this set of possibilities involves turn-ing attention to the roots of psychoanalysis in the humanities. These roots have been all but lost sight of in this, the heyday of the medical-scientific program for psychoanalysis. And by roots in the humanities I am not referring to applied psycho-analysis: that is rooted only in psychoanalysis. Psychoanalysis is necessarily closely related to the humanities in that its raw data are meanings and subjective experience, and its methods are those that promote the clarification and organization of meaning and experience along certain lines. Psychoanalysis is a special form of knowing about human existence and history. Berlin's (1969) discussion of historical knowing is relevant in this regard (see also Novey 1968). In my estimation, this close relation tends to be denied or obscured by the current fashion of limiting theoretical discussion to a rigorous application of abstract metapsychological principles that are themselves adaptations and applications of concepts drawn from other fields of study, namely biology, chemistry, and physics. The relation of the biological and the physicochemical to humane studies that is optimal for psychoanalysis still remains to be worked out. If my approach does clarify and strengthen the rationale of specifically Freudian clinical psychoanalytic methods and goals, and perhaps even adds a bit to ego psychology, then it may contribute something to the larger task of systematically diversifying the conceptual tools and thus enlarging the scope of psychoanalytic theory.

At this point, of course, I am in no position to assert that comic, romantic, tragic, and ironic are the most useful terms for my purpose. A further difficulty is that there are no terse definitions of these terms on which philosophers and critics generally agree. These scholars have as much, if not more, trouble arriving at terseness and agreement as psychoanalysts do. This common difficulty stems from the nature of our methods and materials and also from changing times and aims. However, it would be out of place for me to attempt a comprehensive presentation of previous discussions of these visions. A final conceptual difficulty is that the visions join together in certain respects—for example, the tragic and romantic, the comic and romantic, and the tragic and ironic. Consequently, my definitions, like all others in this realm of ideas, will necessarily be selective, provisional, somewhat labored, and controversial; it is their aptness and usefulness that must be demonstrated in what follows.

2. The Comic Vision

The comic vision seeks evidence to support unqualified hopefulness regarding personal situations in the world. It serves to affirm that no dilemma is too great to be resolved, no obstacle too firm to stand against effort and good intentions, no evil so unmitigated and entrenched that it is irremediable, no suffering so intense that it cannot be relieved, and no loss so final that it cannot be undone or made up for. The program is reform, progress, and tidings of joy.

The comic vision maintains itself by emphasizing in a highly selective way the external, familiar, controllable, predictable aspects of situations and people. It celebrates "the power of positive thinking." It sees conflict as being centered in situations and as being eliminated by effective manipulative action. Thus, the protagonist in difficulty is regarded as being blocked in the pursuit of his or her goals by representatives of an obstructive society and as ultimately triumphing over these representatives and becoming the center of a new and better one. As one makes one's way to the influential center of affairs, one's attitude toward the blocking figures changes for the most part from opposition to their exclusiveness to acceptance and inclusiveness. Antagonists are found to be rigid and ridiculous rather than evil and truly dangerous and so they are generally considered to be open to self-improvement. Ultimate reconciliations tend to be important, although particularly objectionable opponents (e.g., those too possessed by their "humour") may have to be made scapegoats and excluded from the new society. Social cohesion, if not conformity, is a guiding value, as is pragmatism.

The program of the new society is, however, not ordinarily carefully defined. For the protagonist, finally, there are prospects of freedom, understanding, good will, selfhood, and worldly success and sexual gratification unburdened by pain, guilt, or anxiety—the happy ending is a utopian beginning, a rebirth, a heaven arriving on earth—but these prospects remain vague, the chief comic interest remaining focused on arriving at the point of having prospects. (From the tragic and ironic points of view, to anticipate a bit, the prospects had better be left vague as they are largely simplistic and illusory—happy daydreams, hopes, and prayers. Analysts might call them manic defense, hypomanic denial, or quasi-hallucinatory fulfillment of infantile, libidinal, and aggressive wishes.)[3]

Black comedy or, more exactly, the degree of blackness of comedy or comic vision, amounts to a questioning of the comic premise, and so belongs to the ironic vision.

Laughter and gaiety are not considered essential to the comic. Worldly gratification and security are. Kris (1937) has clarified the extent to which the comic is grounded on partly mastered dangers concerning security and gratification.

3. As my concern is with perspectives on the Freudian psychoanalytic process, I shall only mention here that the vision of mental-health enthusiasts, community mental health enthusiasts and certain neo-Freudians may be characterized as being restricted to a simple version of the comic.

Does the Freudian analytic undertaking have comic aspects? Are reform, progress, and hope part of the analytic contract? Does the analysis get organized around what is familiar, controllable, predictable, and pragmatic? Do we have analysands who are blocked in the pursuit of their goals? If so, are they blocked by an obstructive society? Does treatment help them triumph and become the center of a new society? Are they finally orientated toward reconciliation, inclusiveness, and worldly gratification? Are they, so to speak, reborn? I believe the answer to these questions to be both yes and no, and I suggest that, insofar as it is yes, the psychoanalytic process conforms to the comic archetype or is shaped by a comic vision.

To begin with the affirmative answer: the fact that psychoanalysis is offered and accepted as a treatment for a troubled life implies a shared melioristic orientation. It is an orientation that many in this world do not share. And analysis is concerned with correcting rigidities and clearing the way toward sustained hopefulness and the experience of progress, security, and pleasure. Then, too, there is the concept of cure, a concept that is still part of the analytic vocabulary long after a consensus has developed that the proper primary concern of analysis is not removal of symptoms but modification through understanding of disturbances in the structure of the personality—which is to say, troubled and handicapped lives. That "cure" is still with us is attributable in part to the comic (but not funny) prejudice that psychoanalysis is a form of medical practice.

As for the analysands, upon beginning analysis, they tend to see themselves, and to some extent, though much less so, to be seen by the analyst as being blocked in the pursuit of their goals by obstructing figures of an existing society. As the resistance and transference intensify, the obstructive environment is felt by each analysand to be embodied in the analyst, though the analyst also comes to be represented in the transference as the analysand's wily provocateur and ally. And to judge by the analysand's subjective experience upon approaching the termination of a benignly influential analysis, that analysand does feel in certain respects that he or she has become, or is on the way to becoming, the center of a new society. This feeling refers to a new and legitimate sense of secure self in the external world, a fresh view of that world, and a more confident, assertive, alloplastic, and pleasurable involvement in object relations. And the analysand's attitudes toward hitherto feared, hated, and despised parents, siblings, workmates, superiors, spouse, children—and analyst—are likely to be considerably more reconciled and inclusive than when the analysis began. In all this change he or she conveys a sense of the end of exile, or rebirth, or life now lying ahead—and life not too strictly or clearly programmed inasmuch as the need for rigid programming itself may well have been found during the analysis to be one of the old-society obstructions to be overcome. After sufficient analysis of the transference and resistance aspects of "getting better," the analyst may share with the analysand this sense of real change for the better.

Rebirth is related archetypically to spring and the world view of cyclic return. Thus, another chance, another time around, an end to the winter of discontent, and a fresh blossoming often characterize the mood and imagery of the analysand contemplating his or her analytic gains. The view of cyclic return implies that the past can be redone, if not undone. Thereby it implicitly denies the passage of time. It cancels out pastness. Its perspective is timeless. There can be and there is, again and again, what Balint (1952) has termed a "new beginning." As analysts, we will be alert to the manic defense or attempted flight to health in the rebirth experience and to the regressive wish-fulfillment in it.[4] Yet have we not, by engaging in the analytic enterprise, based ourselves at least partly on the assumptions of the timeless cycle? After all, it is part of our technique to work back and forth over the analysand's life as if almost all parts of time are potentially recapturable, redo-able, improvable, even though they may not all be equally so in the particular case. In this respect we proceed as if time were not time at all.

The unconscious, we say (following Freud), is timeless. True enough, but is a life timeless? Is the external world? Is the so-called rational ego? There is something amiss in this comic

4. We may also surmise that the cyclic sense of time is founded on the waxing and waning of subjective tension associated with rhythmic bodily processes—hunger and satiation, wakefulness and sleepiness, and the various forms of oral, anal, and genital excitement. The days and seasons and their often crucial ecological implications, so often emphasized in the literature of criticism, are not the only basic reference points of cyclic experience. Appreciating the role of body time does not, however, compel us to accept the cycle as the true or full story of time in the analysand's life.

vision of a green world revisited or restored through analysis.
Kris (1956b) has clarified how it is that analytic penetration to
the deepest layers of the transference neurosis and the resistance establishes dynamic conditions sufficiently similar to
those that prevailed in childhood to facilitate the approximate
recovery of crucial early memories; and Loewald (1960) has
described essential aspects of how this regressive penetration
leads to the points of arrested growth and the undeveloped
"ego core" from and around which resumption of growth may
proceed. But neither of them asserts, and no one can rightly
assert, that analysis has brought about an exact return to, and
reproduction and correction of, infantile life.

Among recent contributors to this topic, Stone (1961), in
particular, has emphasized how much the analytic situation
depends on the presence of an adult analysand with relatively
intact ego functions collaborating verbally and reflectively
with the analyst in the work of exploring and re-experiencing
the past. The adult ego must be there to reunderstand the past
or to understand it for the first time. Psychic structure is not
abolished during analysis. The analysand can never be a child
again and, so to speak, grow up right the second time around:
he or she can only feel and remember or reconstruct something
of what life was like in the remote past. The intensity and
productive influence of the regressively revived feelings and
memories is no proof of exact reproduction. And the liberating
effect of some of these revivals is no proof that a second and
better childhood is being traversed. We are here at a point
where the tragic sense of life would have something to say
about time—linear time as opposed to cyclic time, that is to say,
unrecapturable time, true time within which events are im-
movably located (Jaspers 1952, Watts 1955). We shall return
to linear time in the discussion of the tragic.

The implication of timelessness is not the only problem for
the comic vision. Another is its conception of conflict. During
the analysis a radical change takes place in the picture of the
analysand as a hero matching wits with an obstructive environment. The analysand's goals are found to be contradictory
and ill-defined. Owing to fixation and regression, these goals
prove to be appropriate to different, uncoordinated phases of
his or her development. Further, insofar as the analysand
presents a neurosis or a character disorder, the obstructing

figures are found to be largely, though not entirely, internal; they exist as introjects or unintegrated identifications in the ego and superego systems and also as projective transferences wrought in the analysand's imagination. Thus it emerges that the analysand is simultaneously an ardent defender of the existing society that is to be reordered or replaced as well as the potential center of the new society he or she is determined to bring about. There is an inner hell to be traversed and an inner society to be transformed. With the reversal of the analysand's externalizations and external manipulations, and with the reduction of repressions, the analysand moves beyond the comic vision of self, analyst, and existence into the tragic and ironic world of inescapable conflict and costly and uncertain reconciliations.

A legitimate comic element is preserved even here, however, in the acknowledged possibility of accomplishing some revision of this inner world—of developing a fresh view of it, and, through that, a healthier narcissism and social existence. In this respect the analysand can rightly come to feel that he or she has moved to the center of an inner society. This move will be evidenced, for example, by a sense of being more at one with one's body and one's heritage, more alive in one's senses and sensuality, more worth one's own benevolent attention, and freer to pursue and enjoy success and security, however one now defines them. At least, if the analysis has gone well, one moves *toward* that center, and one is better able to maintain or regain initiative in the face of difficulty. Yet Freud, ever mindful of the tragic and ironic, said with regard to the permanence of analytic gains that much depends on whether the analysand after analysis is spared "too searching a fate."

3. THE ROMANTIC VISION

In the romantic vision, as conceptualized here, life is a quest or a series of quests. The quest is a perilous, heroic, individualistic journey. Its destination or goal combines some or all of the qualities of mystery, grandeur, sacredness, love, and possession by or fusion with some higher power or principle (Nature, Virtue, Honor, Beauty, etc.). The seeker is an innocent, adventurous hero, and the quest ends, after crucial struggles, with exaltation. The romantic vision, too, characterizes certain significant aspects of the analytic undertaking, and it, too, soon reveals its limits. As with the limits of the comic vision, the definition of these limits will indicate the necessity of particularly emphasizing—but not substituting—the tragic and ironic elements of the psychoanalytic vision of reality in general and the psychoanalytic process in particular. The standard cowboy movie is a commonplace, communal American expression of romantic vision.

The quest follows the pattern of the wishfulfilling daydream (Frye says dream and the analyst would add masturbation fantasy). In this daydream, ideals are represented by virtuous heroes and heroines while threats to the ascendancy of these ideals are embodied in villains. The romantic vision is, implicitly if not explicitly, regressive and childlike, particularly in its persistent nostalgia for a golden age in time or space that is the essential destination of the quest, the prize for the counterphobic victor in the central conflict. Outwardly, it may proclaim as its achievement a discontinuous leap forward in existence and thereby an emancipation from history; but this proclamation only obscures its regressiveness and the quality it shares with the comic vision of being ultimately atemporal or ahistorical.

Other common manifestations of the romantic vision are the idealization of individuality and "nature": self-expression is uncritically and totalistically equated with triumph, and narcissistic or impulsive action with being "natural" (or "authentic" or "with it"). In fact, idealization of any sort is a romantic phenomenon. Sooner or later experience becomes a failed quest as "nature" and "triumph" remain ambiguous, elusive, and costly. Many analysands seek analysis with a sense of failed quest, which they may verbalize as a search for authenticity, identity, dedication, and aspirations to be more at one with the world around them.

The archetype of the quest certainly embraces essential aspects of the analytic process. For the analysand, analysis is initially a quest for a lost golden age, whatever else it may signify. Freud's (1937a) comments in "Analysis Terminable and Interminable" on the female analysand's unappeasable wish for her lost penis, for example, imply that a romantic quest is an essential organizing principle of her analysis; we may say the same for her unappeasable wish to bear her father's child.

Another example is the extent to which persisting early infantile wishes to fuse with a nurturant breast-mother generate an essential part of the impetus of the analytic process for male and female patients alike. And, with regard to ego-superego relations, the analysand's quest for purification, absolution, and redemption through analysis can hardly be overemphasized.

Yet fundamental changes take place in the course of a benignly influential analysis: the quest continues, but, for the analysand, the dragons change, the modes of combat change, and the concepts of heroism and victory change. More and more the dangers and adversaries are seen to be repressed infantile experiences and fantasies, unconscious identifications and introjects, and infantile defenses and motives for defense —hence meanings, aims, self-representations, and object-representations hitherto denied access to conscious or preconscious expression. As the analysis deepens, the ordeal to be lived through and the victory to be won concern not so much a hostile and rigid environment, and not so much reaching the analytic "moment of truth," but immersion into a disturbing inner world that is a highly distorted version of an earlier environment and earlier selves. Gaining insight into this world replaces much interpersonal and intrapersonal aggressive and libidinal manipulation as the way to fight it all out. Heroic fulfilling of tasks becomes "working through" in the face of sometimes almost intolerable anxiety, guilt, grief, yearning, and despair. And the actual reward? A more united subjective self, one which has more room in it for undisguised pleasure, to be sure, but also for control, delay, decisive renunciation, remorse, mourning, memories, anticipations, ideals, and moral standards; and more room, too, for a keen sense of real challenges, dangers, and rewards in one's current existence. The childlike, regressive nostalgia is reduced in influence as is the attachment to dragons—for what is a nostalgic counterphobic hero without a dragon?

How does the quest look from the standpoint of the resistance and transference? As the resistance and transference develop, the analyst, now perceived regressively by the analysand, becomes the goal of the quest, though simultaneously he or she serves as its guide, its objective critic, and, through the rule of abstinence, also its terrible adversary in the realm of

bodily activity and gratification. The dangers in the transference neurosis—the sense of life-and-death struggle that may
enter into this crisis—are like the monster that has to be slain,
the ring of fire to be penetrated, the tasks and trials and ordeals
that the hero must master en route to the goal. And the resistance takes on a desperately heroic, "last stand" quality. The
analyst becomes simultaneously the enemy and the ally, the
villain and the benevolent wise man or "earth mother." In terms
of Lewin's (1952) likening the analytic situation to the state of
sleeping and dreaming, which is akin to the romantic experience, the analyst is both the soothing sandman and the harsh
awakener. The simplifications of romance break down.[5]

Looked at from the standpoint of enhanced reality-testing,
the analytic quest becomes more and more the search for meaning, understanding, or insight, through consciously reencoun-
tering significant feelings, memories, and desires, and defining
their place and influence in one's past and present life. Analysis
as investigation is the quest, however variable the motivating
influence of the need to know on the course of the analysis. On
this point of investigative zeal analytic authors differ in emphasis, though none deny it a dynamic place in the rationale of
the analytic process.

In the end, just as a central and valuable element of the comic
persists as the analysis moves deeper into the tragic and ironic
realms, so a central and valuable element of the romantic persists. The analysis remains a quest just as it remains an opti-
mistic, assimilative, revisionist enterprise. At the same time,
these visions influence much of the analysand's sense of his or
her own life outside the analysis: courageous (inner and outer)
quest and determined recentering of (inner and outer) society
do not lose their importance. Yet insofar as the analysis has
genuinely deepened, all the terms have also changed in the
direction of the complex, ambiguous, paradoxical, and inexorable. Changed, that is, in the direction of the tragic and ironic
visions. What remains of the comic and romantic is no longer
naive and unqualified. It is as simplistic to characterize psychoanalysis as merely romantic on account of its individualistic
aspects, as it is to characterize it as comic on account of its em-

5. Compare Jacobson (1964) on the crucial developmental problem of representing
the "good but also bad" object (and self), and Melanie Klein (1935) on similar problems in the "depressive position."

phasis on healing and gratification. This point may be more
fully appreciated once the tragic and ironic visions have been
discussed.

4. THE TRAGIC VISION

I should like to begin this section with a marvelous little story
told by Unamuno (1921) in his discussion of the tragic sense of
life. "A pedant who beheld Solon weeping for the death of a
son said to him, 'Why do you weep thus, if weeping avails
nothing?' And the sage answered him, 'Precisely for that reason—because it does not avail.'" No story can tell "the whole
story," but this one conveys something essential to the tragic
vision as it shall be represented here.

The tragic vision is expressed in a keen responsiveness to the
great dilemmas, paradoxes, ambiguities, and uncertainties per-
vading human action and subjective experience. It manifests
itself in alertness to the inescapable dangers, terrors, mysteries,
and absurdities of existence. It requires one to recognize the
elements of defeat in victory and of victory in defeat; the pain
in pleasure and the pleasure in pain; the guilt in apparently
justified action; the loss of opportunities entailed by every
choice and by growth in any direction; the inevitable clashes
between passion and duty; the reversal of fortune that hovers
over those who are proud or happy or worthy owing to its being
in the nature of people to be inclined to reverse their own for-
tunes as well as to be vulnerable to accident and unforeseen
consequences of their acts and the acts of others. The person
with a tragic sense of life knows the renunciations that are in-
termingled with the conditions of gratification; the necessity to
act in ignorance and bear the fear and guilt of action; the
burden of unanswerable questions and incomprehensible afflic-
tions; the probability of suffering while learning or changing;
and the frequency with which it is true that only in the greatest
adversity do people realize themselves most fully. Of all the
perspectives on human affairs, the tragic is by far the most re-
morselessly searching, deeply involved, and along with the
ironic, impartial.

Linking these terms to psychoanalytic variables, it may be
said that the person whose vision of reality is tragic is keenly
responsive to the terrible power of fixation, repression, regres-

sion, and repetition; the insidious influence of unconscious processes; the petrifying spectacle or anticipation of loss of self and objects, castration, and superego condemnation, in all their direct and symbolic forms, including death; the ever-present conflicts among id, ego, and superego tendencies; the ultimate unreachability of the ego ideal or ideal self; and the unshakable ambivalence in human relationships. One is constantly aware that these are among the essential conditions of love and hate alike, of illness and health, and of failure and the most sublime achievements. One knows adaptation to be a costly and endless struggle with uncertain results. One has no illusions about gaining complete and stable insight into and mastery over the mysterious unconscious. The well-analyzed person no longer has to deny or merely pay lip-service to the fact that his or her existence has been shaped, and in every respect continues to be shaped, by specific factors of this sort. I do not, of course, imply that analysis is the only route to a developed tragic sense of life or that it can impress this sense on a mind not receptive to it. At the same time, I am mindful of the fact that it is far easier and far more common to pay lip service to the tragic vision than to be deeply imbued with it.

The tragic sense of time is linear rather than cyclic: time is seen to be continuous and irreversible; choices once made are made forever; a second chance cannot be the same as the first; life is progression toward death without rebirth; rebirth is an illusion—which is not to say that newfound freedom must be illusory. Earlier, in my discussion of the comic vision, I mentioned the complicating factor of the obstructing figures' being mainly internal, which is to say that both the opposing society and the new society are simultaneously represented by the hero. This internal split or opposition is essential to the tragic vision, according to which the protagonist is inevitably divided internally, some rights, values, duties, and opportunities necessarily clashing with others, and the choices made consequently always entailing sacrifice, ambivalence, and remorse, if not guilt. Scheler (1954) extending Hegel's (Abel 1967, pp. 367-416) line of thought, speaks of the "tragic knot," which expresses "the entanglement between the creation and destruction of a value"; by this he refers to the coinciding in an event, person, or thing, and, above all, in one quality, power, or ability, of the influences that both champion the value and destroy it. Much of analysis is concerned with tragic knots.[6]

Freud (1915d, 1927, 1930) conveyed his sense of the tragic in psychoanalytic understanding most clearly in his essays on the discontents inherent in civilization and on the infantile foundation of the need for religion, traditional Christian religion, at least, being in the terms of this discussion, a mixed comic and romantic vision; it is a denial of the tragic inasmuch as it promises a happy ending, a negation of worldly existence, a clear ultimate meaning or a grand design. The tragic spirit in Freud can also be found between the lines of many of his clinical and theoretical discussions. It is an internally consistent vision from which Freud sometimes departed in his gloomy and contemptuous remarks about people in the mass. His need to theorize in terms of great polarities, and particularly his finally pitting a death instinct against a life instinct, may well have been partly determined by his tragic vision. But the polarity of the death and life instincts, being a biological and not a psychological hypothesis, does not qualify as a directly tragic conceptualization. I do not imply that the tragic describes the totality of Freud's outlook.

One must exclude more than religious consolation, contemptuous generalization about people, and biological speculation from the tragic vision. The melodramatic and the pathetic must also be excluded on the ground that they belong to the naive, unqualified comic and romantic modes of comprehension; this is so because the melodramatic and pathetic stress a clear division between the good and the bad, and always imply the possibility of the triumph of the pleasure principle, of clear and simple choice and consequences, and of endings that are simply happy—e.g., fully satisfactory endings of sleep, nursing, excremental functioning, and oedipal conflict. This point is important for identifying the tragic perspective in the psychoanalytic process.

How might one describe that clinical perspective? I mention first that applying the genetic point of view of psychoanalysis does culminate in a rough sense of the necessity of the neurotic maladaptation that is being studied, that is, of the inevitability of its presence, form, and severity (Hartmann and Kris 1945). And certainly, the genetic point of view is consistent with the

6. Earlier papers of mine on ideals (1967b), affects (1964), and defenses (1968a), though developed for different purposes, illustrate this point.

tragic sense of time as linear. For while the past may be partially re-experienced, reviewed, and altered through reinterpretation, it cannot be replaced: a truly cold mother, a savage or seductive father, a dead sibling, the consequences of a predominant repressed fantasy, years of stunted growth and emotional withdrawal, and so forth, cannot be wiped out by analysis, even though their hampering and painful effects may be greatly mitigated, and the analysand freed to make another, partly different and more successful try at adaptation.[7] The analysand whose analysis has been benignly influential retains apprehensions, vulnerability, and characteristic inclinations toward certain infantile, self-crippling solutions, however reduced these may be in influence and however counterbalanced by strengthened adaptiveness. This is one implication of "analysis interminable" (Freud 1937a). This is why we retain defenses after analysis and continue to censor our dreams. To say this is in no way to minimize the gains that may be made through analysis—and, so far as adults are concerned, probably only through analysis. Analysts have enough to be proud of to be open, as Freud was, to the recognition of the limits of their work. Indeed, consideration of its limits is essential in clarifying the nature of the work itself.

I go on therefore to ask: who among reasonably well-analyzed analysands is invulnerable to a painful stirring up of preoedipal and oedipal conflicts by, for example, his or her children—their birth, their infancy, their instinctual moving away during adolescence? Who is immunized by analysis against neurotically colored responses to the advance of age, the disharmonies of marriage, the death of parents, and the limits of career? Freud did not fully represent his understanding of these matters when he said that analysis frees one from neurotic misery so that one can deal more directly and effectively with the miseries of everyday life. He himself taught us

7. Already in 1893, Freud concluded his chapter on the psychotherapy of hysteria with this account of how he answered the objection frequently raised by his patients when he promised them help or improvement. The objection would be: "Why, you tell me yourself that my illness is probably connected with my circumstances and the events of my life. You cannot alter these in any way. How do you propose to help me then?" To which he would reply: "No doubt fate would find it easier than I do to relieve you of your illness. But you will be able to convince yourself that much will be gained if we succeed in transforming your hysterical misery into common unhappiness. And with a mental life that is restored to health, you will be better armed against that unhappiness" (Breuer and Freud 1893, p. 305).

that the miseries of everyday life do not ordinarily impinge on us simply with their own force, even when they are extreme; he showed that, from the strictly analytic point of view, they are always in the nature of day residues that come into connection with the permanent, unconscious infantile conflicts, and that they gain much of their meaning and influence through that relation. The adaptational point—Freud's point—is that one need not then lose sight of the immediate situation and its real potential for resolution—or lack thereof.

In the comment under consideration Freud also neglected to point out that the neurotic misery is also the neurotic love-life and work-life—something he demonstrated in other connections—so that to complete his formulation one would have to say that analysis frees one for the everyday love-life and work-life, too. Freud was referring to the analyzed person's diminished inclination to express misery, love, and work in symptoms—and, I would add, in repetitively melodramatic and pathetic forms of action and subjective experience.

Other aspects of the tragic clinical perspective will become clear if we consider more closely the place in analysis of the tragic, the melodramatic, and the pathetic. From the point of view presently being developed, the person comes to analysis caught in a tragic situation. This tragic situation exists with greatest force in his or her inner world, although the external world may have its own share of partly independent tragic elements. Those who appreciate the vivid, populous, grim, and psychically real aspects of this inner world will not object to the idea of internal tragic situations. With what else could an audience appropriately and intensely go out to meet a tragedy on the stage? One may say, therefore, that the analysand is a tragic hero. But, to begin with, and for a long time, one does not usually see or present oneself that way; nor does one ordinarily participate in analysis that way. One's approach is likely to be pathetic and melodramatic, whether it takes the form of fearful and excited cruelty toward others or oneself, helpless dependency, grandiosity, depression, servility, shame, coy seductiveness, or something else. If anything, one is outwardly an anti-hero. At first the analyst, too, does not see the analysand's tragic situation, though he or she might sense it, and would be right, I maintain, to assume it a priori. It is the work of the analysis—an essential part of its quest—to define

that situation and to bring out into the open the analysand as
tragic hero, however that development may be worded. I am
not idealizing analysands in saying this; for, according to
Freud's tragic vision, we are all caught up in a tragic situation
simply by being alive, growing up in civilization, and trying to
make our way in it. In the analysis the analysand is the tragic
protagonist or hero—the center of the plot, the prime mover
and the one moved, creature as well as creator, the victor and
the victim.[8]

This view of the analysand makes it possible as analysis
deepens for the analyst to feel with more force and precision
the emotional foundations of the phenomena he or she encounters, and thus at times to feel at one with the analysand
through empathy. This is not simple countertransference as it
would be early in the analysis, that is, at a time when the analysand has not yet emerged into a tragic world, when he or she is
still predominantly engaged in being neurotically miserable or
defending against disclosures of neurotic wretchedness and
thus playing a part that is exaggeratedly comic or romantic,
pathetic or melodramatic. Especially at that early time, any
significant emotional involvement on the analyst's part in the
manifest material is likely to be in the nature of sentimental,
self-pitying, and defensive identification with, or reaction
against, the analysand. This involvement is bound to betray
itself as a kind of countertransference by its urge toward personal rather than analytic intervention or non-intervention.
The analyst's truly tragic vision of the analysand, on the other
hand, is not a call to personal intervention or inaction, but a
stimulus to empathy, reflection, and inquiry. In this respect it
parallels the frequently emphasized response appropriate to
tragic drama: in its fully developed form that response, too, is
not toward intervention; instead it is characterized by deep
empathy, sober contemplation, containment of tension, working the experience over in one's mind and heart, and humility
acting as a brake on hubris or grandiosity, all in the face of the
awesome power, complexity, and unpredictability inherent in
human affairs (cf. Kris 1952).

8. It is this view of the patient as tragic hero that is involved in what I have called
elsewhere (Schafer 1959) the analyst's generative empathy. It is also implied, I believe, in Loewald's (1960) reference to the analyst' holding the patient's ego core in
trust through all the adversities of the analysis.

Here is where some non-analytic and neo-Freudian therapeutic approaches are prone to go astray: in their tendency to
prescribe closeness and intimacy of feeling as a fixed therapeutic attitude, they require the therapist to remain oblivious
to the initial and changing atmosphere of the psychoanalytic
situation—if not of human relations in general. Love is not a
substance that one has "to give." In effect, these approaches
deny that the empathic closeness I have described must grow
through adversity and crisis. The analysis of resistance is an
instance of analytic adversity and a series of crises. Erikson
(1959, personal communication) has commented that empathy
grows out of crises. Nor do these approaches see that this closeness must remain subject to certain strict limits of expression
on the analyst's part. The limits themselves help empathy
grow, for abstinence is, in short-range terms, productive adversity, too; it is a precondition of internal elaboration and
deeper understanding.

Having mentioned now responses to tragic drama, I shall
discuss this topic briefly before returning to the analytic process. Rather than its being a digression, this discussion is intended to be another stepping stone toward a formulation of
the dynamic and structural aspects of the tragic vision. Some
analysts, including Freud (1905c, 1916a, 1928), have tended
rather too narrowly to interpret tragedy as a dramatization of
masochism and guilt, or at least to interpret the audience's
response to tragedy as fundamentally masochistic or guilty,
that is to say, as the enjoyment of identifying with the suffering
and defeat of a guilty hero. The reductionist approach in analysis (the "nothing but" fallacy) has been shown by Hartmann,
Kris, Rapaport, and others to be unsatisfactory in that it neglects ego psychology and the questions of autonomy, change of
function, and multiple function. I would add to this list of variables that special instance of multiple function, the "multiple
appeal" of interpretations: Hartmann (1951) spoke of "multiple
appeal" in showing that interpretations necessarily impinge on
a field of forces which originate to one degree or another in
each of the psychic systems. No doubt, masochistic and guilty
fantasies can be excited by seeing Oedipus self-blinded and
banished, or Hamlet joining all those other corpses on the floor.
Yet if we bear in mind the advances of psychoanalytic theory,
can we say that this is all there is to the dynamic and structural

implications of the audience's experience? I think not. Like an effective interpretation, a stirring dramatic spectacle, whatever its content, is bound to have "multiple appeal," that is, to impinge on a field of intersystemic and intrasystemic forces. Kris's (1952) appreciation of this point is evident throughout his writings on the psychology of art and the comic (see also Lesser 1957).

A more important question than the primacy of masochism and guilt in tragic experience is this: are the masochistic or guilty components of the enjoyment of tragedy a true part of the tragic vision of reality? Again, I think not. Masochistic and guilty tendencies are melodramatic and pathetic; they depend on the illusions that complete fulfilment, union, and victory are possible, and that people, situations, acts, and consequences are simply either good or bad. Masochism and neurotic guilt support the maudlin and mocking spirit, not the tragic, and in one way or another may be so interpreted during analysis, though not only so. In these ways masochism and guilt pertain more to the naive, unqualified romantic and comic visions than to the tragic.

I return now to a direct discussion of the analytic process. I have so far discussed the tragic implications of the genetic point of view and the tragic as distinct from the pathetic and melodramatic. A third aspect of the tragic view of the analytic process is the analyst's recognizing that suffering while learning and changing cannot usually be avoided, nor can the analysand realize himself or herself most fully and resume growth in the absence of adversity and deprivation. Of course, adversity and deprivation do not guarantee learning and self-enhancement; as a rule, they make people mean. But, in the context of the analytic interpretation of resistance and transference, this suffering is given the best chance to promote learning and beneficial change. It should go without saying I am not advocating that the analyst be on the alert for opportunities to make the analysand suffer or improvise special means to intensify this effect. When carried out analytically, an analysis contains enough potential for suffering on the analysand's part to take care of this requirement (cf. Stone 1961).

As issues of responsibility and choice enter into an analysis, additional emphasis falls on tragic comprehension. During analysis, one realizes that one has been playing an active role in bringing about apparently passive suffering. One recognizes one's unconscious sabotage of love and work. One sees the relation of this sabotage to neurotic anxiety, guilt, masochism, and compliance, and to one's having continued to experience the present predominantly in terms of the threatening, disappointing, or traumatic past. This increased realization of having participated decisively in one's fate, even if not from its very influential beginning stages, necessarily brings with it an intensified and genuine sense of choice and responsibility. Contrary to popular distortion, which is a kind of extra-analytic resistance, the deterministic probings of effective analysis ultimately enhance rather than eliminate the analysand's sense of self-rule and the capacity to have a rationale for self-rule. They also enhance a realistic consideration of others, in whose feelings and welfare one now has a more definite and objective stake. The analytically enhanced sense of responsibility and choice is an alternative to neurotic guilt, masochism, dread, and compliance; it, too, has its infantile origins, but, having greater adaptive potential, it may achieve relative autonomy from these origins. Then, the analyzed person may even knowingly and regretfully—but rightly—make choices that he or she knows will involve suffering, while at the same time he or she will also be much freer to foster the possibilities for pleasure in life and reduce the objective danger and pain he or she encounters.

It has been said, "Tout comprendre, c'est tout pardonner." That easy way out is not in the spirit of analysis as it is not a part of the tragic sense of life. Understanding in depth seems rather to support a sense of one's own obligations and culpability and one's right to expect others to feel their obligations and culpability.

Another consideration that stands out in the tragic vision is that the very ego functions and interests that collaborate with the analyst in the analytic quest have been shaped ("deformed") to some extent by just those disturbing influences on personal development that the analysis is trying to define and reduce. The problem is not just that other aspects of ego functioning, such as the infantile defenses, impede the work of analysis; it also seems to be the case that the healthier or more mature ego functions and interests are themselves limited, imperfect, inconstant, and unreliable allies—somewhat like

mercenary soldiers or double agents. In this respect, a well-
chosen analysand is one whose so-called rational ego is not so
compromised that analysis is impossible; yet even the best of
analysands cannot be perfect in the part and so cannot have a
perfect analysis. I need not elaborate how the same considerations apply to the work of analysts. The perfect analysis may be
a useful theoretical standard, as in Eissler's (1953) discussion,
but it does not seem to exist in nature. And the tragic vision
sees through any gloss of perfection whatsoever. Again, however, I do not imply that essential, fairly comprehensive, and
benignly influential analytic work is generally out of the question.[9]

In order to develop further the tragic perspective on the
analytic process, I would like to come back to the question of
time, now in its relation to the compulsion to repeat.[10] We conceptualize the unconscious (or primary process) as timeless,
and we find the life of the neurotic analysand to be so dominated by unconscious (primary process) conflicts, and anxiety
and guilt, that he or she seems doomed to continue expressing
these conflicts apparently blindly and in infinite variety. Again
and again, for example, one must bring about the loss of the
needed breast or the enactment of one's own or someone else's
castration or rape. This compulsion to repeat gives emotional
life a static quality. Insofar as one is neurotic, all the action and
achievement in the world does not alter this static quality.

We know what this timeless, static quality is founded on: repression; fixation; the pleasure and security gained through
suffering; the peremptoriness of the primary process; the primary-process equivalence of wish and deed, or thought and
actuality, and the assumption of omnipotence implied by this
equivalence; also, the readiness with which objectively distinct
persons, things, and acts may come to stand for each other
through unconscious displacement, condensation and symboli-
zation and the non-intervention of reality-testing. The static

9. It is to be noted that I am speaking of degree of change. I do not intend to roman-
ticize (idealize) the outcomes of analysis. For example, I have chosen to speak of a
"benignly influential analysis" to get away from other locutions that refer to cure,
success, completion, or permanent and thoroughgoing change of structure or character. My caution expresses an aspect of the tragic and ironic visions of analytic work.

10. I do not mean the biological explanatory concept "repetition compulsion"; I
mean the regularly observable repetitiveness of neurotic behavior and its being "compelled" by the pressures of anxiety and guilt.

quality we call the compulsion to repeat signifies that the analysand is endlessly enacting the same ritual at the same point in time and with the same persons and consequences as obtained at the times of fixation. In this crucial respect—not, of course, in every respect—the analysand lives essentially out of time. Nothing changes. Indeed, from the standpoint of the defensive ego interests, change must be forestalled; for the prospect of change means exposure to greater danger and loss of secret gratifications; in either respect it means the analysand's applying his or her objective sense of reality to autoerotic or asocial fantasies of omnipotence, self-sufficiency, revenge, self-punishment, safety, and so forth. In this light the resistance, in protecting the compulsion to repeat, protects the static, out-of-time quality of the analysand's existence. It opposes reality-testing.

The compulsion to repeat is at the basis of much of the conscious and apparently passive suffering experienced by the analysand. It lacks the quality of a tragic phenomenon, however, owing to its repudiation of time and change, and its denial of the wilful, pleasurable, and reassuring elements of the repetitions. It may involve cyclic elements in having phases—for example, the obsessional phases of doing and undoing; and it may involve necessarily futile romantic quests—for example, for the oedipal mother: but in neither respect does the repetition embrace linear time. Progress in the analysis reduces the scope and urgency of these pseudo-blind, pseudo-passive, timeless repetitions. Loewald (1960) speaks of ghosts being transformed into ancestors during analysis (cf. my discussion of "presences" in *Aspects of Internalization,* 1968b). Analytic progress allows the wishes and fantasies on which the repetitions are based to be included in one's temporal view of one's own life and goals. It helps one see the necessity, the exaggerations, and the value of the comic and the romantic in both the disrupted and successfully adaptive aspects of one's life. Analytic progress dignifies the analysand by allowing sophisticated and controlled comic and romantic visions a place in life, while at the same time bringing him or her closer to a consciousness of the status of tragic hero in the inner world.

If this much is accepted, it seems warranted to propose that *the tragic vision is an accomplishment in the ego system.* Its impartiality is an expression of the ego system's recognizing

the exciting, dangerous, ambiguous, and contradictory influences of id wishes, superego strictures, the demands of, and
opportunities in, external reality, and the obscurities of its own
organization, as well as the inexorable passage of time. When
Freud said of the effects of analysis that were id was there shall
ego be (or become); when he specified that a similar transformation takes place in the ego's relations to the superego;
and when he said further that analysis puts the ego in the best
position to deal with its various problems or masters—in all
such statements he was, I believe, providing the foundation for
the assertion I have just made: that far from being a masochistic or guilty treat, tragic dramas and the tragic sense of life represent the ascendancy of objectivity in the ego system—what
we call good reality-testing and the dominance of the reality
principle. We see—and value seeing—that which we are most
powerfully disinclined to see.

It is not the immature, after all, who enjoy tragedy most in
the theater, though they may unconsciously enjoy the pathetic
side of the tragic developments they witness. Even so, the audience for tragedy is relatively small—much smaller, of course,
than the multitude of persons in our civilization who are inclined toward excessive neurotic guilt and masochism. En-
hancement of the tragic vision is an essential aspect of the
analytic goal of expanding the scope and sway of the ego system. This proposition should not be construed to mean my
advocating that philosophical discussions of "life" take place
between analysand and analyst, nor the words like "tragic"
become part of the vocabulary of interpretation: I am trying to
get at something that is implied—between the lines, so to speak
—in the analytic mode of understanding.

Effective analysis, it can now be said, alters not only the
analysand's past by helping fill in and organize its content
along certain lines but also transforms the way the analysand
acts in the present and in the future. It alters the mind that con-
templates the past, present, and future. It decisively influences
the way one views a life, and thereby it promotes that sense of
integrity which Erikson (1950) stressed as the positive pole at
the culmination of the psychosocial development. Erikson's description of the sense of integrity is, I believe, shaped by a
tragic vision. In fact, tragic and ironic perspectives are implied

throughout his developmental sequence of inescapable anti-thetical positions (trust-mistrust, etc.).

For the analysand, then, analysis represents a rise toward the possibility of tragic experience. Tragic heroes in drama, too, must rise to that status: Oedipus, Antigone, Hamlet, or Lear, all must struggle toward that naked yet magnificent position. Its spirit is summed up in Hamlet's "the readiness is all."

In the analysis of the neuroses it is especially the oedipal defeat and its consequences that must be relived and reunder-stood in the transference and termination before it can become a tragic experience (cf. Loewald 1962). Contrary to popular usage, tragic does not necessarily imply unhappy or disastrous outcomes. The working through of the termination of analysis both measures this transformation and consolidates it. Termination is, in one of its aspects, a tragic event; for the very process that brings the analytic relationship to its most profoundly meaningful, rewarding, and objective status also brings that relationship to an end. Both analyst and analysand share this tragic experience. They lose each other in finding each other. The conclusion of the analysis combines fulfilment and deprivation. The analysand feels this much more acutely than the analyst, and he or she expresses the rise to the tragic vision in an objective recognition of the value of terminating, and in an ability to persevere in the analytic work while mourning its ending. It is not that the analytic relationship has come to a complete end—and not only because the transference has not been totally resolved; as Loewald (1962) has shown, there is also a kind of internalization of the analyst as analyst into the analysand's ego and ego ideal organization that has much to do with his or her subsequent capacity for, and interest in, benignly influential self-analysis (see also Myerson 1963, 1965).

As for the analyst, his or her tragic vision (along with the ironic) is the foundation as well as the safeguard of neutrality toward the analysand and toward the role of analyst. This way of looking at reality counteracts tendencies to think of oneself as a god and to demand god-like achievements of the analysand: both are human beings, neither is omnipotent; blows to infantile narcissism must be suffered; and the best of analytic indications, intentions, and interventions may not pay off to the degree or in the way one expected. Moreover, the tragic per-

spective confers poise on the analyst in the face of the grotesque, terrible, and painful elements in the analysand's material; it makes it less tempting to be carried away regressively
by intense emotional responses to the analysand's suffering.
Against the impact of this suffering, the naive unqualified
comic and romantic visions offer only the flimsy protection of
avoidance, denial, and sentimental heroic daydreams. I think it
not unlikely that selection of analysands and analytic candi-
dates is often influenced by analysts' preconscious estimates
of their actual or potential capacity for a tragic (and ironic)
sense of life—sometimes subsumed under "psychological-
mindedness."

A particularly important tragic element in the analyst's sense
of his or her own role in the analysis is the awareness that, notwithstanding a close adherence to classical and well-founded
principles of technique, one remains the tool of one's own work
and so can analyze only in one's own way. One's use of the established principles and one's way of recognizing and verbalizing fundamental trends in the analytic material ought to be not
too different from the next analyst's, and so the insights and
changes achieved during the analysis ought to be not too different from what one could expect them to be if the next analyst
had this case. But differences there will be. These differences
exist partly because analysts differ among themselves in their
life histories, their talents and training, and their id, ego, and
superego organizations; and partly because the analysis of the
ego system, insofar as it can be sorted out of the analytic process as a whole, necessarily involves the analyst in a great
variety of highly individual variables. He or she is, for example,
attempting to clarify and account for very particular definitions
of danger, defenses, shifts of level, preferred shades of feelings,
interests, and values. Each analyst's sensitivities, interests, and
cultural scope are bound to influence the exploration and comprehension of this material. And there is no way of measuring
the resulting differences among analyses. One cannot experi-
ment with analyses. In this respect clinical analysis does not
meet the scientific requirement of being amenable to replication. Yet a second analysis, though not a replication, may high-
light some of the special characteristics of a first analysis and
may partly identify the particular slant given to it by the individuality of the first analyst. Similarly, the analyses of any

one analyst differ to some extent according to whether they were carried out early in his or her career or later on.

Thus it is a necessary part of the analyst's vision of the work to recognize that no matter how objectively one carries out analyses, no matter how far above reproach by colleagues the essentials of one's technique may be, and no matter how satisfactory the results, each analysis will bear a trademark or one of several trademarks. When asked in our circle, the question, "Who was the analyst?", can be meaningful in this connection, whatever its other, infantile implications. Implicitly, the question acknowledges the place of fate in one's personal analytic history.

I just used the word trademark. It is not the best word for what I have in mind in that the influence I am referring to pervades the analysis and is not simply stamped on its exterior. Analysis creates a new or another version of the life and mind of the patient. I have just been emphasizing that this version is a joint product of analyst and analysand, and that it would read somewhat differently if it had involved a different analyst.[11] What I want to emphasize next is my allusion to a creative element in this work. The analytic process creates a more comprehensive, unified, and intelligible past and present for the patient than was available to begin with, and, on this account, it even provides some vague outlines of a future. It does this by filling in crucial gaps of a particular kind in the analysand's memory, in the awareness of certain crucial meanings and connections, and in intrapsychic and interpersonal experience; also, by correcting old and new, inadequate and distorted meanings and connections and enriching accurate ones; and, further, by helping find an appropriate and useful language of words, images, and feelings through which to organize, modify, and communicate the life and mind in question. Neither the analysand nor the analyst has an infinitely plastic psychological vocabulary to draw on. For purposes of bringing about beneficial effects through analysis, they do not need that rich a vocabulary.

But I am concerned at the moment not so much with problems of technique as with an understanding of what analysis necessarily is. I propose, therefore, that the analytically created

11. This point may help explain why supervision of therapy and analyses is more effective when the supervisee presents *his* or *her* version of the material and not a tape-recording or a facsimile thereof in over-detailed, noncommital notes.

life history, while not fictive, is also not what one might call the absolute truth. How could it be when it has been wrought by two specific collaborators working at a specific point in time, under specific conditions; and also when, as I mentioned earlier, the collaborating side of the analysand's ego itself has been shaped by the influences it is the business of the analytic collaboration to modify? Genuine self-analytic progress during the post-analytic years, and also second analyses, can modify some aspects of the version that was worked out initially. If it is permissible to say so, the version becomes less fictive as the analysis is extended in range and made more precise. To some extent, the working through of termination can also play a part in this process. Nevertheless, however close the approximation to truth—and it can be considerable and of considerable value to the analysand—in the end, one is still left with a version of one's life and mind. It cannot be otherwise. It is, I submit, part of the tragic outlook of both analysand and analyst to recognize this necessity and be reconciled to it, which is not to say be passive, apathetic, or dismissive in relation to it. As I understand it, this point of view is generally accepted in other branches of historical inquiry.[12]

6. The Ironic Vision

The ironic vision I shall characterize chiefly as a readiness to seek out internal contradictions, ambiguities, and paradoxes. In this respect it overlaps the tragic vision.[13] The difference between the two lies in their aims. The tragic vision aims at seeing the momentous aspects and implications of events and people; it values total involvement and great crises; wherever it looks, it focuses on the simultaneous presence or interlocking of the noble and the demonic, the greatest achievement and the greatest waste, pity and terror, complete being and complete

12. Novey's (1968) discussion of psychoanalysis as historical inquiry throws much light on these problems. And, in this regard, Loewald (1969, personal communication) has said: "In a sense, every patient, and each of us, creates a personal myth (Kris 1956a) about our life and past, a myth which sustains us and may destroy us. The myth may change, and in analysis, where it becomes conscious, it often does change. The created life history is neither an illusion nor an invention, but gives form and meaning to our lives, and has to do with the identity Erikson (1956) speaks of."

13. For this reason, contemporary critical discussion has sometimes subsumed under "ironic" much that I have subsumed under "tragic" (see, for example, Brooks 1939). Also, the phrase "tragic irony" is often used for the blendings of these two visions.

annihilation. The ironic vision considers the same subject matter as the tragic but aims at detachment, keeping things in perspective, taking nothing for granted, and readily spotting the antithesis to any thesis so as to reduce the claim of that thesis upon us. In this respect the ironic vision tends to limit (not minimize) the scale of involvement in human difficulty while continuing to insist on the inherent difficulties of human existence. The very terms of tragic thinking—heroic, demonic, achievement, waste, etc.—are challenged by irony as to their largeness, urgency, clarity, meaningfulness. (The pretentious aspects of the romantic and the paradisial thrust of the comic are, of course, even more vulnerable to irony.)

The ironic vision may seem to be in the service of standing completely apart from experience and negating its significance; and the important and frequent contribution of irony to wit may seem to be in the service of taking nothing seriously. Although irony is often used in such fashion—for example, as a type of resistance in psychoanalysis—the ironic vision is not necessarily or inherently a withdrawal from, or mockery of, commitment. Essentially it is a serious business. It is no safe or comfortable thing to challenge firmly held beliefs, established traditions, and cherished illusions (the fate of Socrates might be recalled here), just as it is far from incidental whether and to what degree one can maintain detachment, perspective, and balance during those frequent trials of existence that make dogma, systems, and rigid conventions so appealing. There exists considerable potential for agitated states of conflict in the ironic vision.

The ironic vision is directed not only outward but inward as well. Applied to oneself, irony is self-deprecatory, not so much with the aim of self-abasement or self-ridicule as of not taking any single aspect of oneself too seriously for one's own good. The emotionally overcharged and grandiose inclinations common to all of us incline us to damn and glorify ourselves (and others) recklessly, simplistically, and absolutely; irony moderates these inclinations and thus safeguards good judgment and effective action.[14]

14. It might be argued that the ironic should occupy a superordinate position with respect to specific visions such as the comic, romantic, and tragic; specifically, that it should culminate in not taking too seriously any particular vision inasmuch as a tenable antithesis to it can always be established. The difficulty with this argument is that

Irony says not only that things are neither so simply bad nor so simply good as we would like to have them; ultimately it also questions whether we can be sure what we mean by bad and good, and whether and how far we can use such terms without contradicting ourselves. In this respect, irony leans toward resignation—an active, deliberative resignation, not an apathetic one.

That the ironic and tragic should not be regarded as antithetical is evident in the fact that neither would accept Hegel's synthesis-orientated assertion that, in the end, tragic drama establishes "ethical tranquillity" in the beholder (Abel 1967, p. 376); nor would either vision regard "ethical tranquillity" as a possible or desirable goal in the theater or on the couch; and the ironic vision would recognize that "ethical," like "superego," refers to tension, so that as an idea ethical tranquillity is self-contradictory, though it is common enough as a pose and an ideal.

The ironic and tragic visions are also alike in the relative emphasis they put on reflective thought and inner articulation of feeling. In contrast, the romantic and comic visions tend to emphasize action in the world, people making their places or losing themselves in something outside themselves—in society, nature, a cause, or a conquest. The ironic and the tragic are especially important in the investigative aspects of psychoanalysis, while the comic and romantic have more to do with its healing and emancipating aspects.

The ironic perspective in analytic work results in the analysand's coming to see himself or herself as being less in certain essential respects than was initially thought—less, that is, than the unconscious ideas of omnipotence and omniscience imply. Such terms as neurotic pride, egocentricity, inflated narcissism, infantile ego ideal, and manic defense refer to different aspects of, or different theoretical approaches to, the residual yet powerful core of grandiose self-representations people carry forward from early childhood. To some extent, these representations are brought to light during analysis and seen to be wishful

it expresses a value judgment as to "the best way to be" or "the best way to think," whereas it is my intent to treat visions neutrally as alternatives, any one of which might for certain purposes be set up over the others. It is, for example, equally arguable for certain valuative purposes that the ironic be subsumed under the tragic, or that, as Frye (1957) suggests, all visions be subsumed under a total quest myth. At the same time, however, I am attempting to define differences among these visions in scope, consequences, and adaptive implications.

fantasies which both contribute to and hamper internal integration and effective action in the real world. Their exaggerated influence may be reduced through establishing their presence and through understanding their origins, functions, and consequences in the analysand's past and present life—in other words, by subjecting them to reality-testing.

I have already mentioned that an ironic stance may be largely in the service of resistance. The same is true of the romantic, comic, and tragic stances. Insofar as this is the case, each will betray that it is making a significant contribution to resistance by its being facile or glib, repetitious, too quickly resorted to whenever anxiety mounts, and not leading toward fuller discovery and disclosure of deeply personal, more or less archaic fantasies, wishes, and feelings. They are then revealed to be rigid postures rather than searching visions—ways of staying on the surface or of hastily resurfacing. When less resistant in intent, the ironic vision facilitates deepening of the analysis: it helps it feel safer to enter into regressive processes, especially in the transference, by its assurance that, while not unreal or unimportant, the experiences encountered are part of a program of investigation and treatment; that they include an "as if" quality along with a "true" quality; and that they are not a total, absolute, and overwhelming new reality.

A useful capacity for irony is not reliably available to psychotic patients undergoing treatment.

On the analyst's part, his or her capacity for irony makes it more possible to appreciate that, on the average, the crises, retreats, and advances to be dealt with are great and not so great at one and the same time. When Freud referred to the saying that every advance is only half as great as if it appears to be at first, he was, I would say, expressing an ironic vision of the analytic process. Similarly when he said, with regard to the addition of superego analysis to id analysis, that psychoanalysis shows people to be more moral as well as less moral than they have thought.

The effectiveness of interpretation sometimes depends on its being touched with irony; if not too heavy and thereby self-canceling, irony can make certain analytic discoveries tolerable enough to be usable. Tact in interpretation (Loewenstein 1951) involves more than timing and choice of dynamic content and level. But whether or not ironic tone is used or should ever be used, ironic vision is essential in psychoanalytic interpretation.

7. VISION AND VALUES

Finally, I should like to direct your attention to certain valuative implications of the main thesis of this chapter. Clinical analysis strengthens the analysand's sense of reality and makes the operation of his or her version of reality-testing more efficient. In this chapter I have pointed out that in so doing clinical analysis modifies one's view of the world in such a way that when important problems arise one can intensify one's own tragic and ironic probings. And it is often adaptive to intensify these probings. I remind you that tragic by no means implies overriding despair, bitterness, or horror; nor does ironic imply any simple facetiousness, aloofness, or cynicism. The fact of this shift says something about the view of reality implicit in psychoanalytic understanding, though not in that approach to life alone, for it pervades the large body of myth, literature, and philosophy, too.

Psychoanalytic thought is deeply colored by tragic and ironic visions of the world. Therefore, for the analyst to recognize and declare that this is so, as I am doing, is not to step outside the role of analyst: it is to affirm that role as well as to put additional content into those abstract, formalistic terms—the average expectable environment, the life cycle, reality-testing, and the reality principle. This content is not simple, specific, and uniform. If it amounts to a *Weltanschauung*, it does so only in a very general, unconfining sense. It does not prescribe a particular consensus. But, to one degree or another, this content is defined and organized primarily by tragic and ironic principles. These principles are implied, I believe, in Hartmann's (1939a) proposition concerning the concept of health: "[A] healthy person must have the capacity to suffer and to be depressed" (p. 6).[15]

15. The mixture of tragic and ironic perspectives in Hartmann's (1939a) approach is evident in his amplification of this proposition: he refers to what clinical experience has taught us regarding the inability "to admit to oneself the possibility of illness and suffering. It is even probable that a limited amount of suffering and illness forms an integral part of the scheme of health, as it were, or rather that health is reached in indirect ways. We know that successful adaptation can lead to maladaptation—the development of the superego is a case in point....But, conversely, maladaptation may become successful adaptation....We discover a similar state of affairs in relation to the therapeutic process of analysis. Here health clearly includes pathological reactions as a means towards its attainment" (pp. 6-7).

If this be granted, it seems to follow that as a system of observations, methods, and hypotheses, psychoanalysis leans
toward certain values and away from others. It leans toward
values that support the recognition of the depths of the inner
world, complexity, ambiguity, conflict, the ubiquity of the demonic and of suffering, the frequent interpenetration of victory
and defeat, unremitting questioning of absolutes, and the like.
These would be the values inherent in the reality principle,
broadly conceived, along with those values (related to the
comic and romantic) that emphasize taking remedial action
and taking chances. Any system of thought that denied or
opposed these values would be an enemy of psychoanalysis. In
this sense, although psychoanalysis is not synonymous with
absolute truth, it is the manifestation of Freud's love of truth.
Psychoanalysis is the expression and weapon of a value—or,
more exactly, of a body of values contained within love of
truth.

8. SUMMARY AND CONCLUSIONS

The concepts reality relations and reality-testing should
cover broad views of inner and outer reality, as well as the details of concrete, immediate perceptions of, and interactions
with, these realities. The broad views vary among people who
qualify as being generally objective, so that any absolute standard of objectivity in this regard is not tenable. These views are
termed here "visions of reality" to emphasize that they are
partly subjective, or not completely disprovable, ways of looking at experience and imposing meaning on it. I have maintained that there is a vision of reality characteristic of psychoanalytic thought and that this vision combines comic, romantic,
tragic, and ironic modes or partial visions. I have supplied definitions of each of these partial visions and have applied them
particularly to pertinent aspects of the psychoanalytic process—
that special reality about which analysts are most knowledgeable. The comic vision, with its emphasis on optimism, progress, and amelioration of difficulties, and the romantic vision,
with its emphasis on the adventurous quest, are related especially to the curative, liberating, and alloplastic emphasis in the
analytic process. The tragic vision, stressing deep involvement,
inescapable and costly conflict, terror, demonic forces, waste,

and uncertainty, and the ironic vision, stressing detached alertness to ambiguity and paradox and the arbitrariness of absolutes, are related especially to the investigative, contemplative, and evaluative aspects of the analytic process. Particularly the tragic and ironic seem to be distinctive features of the Freudian psychoanalytic outlook. Resistance, transference, countertransference, empathy, and pathetic, melodramatic and masochistic coloration of analytic behavior, have been considered within the framework of these components of the analytic vision of reality. I have also discussed representations of experience and life history as being atemporal, cyclic, and linear, and the significance of the compulsion to repeat. The emerging analytic life history is to be viewed as a joint creation of patient and analyst—not a fiction but not simply factual either, being subject to a degree to the limitations, individualities, and visions of the two participants in the analytic process. Finally, I have called attention to certain valuative implications of the psychoanalytic vision, especially those pertaining to "love of truth."

The analytic standard of objectivity demands that we confront and contend with much unavoidable pain, uncertainty, paradox, defeat, and disillusionment in our existence, which, helped by our defenses, inhibitions, illusions, and symptoms, we might otherwise avoid recognizing, experiencing, and modifying. In this respect, the standard calls for tragic and ironic views or visions of reality. However, the impartial and elastic approach of psychoanalysis implies a more inclusive vision of reality than that provided by the tragic and ironic, in that it also appreciates and relies on the contribution of the sophisticated, controlled romantic and comic visions to adaptive strivings.

In the end, the analytic approach to inner and external reality is not a simple matter of fact-finding and fact-organizing. When one steps back from the immediate and specific, the approach is a matter of vision, too.

4 An Overview of Heinz Hartmann's Contributions to Psychoanalysis*

1. INTRODUCTION

Heinz Hartmann's contributions to psychoanalytic theory (1939b 1960, 1964) rise up before the student of psychoanalysis as a mountain range whose distant peaks with their immense vistas and rarefied atmosphere one can scarcely hope to reach. And yet the student must not only attempt the arduous climb, he or she must try to get above that range in order to be able to include Hartmann's work within his or her own vision of psychoanalysis, for that work is not the whole of psychoanalysis, nor can it be the last word on psychoanalytic theory; it is and can only be part of the terrain of scientific psychoanalysis and of science generally. (Nietzsche said: "One repays a teacher badly if one always remains a pupil only.") The high probability of being presumptuous and unfair in the attempt— or of being thought to be so—is exceeded by the even higher probability that in the absence of such attempts psychoanalytic thinking will stagnate in the lowlands of orthodoxy. Hartmann as much as anyone in the field was alert and responsive to the latter danger, and there can be no doubt that long ago he saw the necessity of setting himself up above Freud, at least provisionally, in order to further the development of psychoanalysis.

It is my purpose in this chapter to define and discuss from a vantage point somewhat different from that usually taken (e.g., Rangell 1965; Loewenstein 1966) certain essential contributions Heinz Hartmann made to psychoanalytic theory. The difference in vantage point is this: instead of summarizing Hartmann's ideas in order to show that they *are* contributions, I shall be mainly concerned with the nature of these ideas (their

*This is a modified version of a paper first published with this title in the *International Journal of Psycho-analysis*, 51 (1970): 425-46. Even more so than in Chapter 3, I have let stand the bulk of my own formulations that conform to traditional metapsychological usage; see, however, the shift of emphasis that I began in the discussion of neutralization (section 5) and thereafter.

internal logic); with the question *Contributions toward what end?* (their strategy); and with some criticisms to which they are open (their vulnerability). For the time being, then, I have chosen a vantage point above Hartmann's contributions to psychoanalysis.

That my endeavor is in the spirit of Hartmann's thought will be apparent if one remembers his consistent attempts to state his own objectives, strategy, and criticisms (e.g., "synchronization" of Freud's unsystematized and unevenly developed contributions, and formulation of psychoanalytic propositions in a manner suitable for establishing psychoanalysis as "a general psychology"). It is, however, in the nature of criticism not to rest with an author's statements about his or her work. One must directly examine the corpus of these works, which includes the author's own view of it as one item among others, in order to arrive at an independent judgment as to its design, value, and success. Just as poets do not have the final say about their own poetry, psychoanalytic theoreticians do not have the final say about their own theorizing. I do not, however, present this paper as a *complete* overview of Hartmann's contributions; rather as a consideration of certain defining features of Hartmann's thought.

It is evident that from the first Hartmann was keenly aware of the lack of elegance in psychoanalytic theory as it stood at the end of Freud's life and work, and that he set about systematically to develop the elegance that psychoanalysis, by virtue of its tremendous insights, so richly deserves. He found the theory crude in every one of its metapsychological aspects. *Dynamic* propositions, especially those concerning aggression, were in a state of disorder: the many types of aims they covered were not hierarchically arranged, they were defined on many levels of abstraction, and they were not always clearly related to basic concepts concerning the driving forces of the personality; moreover, the conceptualization of these driving forces, especially the instinctual drives, was itself in need of considerable repair. The *structural* theory contained comparable weaknesses in its treatment of the development and functions of the id, ego, and superego alike; especially intrasystemic issues had been neglected. The *economic* point of view (and, with it, the structural) was unworkable without considerable articulation and amplification of energic concepts. *Genetic* propositions were uncoordinated and unevenly developed, especially in the case of narcissism, aggression, and preoedipal development. *Adaptive* propositions concerning relations with the real world were lacking in theoretical stature and systematization and required an approach through the biological concept of adaptation.

I shall be detailing some of these statements below. I want to mention now that, whatever his reasons, Hartmann rather consistently underestimated (or underemphasized?) the extent to which he disagreed with Freud, correcting him, altering some of the foundations of his theory, and perhaps above all establishing a basis for a continuing challenge of psychoanalytic theory by psychoanalysts. The grounds of that challenge are that psychoanalysis is a scientific endeavor, and that, along with formulation of theory, challenging its own theories is of the essence of any science. Which is to say that Hartmann was engaged in revisions in psychoanalytic thought and modes of thinking about psychoanalysis that are, in some respects at least, revolutionary, their modest and emendatory tone notwithstanding. I shall return in several places to this assertion, too.

Unfortunately, it seems to be the case that Hartmann's writings have tended to be made the center of a new orthodoxy in psychoanalytic theory. Viewed historically, it is not surprising that what started out as a fresh look at psychoanalysis, and indeed continued to be amazingly fresh over the years of its development, should now threaten to become an institutionalized blindness to the need for continued critical and original thought. Open-mindedness is one hallmark of Hartmann's work. It can, I think, be shown that in part Hartmann was spurred on in his pioneering efforts by his recognition that the neo-Freudians on the one hand and the Kleinians on the other have been directing challenges to Freudian analysis that have to be faced. This is so because these challenges owe their existence to defects in the Freudian theory (e.g., its neglect of a systematic consideration of adaptation and the environment, values, aggression, and the earliest phases of development, including superego development).[1]

1. Although Hartmann was also aware of challenges emanating from phenomenological and existentialist thought (e.g., with regard to the self and questions of intentionally and meaning), he devoted little attention to these challenges which are still with us today—and rightly so.

In his role as theoretician Hartmann did not write off radical dissent as madness, ignorance, or unanalyzed resistance and negative transference. His taking dissent seriously for what it can teach about deficiencies in one's own thought was as much a part of his greatness as his readiness to question and revise formulations held precious, if not sacred, by generations of analysts. I do not get the impression from his writings that he enjoyed assuming this critical obligation; be that as it may, what matters is that he assumed it, even while softening somewhat the impact of his so doing. Thereby he set an example of manliness and scientific clearsightedness for all of us. Those who would make him the center of a new orthodoxy contradict what his own work stands for. He was an inspiring and irreplaceable teacher of modes of elegant scientific thinking as well as of fruitful and progressive formulations in all aspects of psychoanalytic theory.

I shall be taking up in turn Hartmann's assault on dualism; his recognition of options in psychoanalytic theorizing; his anatomizing of psychoanalysis; his psychoeconomic contributions, particularly his conceptualization of neutralization; and his model of mind.

I know I shall be being unfair to Hartmann's frequent collaborators, Kris and Loewenstein, by usually attributing to Hartmann alone the ideas to be discussed below. My doing so is, however, warranted by three considerations: Hartmann acknowledged his debt to these men; in turn, these men have in various ways given pride of place to Hartmann (e.g., Loewenstein, 1966, p. 477n); and, above all, the main outlines of the conceptual approach in question had already been set forth by Hartmann independently, in 1939, before the remarkable collaboration began (see Hartmann et al., 1964).

2. The Assault on Dualism

One of the fundamental revisions in Freudian thinking undertaken by Hartmann is the dissolution of its dualistic framework, its crudely dialectical bias, its orientating itself so far as possible by means of great polarities. To recall the main polarities, I mention pleasure principle-reality principle; sublimated-unsublimated; id impulse-ego defense; cathexis-anticathexis; ego cathexis-object cathexis; instinctual drive-hostile reality; life instinct-death instinct; libido-aggression; biological-psychological. And there were some polarities that had fallen into relative disuse in psychoanalytic theorizing but had not yet been systematically disposed of, such as phylogeny-ontogeny and sexual instincts-ego instincts, to which Hartmann administered the coup de grâce.

Hartmann revised some of these polarities by introducing notions of degree; some by establishing the equal theoretical dignity of third factors or multiple factors; some by showing that one of the terms could subsume the other; still others by thoroughly discrediting one or both of the dialectical opposites, either by showing that the concepts had been superseded or that one concept was not on the same conceptual plane as its opposite.

I shall be told that I am overstating the case, that neither Freud nor his distinguished followers really let themselves fall victim to dualistic oversimplifications or constraints, that the polarities were useful as flexibly managed reference points. I wish it were so. One has only to compare Freud's and Hartmann's metapsychologies to realize the extent to which dualism has been forced to give ground.[2] It is just because Freud's *clinical* discussions and low-level empirical generalizations are not constrained by his a priori dualistic orientation that his general theory may be seen to be problematic; that is to say, the general theory corresponds not to Freud's psychoanalytic understanding of specific people but to his views on human nature and science.

Later I shall detail some of these revisions of dualism systematized by Hartmann. (I recognize that others—e.g., Waelder 1930—have made significant but less systematic and systematized contributions along these lines.) Here I want to say that, taken together, these revisions, aimed in part at establishing a field-theoretical orientation, helped to free psychoanalytic theorizing from the binary straitjacket. The study of the central conflicts of the personality remains the hallmark of psychoanalysis, but now two-factor conflicts can be considered only one among many types of conflict, and, more important, dichotomies can be seen to be often ill-suited for organizing psycho-

2. Overdetermination, though non-dualistic, is not central to Freud's *meta*psychology, and the forces to which it refers are conceived dualistically by Freud; consequently it does not count against my present thesis. The importance of overdetermination is recognized in the discussion of psychic reality in section 5 on neutralization.

logical data. To give only two examples at this point: the hypothesis of primary neutral energy added a third type of energy; and the hypothesis of primary autonomous functions added a third factor to the drives-reality configuration.

I stress this point: to acknowledge that psychoanalysis is, above all, the study of conflict is not necessarily to agree that the most useful model of conflict is binary or that life is organized around and in terms of polarities. The latter propositions are philosophical a prioris, not scientific findings, and they seem to ride roughshod over the results of refined observation and to restrict the generation of new hypotheses. In fact, many of the charges of crude reductionism leveled against psychoanalysis seem to pertain not to genetic reductionism but to the view of the person as a bundle of familiar dichotomies. (There is, of course, an age-old philosophical tradition of dualism that lies behind Freud's particular attempts to bring order into his clinical observations; the psychology of that tradition deserves full study in its own right.) I am also aware that for many ordinary clinical purposes it is useful to analyze conflict in two-factor terms, though at the same time I would emphasize that by the end of a searching analysis two-factor explanations of any significant problem will—or should—appear to be trivial, false, and mechanical.

Not only conceptualization but observation as well has been freed by the assault on dualism. The field-theoretical approach is not less dramatic, less appealing to the imagination than the dualistic; it is less *melodramatic* because more subtle, more demanding of wit and intelligence, more ironic in its multifaceted emphasis, even more tragic in its appreciation of the intertwining of influences and consequences to the point where clear categorizations, explanations, and evaluations (e.g., of adaptation, health, defense, etc.) are not easily come by and most likely inexact. A different vision of reality is implied (see chapter 3). One encounters this vision in Freud's clinical discussions.

In order to clarify how Hartmann cracked the dualistic mold, I select for discussion some aspects of his structural propositions. (An examination of his economic propositions could serve the same purpose; see section 5 on neutralization.)

First, however, I must provide some background for my discussion of this point. I must point out that we are not exact in attributing the tripartite structural theory to Freud, even though we are not far wrong in so doing. There is much reason to think that for Freud the structural theory was dualistic in nature. Freud subordinated his treatment of the superego to dualistic necessities; I say this in full awareness of his many and well-known statements concerning the superego's independence (e.g., the superego as one of the three masters served by the ego); Freud was often inconsistent in his theorizing. For one thing, he entitled the book in which he set forth the theory of the superego *The Ego and the Id*. Moreover, he chose there to characterize the superego merely as a grade (or differentiation) *within* the ego and as a precipitate *in* the ego. Further, when he considered the superego's enmity to the ego, he did so in terms of his dualistic instinct theory; he portrayed it as a new form of the struggle between Eros and the death instinct. In this respect, Freud also stressed the superego's closeness to the id—almost as a grade within the id as well as within the ego—and so still not really an autonomous organization. And finally, as I have argued elsewhere (1960), Freud had great difficulty in recognizing how some of his formulations concerning the superego implied that it worked with libido as well as agression; this difficulty, too, is a consequence of his penchant for dualism. He attempted to arrange all his major general theoretical propositions in accordance with the logic of the libido-aggression or Eros-death instinct polarity.

Dualism cannot survive if close and systematic examination of each of its components shows it to be internally heterogeneous, multidirectional, conflicted, or caught up in self-contradiction. And this is precisely the kind of examination that Hartmann, unlike Freud, undertook in a rigorous manner —an examination, I might add, that is eminently clinical as well as theoretical.

I shall refer only briefly to another crucial aspect of the dualistic cast of Freud's structural theory, namely its treatment of the ego as a cohesive, unitary, or monolithic system. Despite his profound discoveries concerning irrational defensive ego activities and the splitting of the ego, and despite his *clinical* awareness of intrasystemic conflict (e.g., conflicting identifications in the ego), Freud never gave a prominent place in his theory to intrasystemic relations. His mind was ever on inter-systemic relations. Although we can appreciate the historical grounds of his preoccupation with intersystemic relations, we must also bear in mind that the alleged cohesiveness of the ego followed from theoretical preconceptions and problems and not from psychoanalytic discoveries proper. The cohesive ego was the embodiment of Eros—one of the two poles of life.

Hartmann articulated certain key structural concepts in such a fashion as to prevent the careful thinker from resorting to the common simplification of treating psychic agencies as homo-geneous, unidirectional, monolithic entities (e.g., to speak of "the ego"). It does not matter really that, as Hartmann was careful to note, Freud indicated in many places his awareness that the polarities were temporary theoretical scaffolds, or that empirically things are always considerably more complex and ambiguous than the binary framework suggests. It does not matter, that is, when we confront Freud's formal theorizing and Hartmann's formal critiques and revisions of them, though it can matter in one's estimate of Freud the man, which is an altogether different subject. And it does not matter that, de-spite his own systematic demolishing of the hidden myth of monolithic psychic structures, Hartmann himself resorted in many places to locutions concerning "the ego" or "the id" (see the following section).

What does matter is that Hartmann laid the groundwork for systematic study of the conflict-free functions of the ego, the change of function and secondary autonomy of ego functions, the rank order of their importance, their hierarchical arrange-ment, and the increasing internalization and centralization of control in superordinate regulating functions that characterize human development; additionally, he pointed to the necessity of assuming that different ego functions work with different degrees of neutralized energy and hence are at variable dis-tances from the drives and the primary process, and he also showed a similar necessity regarding the superego functions; further, he made the role of aggression in the ego as important as the role of libido; and he also clarified that certain aspects of ego function rather than id function correspond to the action of instincts in lower animals. Once he had made these and similar contributions, it simply made no sense ever again to speak without qualification or specification of "the ego," "the super-ego," and in certain respects "the id." Psychoanalysis was in new theoretical terrain.

This theoretical progression has not, I would say, reduced the systemic concepts to the status of handy metaphors or arbitrary shorthand references to complex matters. The concepts have retained empirical content and theoretical value. Hartmann fully appreciated the fact that certain functions are more like each other than they are like other functions; for instance, they resemble each other in the types of aims they are suited to and their closeness to or distance from the primary process or primitive modes of "discharge." He was also well aware of observations the theoretical implications of which were developed at length and in related ways by Rapaport (1951, 1959, 1967), namely that these similar functions tend to be interrelated and subject to the same superordinate regulations or principles, so that they can take on the quality of organized groupings of functions.

On these grounds Hartmann argued the necessity and value of the concepts id, ego, and superego—the tripartite structural point of view. In fact, it was only after Hartmann (with his collaborators Kris and Loewenstein) expounded his views on structural development (1946) and the superego (1962) that the superego was fully established as an independent psychic structure equal in *theoretical* dignity to the id and ego. And yet, by developing his differential intrasystemic propositions, Hartmann also showed that each structure is at least as heterogeneous in its make-up (its referents) as it is homogeneous. Not only at the borders of each structure is it difficult to lay down clear lines of demarcation, but at its very center; for example, the simultaneous position of certain processes as impulse and defense renders systemic classification ambiguous, if not arbitrary. Fenichel (1941), among others, had recognized this simultaneity long ago but had not seen its systematic implications.

Further, in his discussion of intersystemic relations and his regard for the principle of multiple function (see Waelder 1930), Hartmann developed propositions concerning specific phenomena, processes, or structural factors which establish that they cannot be assigned to any one of the psychic systems.

I have in mind, for example, his discussion of moral codes (1960): he conceptualized these codes as quasi-autonomous structures that are joint products of superego and ego, which means that they cannot be assigned to either of these structures alone; further, he pointed out that in different people or at different times moral codes shade over more to ego or superego, and thus clarified that matters of degree as well as kind are involved in the structural position of moral values.

Hartmann's concept of the multiple appeal of interpretations reflects the same recognition of multiple-systemic belongingness of specific events.

His conceptualization of aggression in the ego destroys the assumption of a built-in, Eros-derived cohesiveness of the ego.

Thus, while not minimized, the structural concepts were shown by Hartmann to require considerable qualification in particular explanatory propositions. Especially is this true of ego and superego (see, for example, Hartmann 1964, pp. 138-41; Hartmann and Loewenstein 1962). Although the observations in question had been familiar for a long time, they appeared in a somewhat new light in Hartmann's discussions, and so were partially transformed, as facts or observations will be once new questions are asked about them and new hypotheses developed concerning them. More important, however, is that the theoretical language of psychoanalysis was transformed in order simultaneously to see things in a new light and to assimilate the results into a theory adequate for them. *That* theory had to be thoroughly emancipated from dualism and its by-products (e.g., simplistic structural concepts).

If, in being thus elegantly articulated and complicated for empirical as well as theoretical reasons, the structural theory has not been undermined, it has been, ironically, put in its proper limited perspective by this, its most polished formulation. It is subject now to stringent limits and internal paradoxes. I shall try to show later that a similar ironic consequence characterizes Hartmann's elaboration of psychoeconomic theory. It is a contribution to science of the first order so to crystallize its propositions that their vulnerability to criticism and modification is maximized. (This point is not always appreciated in the psychoanalytic literature, which often tends to be self-congratulatory in tone.) Upon reaching the heights of formalization, one finds not security or invulnerability but new problems and new possibilities of solving them. Hartmann moved psychoanalytic theory into a new, more advanced phase of insecurity.

3. Adaptation Theory as a Scientific Option

Hartmann accomplished another of his fundamental revisions of Freudian thought through his remarkable method of setting all of psychoanalytic theoy within the framework of biological adaptation theory. Clearly, this was a carefully considered choice. Freud (and others after him) had been at pains to adhere to a biological model of conceptualization, and assumptions about adaptation can be found in every major aspect of Freud's theorizing. The difference is this: until Hartmann made the attempt, the biological mode of thought and the regard for adaptation had been improvised and uncoordinated, fragmentary and groping. Freud needs no apologists in this regard. It is to Hartmann's credit that he recognized that the biology in psychoanalysis was in bad shape, loosely used, and not up to date. He saw that Freud had employed a great variety of biological concepts and propositions in response to his confrontation of myriad clinical observations and problems, and he knew that these concepts and propositions had to be aligned, realigned, modified, reformulated, and in some cases discarded on the basis of a systematic application of biological principles, particularly those concerning adaptation. Being also keenly aware of the history of Freud's thought and Freud's tendency to follow new lines of thought without systematically reformulating earlier conceptualizations while so doing, Hartmann could speak out for the need to synchronize, coordinate, and amplify Freud's theoretical contributions, and he could embark on this program in a consistent and consistently illuminating manner.

The profoundly important step Hartmann took was this: he did not, as others had been content to do, take psychoanalysis as a scientific enterprise that was a law unto itself; he recognized that, in science, observations are made and ordered, and propositions and hypotheses formulated, according to a priori basic assumptions. These assumptions dictate certain theoreti-

cal strategies, and they establish the decorum of conceptualization, the "right" language for the science. In other words, he
saw that for science it is always a question of vantage point.
References to vantage point abound in *Ego Psychology and the
Problem of Adaptation* (1939b). Having chosen the biological-
adaptational vantage point, Hartmann proceeded to demonstrate in his papers and monographs what psychoanalysis
could be as a scientific theory *of a certain sort.*

The point I want to emphasize is that by setting an example
Hartmann helped establish the legitimacy of recognizing that
one does have options in choosing one's vantage point. One
does not, of course, have unlimited freedom. The choice of
vantage point cannot be arbitrary if it is to be useful. In order to
facilitate the coordination and amplification of concepts and
hypotheses, a vantage point must bear some close, compelling
relationship to the conceptual and observational material already at hand. Hartmann's contributions put an end to the
period when psychoanalytic theorizing was a law unto itself.
He brought psychoanalysis into the world of modern natural
science. Although I would judge from his writings that Hartmann believed options to be available only *within* the natural
science approach. I propose that by his deliberate *choice* Hartmann also made it clear that vantage points other than that of
natural science may also be considered. I regard this as another
of his revolutionary contributions.

To date, the chief psychoanalytic questioners of the commitment to the natural science model have been the existential
analysts, notably Binswanger (1963, pp. 149-81). One need not
subscribe to existential-analytic thought to recognize the
merits of the point that the natural science approach itself is an
option, one that is useful and costly at the same time. And so,
though Hartmann does not seem to have carried his reasoning
this far, he contributed to putting the thinker, the self-aware
and purposive observer, back in the driver's seat, where he or
she was anyway—though often it was as if we were supposed to
think he or she was simply being driven by the data.

It must be emphasized that by his example Hartmann
demonstrated how great a challenge each choice of vantage
point entails. That challenge is none other than a life's work of
rethinking the basic problems, findings, and explanations of
psychoanalysis in the terms of one's new vantage point.

There have always been dissidents, deviationists, revisionists in psychoanalysis, and there always will be; however, so far as I know, none of them has assumed the burden of thinking through the consequences of one's choices. It is not even clear that any one of them has been aware that he or she was making a scientific *choice*, for each has justified departures from Freud on empirical, technical, or humanistic grounds, none of which are germane. No one has said: "Let's make a different set of basic assumptions, which we are free to do prior to any empirical or valuative decision—prior to experience, if you will—and let's see how that works out." From a systematic point of view the assumptions precede experience, though, of course, in fact it does not happen quite that way. The existential-analytic approach is, as already noted, an exception to what I just said; however, for reasons I cannot go into here, that approach is not—or not yet—psychoanalysis as I understand it, and my discussion pertains to modes of theorizing used by those we would agree on as being psychoanalytic.

By what he self-consciously chose to do, Hartmann made it possible to turn the assumptions of psychoanalysis inside out, to stand them on their heads, to throw them out, and to bring in new ones—provided that the changes can be justified by showing that the new assumptions do some work that the old ones did not do and at the same time do a lot of work (not necessarily all of it) that the old ones did do. Thus it has become possible to say, as I believe Novey (1968) began to do: "Let's take history rather than biology as our vantage point." It is even possible to say: "Let's assume psychoanalysis is not a science and cannot be a science, except perhaps in only some of its aspects, and for only certain purposes." Even that is allowable; for viewed in its broadest aspects Hartmann's contribution amounts to introducing psychoanalysis firmly into the world of intellectual history and not just the world of scientific ideas. I shall return to these options briefly later on.

In this connection I must mention my judgment that Rapaport and Gill (1959), in their discussion of the metapsychological points of view, misconstrued Hartmann's contributions. Basing their argument on Hartmann's discussion of adaptation, they proposed that the adaptational perspective be accepted as a metapsychological point of view along with the economic, dynamic, and structural—the three points of view retained by

Freud in his final theoretical formulations. Freud regarded these three points of view as sufficient for the explanation of psychological processes. According to my argument, adaptation, in the broad sense generally used by Hartmann, is a point of view that is located outside the field of psychoanalytic propositions, whatever their degree of generality or abstractness. Adaptation is a natural science—specifically, biological—point of view with the help of which one may systematically select, formulate, arrange, and interrelate psychoanalytic propositions. Adaptation theory starts with the proposition that if one regards people as biological entities, one's language for discussing psychology should consistently reflect the fact that psychology deals with one facet of biological existence. Hartmann went further than this to propose that sociology, too, be viewed as dealing with still another facet of biological existence (1964, pp. 31-32), and then went even further, marvelously, to propose in the same statement that drives are as sociological as social factors are biological, i.e., that it is always a matter of theoretical vantage point. But his main point was that the language of psychology should derive from, or be consistent with, or at least make good sense with respect to, biology. Hence Hartmann's continued close attention to the language of "functions." Concepts such as psychological structure and psychological conflict are, in this respect, within psychology and not outside of and prior to it; this is not true of the biological-adaptational perspective.

It is, however, demonstrable that Hartmann used adaptation not only as an a priori vantage point but in a narrow clinical or descriptive sense as well. In this narrow sense adaptation refers to "functions" concerned with maintaining the stability and efficiency of psychological organization in relation to environmental organization. Although in this sphere Hartmann contributed many acute perceptions, thoughtful differentiations, and searching questions, he did not always make it clear when he was working within the context of psychoanalytic theory and when he was developing orientating propositions to analytic theory and observation as a whole.

This narrow view of adaptation points to variables and leads to propositions that articulate and amplify the structural—specifically, ego-psychological—point of view. Consequently it does not call for the designation of a new metapsychological point of view. Hartmann never proposed this addition—and he was right about that.[3]

While on this critique of Rapaport and Gill, which I make as a step toward clarifying the nature of Hartmann's contribution and not for its own sake, I will add that, in my judgment, their proposal that the genetic approach be regarded as still another metapsychological point of view misconstrues the place of genetic considerations in psychological explanation. The genetic emphasis in the traditional psychoanalytic explanation is methodological: it represents the recognition that it is usually necessary to study the past and present life-historical contexts of the component factors of any psychological process in order correctly to identify, characterize, and assess their influence. Traditional explanation concerns immediate fields of force; history helps to determine the nature of these fields of force. The component factors of the field are necessarily *current* factors and these are, in the final analysis, to be explained in terms of aims (dynamics), emphases (economics), and organizations with varying degrees of independence, integration, stability, and influence (structures).

I am aware that psychoanalysis has been characterized by a strong interest in longitudinal studies. Especially is this so regarding developmental continuity and the profound consequences of radical attempts at personal discontinuity. I also take into account that expositions of psychoanalytic discoveries and clinical work necessarily include rough accounts of personality development viewed over time. However, that interest and those longitudinal accounts are not explanatory; their purpose is to provide a basis for summaries of many explanatory propositions appropriate to different phases, types, and contexts of development. Genetic propositions refer descriptively to temporal sequences and to the regressive and progressive directions of influences on, and modifications of, functioning. Therefore I think Freud right in indicating that, in terms of his scientific approach, any aspect of functioning, including its amenability to influence and its direction of

3. One can easily recognize in the argument of Rapaport and Gill special pleading on behalf of the metapsychological legitimacy, compatibility, and usefulness of Erikson's psychosocial propositions. In my view, the thrust of Erikson's thinking is clearly away from the natural science model that has exclusively shaped Freudian thought until recent years; consequently, it is incompatible with the received metapsychology, which is not to say that it is not or cannot be psychoanalytic.

change, is sufficiently explained by dynamic, economic, and
structural propositions. Despite his occasional references to
genetics as being on a par with the three points of view, Hartmann's preference for field-theoretical formulations suggests
that he was clear about the special place occupied by the dynamic, economic, and structural in psychoanalytic explanation.
Consequently, the developmental story does not justify a
"genetic point of view" in the sense argued by Rapaport and
Gill. The proposed metapsychological "genetic point of view"
is to be distinguished from the "genetic approach" (Hartmann
and Kris 1945).

It should be clear that I am in no way questioning or minimizing the methodological and clinical importance of the
genetic approach. A psychoanalysis without a genetic methodology is inconceivable. Nor am I minimizing the importance
of adaptational propositions in the narrow, ego-psychological
sense in which Hartmann often used them; they, too, are indispensable to psychoanalytic thought.

4. The Anatomy of Psychoanalytic Thinking

Perhaps the most common complaint against Hartmann's
writings is that he fashioned a theory so abstract, so far removed from concrete phenomena, and so complex, with hypotheses piled on top of hypotheses, that commonsense, down-to-
earth, directly grasped reality has been devalued, virtually
forgotten, and the way back to it blocked. In this view Hartmann was the austere impersonalizer of psychoanalytic thought
and clinical work, and therefore he was, so to speak, guilty of
crimes against the humane spirit of psychoanalysis. I do not
think this complaint justified in the least. To me it is equivalent
to the complaint against an anatomist of the human body for
showing how complex are its parts and their interrelationships.
Among other contributions, Hartmann served as an anatomist
of the structure of psychoanalytic thinking. Simplicity and easy
accessibility were not among his primary goals in this endeavor,
for he recognized that the proper goal of scientific thinking is
theory of sufficient preciseness and coherence to do full justice
to the information and methods at hand. If the resulting theory
is simple and easily accessible, so much the better, but the

theoretician has to let the chips fall where they may. Illusory parsimony is no help.

As an anatomist of psychoanalytic thinking Hartmann was centrally concerned with its lack of preciseness and coherence in key places, and he sought to make necessary improvements. In so doing he was not less mindful of concrete phenomena but more mindful of them than those who complained against him. For example, there was his interest in the concepts and findings of neighboring disciplines and of splinter movements within psychoanalysis. There was also his associated interest in expanding the observational sphere of interest in psychoanalysis to include infant observation, longitudinal studies, and the non-conflicted spheres of function. These interests, which foster the development of "psychoanalysis as a general psychology," should not be thought of as a kind of psychoanalytic imperialism, nor should they be thought of as leading to superficialization of psychoanalysis or making it too philosophical (whatever that means). Rather they must be understood as helping to realize the aim of increasing the preciseness and coherence of the central theory of psychoanalysis.

Clinical provincialism stands in the way of increased preciseness and coherence. How is that so? Quite simply, specifying the qualities of the phenomena studied in psychoanalysis depends in large part on one's being able to say how these phenomena are different from other related phenomena; it depends, too, on coming to grips with the various sides of these phenomena. We cannot be precise in speaking about ego functions caught up in severe conflict, if we cannot say much about them when they are caught up in mild conflict or not caught up in conflict at all. We cannot be precise about unhealthy development and the pathogenic influences it reflects, if we cannot at the same time say much about more or less healthy development of different kinds and about varieties of health-fostering influences and contexts. And we cannot comprehend adequately the asocial aspects of neurosis and psychosis without comprehending types of relatively undisrupted social relations. The data (and concepts) of approaches to human beings other than clinical psychoanalysis are indispensable to adequate—comprehensive and precise—analytic observation and theory.

Many of the classic formulations in psychoanalysis have been less applicable to healthy functioning than to unhealthy functioning. To explain a disrupted marital relationship in terms of its oedipal significance to one or both partners is simply imprecise and inadequate explanation, in that, so far as psychoanalysis is concerned, there are few if any marital relationships in which oedipal significance is absent. Inevitably, then, the question arises why this significance is disruptive in one case and not in the next. And it is not much of an explanation automatically to say that it is a quantitative matter, that the oedipal significance is greater in the first case than the second, though, of course, one can be justified in making that statement in certain cases. I might be told at this point that, in recent years at any rate, no sensible psychoanalyst would use the simple-minded oedipal explanation of my example; to this objection I would (only for the sake of argument) agree but then go on to emphasize that the theory of psychoanalysis had been much less adequate before Hartmann's work than it is now to deal with this clinical sophistication.

Even the additional proposition that the undisrupted marriage is based on stronger defenses against its oedipal significance would still be imprecise and inadequate, for it would only lead into a group of further questions. For example, what makes one defense stronger than another; what makes one strong defense less impoverishing to a relationship than another; and how it is that some marital relationships with rather conspicuous manifest oedipal derivatives (i.e., apparently less defended relationships) are less disrupted than others in which these derivatives are rigidly defended against?

Attempting to answer these questions, which arise out of broad clinical observation as well as careful thought, and doing so with an eye to theoretical coherence, requires additional hypotheses and sometimes new terminology. The consequence is a more complex theory. But that theory, in turn, both reflects and points to a more complex and sharply seen reality. Often a simple theory is a know-nothing theory as well as a carte blanche for technical crudeness.

An anatomist of theory will lay bare the bones of that theory and examine both its gross and fine structure. What is called the introduction of new hypotheses is often no more than (a) making explicit the assumptions that have been made or must be made; (b) eliminating assumptions that are unnecessary because redundant, or undesirable because inconsistent; and (c) revealing both ignorance and knowledge that have heretofore not been clearly seen or even suspected. The complaint against Hartmann's complex formalism amounts then to criticizing him for having shown how ambitious, complex, multilayered, and incomplete psychoanalytic theory was and *is*. The same complaint may be made against the seventh chapter of *The Interpretation of Dreams* and its complex theory of memory function.

The example of memory function will serve to make my point more specific. Psychoanalysts know a lot about how and why crucial memories remain unconscious. Yet, as G.S. Klein (1966a) pointed out, they know much less about normal memory function. Knowledge of normal memory function helps to specify just how and where memory may be disrupted and how it may be repaired. Further, psychoanalysts have found not only that certain memories are lost to consciousness, but also that the memory function itself can come to be treated as dangerous, regardless of the manifest content with which it deals (see Kris 1956b). Consequently, within the natural science framework, the theory of functions and their standing in mental functioning generally must be as well developed as the theory of content and its relation to conflict. Much of Hartmann's work amounted to developing an adequate theory of function—its initial status in development, its energy supply, its relation to the content with which it deals and also to the outer world, its stability and autonomy, its regressive transformations, and so forth. Certainly, if the ego is defined as a coherent group of functions, the psychoanalytic psychology of functions must be well developed. There are, however, many analysts who, disregarding the anatomical logic of theory, are readier to accept the first part of this proposition than the second.

The example of memory function also illustrates the intimate relationship between natural science theory and observation in Hartmann's thought. This is so because the differentiation of function and content reflects careful attention, *along certain lines,* to mental activity in the analytic hour just as much as it reflects careful attention to problems of completeness and coherence in theory construction. (As noted earlier, the definition and selection of data are those dictated by the natural science model.) The appearance in Hartmann's work of rarefaction of psychoanalytic thought is misleading. The way back to clinical phenomena is not difficult to find, provided that Hartmann's sophisticated contributions are studied closely enough. Obviously, Hartmann counted on its being so. He was, after all, writing primarily for psychoanalysts. That nevertheless Hartmann's natural science theorizing *does* encounter difficulties in clinical application I shall attempt to show at the end of this section and in section 5 on neutralization.

Among the results of Hartmann's studies are the following. From the conflict between reality and drives one cannot derive psychic structure, a reality principle, sublimations, or communication. One therefore has to introduce (or make explicit) the assumptions of primary autonomous apparatus and functions. These are factors which, as Hartmann said, "speak out for reality." And if there are these factors, which exert their own kind of influence, and if the theory ascribes influence to accumulations and expenditures of psychic energy, then one must also assume the accumulation, expenditure, and influence of primary neutral energy, i.e., energy of non-instinctual origin.

Hartmann also showed that if one follows Freud in assuming that libidinal energy may be desexualized—a proposition in *The Ego and the Id* that is central to our received version of psychoanalytic theory—one must make two additional assumptions: the same loss of instinctual quality may happen to aggressive energy; and both energic changes, subsumed under the terms neutralization and de-instinctualization, may be a matter of degree. One advantage of the concept of degrees of neutralization is its freeing of discussions of ego function from the investigator's value judgments, especially in the regions of sublimation, reality relations, and moral values.

I shall not say more about neutralization now, for I shall deal with it extensively in the next section of this chapter. About aggression, however, I shall add this: Hartmann recognized that psychoanalysis requires a theory of aggression equal in dignity to that of libido, and so (with his collaborators) he attempted to give aggression the full theoretical treatment already accorded libido; in so doing he detached the concept of aggression from the extremely problematic hypothesis of a death instinct, which, from the time of its introduction, had stood in the way of coordinating the theories of the two energies.

Hartmann also demonstrated that the reality principle, as usually construed, is not on the same theoretical plane as the pleasure principle and so cannot stand as its opposite pole. There is a broad reality principle, corresponding to the concept of biological adaptation, and a narrow one, corresponding to certain ego functions.

I have already mentioned some other results of Hartmann's studies: his administering the systematic coup de grâce to the ego instincts or instinct of self-preservation and to the phylogenetic transmission of psychic contents; his establishing systematically the status of the superego as an independent structure; and his differentiating cathexis of contents and cathexis of functions. In connection with the latter he also established that the cathexis of functions and contents may vary within single psychic systems and at different times and may do so more or less independently in each instance. These concepts, along with the concepts change of function and secondary autonomy, correspond to the fact that much of the time while doing clinical analysis we are concerned with the pleasure-unpleasure or danger-security aspects of ego functions, or their high or low "discharge" potentials, as issues quite apart from the specific contents with which these functions might be occupied (though, once the matter is understood, there is usually a significant relationship between the two). The crucial question of dynamic content analysis of functions themselves will be dealt with below.

I have also mentioned Hartmann's alertness to the challenges posed by the neo-Freudians and the Kleinians. This alertness expressed his recognition that these challenges, however simplistically, fantastically, or unscientifically executed, have been responses to theoretical vacuums left behind by Freud and not yet filled by Freudian propositions. Additionally, Hartmann legitimized the language of representations through his study of narcissism. There he clarified the necessary distinction between ego and self-representations, and thereby made possible by a systematic study of mental contents, which, while exceedingly narrow in certain respects, can be carried through in a manner consistent with a natural science metapsychology. As I shall argue later, this metapsychology has no means of dealing with meanings and subjective experience in their particularity, nor does it aim to do so.

Finally, Hartmann's analysis of psychoanalysis also made it possible to coordinate and compare many psychoanalytic propositions that previously had remained isolated from each other owing to differences in the modes of their conceptualization. In the long run, this advance in internal coherence of the theory must also enhance the observational aspect of psychoanalysis, for it alerts analysts to connections between phenomena and between explanations that they might otherwise miss.

It remains to take notice in this connection of certain arbitrary tendencies in Hartmann's anatomizing. One such tendency is his a priori commitment to symmetrical conceptualization. Proceeding under the banner of the need to synchronize concepts, Hartmann, alone and with his collaborators, attempted to lay out symmetrically structured theories of aggression and libido, and also of the three psychic structures. In the former instance, starting from the already more fully developed theory of libido, Hartmann strove to develop point-by-point correspondence between it and the theory of aggression. Though he recognized many difficulties in the way of carrying through this program successfully, Hartmann persisted. Particularly when confronting such variables as periodicity, pleasure in discharge, and zonal referents, his argument became strained, tentative, and overburdened with both provisional hypotheses and unconvincing references to parallel phenomena. Clearly, symmetry had become a must. Here Hartmann missed (or bypassed) an opportunity to use the consideration of aggression as an occasion for further innovative thinking concerning drive theory generally. Although the theories of the two basic drives would, of course, have to be cast in the same general conceptual terms, there is no necessity to match or symmetrize the detailed propositions in every respect.

Similar problems arise in the papers that attempt to symmetrize the theories of the id, ego, and superego. (See especially in his *Essays* (1964) "The Mutual Influences in the Development of Ego and Id" and "Notes on the Superego.")

A second and related arbitrary trend is evident in Hartmann's treatment of the structure of the ego. I have already pointed out (see section 2 on dualism) how Hartmann's lucid and disciplined theorizing laid the groundwork of the conceptual dissolution of *"the* ego"; yet he persisted in many places in emphasizing the unity of the ego. He spoke of the ego as being defined by its functions, the coherence of these functions being established by their usually being found on the same side in conflicts (Hartmann et al. 1946). At the same time, he noted that thinking, perception, and action frequently serve the id and superego, in opposition to the ego; and elsewhere he developed at length the importance and inevitability of intrasystemic conflicts, the most notable of which arise between the defenses and other functions and interests of the ego, such as reality-testing and synthesis. How then are we to understand and accept "coherence" as a defining characteristic of ego constituents?

I venture to suggest that these arbitrary tendencies reflect an intrasystemic conflict of Hartmann's—that between holding fast to Freud's basic concepts concerning psychic structure and his pressing ahead with his own observational and theoretical explorations. (This conflict is even more apparent in Hartmann's psychoeconomic theorizing.) Having chosen to be both a steward of an old order and a leader of a new, Hartman had at times to contradict himself and confuse his readers. To the objection that I am being unfair to Hartmann, since, in some contrast to Freud, he presented a model of very orderly and faithful progress, I reply that much of this chapter is devoted to demonstrating just that point—*among others.*

5. Neutralization

Many of Hartmann's endeavors and attainments centered on psychoeconomic issues. In order to appreciate the nature of his contributions in this respect, it is necessary to be clear about the structure of psychoanalytic metapsychology. About that structure something needs to be said which, so far as I know, has not been said so plainly, or perhaps recognized, by contributors to psychoanalytic theory, namely that the entire metapsychology is committed to and organized around one basic assumption: this assumption is that it is necessary to postulate psychic energy for explanatory purposes. It is specifically to this postulate that Freud referred when he invoked "the witch metapsychology" (1937a, pp. 225-30). Psychic energy was the impetus factor of instinctual drives which were conceived as analogous to mechanical forces; but, as we shall see, far more than impetus was to be ascribed to this energy factor.

In its original form this postulated psychic energy was a cathectic charge corresponding to unexpressed affect. Soon cathexis became primarily libido and secondarily anti-cathexis derived from the ego instincts (presumably without quality, unlike libido). Psychic energy was embedded in part in the concept of primary process, and in part in the concept of instinctual drive or the component drives. Anti-cathexis was secondary, not in its explanatory usefulness, but in its theory, being for the most part left undeveloped in comparison to the theory of the libidinal cathexis to which it was opposed; secondary also because its very name gave it a reactive, if not negative, definition in that it was defined by its oppositional deployment.

It is true in this regard that attention cathexis, which presumably also derived from the ego instincts and lacked quality, implied a positive definition—something like neutral energy available, through the sense organ *Cs.*, for adaptation (perception, memory, etc.). But here, too, systematic development of this concept was lacking, as is evident in the crudeness of the concept of the sense organ *Cs.* and the temporary place occupied by that concept, along with the ego instincts, in Freud's major theoretical efforts. Presumably, attention cathexis was the same cathexis as that involved in the secondary process that partially supplanted and also confined the primary process; in so far as the secondary process served as a kind of regulatory principle (partially redundant with the subsequently introduced reality principle and ego), its cathexis was necessarily, whether so stated or not, non-libidinal and purposively deployable along adaptive lines.

To get now to the point: once cathexis had become mainly libido or instinctual energy, a whole set of properties other than impetus was ascribed to it. And it is around these properties particularly that the complex edifice of metapsychology has been erected. These properties, which are qualitative, not quantitative, are: *direction* (sexual gratification), *urgency* or *peremptoriness* (unremitting pressure for discharge), *mobility* (readiness to divert itself into indirect channels when direct channels are blocked), *dischargeability* (its being reduced in quantity, hence in impetus, following certain activities), *bindability* (its being maintained in a fixed or blocked position by opposing energy), *transformability* (loss of its properties of direction, peremptoriness, mobility, and dischargeability—a loss known as desexualization or de-instinctualization), and *fusibility* (its capacity to blend with the energy of aggressive impulses—later, aggressive energy proper). Dreams, symptoms, parapraxes, jokes, primitive rituals, psychoses, perversions, narcissism, object relations, falling in love, ego ideal (superego) formation, sublimation, abreaction, therapeutic effects: all this and more was to be explained by these qualitative aspects of libido (as influenced more or less by deployment of anti-cathexis and hypercathexis).

These properties of libido constituted or became manifest in the primary process and were modified or contained in and by the secondary process (or the ego or the reality principle). Clearly, one could not derive the organized or developed personality from libido alone: something so fluid, imperious, and mercurial was a principle of chaos, a Dionysian element that required an Apollonian counterpart before development could occur. Also, with regard to this libido, external reality could only be hostile (a proposition the modification of which was much on Hartmann's mind), for external reality had to "bring up" the instinctual infant, whether purposively or not, by imposing delay, restraint, deprivation, fear, the necessity for detour, compromise, renunciation, and taming. And as the preconscious (later the ego) was the representative of external reality and was by definition a principle of organization, it was necessary to stress its primary enmity toward libido (A. Freud 1936). This enmity would obtain even when the preconscious was facilitating discharge, for preconscious implied conditional discharge, and libido was by definition intolerant of being subject to conditions.

When the energy of the death instinct, or aggressive energy, was added to libido as a basic impetus factor, it, too, had the same set of properties ascribed to it. Hartmann and his collaborators attempted to state these parallels systematically.

I shall not attempt to trace the history of Freud's attempts so to devise a theory of transformation of instinctual energy that he could construct a general theory of development and organization of the personality. Bibring (1936) and Rapaport (1959), among others, have assumed this responsibility and produced excellent summaries and critical analyses. I need only say that, upon reading Freud's metapsychological discussions from beginning to end, one can see how he was laboring over the consequences of postulating psychic energy for explanatory purposes. One might say that he was in the toils of this postulate. And his labors were not finished when he finally laid down his pen.

More than anyone else, Hartmann continued those labors and brought them as close to completion as it has yet been possible to do. His ideas on functions, structures, adaptation (in the narrow sense described above), reality relations, narcissism, and so forth, depend on his version of the transformations, origins, distributions, and regulations of this energy—this primary, mobile, inherently vectorial, peremptory, dischargeable, bindable, transformable, and fusible energy. That is, he accepted Freud's basic assumption concerning instinctual drive energy uncritically and conservatively while he displayed remarkable freedom in reconsidering, reformulating, or revising so many other basic or ancillary assumptions inherited from Freud. And nowhere, to my knowledge, did he present a full review of the arguments in favor of the concept of psychic energy and then weigh those arguments against others that favor explanation without recourse to psychic energy. It has been as if without psychic energy there can be no recognition of the central roles of sexuality and aggression in human life and thus no possibility of psychoanalytic explanation. And if psychoanalysis is to be recommended as a general psychology and a depth psychology on the basis of its explanatory propositions, then, of course, psychic energy has to be part of the package.

I have argued elsewhere (1968b) that, rather than its being necessarily part of the package, it is a theoretical *option,* and I remind you here of my emphasis earlier in this chapter on Hartmann's having shown by his example that psychoanalytic theorizing is a matter of the options one chooses. Although my argument against postulating psychic energy cannot be reproduced here in detail, I shall summarize some of its salient points in order to throw into sharp relief the problematic aspects of Hartmann's psychoeconomic contributions.

The conclusion I came to is that rough *quantitative* comparisons of the order of "more than" and "less than," or "stronger" and "weaker," seem to have a definite place in any dynamic psychology. This is so because in particular cases some factors under consideration seem to exert more influence than others over the course of events. These quantitative judgments may be made without recourse to "psychic energy" possessed of various properties. I tried to show that although mobility of emphasis and changing forms of gratification and functional application must be recognized when dealing with concrete cases, these elements can be conceptualized in terms of equivalent, substitute, and competing aims or confluent aims (*dynamics*) being pursued under varying organizational conditions (*structure*), both of which—aims and organizations—are accessible and understandable through their history (*genetics*), and both of which are more or less attuned to the stringencies of organization and reality relations (*adaptation* in the narrow sense). The approach to psychological processes by means of these four types of considerations plus some specification of relative strength or degree of influence of the factors (a simplified *economic* consideration) is sufficient for purposes of psychoanalytic explanation.[4]

According to this way of looking at it, a "psychic energy" with qualitative aspects is not needed. It is not even needed to make the theory *truly* biological or natural scientific. Such concepts as directedness, organization, regulation, development, and adaptation are independently useful biological or natural scientific concepts. In this proposed revision of Freud's and Hartmann's metapsychology, sexuality (libidinal emphasis) is in no way minimized. The unconscious continuation of infantile sensual pleasure-seeking and fantasy, with all their urgency, conflicts, transformations, disguises, and contributions to development, remains a central reference point. It is the same with physical, especially sexual, maturation and change and the bodily feelings and fantasies that accompany them; the anatomical differences between the sexes; aggression; defense; early object relations and their internalization; etc. And those variations of zest and impetus in feeling and behavior, which

4. In action language, such terms as dynamics and economies no longer have a place; see e.g., chapter 10.

have been the phenomenological basis for psychic energy concepts throughout the ages (Jackson 1967), remain to be an-
analyzed in terms of both their representational significance
(versions of impotence, castration, arousal, hunger or satiety,
depression or elation, self-punishment, etc.) and the confluence or contradictoriness of "ego" aims concerning self-feeling
and overt action. Although we have been told repeatedly that
it is otherwise, clinical *interpretation* has never really depended on complex psychoeconomic theorizing.

And with respect to the objection that this approach introduces an infinity of aims to contend with, it can be said that
that phenomenological infinity is exactly what analysts have
always had to contend with, and that analysts have always
managed to cope with it by grouping specific aims under headings according to their common genotypic features (e.g., the
myriad aims subsumable under the heading of the need for
punishment). In other words, no obstacle is being put in the
way of analysts using their powers of concept formation and
memory.

To return to the biological vantage point: Hartmann made it
clear that ultimately everything said about the human being
can be viewed as a biological proposition. That is not in question at this point. From Hartmann's vantage point what matters is whether a proposition is good biology or bad biology or
the only possible biology. It matters, that is, *if one wants to
conceptualize human beings as biological entities*. That they
are also social entities, historical entities, and metaphysical
entities is also true, and Hartmann was well aware of that fact.
In each of these latter instances, other systems of thought and
other vantage points would be invoked and other kinds of
hypotheses generated, the value of which for psychoanalytic
understanding remains to be determined. It would be naive to
claim the priority of any vantage point for explanatory purposes. Hartmann's vantage point was biology. It is not the
same biology as Freud's in many respects, but it is the same in
one inessential respect, the one that has created more theoretical problems than it has solved in psychoanalytic thinking, i.e.,
the assumption that the postulating of "psychic energy" with
qualitative aspects would be a help in theory development and
would be essential to a natural science approach to the psychology of human beings.

From this carry-over of Freud's "biological" metapsychology flowed Hartmann's propositions concerning neutralization; degrees of neutralization; neutralization as a continuous process carried on by the ego exclusively; primary neutral energy; cathexis of functions as differentiated from cathexis of contents; the "reservoir" of neutralized energy available to the ego; varying degrees of neutralization of the energies feeding and expended by ego and superego functions; partly neutralized aggression in defensive function; and the difference between fusion and neutralization.

Out of this array of psychoeconomics propositions I shall select for close examination only the differentiation between cathexis of functions and cathexis of contents. An examination of this differentiation, on which Hartmann correctly placed so much emphasis, brings to light a crucial problem in his economic theorizing.

According to Hartmann the same function may be energized by and expend libido and aggression of different degrees of neutralization. For example, looking may be energized by and expend relatively neutral energy or relatively unneutralized energy; in the latter instance the function of looking is said to be sexualized or aggressivized or both. These formulations are supposed to help explain why certain functions get caught up in conflict and become unstable or inhibited. If one is working with functional concepts and energy concepts of the sort described above, these formulations seem to make perfect sense.

Is there an alternative? That there is can be shown by introducing some clinical psychoanalytic considerations. One set of problems comes to light if we consider the example of a certain patient's struggle against homosexual transference. That struggle frequently took the form of his promptly forgetting major developments in his analytic hours. Upon analysis, it seemed that: this forgetting defended against his getting more deeply involved in his analysis since that involvement would lead into experiencing and disclosing the homosexual transference; it represented him as a woman with a vagina, i.e., suitable as a homosexual object; and the forgetting was intended to provoke attacks by the analyst, thus bringing about repetitions of sadomasochistically colored attacks by his father, and thereby amounted to an unconscious homosexual seduction. Now, from the standpoint of biologically adaptive function, one could say that the ego function of memory was disrupted owing to its having been instinctualized. In clinical analysis, however, one works out what remembering and forgetting have come to mean, how that meaning has developed, and why it is being emphasized so much in the present. In this regard, the analyst remains steadily aware that the phenomenon in question pertains to pleasure-seeking, pain-avoidance, defense, punishment, revenge, and adaptation in the narrow sense (maintaining security and stability within the limits of the patient's tolerance for the homosexual themes). Even to characterize the matter in traditional energic terms one would have to speak of the memory function's simultaneously being "fed" by and expending libidinal and aggressive energy of *many* degrees of neutralization and emanating from a number of sources in all three psychic structures—and what would that formulation amount to but restating the variety of unconscious aims and meanings of remembering and forgetting? Moreover, to speak of instinctualization of the function simply would not convey what the clinical analyst understands (e.g., that both remembering and forgetting are defensive and gratifying at the same time and in various ways). We see then that these crucial energic formulations concerning ego functions do not even do the work they are supposed to do. They give the illusion of deep and exact "scientific" understanding when in fact they are blurs.

Additionally, the anthropomorphism that was to have been expunged by energic-functional conceptualization now resides in the mentality implicity ascribed to functions and energies. Although the language is less dramatic, the mind remains an assembly of minds working together and at cross-purposes. A natural science approach cannot escape this problem. (I shall focus on this problem in the next chapter.)

Still other major problems emerge if we consider the example of instinctualized looking. In this connection clinical analysis will usually reveal that the function of looking is unconsciously equated with, or not differentiated from, the activity of sexual penetration or oral incorporation, to mention only two possibilities. What then is the "function" in this case? Clinically we would say that the dynamically important function is not the manifest one but the latent, unconscious one. We would say then that the ostensible function of looking has become caught up in conflict and has been disrupted, renounced, or has occasioned suffering because its latent function (or latent meaning) is too close to instinctual drive aims (sexual penetration, oral incorporation). From this perspective one can see that Hartmann based his argument on manifest content, contrary to the nature of empirical psychoanalytic understanding. He would not, of course, have denied the latent functions their place in a full clinical interpretation. Yet for purposes of biological-functional systematization, and in the light of his having accepted the postulation of psychic energy and all the properties that have come to be ascribed to this energy, he subtly shifted the emphasis to behavioral observation (manifest content, ostensible function) away from psychoanalytic observation which takes into account the latent as well as the manifest. His attempt to come to grips with this issue, on which so much depends, was singularly unfocused and inapposite as well as inappropriately brief (Hartmann 1964, pp. 217-18).

In explaining why a person gives up the efficient use of his or her eyes, we would base our clinical explanation on that which has found disguised expression in "looking," which is to say, the latent *meaning* of looking. We would say that having taken on the significance of certain drive activities and gratifications, looking was being dealt with as if it were these very activities and gratifications—*which, in psychic reality, it is.* As Hartmann was well aware, the adaptational-biological point of view is conducive to behavioristic formulations in that it relies heavily on what can be seen or evaluated from the outside. Yet despite his awareness of this danger and his own contributions to grasping psychic reality, Hartmann here, as in other connections (e.g., activity-passivity, "functional pleasure," and "free aggression"), lapsed into propositions "from the outside." The lapses, the subtle shifts from psychic reality to behavioral reality, are attributable, I think, to Hartmann's having been, as Freud was, "in the toils of" the energy postulate and its inevitable consequences. While his being in this difficult position was facilitated by his commitment to the biological language of functions, it was a systematic consequence of the energy postulate.

I mentioned before the irony of Hartmann's systematization of structural theory containing the potential for undermining much or all of that theory. Here, in the psychoeconomic realm, we encounter a second great irony, namely the finding that psychic energy—the presumed impetus factor of instinctual drives—has driven psychoanalytic thought back to the outside surface of the human being. More exactly, it is the analyst committed to the natural science approach to explanation, as manifest in the "psychic energy" postulate, who, while working "inside," thinks "outside."

A defender of Hartmann might counter this criticism in the following manner. He or she could argue that what I refer to as the latent function or meaning of ego function is only a dynamic characterization of the events in question and that it must be completed by a coordinated economic characterization. That economic account would speak of the function's being fed by and expending relatively unneutralized energy. Kris (1956b) discussed disturbed memory function in just this way. My rejoinder to this objection is this: the economic account can only *follow* the discovery of the unconscious meanings or "psychic reality" of the function; economic propositions about specific events invariably *follow* their clinical analysis, and so amount to no more than a restatement of the discovery; moreover, the economic proposition in this instance concerns the behavior function, not the psychological event. As G.S. Klein (1966b) has put it, we are on a "one-way street" in this regard: we understand why looking is disrupted once we know that it has taken on sexual *meaning* or *too much* sexual meaning relative to other, more neutral meanings. "Too much" is the kind of rough quantitative statement I recommended earlier as a simplified economic point of view; it says that some meanings carry more weight or exert more influence or are more strongly reacted against than others.[5] Going beyond a statement of this sort into energic qualities results in no gain in explanatory power.

At this point, in speaking of meaning instead of properties of psychic energy, I seem to be changing some of the language of psychoanalysis. In fact, however, I am re-establishing the importance of "psychic reality" in the psychoanalytic vocabulary. Although much in the fore in clinical work, the concept of

5. In action language, one would say that the person emphasizes these meanings more, defining more actions and modes of action in their terms; one would not ascribe weight or the exercise of influence to the meanings themselves.

psychic reality has lost its place in the general theory of psychoanalysis. "Psychic reality" refers to subjective meaning, especially unconscious meaning. Its usefulness resides in its reminding us that psychoanalytic explanation depends on our knowing what an event, action, or object means to the subject; it is the specifically psychoanalytic alternative to descriptive classification by a behavioristic observer (see Kohut 1959, for a similar view).

Now, in psychoanalysis, as elsewhere, meaning is no simple concept. What something means to a subject includes two sets of interrelated factors: first, conscious and preconscious apprehensions of it, which may be more or less objective by ordinary standards and also more or less complex; and, second, unconscious apprehensions of it, which usually follow the lines of the primary process and so are usually irrational and inaccurate by ordinary standards and also more or less complex. I say complex in both instances because the same event is given meaning by the subject according to the variety of conscious, preconscious, and unconscious wishes, fantasies, and perspectives operating at any one time and also at different times and in different contexts. Although some meanings will prove to be of more importance and more durable than others in any one instance, they may not be said to constitute *the* meaning of the event. Thus meaning is a matter of levels, perspectives, and temporally extended emphases.

The biological language of functions cannot be concerned with meaning. And Hartmann always bypassed the question of meaning—rightly so, in terms of his vantage point. In functional-adaptational language, looking is looking (or perception, however experimentally refined the breakdown into constituent functions), and defending is defending. The language is behavioristic, as suits a natural science approach. In contrast, the primary psychoanalytic language is a language of and for meanings and the changes they undergo during development and during the psychoanalytic process. Aims are meanings. Looking is disrupted in so far as it means something else, provided that that something else is caught up in serious conflict. Even where being clear-sighted itself has been made a matter of conflict by coercive parental lying and denials, we find in analysis that it is the meanings of clear-sightedness that are at the heart of the trouble: these meanings may include

overthrow of paternal authority (castration of the father) combined with insistence on one's own phallic claims and running
the risk of castration oneself; and/or rejection of identification
with the mother and running the risk of loss of love, nourish-
ment, and security; and so forth. Through analysis of these
meanings, which is what clinical analysis is about, we enable
the analysand to differentiate them from behavioral acts and
thereby to become able again to act or function adequately—
in some cases even when the conflicts remain intense. We
speak of these analyzed meanings as the analysand's psychic
reality. We could say that functions have meaning in psychic
reality—we represent them to ourselves—and so the fate of
functions is determined by how we represent them.

Elsewhere (1968a) I have discussed this proposition in connection with the mechanisms of defense. There I followed some
undeveloped ideas of Freud's and some fundamental applications of these ideas by other analysts, including the Kleinian
analysts. For example, to deny may be to destroy by incorporating or expelling; and to project may be—as Waelder (1930)
pointed out long ago—unconsciously to bring about fantasized
homosexual penetration.

All of which indicates that functions, as they are represented
in psychic reality, correspond to dynamic processes characterized by their aims and influence. Accordingly, the vicissitudes
of functions may be accounted for in terms of the closeness of
these aims to instinctual aims and the types and degrees of
conflict into which these aims enter. So far from there being
any need to assume that the energy feeding and expended by
the disrupted function has been instinctualized, that very assumption represents a departure from consistent, specifically
psychoanalytic explanation. It substitutes the theoretical
necessities of the natural scientist observing the surface of
things for the psychoanalyst's grasp of multilayered and multifaceted subjective experience. In Kris's (1956b) excellent discussion of memory from a dynamic point of view, he seems to
have been reduced to throwing in some remarks on cathectic
processes almost as afterthoughts and as if meeting an obligation that has lost its force. The obligation—which I here question—is to transform psychoanalysis proper into a general
biological psychology.

In other discussions (1960, 1964, 1967b, 1968c), though not

as pointedly, I have tried to show how the conceptualizations of the superego, affects, ego ideal, and activity-passivity have suffered from the same or similar confusion as to what is specifically psychoanalytic. Here I have wanted to show that this confusion, based often on an unremarked shift of vantage point, is a direct consequence of the basic psychoeconomic assumption made by Freud and elaborated most of all (and best of all) by Hartmann.

Finally, to illustrate my alternative further, I offer a few brief comments about two other psychoeconomic propositions used or developed by Hartmann: fusion and the use of partly neutralized aggressive energy in defense.

The concept of fusion of aggression and libido contains an unnoticed internal contradiction. It is this: although the fused energy should constitute a new kind of energy (what else does fusion mean?), it is always treated as combined libido and aggression—combined, that is, as contrasted with certain types of ambivalence in which aggression and libido presumably work against each other. "Fusion" is somehow supposed to account for why they do not work against each other in certain instances. According to my argument, fusion may be understood differently and without self-contradiction and obscurity. It would refer to a coordination, condensation, or confluence of the meanings of an action of fantasy such that libidinal and aggressive aims may be served simultaneously by it.

As to relatively neutralized aggression providing the impetus of defense, I would point out two things: first, this proposition can be recast in terms of analytically accessible aggressive meanings of defensive activity, such as to cast out, annihilate, or repudiate—especially in zonal terms; second, defensive activity can have libidinal meaning as well as or instead of aggressive meaning, as in the instance of denial implying the experience in psychic reality of being orally gratified and sleeping at the breast.

The apparent unity and degree of success of Hartmann's systematizing efforts, especially in the economic realm, depended on his bypassing the ubiquitous problem of meaning. He pursued his objectives by distinguishing between functions and content, and then concentrating on functions and their supply and expenditure of energy; he treated content almost as a peripheral issue *for theory*. According to Hartmann, the language of functions helps to avoid the anthropomorphism that tends to creep into references to the psychic structures. Is it, however, any the less anthropomorphic to speak of functions as intentional, self-steering entities that can collaborate with or oppose or suspend other functions? What is the difference between saying that the ego revolts against the tyrannical superego and saying that the defensive functions of the ego direct countercathexis against superego influence? I maintain that the anthropomorphism has merely been concealed behind aseptic language (see chapter 5).

The ubiquity of the problem of meaning may be gathered from a consideration of the following list of propositions culled from Hartmann's writings in general.

(1) Hartmann works with the concept of "phase specificity," which in the genetic approach refers to the child's giving meaning to experience of every sort according to its phase of development. But he cannot sensibly attribute this giving of meaning to the drives or the maturational equipment. Even the ego functions will not serve in this regard in that ego function is a concept of a different order, a biological order; meaning is a concept that requires a different kind of conceptualization, one in which it is proper to say that it is the child who gives meanings.

(2) Hartmann emphasizes that learning is important throughout development. Here one must ask whether it is not the child who learns and organizes meanings according to its present modes of understanding. It is odd to attribute learning to drives, equipment, or functions.

(3) In Hartmann's discussion, drives are now to be classified and understood primarily in terms of aims and objects. But aims refer to meaningful purposes or actions and objects refer to persons in the world of the child at that time.

(4) Behavior is to be described and explained in terms of its being invested with, and its resulting in expenditures of, aggression and libido of varying degrees of neutralization. These descriptions and explanations depend, however, on the prior discovery or definition of the meanings of the behavior in question; for the same manifest item of behavior may prove, once it has been interpreted, to be either aggressive or libidinal or some mixture of both.

(5) In order to be influential, knowledge requires substantial

quantities of cathexis and considerable integration. But here the question is being begged in that to assume a quantity of cathexis is to imply that somehow the knowledge has already been deemed important in some sense, and to assume a degree of integration is to imply that the relevance of this knowledge to certain critical issues has already been remembered and appreciated. Can it be the energy itself, one must ask, that assigns the importance? And can it be a contentless function that remembers and appreciates relevance? Or is it not better to say that it is the person who does both—the person viewed as the finder, assigner, and creator of meaning?

(6) Hartmann treats intentionality, in the sense of conscious setting of goals, as one ego function among others. In so doing, he makes of intentions a distinct subclass of dynamics the significance of which is ambiguous. He implies thereby that the other and major dynamic factors somehow lack intentionality even though they are characterized as having aims. He further implies that dynamics, as opposed to functions and interests, are not to be part of the vocabulary of ego psychology. That this implication is unsatisfactory in fundamental respects I have argued in my paper on the mechanisms of defense (1968a); there I proposed that an internally consistent language for conflict would have to include ego and superego wishes along with id wishes, which is to say dynamic factors straight down the line. We see in Hartmann's use of intentionality both a narrowing of the scope of a concept with a broad and significant philosophical background and the sacrifice of metapsychological consistency in one important respect in order to be able to work consistently with the language of functions and energies.

(7) Especially in one place (1964, pp. 217-18), though also generally, Hartmann dismissed the question of the personal meaning of functions: he said that the concept of meaning is unclear; that it may be addressed in terms of unconscious genetic determinants; that the metapsychological concepts of primary and secondary processes and reality-syntonicity are already available as alternatives to "meaning" to deal with the phenomena of sexualization and non-sexualization of functions; that undesirable value judgments may be introduced into psychoanalysis through the concept of meaning; and that the stability or secondary autonomy of ego functions with very

similar instinctual cores may vary considerably. The consequence being that the meaning of a function is too variable a
matter for psychoanalytic theory. That there are difficulties
and hazards in working with the concept of meaning cannot be
denied; but it does not follow from this recognition that the
concept should be dismissed. In effect, Hartmann was arguing,
as Freud had earlier, that the metapsychological language can
include meaning only as a phenomenon to be discussed and
explained in other terms. Although correct in this systematic
position, he did not make it clear that he was settling a problem
of language rules and that the rules he was advocating, Freud's
rules ultimately, entail this arbitrary disposition of the concept
of meaning and the limitations of discourse attendant upon it.

The preceding extended discussion of neutralization should
serve to coordinate the general theory of psychoanalysis with
psychoanalytic technique and interpretation more closely than
has been the case up to now. At this time in the history of
psychoanalysis, psychic energy—the key concept in natural
science analytic theorizing—stands in the way of that coordination. Bridges between body (or brain) and mind cannot be built
by a priori commitments to a scientific rhetoric. First we need
suitable languages for the disciplines with which we are concerned. Moreover, it is debatable whether the idea of a bridge
between these disciplines makes sense. But in any case, one
must start with languages congenial with the methods and data
of each of the disciplines in question. The supports of any attempted bridge must stand on solid ground. The metapsychological language no longer appears to be so solid a ground as it
has been thought to be.

6. MIND AS GOVERNMENT

In this final section of my overview, I shall attempt to throw
some new light on the overall scheme of Hartmann's contributions. Clearly, Hartmann's manifest goal was increased systematization of the psychoanalytic theory of mind or the
development of psychoanalysis as "a general psychology." (To
say this is not to be blind to the original ideas and expansion of
observational power that underlay and accompanied his systematizing efforts.) To be systematic and comprehensive,
thinking must observe the stringencies imposed by some model

or prototypical thing, process, or organization. Rather than this model's simply being dictated by the data, it establishes the language used to specify, select, and interrelate observations so that they become data. Thus, with a psychoanalytic model, the observer specifies, selects, and interrelates observations of people differently from how he or she might as a teacher, citizen, or parent.

On the face of it, Hartmann's model is a biological one in which evolutionary, organismic, and ecological processes play crucial roles. And up to this point I have discussed it as such. I am, however, not persuaded by Hartmann's language and assertions that his adaptational model is intrinsically or totally biological. I should like to suggest rather that it has the features of a socio-political model; specifically, that it implies a governmental model.

To see how this might be so, consider the governing of a nation. Those who govern are concerned with both the internal processes and organization of government and its relations with neighboring governments. They attempt to promote certain domestic and international interests and to ward off internal and external threats to the stability, unity, and economy of their government. They have to reconcile conflicting interests so far as they can and to draw lines as to what is permissible or safe. Those who govern must also generate their government's own strength from within, though they may also increase its strength through external alliances: they must generate the government's means, which include its finances and its traditions, national goals, and pride. They are necessarily concerned with efficiency, coordination of functions, rank orders of importance. A balance between specialization of functions and centralization of control and planning must be achieved. They are aware that the national problems cannot be understood and governmental modes of coping with them cannot be used effectively without taking into account the nation's history. Governmental practice sometimes involves establishing and implementing policies which sacrifice certain aims or values in the interest of promoting others; indeed, sometimes the same policy has disruptive as well as stabilizing or progressive consequences, so that ambiguities as to the rational course of action to pursue are bound to arise, as are conflicts between values concerning the national interest (its "health") and other values.

Those who govern must direct sources of unrest and national division into useful channels and thereby build up impetus steadily for what they consider desirable programs. They must see to it that the government has strength in reserve to deal with a wide variety of crises. They must be concerned with the stability of governmental functions as a matter distinct from the particular issues or content being dealt with by these functions (agencies, committees, posts, etc.). Moreover, in governing they must take into account irrational elements within the nation, and they cannot afford to assume that the most knowledgeable and reasoned policy is the best one at any given time. And policies (or taxes) instituted once for certain purposes may later come to serve other purposes and be justified and continued on new grounds.

I shall not lengthen this list, though it would be easy to do so, for I believe my point will be clear to those familiar with Hartmann's main conceptual concerns. Problems of organization, structure, control, central regulation, and adaptation in the narrow sense; problems of functions and contents and the energic supplies with which these work or by which they are sustained; problems of health, rational action, moral codes, rank order of functions; the necessity of not mistaking any part of the psychic apparatus for its totality so that, for example, neither instinctual drives, nor ego interests, nor superego imperatives, will be minimized or exaggerated in importance; issues of friendly or peaceful relations between the psychic systems and within them (presence or absence of intersystemic and intrasystemic conflict); matters of autonomy and change of function; a "genetic approach"; and so forth: all closely parallel the stringencies of governmental evolution, survival, and success outlined above.

According to this model, then, mind was for Hartmann a government; its growth, direction, strength, and network of relationships are most comprehensible and most consistently surveyed from this socio-political vantage point. And yet Hartmann consistently emphasized that he was thinking biologically! How might the governmental and biological models of mind be reconciled in this case? I submit that there is no irreconcilable difference between the two; that the adaptational point of view which stresses evolutionary, organismic, and ecological regulations is one which might well draw on governmental models or parallels; that the very choice of the adaptational vantage point may have been dictated by, or at least supported by, its compatibility with governmental analogies. In making this claim, I am not downgrading the scientific utility of the adaptational-governmental model. I am merely trying to define the nature of this model in order better to understand the program adopted and carried through by Hartmann.[6]

Will it help matters to entertain this governmental analogy? I submit that understanding, using, and evaluating theory—especially complex theory—is a matter of grasp as well as reason, and that this analogy helps me, at least, to grasp Hartmann's contributions as a network of propositions and not patchwork. Perhaps some such grasp is derivable from the biological model that Hartmann professed, but I do not find it so. To me the biological model often seems to be stretched, if not tortured, to make its uses seem unified and profitable. The ostensible commitment to natural science models has been costly indeed to psychoanalytic thinking.

More than comprehensive grasp is at stake, however. The governmental model is by definition purposive and intelligent (though, of course, specific governmental acts may be ill-informed, ill-advised, ill-planned, and ill-intentioned). Government is an aggregate or ensemble of people acting within a certain organizational context intending certain actions that lead toward certain goals. This is in contrast to an aggregate or ensemble of impersonal forces, energies, functions, and apparatus somehow evolving into a purposive personality, which is to say, into a person as a meaning-creating and choice-making entity. Trying not to ignore this consideration, Hartmann explicitly provided for certain regulations or organ-

6. Hostile critics of psychoanalysis have often referred to its theory as *hydraulic*, which indicates another possible prototype. I consider this analogy too narrow, though it does fit some psychoanalytic theorizing, such as Fenichel's (1945) basic reliance on "damming up" as an explanatory concept. One could also develop a *fiscal* analogy. Again, however, this analogy would be too narrow, sufficing only for energy concepts, and anyway having to invoke governmental structure of some sort in order to be carried through adequately. This is so because money and credit, unlike psychic energy, are not thought to distribute and transform themselves; they do not possess and direct their own urgency. Rather they are recognized to exist and take on value and meaning within and between societal structures. It is unfortunate, as I have argued above and elsewhere (1968b), that this recognition has never been carried over to the basic theory of psychic energy.

izing functions in his theorizing; however, he said little about them except to indicate that they constitute a steerihg apparatus for the developed personality. Despite its lack of amplification, central regulation is a key concept in Hartmann's theorizing; his version of ego psychology cannot work without it. (His 1939 monograph relies heavily on "intelligence.") Yet these processes cannot be derived from the drives, energies, apparatus, functions, and object relations that are the elements of his ego psychology. The entire topic of the purposive, meaning-creating, choice-making person requires further exploration in psychoanalysis.[7] I have touched on some aspects of this exploration in the preceding section on neutralization.

In stressing the idea of mind as government I have in mind Hartmann's biography. He was the son of an eminent historian (a historian of Rome, especially), who also served after World War I as ambassador to Germany; in addition, his father was "the principal organizer of educational centers at university level for the laboring class" (Eissler and Eissler 1964, p. 289). His paternal grandfather was a leading politician of his time. Hartmann worked as secretary to his father while the latter was ambassador in Berlin and Hartmann was pursuing his own medical education: "In this way, Heinz Hartmann was able to study history as a living process, meeting the foremost politicians of the new German Republic. It was an enriching experience to be able to feel the pulse of a historical center— particularly for a young man whose background must have created in him a disposition toward theory" (Eissler and Eissler 1964, p. 291).

According to the Eisslers, Hartmann never contemplated a career in politics. A career is, however, not the only outcome to consider with respect to this exposure. The exposure was intensified especially during that period of development when, as Erikson (1956) has so ably argued, lasting forms of world outlook are being laid down by the interaction of phase-specific internal factors and environmental influences. Having these background factors in mind, I am disposed to look for historical-political or governmental models in Hartmann's conception of systems and systematization. All the more so in view of the heterogeneous composition and interests of the Austro-Hungarian Empire of that time and the aftermath of its dissolution,

7. Here I anticipate my task in this book.

and the basic position of the Roman Empire in the history and procedure of modern national governments. While recognizing that both models—the adaptational and governmental—are compatible with a more fundamental equilibristic, homeostatic, or cybernetic model, I intend to stress here only the probable contribution of the personal-societal context of Hartmann's own development to the psychoanalytic model he so assiduously and inventively worked out.

The merit of my analogy does not, however, depend on the validity of this genetic interpretation of Hartmann's model of mind; nor am I unaware that my point involves running the risk of committing the "genetic fallacy" so much emphasized by Hartmann in his writings. The "genetic fallacy" amounts to reducing later modes of functioning to their genetic antecedents without regard for a whole series of factors: possible changes of function; secondary autonomy; synthesis with additional determining factors including the nature of external reality and, according to Kris (1952), the possibilities and problems posed by the materials with which one is working (much of which had, of course, come down from Freud). But whatever its origins and evolution, Hartmann's model of mind fits the governmental model as though it had been derived directly from it; and the governmental model assumes meaning and purpose in a way that the natural science model cannot accommodate.

7. SUMMARY AND CONCLUSIONS

Heinz Hartmann was the guiding genius of modern metapsychology. He attempted to develop to its highest possible point Freud's natural science model of mind. With rare consistency he formulated his metapsychological contributions from the specific vantage point of biological adaption. Thus he emphasized evolutionary, organismic, ecological, and functional modes of conceptualization. The adaptational vantage point was deliberately chosen by Hartmann; it is not the only possible vantage point for psychoanalytic theorizing. Indeed the natural science model itself is a theoretical option: rather than its flowing from "the data," it is an a priori that determines the definition, selection, and arrangement of data. Other a priori models, such as the historical and existential, though their adequacy for dealing with the full range of phenomena defined in Freud's psychoanalysis has not yet been established, are available as options for the psychoanalytic investigator and remain to be worked out and evaluated comparatively.

I discussed the following aspects of Hartmann's contributions: (a) his assault on dualistic constraints in Freud's thinking; (b) his establishing or making clear the legitimacy of different modes of psychoanalytic conceptualizing; (c) his laying bare the anatomy of the natural scientific Freudian metapsychology as a necessary step toward elegant systematization and detailing of that theory; (d) his synchronization, refinement, and amplification of Freud's psychoeconomic propositions, especially through the use of the concepts of neutral and neutralized energy; and (e) his seeming to follow or parallel implicitly a socio-political model of mind as (meaningful and purposive) government.

I attempted to convey not only the range and many merits of Hartmann's mode of theorizing but also its problems. Some of these problems arise from this mode's being simultaneously conservative and revolutionary. Many problems arise from Hartmann's adherence to the postulate of psychic energy and his attempts to maintain the traditional tripartite structural model despite his having thrown key aspects of that model into question. Certain problems stem from too fixed an interest on his part in establishing a thoroughgoing symmetry in the conceptualization of libido and aggression and also of id—ego—superego.

Broadly viewed, however, the problems arise from Hartmann's commitment to the natural science approach to conceptualization. This approach excludes meaning from the center of psychoanalytic theory. It deals with meaning only by changing it into something else (functions, energies, "principles," etc.). But meaning (and intention) is the same as "psychic reality"—that which is at the center of clinical psychoanalytic work. Consequently a radical split between the mode of theorizing and the mode of investigation is a major consequence of adhering to the natural science model. Hartmann's emphasis on functions and varieties of psychic energy is shown to lead in certain instances to behavioristic, as opposed to truly psychoanalytic, formulations. It also retains the anthropomorphism it is intended to expunge from metapsychology. And finally it is inadequate *on its own terms* for rendering the complexity of clinical understanding and thus to support claims of exact explanation. Hartmann's contributions to psychoanalytic theory of increased orderliness, subtlety, and comprehensiveness have continued and even added to some difficulties, while diminishing or resolving others.

We are all much indebted to Heinz Hartmann. He gave to new generations of those interested in psychoanalytic thought a multitude of solutions, suggestions, opportunities, ambiguities, and problems that demand to be sorted out, appraised, and dealt with further. For this continuation of his work to be executed correctly and profitably we must remain aware that Hartmann's is not *the* general theory of psychoanalysis; it is, as anyone's theory (Freud's, too) has to be, *a* general theory of psychoanalysis. By his boldness and vision, Hartmann made it possible to consider alternative conceptual approaches, other a prioris and their consequences, and to do so without having to ignore or reject the basic clinical understanding and methods of Freudian psychoanalysis.

5 The Mover of the
Mental Apparatus*

1. INTRODUCTION

In this chapter I focus on the anthropomorphism that both pervades and artificially sustains Freudian metapsychology. I identify the manifestations of this anthropomorphism and argue that it is an inescapable consequence or correlate of Freud's mechanistic and organismic mode of theorizing. The reader will do well to consult also the excellent article on this topic by Grossman and Simon (1969).

I go on to argue two propositions concerning the growing appeal of such concepts as *ego autonomy, identity,* and *self* within the field of Freudian psychoanalysis: first, that this appeal represents a reaction against the mechanistic-organismic mode of conceptualization owing to that mode's great distance from, and apparent unrelatedness to, the subjective experiences and their interpretation that make up the primary data of clinical psychoanalysis; secondly, that this reaction typically miscarries owing to the continuing use of mechanistic-organismic modes of thought by those who are reacting against them. In regard to the second proposition, much of the problem resides in the extent to which mechanistic, organismic, and anthropomorphic modes of thought make up a large part of our common language, the language in terms of which, from our psychological beginnings, we learn to think about ourselves and the world around us; the extent to which this is the problem should become increasingly plain as one reads the remainder of this book.

*This is a revised version of the first portion of a paper entitled "Action: Its Place in Psychoanalytic Interpretation and Theory," which appeared in *The Annual of Psychoanalysis*, 1: (1974), 159-96. The other major portion of that paper is the basis for chapter 7 of this book. Together, these two discussions constitute a modified version of the Third Fenichel-Simmel Lectures, given in November 1971, before the Los Angeles Psychoanalytic Society and Institute. I am grateful to the officers and members of that group for the honor they bestowed and the opportunity they offered to present and elaborate my ideas on that occasion.

2. Conceptual Difficulties in Freudian Metapsychology

The terms of Freudian metapsychology are those of natural science. Freud, Hartmann, and others deliberately used the language of forces, energies, functions, structures, apparatus, and principles to establish and develop psychoanalysis along the lines of a physicalistic psychobiology.

It is inconsistent with this type of scientific language to speak of intentions, meanings, reasons, or subjective experience. Even though in the first instance, which is the psychoanalytic situation, psychoanalysts deal essentially with reasons, emphases, choices, and the like, as metapsychologists they have traditionally made it their objective to translate these subjective contents and these actions into the language of functions, energies, and so forth. In this way, they have attempted to formulate explanations of action in the mode—actually it is only one of the modes—of natural science explanation. They have suppressed the intentionalistic, active mode. In line with this strategy, reasons become forces, emphases become energies, activity becomes function, thoughts become representations, affects become discharges or signals, deeds become resultants, and particular ways of struggling with the inevitable diversity of intentions, feelings, and situations become structures, mechanisms, and adaptations. And, in keeping with the assumption of thoroughgoing determinism, the word *choice* has been effectively excluded from the metapsychological vocabulary. Action, if it is not used in the sense of acting-out, is understood merely as motoric activity with respect to the so-called external world (Hartmann 1947).

It is curious, to say the least, that practitioners of a discipline that is so specifically concerned with human subjectivity and action should have continued to devote themselves to the impersonal rhetoric of natural science. The discrepancy is all the more curious in view of the close parallels between this language and what I shall discuss in chapter 7 under the heading "disclaimed action" (e.g., "My unconscious made me do it, so don't blame me!"). Analysands and metapsychologists sound strangely alike.

In what follows, in addition to continuing my critical review of the work of Freud and Hartmann, I shall take up or at least touch on certain related aspects of the work of Waelder, Erikson, Kohut, Guntrip, and Laing, among others.

There was something about this discrepancy between practice and theorizing that seemed to trouble Freud. We are all aware that Freud did not adhere consistently to the scientific model on which he had pinned his theoretical hopes. While using it, he "anthropomorphized" it. In doing so he made some of his most memorable statements—for example, when he spoke of the superego as the heir of the Oedipus complex, and of the ego's serving three masters, or letting itself die, or deforming itself. Freud often spoke in this way of the psychic structures, the topographic systems, the primary and secondary processes, the great principles, and the instinctual drives and energies: he spoke of all of these as if they were purposive, meaning-creating, choice-making, action-oriented entities, which is to say, as if they were minds within the mind, or homunculi.

Was this anthropomorphizing mere carelessness or indifference on his part, or metaphorical embellishment, or inevitable conceptual impurity retained in the process of developing a new field? Although I would say that the answer to each of these questions is yes, I do not think any or all of these characterizations is sufficient. I would emphasize as well that Freud felt his powers of understanding to be too confined by the natural science model. It is as if he sensed that this model excluded something essential, something it had to exclude owing to its internal logic, and yet something that psychoanalytic propositions could not do without, namely, the purposive agent, the experiencing human being, the active self, the "I," or whatever one chose to call it. To put the matter in terms of Binswanger's (1936, 1946) later discussions, Freud must have sensed that natural science theorizing necessarily reduces that personal "I" to a clinically unwieldly or unsuitable thing, organism, or apparatus; or in Buber's (1923) term, to an "it."

When Freud was not being self-consciously theoretical, he spoke a different language—a purposive or intentionalistic language, or, in my terms, a rudimentary action language. Consider, for example, these two excerpts from his stunning papers on technique:

It must be understood that each individual, through the combined operation of his innate disposition and the influences brought to bear on him during his early years, has acquired a specific method of his own in his conduct of his erotic life—that is, in the preconditions to falling in love which he lays down, in the instincts he satisfies and the aims he sets himself in the course of it (Freud 1912, p. 99).

The more plainly the analyst lets it be seen that he is proof against every temptation, the more readily he will be able to extract from the situation its analytic content. The patient, whose sexual repression is of course not yet removed but merely pushed into the background, will then feel safe enough to allow all her preconditions for loving, all the phantasies springing from her sexual desires, all the detailed characteristics of her state of being in love, to come to light; and from these she will herself open the way to the infantile roots of her love (Freud 1915a, p. 166).

Consider, too, this excerpt from "Beyond the Pleasure Principle":

What psycho-analysis reveals in the transference phenomena of neurotics can also be observed in the lives of some normal people. The impression they give is of being pursued by a malignant fate or possessed by some "daemonic" power; but psycho-analysis has always taken the view that their fate is for the most part arranged by themselves and determined by early infantile influences (Freud 1920a, p. 21).[1]

"A...method of his own"; "preconditions...he lays down"; "she will herself open the way"; "their fate is for the most part arranged by themselves"! Thus Freud the clinical analyst, a striking contrast to Freud the scientist. Yet, as I have mentioned, Freud the clinical analyst had his say in the theory through his anthropomorphic rendition of his metapsychology.

Let us move on now to that outstanding theoretician, Robert Waelder. He, too, could not escape this difficulty in conceptualization. Consider, for example, the following two interrelated passages, which, despite their awkward construction, count among the theoretically most suggestive and clinically most useful statements in the psychoanalytic literature:

1. Although Freud went on in this connection to begin arguing for some principle "beyond" the pleasure principle, or, as it turned out, antithetical to it, he nowhere modified his assertion that, clinically, the analyst may look at normal and neurotic lives as actively chosen or "arranged."

According to this principle of multiple function the specific methods of solution for the various problems in the ego must always be so chosen that they, whatever may be their objective, carry with them at the same time gratification of the instincts. However, in the face of the dynamic strength of human instinctual life this means that the instincts play the part of choosing among the possible methods of solution in such a way that preferably those attempted solutions which also represent gratification of the dominant impulses will appear and maintain themselves (Waelder 1930, p. 56).

In a situation of conflict each method of solution which perceives an experience as coming from the outside and itself passively surrendering to these outside forces, is an attempted solution for certain problems, is gratification of love and hate relationships, defense reaction and others such (Waelder 1930, p. 60).

Notice how Waelder was driven to anthropomorphize what he calls "methods of solution." According to him, these methods maintain themselves; they perceive experiences and perceive themselves; and they passively surrender. In this passage, in a similar but less obvious anthropomorphizing vein, he also indicated that instincts have preferences and make choices. I think it fair to say that Waelder could not see that there are more things in heaven and earth than can be spoken of in the natural science rhetoric of metapsychology, and that, as a consequence, he, like Freud, had to anthropomorphize the established mechanistic-organismic concepts.

What of Heinz Hartmann? He did make extensive efforts to deal with this problem systematically. First, he explicitly devoted himself to purging metapsychological discourse of anthropomorphism. He did so particularly by working out refined conceptualizations of functions, psychic energy, and intrasystemic heterogeneity, and by his consistent application of these conceptualizations. Consider, for example, the following contrast. On the one hand, Freud (1928) had spoken of the ego's submitting itself masochistically to a tyrannical superego, with both ego and superego playing son and father simultaneously in that interaction. On the other hand, Hartmann, together with Loewenstein (1962), tended to speak of interactions between ego functions and superego functions; he proposed that each function was fed by and expended libidinal and aggressive energies of varying degrees of neutralization; and he further proposed that the proportions of pleasure and pain in the interaction could be accounted for by the types and degrees of energy discharge involved in these mutual influences. The difference between the two approaches is plain enough. Hartmann certainly seems to have succeeded in eliminating Freud's anthropomorphism from metapsychology. (However, that he still retained it in a subtle, yet central, way will soon be made plain.)

Hartmann was too wise and conscientious a thinker to consider the job finished at this point. As his second contribution in this respect, he attempted to find a place for whatever it was that the anthropomorphism was supposed to have informally retained in the theory. He did this in several steps. One step, represented throughout his writings (Hartmann 1939b, 1964), is his emphasis on higher-order, central-regulating, and organizing functions. These are the functions that differentiate and synthesize mental processes and contents and also control other functions by setting aims, establishing rank orders of functions, and controlling expenditures of the neutral and neutralized energies that are freely available to the ego for carrying out its activities. For example, these are the functions that suspend certain rational and defensive functions in "adaptive regressions." Essentially, they constitute what Hartmann (1939b) termed, in his great monograph on adaptation, the "intelligence" of the organism. But, although he placed these functions at the top of the hierarchy of functions, Hartmann never amplified this conceptualization in proportion to its obviously central strategic significance. It is a most striking gap in his theorizing!

The second step Hartmann took to recast Freud's anthropomorphic formulations was this: he acknowledged intentionality as a human characteristic and classified it as an ego function (1952, p. 173); however, he defined intentionality quite narrowly as one function among others—a direction-setting function—and he did not discuss it at length. Moreover, according to my reading of his somewhat ambiguous discussion, he seemed to be restricting intentionality to the defining of *conscious* intentions. This view of it, which does not violate the logic of natural science theorizing, is considerably more restrictive than the one derived in part from Brentano and Husserl and their modern followers according to which intentionality is the defining feature of every psychological act. For psychoanalytic psychology, then, if "intentionality" is to be used at all, it ought to refer to something universal; it should define our subject matter entirely. Hartmann's including so shrunken a version of intentionality in psychoanalytic theory could not go far toward dealing with problematic anthropomorphizing (see also chapter 10, section 3).

In a third step, Hartmann emphasized functions of primary and secondary autonomy. This step seemed to allow recognition of apparently "free" or conflict-free behavior without any compromise of the natural science, deterministic model of explanation. Two points must be noted here: if "autonomy" is to retain any meaning, designating these functions "autonomous" amounts to stating that they are or can be self-activating and self-regulatory; and to speak of "relative autonomy," though it represents hedging to the point of self-contradiction, is still a way of ascribing freedom to functions. I shall return to autonomy concepts soon, and again in section 3 of this chapter.

Although Hartmann seems to have considered taking a fourth step against anthropomorphic theorizing, he never quite took it. This step would have been a full discussion of the problem of meaning. (Here I shall briefly review and then go on to supplement what I have already discussed in chapter 4, especially in its section 5; see also chapter 10.) Hartmann referred to *meaning* in a number of places, but he discussed its concrete application only in one place and there only briefly (1955, pp. 217-18). He merely stressed that *meaning* is an unclear concept, and he suggested that the established metapsychological concepts, such as the functions and regulating principles, are the appropriate and adequate ones to deal with its referents. In another place (1959, p. 346), he said that "the same manifest action, attitude, fantasy may have different 'meanings' (that is, may be the result of the interaction of different tendencies)." Here, in equating meaning with the resultant of forces, he took the position he had worked out long before (1927) and was never to depart from. This is the position that psychoanalysis is and must be a natural science theory, that is to say, one that is cast in terms of forces, energies, functions, etc. One major consequence of taking this position is that "understanding," "meaning," "reasons," and suchlike are to be regarded merely as subjective mental contents, not yet "objectified" in the language of scientific causality. I believe that had Hartmann explored the idea of meaning, he would have had to acknowledge more openly than he ever did the fact that mechanistic-organismic theory is merely an option, not a necessity, for psychoanalysis; and he might have moved toward the type of mixed economic-experiential conceptualization most recently attempted by Ricouer (1970).

Hartmann's treatment of this central problem of meaning may be interpreted in the following manner. He wrote as if he had seen, correctly, that a full, direct consideration of meaning would require a theoretical model radically different from the traditional natural science model, and as if he had concluded that, for the sake of consistency in his own (and Freud's) systematizing efforts, it was best never to get deeply into it. He committed himself to Freud's model.

I have sketched Hartmann's efforts systematically to expunge anthropomorphic formulations from metapsychology, and I have indicated that as a natural science theoretician he was both exactly right to set this as his aim and impressively consistent in his pursuit of it. But was he really successful? Did he really rid metapsychology of its correlative anthropomorphism? As I have already indicated, I believe that he did not succeed. In the relatively undeveloped concepts of intelligence, central regulating and organizing functions, autonomy, and intentionality as one ego function among others, there remain many residues of this problematic anthropomorphism. Hartmann implicitly ascribed intentionality and choice to the central functions and the autonomous functions. How else can we understand propositions concerning functions that set aims, rank order other functions, or discharge their own noninstinctual energy? In being represented as self-activating and self-regulating, autonomous functions are being implicitly portrayed as independent, symbol-utilizing minds that can make themselves up. I see no way around this anthropomorphic implication.

Despite his sticking to the impersonal language of energy and functions, Hartmann placed in "the ego" a center of actions that only a mentally intact human being might engage in. In the very terms of his own argument, intentionality could not be, as he said, one direction-setting ego function among others; nor could it be restricted to consciousness. Nor could *meaning* be set aside as mere experience or mere content waiting for its scientific conceptualization. Intentionality and meaning were coterminous with ego itself. There was a person loose in the apparatus, a mastermind working the mechanism— what in a general way Ryle (1949) in his important book, *The Concept of Mind,* called "the ghost in the machine," and what, in my adaptation of his argument to this particular metapsychological problem, I shall call "the mover of the mental apparatus."

In this light, it is possible to understand the awkwardness of Hartmann's conceptualization of intersystemic relations: he had to limit himself to speaking of noncognitive "influences" of id and superego on ego functions because he could not attribute perceiving, knowing, and choosing to the id and superego without having to face the problem of anthropomorphism all over again—which is the problem of meaning as well. The consequence of not observing these limits would be that the psychic systems would begin to sound too much like people in relationship to each other—as they do, for example, in Fairbairn's (1952) theorizing. And yet what sense does it make to speak of noncognitive influences in mental functioning? How can the superego influence what it does not know? How can it even choose to exert influence? Who or what activates the superego? How can it be activated? Who or what receives its signal or knows its meaning? Surely, Hartmann was not aiming to set forth a conditioned-response, simple reflex-arc, nonsymbolic neurological theory. In these respects, the purity of Hartmann's natural science propositions rests on an incomplete and inconsistent analysis of the conceptual field.

On the basis of these considerations, I come to this conclusion: however much Hartmann eliminated blatant anthropomorphism from Freud's metapsychological formulations, in certain crucial respects he did not succeed in resolving the problems latent in them. His efforts were incomplete, insecurely founded, and unconvincing. Incorporated in them were the problems they were meant to solve. Further, I believe that *in principle* a mechanistic-organismic model of human psychology, so long as it is an attempt to deal with fundamental and complex phenomena and relations, must in the end turn into an anthropomorphic model. Within any psychology, mechanism,

organism, and anthropomorphism imply each other. Hartmann
had to fail in this respect. He had to hide a mover in the mental
apparatus. For an apparatus cannot move itself; nor can it, like
the human mind, move the world. It cannot, for example, in-
vent psychoanalysis. We shall identify that hidden mover
before we are through.

What follows from this? Most generally, we may take the
state of theoretical affairs described in this brief discussion of
Freud, Waelder, and Hartmann as an indication that it is essential to try out radically different conceptual models. These
models should be tried out with all due regard for their internal
logic, just as Hartmann tried out the natural science model
with all due regard for its logic. The rationale of engaging in
these attempts is simply that we have yet to find a home for the
sense in Freud's unabashed metapsychological anthropomorphic theorizing. After all, Freud's *das Ich* is not ego and self: it
is also "I," the agent, the subject who must always be assumed
in any psychological proposition. This agent is metapsychology's greatest embarrassment; for the theory can only reduce
the agent to anthropomorphized ego functions. Hartmann
(1950) and also Jacobson (1964) attempted systematic differentiations of the concepts *ego* and *self-representation*—the
established metapsychology could accommodate both of these
terms—but where is the "I" (and the "over-I") that Freud could
not do without?

The "I" or agent must remain outside the natural science
language. It should not, however, be left in limbo. Analysands
often try to leave it in limbo, as when they insistently disclaim
responsibility for action. On our part, we analysts try to restore
an unthreatened sense of activity to the analysands and to enhance it as well as preserve it for ourselves against the analysands' assaults and seductions. But we have no theory to
formalize and guide this defining aspect of our work. Our general theory serves other purposes.

Up to now it has been left to the existential psychoanalysts to
develop this theory of agents—persons defined by their intentions, choices, and actions—but it seems to me that these
analysts have been distorting and discarding so many of the
essential Freudian contributions to the understanding of
human development that I cannot consider them psychoanalytic. For example, they generally ignore infantile sexuality or

minimize its significance; moreover, they tend to rely heavily on interpretation of manifest content, and the content in question is likely to have been gathered outside a clinical analytic situation, perhaps from creative writing, autobiographical statements, letters, or Kraepelinian observation from afar. The Freudian analyst is left still confronting the gap between clinical interpretation (with its implied theory of the psychoanalytic process) and the general theory of psychoanalysis.

3. Stopgap Metapsychological Concepts

Where there are serious gaps between theory and observation or application, one may expect that in time various types of efforts will be made to close the gaps with the help of new, supplementary concepts or newly employed familiar concepts. As Kuhn (1970) has demonstrated, in these circumstances one is much less likely to find a fundamental reorientation to theorizing, at least not for a long while. With regard to the agent left in psychoanalytic limbo, the more limited and still problematic attempts at closure are found. I shall now discuss three such stopgap concepts, namely *the adaptive ego, identity,* and *self.*

(1) *The adaptive ego.* Hartmann's systematic introduction of the concept of adaptation appears to close the gap in question. In fact, however, and despite the pains he took to avoid this consequence, he has provided another opening for confused theorizing. Through this opening many psychoanalytic writers have by now attempted to reintroduce the central agent, the embarrassing "I," into metapsychology. The adaptive ego or ego functions, or the autonomous ego functions, have been used to include just what the decorum of natural science conceptualizing is designed to exclude, namely the sentient, self-determining, choice-making, responsible, active human being. In natural science that human being must be made into an object of observation, a mechanical or mindless object, and thus an object of an order different from that of the free observer. It is only on the surface that this use of "autonomy" remains functional and impersonal. Often, the adaptive ego is merely a pseudo-orthodox way of saying "he" or "she"—or, possibly, since analytic self-esteem has gotten hooked up to

being autonomous or "having" autonomy, the adaptive or autonomous ego is sometimes a covert and valuative way of saying "I," that is, the author himself or herself. It is then an instance of the observer's implicitly claiming exemption *as observer* from deterministic propositions.

Additional problems have ensued in this regard. To accomplish their mission fully, the adaptive ego-ists have tended to slip into simple, unsubstantiated assertions that this or that function *is* autonomous and the corresponding behavior adaptive. All too often they do not trouble themselves with noting that they lack clinical evidence to support their assertions. They do not seem to remember that this evidence would have to be collected during clinical analytic investigation of the implicated functions and behaviors (Schafer 1967a). For example, some of the comments included in the panel report in the *International Journal of Psycho-Analysis,* "Protest and Revolution" (Francis 1970), demonstrate this cavalier attitude on the part of analysts who should know better.

Surely, from all we do know as analysts, we should be especially cautious and should be armed with qualifications and question marks when speaking of autonomy and adaptiveness. Freud dealt a great blow to human narcissism when he showed how illusory were many or most of people's claims to conscious functional autonomy and adaptiveness. He showed that the conscious unitary will was not all, and often not much. He dealt another blow when he showed how limited and misleading are impressions of motivation gained through informal social observation and conscious directed report. Freud struck these blows through his clinical method, not through commonsense observation of social behavior supplemented by what we must in all seriousness call "wild ego analysis." In these times of psychosocial variables, psychohistorical explanations, and a widespread professional rage to be relevant—all of which require radical, untested, and highly questionable assumptions about ego autonomy—wild ego analysis may be a greater threat to Freudian analysis than wild id analysis.

It is not, however, Hartmann's conceptualization of adaptation itself that is fundamentally at fault here. The reason for this theoretical "return of the repressed" is this: the anthropomorphic formulations no longer being acceptable, it has become necessary to provide new forms of expression for the irrepressible theme of action, that is, of human beings doing things for specifically human reasons. Anthropomorphism in metapsychology is the archaic representation of the theme of human action. It is ironic that these new forms have been developed at the center of Hartmann's rigorous conceptualizations. There they violate both the decorum of Hartmann's theorizing and the exacting demands of Freud's psychoanalytic method. I did, however, point out in section 2 of this chapter, as in chapter 4, that, careful as he was, Hartmann could not purge his own formulations of anthropomorphic implications.

(2) *Identity*. Some Freudian analysts have used Erikson's (1950, 1956) concept of identity to reintroduce the active person, the "I," into metapsychological as well as clinical discourse. They speak of identity as being, doing, requiring, and effecting various things. In one way this usage makes a new thing or apparatus of identity. Identity becomes something one has or loses or searches for. In this respect identity is being used the way *"the* ego" is used by many analysts, as a machine with a single, central intelligence. Theoretical advance is blocked by this reification.

But in a deeper way, this use of identity is only a breath away from saying "the person" or "the agent." Moreover, I believe it to be true that, as Erikson uses it, and despite his own lapses into reification, identity is more phenomenological and existential-analytic than Freudian-metapsychological. Identity is very similar to the existential-analytic concept of *being-in-the-world* in that both are used to attempt a basic thematic characterization of a person's way of creating, arranging, and experiencing his or her life. Identity is the theme of significant personal actions. Although Erikson retains Freudian drives, defenses, identifications, superego dictates, and stages of development as components of the concept of identity, he tends to view them in the context of life themes and to explain them by reference to these themes. Thus, like the existentialists, he reverses the Freudian priorities which require explanations to move from content to formalistic concepts. Hartmann's translating "meaning" into "the result of the interaction of different tendencies" is an instance of what I mean by the Freudian priorities.

I submit, then, that, as a concept, identity is phenomenological, existential, and intentionalistic at its core. The result of adding identity concepts to the metapsychological vocabulary is theoretical confusion. Erikson has contributed to this confusion by using both mechanistic-organismic and existential concepts in setting forth his ideas.

I should like to suggest in this regard a partial explanation of the wide professional appeal of Erikson's writings. I believe it to stem from Erikson's helping the psychoanalytic therapist to feel that it is all right once again to think about oneself and others as people who do things rather than as organisms or apparatus with functions—while yet retaining Freudian insights! This is the same factor that has led so many otherwise thoughtful analysts uncritically to accept as respectable theory Freud's anthropomorphizing of mechanistic-organismic variables. It seems that, in the final analysis, the important thing is that the person be alive and well in the impersonalized theory, that there be a mover—now called "identity"—hidden in the mental apparatus.

I conclude that identity seems to help close the gap between traditional theory and practice more than it in fact does. Those who use it introduce a second kind of theory without discarding the first. Ultimately, this mixing of forms of theory is more obstructive to psychoanalytic conceptualization than the many loose, ambiguous, repressive, and regressive purposes to which the term identity is currently being put. Nevertheless, identity may be seen as a move toward new theoretical models suitable for human beings and their actions.

(3) *Self.* This is the third and last of the problematic stopgap concepts I shall discuss. For the most part, Hartmann steered clear of self in his systematic writings. As he used it, it was roughly synonymous with the whole biological person or organism, an entity whose existence must be assumed. Accordingly, he differentiated self from self-representation, and emphasized only the latter when clarifying and amending Freud's fuzzy conceptualization of the relation between narcissism and ego. From the point of view of traditional theory, *self*-representation refers merely to one kind of mental content; though a necessary concept, it is not central.

In contrast to Hartmann, another important Freudian theoretician, Heinz Kohut, has become deeply embroiled with self in his recent explorations of narcissism (1966, 1971). He uses the term to refer to a new dynamic and structural entity as well as to a life theme. This usage seems to be in the service of closing the gap between theory and practice while both avoiding anthropomorphism and preserving the metapsychological language. Like identity, however, Kohut's "narcissistic self" mixes two different types of discourse in that it represents an attempt to inject the person as agent into a natural science model.

Additionally, Kohut's weighty and ambitious use of self encounters a problem I could as well have mentioned in connection with identity. The problem is this: descriptively and dynamically, Kohut's narcissistic self overlaps and is confused with the tripartite structure of the mental apparatus. Specifically, Kohut attributes to the narcissistic self features of both the so-called id (e.g., exhibitionism, grandiosity, drive urgency, demands on the ego, and libidinal energy seeking discharge) and the so-called ego (e.g., ambitions, affect signals, and self-feeling). That he treats this self as a new psychic structure, characterized like the others by its independence, is evident in his statement beginning, "The interplay between the narcissistic self, the ego and the superego..." (1966, p. 256). At this point, then, Kohut's carefully worked out conceptualizations suffer from his attempt to mix a phenomenological, experiential, representational concept with the traditional structural-energic metapsychological entities.

Kohut's sophisticated difficulties are all the more apparent when, in one of his central propositions, he says, "At the risk of sounding anthropomorphic, yet in reality only condensing a host of clinical impressions and genetic reconstructions, I am tempted to say that the ego experiences the influence of the ego ideal as coming from above and that of the narcissistic self as coming from below" (1966, p. 250). Again, he mixes experiential and traditional metapsychological terms; now, however, he adds to his difficulties, first by thinking of his argument (or temptation) merely as *risking* anthropomorphism, and then by suggesting in vain that richness of clinical connotation can eliminate the risk of "real" anthropomorphism. Clearly, against his better judgment he is caught up in conceptual conflict.

Consequently, and despite his illuminating discussions of the phenomenology and dimensions of narcissism, by being tied to the ideas of the narcissistic self and by retaining mechanistic-organismic concepts, Kohut has put himself in great theoretical difficulty. The natural science and the experiential rhetorics simply do not mix. Nevertheless, although it does not seem to be his intention to do so, Kohut may yet be contributing to the development of a new theoretical language for psychoanalysis. Like Erikson's "identity," Kohut's "self" seems to be a move toward the model of active persons. To regard Kohut's theoretical contributions on narcissism as transitional to new modes of psychoanalytic conceptualization is to make more comprehensible the unsatisfactory construction of many of his formulations. Although Kohut indicates his appreciation of these difficulties, he continues to employ such formulations as that the grandiose self makes demands on the ego. His transitional position is also evident in his tending to suggest some new interpretation of libido whereby it is equivalent to experience or meaning (see, e.g., Kohut 1971, p. 42n).

The same type of difficulty occurs in a paper on the self by Levin (1969) and in the use of "experiential" and "nonexperiential" by Sandler and Joffe (1969).

Outside the realm of Freudian theorizing, the concept self has enjoyed—or suffered?—wide popularity and usage. Neo-Freudians and existential psychoanalysts seem to like the term because it is so well suited to their generally humanistic, intentionalistic rhetoric. It is obvious, however, that they have used self as an all-purpose term. Like identity, which they also favor, self refers at different times to personality, person, mind, ego, life theme, "I," and subjective life in general. Used this loosely, self is of little use in the quest for clarity of thought.

Furthermore, in these neo-Freudian and existential writings we often encounter the term self as "*the* self." Like the thingness and agency attributed to identity, "*the* self" concretizes or substantializes a term whose referents are primarily subjective or experiential and whose force is primarily adverbial and adjectival. Moreover, in some of its usages, such as "self-actualization," "*the* self" is set up not only as the existential referent of behavior but as, all at once, the motor, the fuel, the driver, and the end point of the journey of existence. It is ironic that self as "*the* self" has become an It: the shadow of natural science theorizing has fallen on humanistic understanding.

As "*the* self," self is also a vague affirmation of the unity of the personality; like "*the* ego" and "*an* identity," it implies a natural state of personal unity and harmony. In its unqualified form, however, that implied affirmation is based far more on hope than on evidence or reasoned argument. A major consequence of this affirmation is that we all quickly become, in Laing's (1969a, 1969b) popular phrase, divided selves, when it would be much closer to the truth to say that the undivided self is at best a possibly useful theoretical fiction and at worst a manic dream of fusion or a new version of the old psychoanalytic dream of perfect and total genitality.

It is perhaps related to this fantasy of undivided subjectivity that self has often been invested with a sentimental glow, if not a quasi-religious halo. Take, for example, Harry Guntrip (1967, 1968). He has written extensively and with much sophistication on a number of the crucial theoretical issues I have been taking up, often along quite the same lines, and we have much to learn from him. Yet he seems to be so concerned with the need for a humane theory of self and others that he argues in more than one place the superiority of his version of object-relations theory—*on humanistic grounds!* It sounds as if kindly theory is better theory, or a kindly theoretician a better theoretician. In my view, his theoretical formulations are implicitly in the service of his aiming to give moral support to the taxing work of deep psychotherapy with schizoid patients. But this is to repeat the same error as that made earlier by Sullivan, Fromm-Reichman, and their followers. Empathy is not theory.

In any case, many writers have been projecting considerable warmth, humaneness, and dignity into the idea of a naturally unitary self shattered by an injurious world. One is made to feel that it is callous and dehumanizing to think about people in other terms, especially as agents of their own lives. In fact, one is at times discouraged from thinking very much at all in this regard. As I suggested earlier, an outstanding example of this anti-intellectual romanticizing of self may be found in the writings of R.D. Laing.

No doubt, all the current enthusiasm for self-concepts as well as autonomy and identity concepts will have to be explained by an intellectual historian of the future. Meanwhile, however, looking at it simply from the standpoint of problems inherent in metapsychology, I propose that, like autonomy and identity, self is the center of some necessarily unsuccessful Freudian efforts to imbue a natural science theory with experiential vividness or excitement—or, from a related vantage point, of necessarily unsuccessful efforts to bring metapsychology closer to the psychoanalytic process itself.

4. The Theory of the Psychoanalytic Process — and the "Mover" Revealed

It remains to consider one more gap between interpretation and general theory. We encounter it in a problematic aspect of the theory of the psychoanalytic process. It is this: the person as human being rather than mechanism or organism, the one addressed by the interpreting psychoanalyst, lurks in the shadows that surround such familiar and useful concepts as the reasonable or rational ego, the observing ego, the ego core, emotional insight, the therapeutic alliance, the working alliance, the mature transference, higher levels of organization, and growth tendencies. Sooner or later, these concepts are used, they have to be used, to imply an agency that stands more or less outside the so-called play of forces, the so-called interrelations of functions, the so-called field of determinants. They have to be so used because they express attempts to avoid, on the one hand, making manifestly anthropomorphic formulations, and, on the other, rethinking the fundamental conceptualization of psychoanalysis. There is the gap: between the person on one side and the natural science apparatus on the other. This split-off agency that makes psychoanalytic work possible is somehow specifically human in that it makes specifically human experience possible and communicable, and specifically human goals definable, maintainable, and approachable. Implicitly, this relationship-forming agency is a whole person. As psychoanalysts, we cannot think about our clinical work without using concepts of this sort. We cannot think that some of the analysand's ego functions have formed an alliance with some of our own ego functions — not, that is, without being anthropomorphic about functions!

We can now identify the mover of the mental apparatus. It is the psychoanalytic clinician's projection of himself or herself into the model of mind. The clinician rightly insists on remaining in the act. It is the analyst who is irrepressible. As analyst, one never really regards oneself as an apparatus or one's work as the resultant of forces or the interplay of functions. One may pay homage to Freud's metapsychology by using these natural science terms when discussing the psychoanalytic process; to oneself, however, one remains an agent, a person who chooses what to do and does it, and who can detect when he or she has chosen wrongly or acted inappropriately, and who can then do something about that. The analyst *as person* is the one who invented the machine, turns it on and off, tinkers with it.

The clinical psychoanalyst does not even really regard the analysand as an apparatus, except perhaps sometimes when thinking in the terms of psychopathology; for "psychopathology" gives all the appearance—but only the appearance!—of being the resultant of forces and defective apparatus. It is a curious kind of isolating or splitting to regard one's analysand as an existential person with mechanistic-organismic psychopathology. But that splitting is necessary only so long as we adhere to the metapsychological model of mind. To be internally consistent, the evolving theory of the psychoanalytic process requires a thoroughly non-mechanistic, non-organismic language. The action language, to which I shall now return, is my attempt to systematize a language of just that sort.

Part III

Essays on Action Language

6　The Essays on Action Language

1. The Challenge of a New Language

In fashioning his metapsychology, Freud used the conceptual tools he had at hand. He relied (as we have, in following him) on a mixture of two languages, one suitable for natural science propositions and the other suitable for the utterly unsystematic discourse of everyday life. But Freud had no warrant to expect either the language of the laboratory or the home to be suitable for defining or expressing his data. He seems never to have realized that the discipline he was creating would have to have a language peculiarly its own before it could attain systematic dignity and elegance. That is to say, it would have to have language rules that were suited to the method he was employing and the kind of observational possibilities he was generating with that method. The method is the interpretation of what people say about their past and present lives, including their lives in the analytic hours, how they say it, and the difficulties they encounter in trying to speak frankly and unprogrammatically, that is, in trying to "free associate" or "follow the fundamental rule." I have tried to show in the preparatory studies of part II that, even in its most advanced form, Freud's metapsychology just does not serve in this regard.

In going on now in part III to present an action language for psychoanalysis, I shall be reexamining psychoanalytic terms of strategic theoretical significance in the interest of eliminating the unsuitable, confusing, unnecessary, and meaningless metaphors and metaphorical preconceptions that are inherent in Freud's eclectic metapsychological language. In this endeavor I shall be building a technical language using plain English locutions. It is one that should make it possible to specify in a relatively unambiguous, consistent, parsimonious, and enlightening way the psychological facts and relations that are of special interest to psychoanalysts and their analysands. One might go so far as to call it a new language, a language devised, as metapsychology was, for the purposes of systematic discourse about human lives as they are encountered in psychoanalytic sessions. According to the rules of this new language, to give but one example, mental actions do not occur in space, are not to be located inside or outside of anything or beneath or above anything, and do not move from place to place—except in fantasy; consequently the concept of internalization can only refer to a fantasy rather than a process—specifically, the fantasy of physical incorporation. (This, in brief, is the line of argument pursued in chapter 8.)

There is no escaping the fact that this conceptual critique and reformulation of psychoanalysis in the terms of action is strong stuff. It undermines our confidence in the sense and utility of such key terms as internalization, drive, structure, and psychic energy, and it leaves us wondering, "What will be left of psychoanalytic theory?" But subtraction is not the point of my project: its point is redefinition, which means that we shall be working with a revised conception of psychoanalytic theory, not a lesser conception of it. Still, the trend of my argument is that many well-established modes of thought will have to be changed and many ideas on many levels of abstraction will have to be reworked. I know from my own labors how difficult it is to change these modes and contents of thought. Effecting change of that nature and that extent requires continuous conscious alertness and self-monitoring. In turn that alertness and monitoring disrupt the ease and smoothness of thought and speech that one has laboriously achieved during one's personal and professional development. The result is a sense of loss and of being at a loss, especially for words. The loss combines "object loss" (the version of psychoanalysis one values and loves) and "narcissistic loss" (the sense of personal unity, worth, and satisfaction associated with thinking psychoanalytically in familar ways). One cannot but fear, resent, and resist such a call for change: what is true for neurotic fantasizing is true for psychoanalytic conceptualizing.

The modes of thought and the terms I am calling into question are those that refer to abstract or nonsubstantial ideas in substantive, animistic, or anthropomorphic terms. Customarily, we speak of thoughts, feelings, motives, traits, and suchlike as though they had the properties of things, such as extension, location, and momentum, or the characteristics of people, such as tenacity, cunning, and wilfullness. This pervasive reliance on what ultimately are infantile or primary process modes of thought undoubtedly adds a certain kind of vividness, charm, and drama to both our everyday discourse and our clinical and theoretical work. As well as being gratifying, it is reassuringly familiar. But in the end we discover theory to be replete with reification and anthropomorphism (Grossman and Simon 1969; see also chapter 5). And we cannot accept this state of affairs.

It would, of course, be absurd to try to legislate in the realms of ordinary everyday discourse and clinical discourse; there, metaphoric thinking of the sort I am challenging is not only inevitable but, need I say, valuable for many different purposes. One may, however, legislate in the realms of theoretical discourse and principles of interpretation; in fact, by their very nature theoretical propositions and principles of procedure are legislative.

2. THE FIVE ESSAYS OF PART III

In turning articles that were written on different occasions into the successive chapters of part III, I have not tried to eliminate the signs of progression in my thinking from one of these chapters to the next. I want the evolution of my project to be visible so that the reader can acquire as full a sense as possible of this being a work in progress; I want not only to be properly frank about the matter, but also and mainly to make plain the problems I have encountered and the solutions I have adopted, thereby putting the reader in the strongest possible critical position.

But I have not hesitated to introduce changes of conceptualization that will, in my opinion, increase the consistency and effect of the entire exposition. That is to say, in the light of later studies as well as further deliberation, I have reformulated some earlier points that seem wrong, incomplete, or fuzzier than need be. I have also reorganized some of the material so as to make the development of my argument more orderly and understandable, and occasionally I have amplified points to strengthen them. In doing this organizational job, which also includes some cross-referencing, I have tried not to obscure the project's progressive nature. And although I deleted some passages that, taking all the material together, are simply repetitious, I do allow a number of restatements of major propositions to stand: in some instances I have done so when I think it will ensure the reader's grasp of the discussion in progress: in others, for the advantage to be gained by reconsidering important points in new contexts. It seems to me that in learning new language it always helps to reencounter key ideas in a variety of contexts; for we really get to know a complex idea only through becoming familiar with the way it appears and the way we work with it in different connections. The result of all these changes is this: while each chapter can stand by itself, its forcefulness and its full meaning depends in some measure on all the other chapters.

In chapters 7 through 11, I shall be taking up the fundamental topics of action and disclaimed action, internalization, self and identity, psychodynamic explanation, and resistance. In one connection or another I shall have occasion to establish, or at least sketch, the application of action language to many more of the concepts and phenomena around which the discipline of psychoanalysis has been organized: slips, conflict, mind, introjects, externalization, affects (a precursor of part IV), motives, the dynamic unconscious, defense, topography, psychic structure, transference, cure, negative therapeutic reaction, and so forth. In the process, I shall continually refer back to metapsychology in order to make clear what is being changed and why: this is the theoretical "thinking through" that is the counterpart of clinical "working through"; and because this "thinking through" returns again and again to the problem of interpretation, it makes some contribution, in my view, to the arduous technique of "working through" itself.

7 Claimed and Disclaimed Action*

1. INTRODUCTION

It is to a certain emphasis in Fenichel's ever rewarding monograph on technique (1941) that I am particularly indebted for a large part of the inspiration of this chapter. I am thinking of his repeated reference to ascertaining the activity that lies behind apparent passivity. He said, for example:

> *How does interpretation work?* We do not want to differentiate at this point between interpretations of resistance and interpretations of instinct, but to ask about the factors common to both. The answer in general is this: the attention of the ego is drawn to a "preconscious derivative." How does this take place? (1) What is to be interpreted is first *isolated* from the experiencing part of the ego. This preliminary task drops out when the patient already has some critical attitude toward that which is to be interpreted. (2) The patient's attention is drawn to his own *activity: he himself* has been bringing about that which up to now he has thought he was experiencing passively. (3) He comprehends that he had motives for this activity which hitherto he did not know of. (4) He comes to note that at *some other point*, too, he harbors something similar, or something that is in some way associatively connected. (5) With the help of these observations he becomes able to produce less distorted "derivatives," and through these the *origins* of his behavior become clear (pp. 52-53: Fenichel's italics).

In brief, the strategy of interpretation is this: to identify a network of intelligible actions where none was thought to exist, thereby expanding the range of acknowledged activity in the analysand's experience of his or her life, and to develop a history of this life as intelligible activity. Although this search for activity has not been conceptualized explicitly and systematically, and indeed has often been lost sight of altogether, it is

*This chapter is a modified version of pp. 174-94 of the article, "Action: Its Place in Psychoanalytic Interpretation and Theory," first published in *The Annual of Psychoanalysis*, 1 (1973): 159-96.

presupposed in the guiding strategy of psychoanalytic work, namely, the analysis of transference and resistance. We regard transference and resistance as activities—as transferring and resisting (see chapter 11). The beneficial change we help bring about in the way our analysands lead their lives may be seen especially clearly in the light of this strategy of interpretation.

I am going to examine some of the essential aspects of the passivity-activity ambiguity as we encounter it in clinical work. After examining this aspect of analytic material and the changes it undergoes, I shall examine similar ambiguities in the fundamental rule we present to analysands and in our interpretations. My discussion of these major aspects of the analytic situation should further pave the way toward my reconceptualization of the psychoanalytic method and its theory. According to this reconceptualization, psychoanalysis will be more clearly recognized to be the study of human action viewed along certain lines. I shall attempt to show that what Fenichel presented as merely an empirical strategy implies a basic model for rendering human events intelligible and thereby amenable to rational and orderly therapeutic influence. Far more than a technique, it is an action language that is distinctively psychoanalytic. This is the native tongue of psychoanalysis.

I shall begin with a brief clinical example. A middle-aged professional man had been unable to work for a number of years following the breakup of his marriage. He presented himself as the victim of a faithless and cruel wife, a very disadvantageous divorce settlement, and the animosity of his children, who had inexplicably turned against him. He stressed that he had been doing nothing for some time—staying at home and sleeping all day, and letting his business affairs, his personal relations, and his professional reputation suffer badly. It is not surprising that during the course of treatment we established that (for the most part unconsciously) he had played an active, intelligible part in bringing about and maintaining this entire state of affairs. He had, for example, offered himself up as a sacrifice to his wife's depriving and humiliating manipulations of him just at the point during the divorce proceedings when he could have easily and rightfully developed his case against her. He had nursed his feeling of having been betrayed and abandoned by family, friends, and colleagues. He had, in fact, regressed to a position modeled after one he had occupied during childhood, when he had had to mother and father himself and had succeeded against great odds in developing and sustaining considerable ambition and interest in intellectual and esthetic matters. Needless to say, he had chosen his wife largely so that he could masochistically enact a repetition of his infantile situation; apparently the crippling divorce settlement had been a climactic consummation of this repetition. We also established that, far from his having been doing nothing during his inactive period, he had been reading voraciously (I use the word advisedly) all night long, thereby extending his intellectual range even further, and he had slept by day both in order to get his needed sleep and to cultivate the conscious and public image of being a derelict. Many other, easily anticipated kinds of details emerged during this investigation.

The point I want to emphasize by citing this example is this: in order to set in motion a specifically psychoanalytic process, I assumed and then sought to establish that, while apparently "doing nothing," this man had remain active all along. He had been doing something important, something ultimately understandable, something that constituted an affirmation, a maintaining and developing of strength. I had to see his passivity as being the most determined activity; his doing "nothing" as doing a great deal. (Psychoanalysts know how that is in their own "doing nothing"—their seeming inactivity in their work.) I shall say more about the specific rationale and advantages of this approach shortly.

As to technique in a situation of this sort, I will mention in passing only one of a number of useful measures. What was particularly significant here was to point out the activity implied in the energetic and emphatic efforts he made, consciously and otherwise, to prove to me that he was a beaten-down, worthless, hopeless, unreliable wreck. In other words, I had to help him acknowledge how actively he was trying to initiate another repetition of abandonment, this time within the transference. Both the harsh judgments he passed on himself and his need to prove anything at all implied that he still maintained aspirations, that he cared what he made of himself.

No doubt the situation I have described represents one instance of the kind of thing Fenichel had in mind when he wrote the passage quoted above. I may mention, again only in passing, that the principle of establishing the activity within apparent passivity is nowhere more urgent and fruitful, when patiently implemented, than in work with psychotic problems. This point seems to me to be better appreciated in certain respects by analysts in the so-called English school than by those Freudians who maintain the traditional emphasis on a weak ego passively overwhelmed by a strong pregenital id. But, in any case, analytic work with psychotics, when it is fruitful, seems to entail establishing that psychosis, too, is intelligible activity. One instance of what I mean is the increasingly common view of psychotic regression as a kind of adaptation—a protection of a true self by a false self as well as a collusion with the desperate needs of family members.

Now, in our daily lives as well as in our clinical work we are surrounded by less extreme instances of masked activity. It is to these that I shall now turn. For reasons to be advanced later, I shall refer to them as "disclaimed actions." The identification of disclaimed action, though it has been conceived in other terms, is central to, if not the center of, the psychoanalytic study of human existence. To make my point I shall discuss three ideas which can be fully understood only in relation to the concept of disclaimed action: *slip of the tongue, mind*, and *conflict*.

2. Slip of the Tongue

If one looks at the idea *slip of the tongue* from the standpoint of disclaimed action, one notices several facts immediately. First, it is being maintained through the use of the locution that it is the tongue, not the person, who (that) has slipped—as if the tongue regulates its own activity. Second, it is being maintained that what has happened is accidental—a slip—and not a meaningful, intended action. (Referring to it as a *Freudian* slip of the tongue, as people do in everyday life, often involves a third disclaimer to the effect that attributing significance to a slip is optional or else that not oneself, but only someone else—a Freudian—would think that the utterance in question had some special significance.)

In psychoanalytic practice, we do not accept these disclaimers. We do not believe that there has been an accident. We do not believe that the tongue has anything fundamental to do with the occurrence. And we do not believe that the attribution of significance is optional. We treat the phenomenon not as a happening but as an action. To us, it is something the analysand has done, something that is intelligible in terms of actions one wishes to perform and the conflicts one experiences in this regard. In effect, in interpreting a slip the analyst affirms the following proposition: while with the help of repressive action, one thought one was intending to say only one thing, one was actually saying two; or, even though one might have been aware of refraining from saying something different or contrary, one nevertheless *did* also say something else that *was* different or contrary. Nothing "slipped out." Words are not furtive entities, nor do they move from one place to another; if spoken, they make public what would otherwise remain private, perhaps unconsciously so. In a verbal slip, then, the speaker simply does two things at once. A two-sided action, and both sides his or her responsibility![1]

More than once I have heard the introduction of a speaker contain the following slip: "It is now my great pleasure to *prevent* our distinguished guest." (I have, by the way, also heard these two words put the other way around: "With only two days left before your vacation, there is not enough time to *present* a catastrophe.") But to return to the "introduction" slip: it is an instance of what I mean when I speak of someone's saying two things at once—the consciously intended statement which we may for the moment believe to have been sincerely intended, and the interpolation of the idea "prevent" with its equally sincere implication of envy, let us suppose, or rivalry. In short, we might interpret that the introducer was acting ambivalently. The slip is not a disrupted action; it is a special kind of action in which two courses of action are taken simultaneously.

It is, of course, wrong to think that the course of action that was taken unconsciously, latently, or implicitly is what the (male) speaker "really" wanted to say; for it was also what he wanted *not* to say. Furthermore, there *was* something else he

1. The issue is, of course, much greater than simply that of responsibility in the usual sense; however, it is also true that in the realm of judgments of responsibility, which includes attributing guilt unconsciously as well as consciously, we encounter disclaimers of the utmost urgency and desperation in psychoanalytic work as in everyday life.

did want to say. It is just that as he worked it out he enacted his dilemma. His defensive action, his conciliatory action, his wretched substitute action—for the psychoanalyst all are equally real; they are to be understood as facets of one complex action.

To return to the man who presented himself as a do-nothing failure, he made the following slip during the analysis of his self-destructive inactivity: "There was nothing I could do that wouldn't make things work—er—worse."

3. Mind

Mind is the second of the three ideas I have selected to discuss from the standpoint of disclaimed action. We are familiar with the great variety of locutions according to which the mind is a place, an autonomous thing, or a part-aspect of one's existence. For example, as to mind-as-place, people say, "I must have been out of my mind," "Suicide entered my mind," "I put that out of my mind." As to mind-as-autonomous-thing, people say, "My mind refused to think about it any further," "My mind is racing," "My mind plays tricks on me." And as to mind-as-part-aspect-of-one's-existence, we encounter the following types of locutions in which the "I" and the mind are thought of as two separate and independent entities: "I am of two minds about it," "I didn't keep my mind on my work," "I wish I knew my own mind."

All such locutions state or imply that there is a subject or agent who exists or can exist apart from his or her mind. Accordingly, the subject can observe mind, comment on it, put it to work, inhabit it, be betrayed by it, limit its scope, and so on. This way of thinking (which, as we have seen, characterizes Freudian metapsychology) has many implications, but what concerns us here is its function in disclaiming action. One may very well take it as disclaimed action upon hearing an analysand split off or split up mind in these ways. One may rightly assume that the analysand is feeling anxious or guilty. Depending on one's psychoanalytic slant, one might think of the event as a defensive splitting of the ego, a regression to primary-process concreteness of thought, or a projective creation of persecutors. In any case, if one takes up this locution at all, one will implicitly or explicitly interpret it as an action; it is an action that disclaims action. One does so, for example, when one responds to "I must have been out of my mind" with such a comment as, "You feel so guilty about what you did that you refuse to think that you were capable of doing it." I do not mean that traditionally analysts have thought of these interventions in terms of disclaimed action. I do mean that the relevance and effectiveness of these interventions stem in significant measure from their treating such comments by analysands as disclaimers. Metapsychological conceptualization has obscured this fact.

Lewin (1971) took up this very subject of mind and its metaphoric treatment. Although both refreshing and informative in his comments on archaic conceptions of mind, his presentation was seriously flawed; for he was, among other things, wrongly encouraging us analysts to use a piece of primary-process thinking both in teaching our theory of mind and in our clinical interpretations; one might say that he was encouraging conceptual acting-out instead of analyzing (see especially his pp. 21-22). Mind is not, as he there suggests, a room or a suite of two rooms; and there is no man or maniken looking in or looking on, or guarding doorways against entities at once mechanical and furtive in their actions. For theoretical purposes, it can be said that mind is an abstract designation of the sense we make of human existence or action; depending on one's approach, it may refer to desires, intentions, aims, reasons, meanings, and cognitive performances such as perceiving and remembering. It has never been helpful to *systematic* explanatory thinking or teaching to resort to these anthropomorphic, spatial, and mechanical metaphors, although I would not question that it has been helpful to *preliminary* explorations, like Freud's, or that it has been comforting to all of us to have them readily available like old friends or dependable escape hatches. As for the usefulness of the two-room and manikin model of mind in clinical interpretations, I shall argue below that the *progress* of an analysis is marked by a diminishing use of this model or any of its variations.

In keeping with the action model of interpretation I have been developing, I would say that mind is something we do; it is neither something we have nor something we are or are not related to or in possession of. And this, I submit, is the sense in

which we do interpret our analysands' thinking, even though
we may obscure the sense of our action by using the inexact
and inconsistent words of everyday speech.

4. CONFLICT

I shall approach the idea of conflict by way of a clinical example. An obsessional analysand keeps interrupting what he is
saying in order to report still another "intruding" thought.
These thoughts, he declares, prevent him from getting to the
point. He insists that he wishes it were otherwise. I remark on
his viewing these thoughts as not his own. He responds that he
does think of it as another person inside him who won't let him
finish what he's saying. He goes on spontaneously to reflect
that he knows that he is thinking all these thoughts, but that it
is impossible to think of himself as doing two contrary things in
this way. (Allow me for the moment to pass over the indication
he gives of an introject fantasy as part of his obsessionality. I
passed over it at the time, too.) I now remark to him that the
tempo of interruptions increases whenever he is telling me
something that might be exciting, such as the topic of the preceding moment, which had been a sexual encounter with a girl,
and that, in keeping with his previously avowed policy of carefully controlling everything, he controls his mounting excitement by interrupting himself frequently. As he had been
complaining earlier in the hour of increased obsessional frag-
mentation of thinking in connection with some research he was
doing, I add that I suppose he had found doing the research
exciting, too, and so had had similarly to control that excitement by stepping up the tempo of his interruptions. He con-
firms the feeling of excitement but quickly goes on to minimize
the significance of what I have said, declaring that he has been
clear about this much all along; in fact, it is what he has been
telling me. He then goes on to some further fruitful elaboration
of the interpretation. I then point out that characteristically he
first has to minimize what I say because he finds it exciting
when I speak to him and because minimizing is his way of
controlling that excitement; once he has it controlled, he can
work with the idea I have presented. After some further minimization, he acknowledges that I am right about that. Here my

account of this incident ends—but not the struggle, obviously.

What is the struggle? Whatever content we ascribe to it, it is an expression in the transference of what we usually call intra-psychic conflict. But we must not forget how we arrive at that interpretation. We must start from the observation that throughout this interchange this analysand is continuously engaged in action. Simultaneously or in alternation, he is attacking and protecting, or, if you will, defying and complying, castrating and being castrated, soiling and being retentive, seducing homosexually and being seduced homosexually, and so forth. On what basis, then, do we say that he is expressing conflict? Not really on the basis that he "has" "conflicting impulses"; for a formulation in terms of impulses, rather than being naively descriptive, can only express an a priori commitment we have made to speak in the mechanistic language of forces and energies. It is as if we had decided in advance that *impulse,* because it has more of an "inside" and "prior" ring to it, was more profound or primary than *action,* which sounds outward, superficial, behavioristic, merely a sign of something else or a resultant of "forces." The fact is, however, that we speak of conflict because we observe the analysand to be engaged in contradictory or paradoxical actions. He conveyed his incipient recognition of this very point when he himself raised the question of his engaging in two contrary actions simultaneously. He could not just then conceive of the interrupting as action, but for the moment it did at least make sense to him that, looked at as a form of control of excitement, it was the kind of action he would engage in under these circumstances. It was a beginning of a new understanding.

Later in the analysis would be the time to get to the interrupting introject he had hinted at. But what, in the end, is an introject? Isn't it a piece of disclaimed action, a fantasy created and invoked by the analysand, a fantasy he takes to be an autonomous happening which he experiences passively? I have discussed this frequently misunderstood issue at length in a somewhat different connection in my book on internalization (1968b), under the heading of *The Power of the Introject.* There I tried to demonstrate that that "power" could only be the subject's own. In the present context my point is that the introject is the fantasied embodiment of one action that the analysand is disclaiming; as such the action can be neither integrated nor rejected by him in a basic way. Considered by itself, the introject experience must be viewed as an action, though an odd and well-disguised one: it is an action open to someone already engaged in paradoxical actions; what the analysand does not allow in speech or other public action, he allows in a sort of projective fantasy.

My obsessional analysand is both telling me and not telling me exciting things. He is both interrupting and protesting his interruptions. He is claiming some of his actions and disclaiming others. In this respect, which, of course, is not the only one of significance for his analysis, the introject experience constitutes his disclaiming strategy. He is constructing or reviving a projective fantasy and, through regression, treating it as real. Thereby he is avoiding experiencing personal conflict consciously. And yet all we have to work with as analytic observations are incompatible actions and a hint of a fantasy about some of these actions.

There is more to be gained by considering the conceptualization of this example a bit longer. In this instance, it may be said that the analysand's initial action is his interrupting himself. This action seems to be modeled in some respects on his sense of having been frequently and meaninglessly "interrupted" by his parents. The introject corresponds to the parents in some of its details. By representing his own interrupting as his *being* interrupted, he is implicitly criticizing these parents as well as controlling them (and me, in the transference). It is an undercover attack, an instance of what another analysand, in another example of disclaimed action, called "sneaky motivations." The fact that it is undercover, that it is represented as the action of an internal presence, indicates the conflict between acting destructively and acting protectively. Being a disclaimer, it also indicates the conflict between consciously acknowledging and denying that in every important detail of his present behavior he is active rather than passive, creator rather than creature, an intentional person rather than a defective apparatus which happens to be under close observation.

However much one might disagree with details of my partial analysis of this introject experience, one would still have to agree that psychoanalytic interpretive work must culminate in formulations that are cast in terms of personal activity. Like slip of the tongue, mind, and conflict, an introject is not something one has or something that happens to him or her; it is something one imagines, which is also to say something one does. The same must be said of any identification.

Conflict, then—to return directly to our starting point—may be conceptualized in the following way. As a psychological event, it involves a minimum of three constituent actions. As agent, one engages in two actions, such as wishing, imagining, or acting overtly, which, in a third, one believes to be incompatible with each other. For reasons which have to be established in each clinical instance, one continues doing both even while believing them to be incompatible. One may or may not acknowledge consciously that one is doing both, that the actions are incompatible, or that one cares whether they are or not; these important variations reflect additional defensive actions, beyond the disclaiming itself, that the agent might take with respect to acting conflictedly.

It might be objected, now, that conflict can exist when no action is being taken, as, for example, in the struggle to resist temptation or to control an impulse. I say that this is a matter of conceptualization and not brute fact. I am suggesting that this situation be regarded not as a struggle between impulses or systems or substructures, but rather as an instance of the person's acting more effectively in one respect than another. The successful resisting of temptation—what we might call inhibition—is one action through which a person has refrained from taking another; at least the person has refrained from taking the action *publicly,* for he or she may still carry out the action in fantasy. An impulse is an action that is not being carried out, and its not being carried out may be due to other actions one has engaged in to that very end; these are the refraining actions. An impulse is an action a person would do were he or she not effectively refraining from doing it (see also chapters 10 and 11).

Impulse is not logically or psychologically prior to, or more internal than, action. We do not, as is commonly said, inhibit impulses; we refrain from actions, and "impulses" are the results of these refraining actions. Nor does one act on impulse, though one might think so, owing to one's awareness of the

effort entailed in refraining from actions one would otherwise
perform. In this view, thought is silent speech (Ryle 1949). I
should say *silenced* speech. I am not as far from Freud's basic
concepts or Fenichel's formulations as I might seem to be at
this point. I remind you that Freud conceptualized thought as
experimental action and, though he did not, of course, develop
an action language for psychoanalysis, he was ever conscious
of the delay of action as the foundation of psychical development and functioning; however, in keeping with his metapsychology, he tended to speak in terms of the delay of *impulse*. In his terms, the secondary process regulates the
primary-process tendency toward immediate discharge; in
action terms, various types of action constitute refraining from
other actions. And, with regard to Fenichel (1941), is there
after all a great difference between demonstrating that unconscious defense is activity, as he proposed, and asserting that
defense is an action taken unconsciously to refrain from taking
another action?

I hope that by now I have made clear the view of interpretation I am developing. As I said, I believe it to be the view that
all analysts implicitly share. I think that by remaining loyal to
Freud's metapsychological ideals we have obscured our recognition that this is our view of interpretation and have blocked
the development of its crucial systematic possibilities. I chose
to discuss *slip of the tongue, mind,* and *conflict* because I believed that in these instances I could easily show the implicit
presence and the utility of the action model of interpretation.
I do not imply that the correct comprehension of just these
three terms is theoretically decisive. And, although I have
tended to speak in terms of two-factor conflicts in my explanations and examples, I have done so only for ease of exposition
and with full awareness that actions are usually a lot more
complicated than that; this is especially true of the actions we
analyze in our work, such as dreams, symptoms, defenses,
and actings-out.

I shall soon discuss briefly the variety of disclaimers we encounter in clinical work and then go on to consider disclaimers
that the analyst may introduce unconsciously or inadvertently.
But first it will be well to pause for a review and amplification
of the concept of action as I am using it.

5. THE CONCEPT OF ACTION[2]

By action, I do not mean voluntary physical deeds only. In my sense, action is human behavior that has a point; it is meaningful human activity; it is intentional or goal-directed performances by people; it is doing things for reasons. There is nothing the psychoanalytic interpretation can deal with that is not action as here defined. For example, to think of something is to do an action; to see or remember something is to do an action; to be silent or otherwise inactive is as much an action as to say something or to walk somewhere. It is one kind of action to say something and another kind to think it and not say it.

The propositions I am advancing are not descriptive, empirical propositions; they are definitions or rules that establish the logic of this psychological language. According to this language, only those human phenomena are not actions that are bodily changes, motoric or otherwise, that take place essentially as normal or pathological neurophysiological processes. On the part of the analysand they involve no mental aim or directionality, no choice, no synthesis of interests, courses of action, and skills. They are devoid of symbolic content. They have no reasons. They are happenings. And events in the environment in the coming about of which the analysand has played no part are also happenings, though what the analysand then makes of them is to be understood as his or her action with respect to them.

I could have chosen the word *behavior* instead of *action*. Actually, both words are unsatisfactory in that ordinarily both imply motor action. However, by using *action* I call attention to the analyst's strategic emphasis on activity within apparent passivity or inactivity. Alternatively, I could have used the word *activity* instead of *action*. However, as I am trying to avoid the ambiguities of traditional activity-passivity discus-

2. Background philosophical discussions of action and related propositions will be found in Anscombe (1956); Aristotle's *Ethics;* Austin (1956); Brand's (1970) collection of essays, especially that by Rescher (1970); Fingarette (1963), Habermas (1971, esp. chs. 10-12), Hampshire (1959, 1962), Kenny (1963), Langer (1967), MacIntyre (1958), Macmurray (1957), Melden (1961), Ricoeur (1970), Ryle (1949), Sartre (1943), Williams (1956), Wittgenstein (1934-35, 1945-49) and Wollheim's (1974) collection of essays.

sions (Rapaport 1953; Schafer 1968c), I prefer the less encumbered and less equivocal *action*. I realize that my choice will be less than entirely satisfactory to analysts; but it is logically permissible and worth the trouble of accepting and using it.

There is a matter far more important than the choice of word. It is the rule, presented in chapter 1, that there is no limit to the number of vantage points from which an action may be regarded, and therefore no limit to the number of ways in which it may be defined or described. Psychoanalysts have not always been sufficiently self-conscious about the fact that they look at their material from only certain points of view and perhaps only on certain levels of abstraction; consequently, they sometimes mistakenly consider their mode of understanding to be the only valid psychology—and a complete one at that! Elsewhere (Schafer 1968b, pp. 161-70), I have discussed how this is the case with respect to motives.

Consider, for example, a male student said to be reading a book. His action may also be described as studying, doing his homework, preparing for a test, competing with classmates for recognition and advancement, complying with his parents' wishes, sublimating voyeuristic tendencies in intellectual pursuits, making rapid and discontinuous eye movements over a page of print, or adhering to the norm of his class. Clearly, what we call an action, how we name it, and the temporal and other boundaries we set for it, depend on the kind and level of descriptive or explanatory context we are trying to establish and maintain. There is no one description of the action that is the only true one, though there are an infinite number that may be false. Indeed, "the action" can refer only to a set of possibilities rather than a unique denotation. To the extent that we discard simplistic notions of fact and truth, we accord proper importance to considerations of consistency, coherence, and usefulness within a systematic approach to psychological reality.

As for the reader in my example, there is at least one description of what he is doing under which he may be said to know what he is doing. If we take into account that, unconsciously, he may simultaneously designate in other terms that which he does knowingly, we may say that there must be more than one such description. But we cannot say that he knows, in any

useful sense of the word "knows," all the possible descriptions
of his action. This means, too, that the agent cannot know all
the possible implications and consequences of his or her
actions. In psychoanalysis, therefore, connections and other
interpretations do not always deal only with repressed material. The "unconscious" is not omniscient. Psychoanalytic
interpretation does uncover other ways in which one defines
what one has chosen to do; that is, it establishes more fully just
what that action means to oneself. But it does a lot more than
that. It also teaches one to see actions in a new light, to be alert
to implications, interrelationships, and consequences of actions
that one never dreamed of, as the saying goes. In this way,
interpretation opens up to the analysand a whole new world of
possibilities—evaluations, goals, and strategies. The analysand's position as historian of his or her life is extended and
made more efficient; the analysand is more aware of having
been making choices all along and that there are now more
and different choices to make (see chapter 3). Of course, much
of the analysand's need for this assistance is itself a consequence of defensive actions and must be so interpreted
throughout the analysis.

I shall not here survey the ways of looking at actions that are
distinctively psychoanalytic. I shall merely mention two of its
goals: the first is to understand action as manifesting or implying the repetition in current life, especially unconsciously, of
infantile conflicts, with all their physically sexual and aggressive, magical, anxious, guilty, defensive, reparative, regressive,
and progressive aspects; the second is to understand action
neutrally, that is, without "taking sides."

I have not forgotten that there are resistances, that is,
actions taken by the analysand to block or retard the progress
of the analysis (see chapter 11). But let me add that not all the
analyst's facilitation of progress consists of clearing away resistant actions through interpretation. As I mentioned, one is
also teaching the analysand a way of looking at his or her own
life and understanding it—as action. This way of looking at
one's life has coherence, consistency, and transformational
effectiveness; that is why the analyst fosters it. I know that in
saying this I seem to be laying the analyst open to the familiar
charge that he or she does indeed brainwash the analysand.
Whatever else that charge might be (political attack, self-

defense, etc.), it is certainly philosophically naive; it misses the point that unless there is some way of looking and understanding, there can be no way of studying any aspect of life whatsoever. "Life" has to be thought; it is an abstract idea. What passes for ordinary everyday understanding of mental life is a mishmash—which means the person is free to conceptualize as he or she pleases and, too often, conflictedly and therefore inconsistently.

Psychoanalytic understanding constitutes a way out of this confusion. It is not a carte blanche approach. It is an arduous discipline distinguished by the cogency of its questions; the emotional significance of its content; the patience it requires in the sorting of material for hypotheses, evidence, and explanations; and the respect it implies for people's desperateness in their human condition, a desperateness that gives rise to a fundamental hatred and mistrust of change and usually precludes even the comprehension of basic change. Through imparting analytic conceptions of this material to analysands, analysts help give new form and significance to the material that is disclosed to them.

In turning to action concepts, I am not advancing a new version of the old misconception of conscious autonomy. Propositions concerning autonomy derive from, and only make sense with respect to, mechanistic drive theories. Action language is unrelated to such theories. Similarly, the issue of free will does not arise for the action language, for free will refers to action being carried out independently of some forces that a natural science, deterministic model must presuppose; consequently, if that model is not adopted, and such forces are therefore not assumed, we are in a universe of discourse in which the idea of free will has no place. In the present context it is a universe of actions by people, actions which by definition are meaningful and goal-directed, actions which have reasons rather than determinants.

The action model does not imply randomness or chaos of events. Although psychoanalysis has always been considered a theory of drives and their development, it does not have to be one; such a theory of underlying drives is only one way of defining and ordering psychological phenomena. The obvious psychological importance of representations of somatic processes does not necessitate, though it does not preclude, adoption of a theory based on bodily drives and their elaboration into psychological motives; it does necessitate a theory that in one way or another deals systematically with the decisive developmental role played by representations of persistent or recurring, intensely pleasurable and unpleasurable bodily sensations, especially those connected with the psychosexual zones. In this regard there is no "mind-body problem." The relation of drive theories to action language will be discussed further in chapter 10.

6. Disclaimers of Action

Each of the following locutions disclaims action in its own way: "The impulse seized me"; "It struck me that something was wrong"; "The words poured out of my mouth"; "My conscience torments me"; "One part of me says yes while the other says no"; "This hour just rushed by"; "The future holds little in store for me"; "I am afraid to let it come out"; "Doubts creep into my mind"; "Something inside resists the idea"; "The excitement slipped away."

I shall only mention in passing the many disclaimers that remain unverbalized, such as self-punishment without confession of guilt and seduction without expressed desire. There are, of course, other disclaimers that are concealed behind words, such as asking, "Would you like to come along?" as a guarded way of conveying, "I want you to come along!" and observing matter-of-factly to the analyst, "You haven't said anything today," as a guarded way of demanding, "Say something already!"

Returning to the verbalized disclaimers, the first thing to note is that they seem to be drawn from a huge supply of such expressions in the language of everyday life. What I cited earlier about mind-as-place, etc., belongs here, too. One can realize at once how frequently or readily we use disclaimers. On closer inspection, one can also note how disclaimers may be classified in terms of the "mechanisms of defense," such as isolation, splitting, introjection, and projection. At the same time, one can further note that these locutions also carry traces of unconscious fantasies of fighting, being beaten, being overwhelmed, copulating, feeding, defecating, being abandoned, and so forth. Putting just this much together, one may safely conclude that everyday language is not only a record of the fundamental, unconsciously maintained desires and conflicts with which people are concerned, but also a record of the many modes that people have developed to ease subjective distress. I particularly have in mind distress felt in connection with being held responsible.

We do use disclaimers to help us "get off the hook." With their help we are able to think and talk about difficult issues in a muted, dosed manner. We use them to protect relationships, to care for the other person as well as ourselves. For example, when a person says "understandingly" to a friend who has disappointed and angered him or her by forgetting an appointment, "It must have slipped your mind," rather than "You forgot me," or when one says about one's own forgetting, "It slipped my mind," rather than "I forgot you," one is in either case protecting the relationship. At least one of the parties is being absolved of responsibility or guilt. To speak plainly of one's "forgetting" the other, unless it is a seduction to a gratifying sadomasochistic interaction, is the sort of directness that ordinarily leads to a quick deterioration of relationships.

Analysands have much reason, of course, to disclaim action. They are resisting analysis all along, though not always in an equally determined and vigorous way. On further reflection, it is in keeping with an action model of interpretation to subsume all our notions of resistance under the heading of disclaimed action, just as it is to subsume insights under the heading of claimed and reclaimed action (see also chapter 11). Defense, for example, is action. The unconscious fantasies informing defensive actions, so much stressed by Kleinian analysts, are the basis for the correct and useful designation of these actions; they are what these actions *mean*, which is to say what they *are* in psychic reality (Schafer 1968a). Ultimately, the analyst should tell the analysand more than that he or she is, for instance, projecting, before going on to analyze when, why, and so forth; assuming that suitable evidence and context are available, one ought to tell the analysand who is projecting that he or she is soiling or bombarding someone else with destructive substances, or setting someone else up as a penetrating, perhaps raping, persecutor, or something of that sort on some level or other.

But it is not only defense that we must be concerned with in this regard. As Fenichel indicated in the statement I quoted above, the so-called impulses or drives are actions, too. In the action model, an anal impulse is an anal action that is not being carried out. A projected anal impulse is an action, or an action one has refrained from taking, that, in a self-protective move, one is attributing to someone else. "I forgot you" may, in psychic reality, be a variant of the action "I killed you" or "I shit you out"; in this sense the so-called impulse is plainly a major (though nonmotoric and unconscious) action, a would-be or conditional action, what one would do if....

By disclaiming actions we limit the excitement and violence of social existence. Human beings have developed and use language to spare themselves from all manner of arousal, pain, anxiety, guilt, loss, and destructiveness. They allude to what they are passing over as they pass over it. This allusiveness is part of what we call unconscious communication. It makes up a large part of what the analyst listens for.

7. CLAIMING AND INTEGRATING ACTION

The analyst works on the assumption that the analysand actively brings about that from which he or she neurotically suffers—not, as Freud pointed out, that all misery is neurotically created and remediable, but that analysis deals with that misery that *is* neurotically created and *may be* remediable. Thus, the analyst *as analyst* sees the analysand as continuously selecting, organizing, and directing a neurotic existence. Through analysis, the nature and occasions of the analysand's activity are defined, and analysand and analyst attempt to arrive at an understanding of the reasons why the analysand arranges his or her life in a particular way. To this end, they examine closely the connections between life in the past and in the present, taking into account the infantile influences to which he or she has, in fact, been subjected, insofar as these influences can be established with any definiteness. Always, however, these influences are understood within the framework of action. That is to say, these influences come to be regarded by analysand as well as analyst as having been jointly defined by circumstance and person, for at all times the analysand, both in the analytic session and throughout psychological existence, is to be understood as being active, goal-directed, choice-making, meaning-creating, fantasying, and responsible. Infantile sexual theories demonstrate this interdependence, one might even say unity, of situation and person (see also chapter 15).

Passive experience—the representation of oneself as passive in relation to events—is, of course, of the utmost significance in psychological development and disturbance. I am emphasizing that it is intrinsic to psychoanalytic understanding to regard passive experience as a mode of representation that can never tell the whole story of any psychological event or situation.

Freud demonstrated that subjectivity, the realm of "experience," is a variable human activity. People engage in subjectivity to different degrees, in different ways, at different times, and for different reasons. For Freud, preconscious and conscious representation and organization required action on the part of the subject. Freud called this action hypercathexis or attention cathexis. He showed that this action cannot be other than inconstant and incomplete. He also demonstrated that the psychoanalytic interpretation of resistances and transference-repetitions expands the scope and amount of action on behalf of subjectivity. And with this change comes a change in the analysand's recognition of action itself.

With progress in his or her analysis, the analysand disclaims actions less flagrantly and less often. At least, he or she uses the kinds of locutions I just surveyed less often at critical junctures in the work. More and more, the analysand indicates a readiness to accept the responsibility of life as action. This acceptance has nothing to do with ideas of omniscience and omnipotence, however, in that it does not imply a belief on one's part that one has caused one's whole life or can cause it from now on. Nor does it preclude one's having "passive" experience (passive self-representations). But more often than before the analysand says, "I will" and "I won't," rather than "I must" and "I can't." More often than before the analysand says, "That's the way I see it," "I decided," "I chose," "I know," and "I prefer." Leaving aside certain expansive assertions of autonomy, we recognize that these are the locutions of insight. They convey that the analytic understanding that has been achieved is not being manipulated by the anslysand as something one "has"; rather, insight has become something one does or one's way of doing or being. I believe this to be the import of Freud's statements that analysis strengthens and expands the ego at the expense of the id and superego: what one presented before as an alien "it"—the aggregate of impulse, defense, conscience, problematic past and future, and external necessity—one now presents as defining aspects of oneself. The person *is* his or her own impulse, defense, insights, and so forth, for they are his or her own actions. A strengthened and expanded ego is a more inclusive subjectivity and with that a more integrated and knowing claim to activity (cf. Freud 1937a).

8. The Analyst's Communications

I turn finally and all too briefly to the analyst's communications. In the light of what I have already said about the analysand's language and the way it may change, I characterize the clinical analyst's ordinary language as both attributing and denying activity to the analysand. In order to develop this proposition, I shall take as models of the analyst's language the fundamental rule of asking the analysand to say "everything that comes to mind" and some representative questions based on this rule; I shall contrast these with a representative (partial) interpretation that the analyst might make, namely, "Because you are afraid to criticize me openly, you keep emphasizing that you couldn't like and admire me more."

First, "Say everything that comes to mind," and its variants, "What does that bring to mind?," "What comes to mind?," and "What occurs to you?" I submit that these questions involve a temporary collusion on the analyst's part with the analysand's strategy of disclaiming action. I say so on the basis of the following action-language considerations: ideas are not entities that transport themselves to places called "mind"; nor do they transport other similar entities into places called "mind"; ideas do not "happen to" the thinker; and the mind is not something other than what the person thinks, feels, wishes, says, and carries out. I remind you of my earlier discussion of the problems of the concept *mind*.

According to the action model, the statement of the fundamental rule should convey the sense of the following ideas: "I shall expect you to talk to me each time you come. As you talk, you will notice that you refrain from saying certain things. You may do so because you want to avoid being trivial, irrelevant, embarrassed, tactless, or otherwise disruptive. It is essential to our work that you do this as little as possible. I urge you to tell me of those instances of selection or omission no matter what their content may be." Similarly, rather than "What comes to mind?," the kind of question that is conceptually and technically exact according to the action model is, "What do you think of in this connection?" or "What do you now connect with that?" or "If you think of this, what do you think of next?" Which is to say that thoughts come and go only as we think them or stop thinking them, or, in other words, that thinking is a kind of action engaged in by persons. We are responsible for all our thoughts, including, as Freud (1925a) pointed out, our dreams. Yet both the fundamental rule as usually formulated and the question "What comes to mind?" imply the negation of this proposition, the very proposition on which interpretation is based. What, then, is the sense of these communications?

I think analysts generally would agree that in their customary form the "fundamental rule" and the questions associated with it facilitate what we call free association. They do so by encouraging the analysand to relax defensiveness and curtail conscious selectivity. They invite him or her to be unreflective and noncritical, to enter upon what Kris (1952) called a "regression in the service of the ego" while talking. Additionally, because they do not challenge the analysand's intent of disclaiming action, of feeling not responsible for what is "going on" in the analysis, they are less likely than a more direct approach to stimulate an immediate increase of resistiveness. This approach is in keeping with the strategy of everyday speech, which, as I pointed out earlier, provides ample room for disclaiming locutions in order that people may adaptively regulate the amount of emotional strain they put themselves and others under from moment to moment. Thus, the question "What does that bring to mind?" helps the analysand approach difficult issues without feeling overwhelmed by them. From this point of view, the analyst's temporary collusion with the analysand is in the service of analytic exploration.

And yet in certain respects the rule and the questions may also be observed to be inconsistent with the aim of developing and maintaining an analytic situation. First, they are a means of circumventing the actions of resistance rather than analyzing them. Secondly, they are seductions to assume a passive

position. Thirdly, rather than analyzing the regressive gratifications implied in disclaiming action, the analyst implicitly
takes their side. Also, the rule and the questions often elicit
defensively isolated indications of issues rather than direct involvement in the issues themselves, and so support an intellec-
tualizing trend in the analysis. Additionally, one will, in subsequent interpretations, hold the analysand responsible as a
person for his or her response to the rule and the questions; one
will do so by interpreting the response as an action, and by so
doing one will give objective support to the analysand's sense
of being manipulated, if not led into ambush. These criticisms
add up to a single, historically significant charge: the fundamental rule and the questions are thinly veiled carry-overs
into analysis of hypnotic technique. And hypnotic technique
encourages one of the purest forms of disclaimed action.

Thus, a case can be made both for and against the analytic
suitability of the usual formulation of the fundamental rule and
the questions associated with it, such as, "What does that bring
to mind?"

Now, we all know that as an analysis moves forward, the disclaiming potential of the rule and the questions diminishes.
The collusion I am describing is in no way fatal to the analysis.
The reasons for this will become clear in connection with our
further consideration of interpretation.

As I have said, a representative (partial) analytic interpretation might be: "Because you are afraid to criticize me openly,
you keep emphasizing that you couldn't like and admire me
more." Notice that the language is entirely an action language.
The analyst addresses the analysand neither as a mind in which
thoughts and feelings happen nor as an apparatus in which
mechanisms operate, but as a person who acts knowingly and
emotionally. Were one to say, "You have a fear that impulses
to criticize me will rise up in you, and this fear makes you act
as if you have only liking and admiration for me," one would be
carrying over into interpretation the disclaiming language of
the question. One would be doing the same were one to say,
"Whenever you show your competence, your anxiety mounts"
rather than "Whenever you perform competently, you feel
more anxious"; and one would be doing so to say, "Your wish
to suck on my penis is expressing itself" rather than "You wish
to suck on my penis" or "You give signs of wishing to do so."

And, certainly, in addition to everything else that would be wrong with it, to speak to the analysand about specific interactions of the id, ego, and superego, *in these very terms,* would be to collude egregiously in the disclaiming of action.

As it is easy to be misunderstood in this connection, I must emphasize that I am not advocating that the analyst enter into an unverbalized contest of wills by opposing the analysand's disclaiming rhetoric with a relentlessly circumspect mode of activistic instruction, questioning, and interpreting. Rather, I am trying to specify the reference point or baseline of the analytic attitude. The analytic attitude is a way of perceiving, reacting, understanding, and communicating developed between the analyst and the analysand as they continue to work together. In the process, the analysand identifies more and more with the analyst as *analyst,* which means that ever more consistently he or she looks at life as largely made up of personal actions, including interpretations of situations; or, as Freud (1920a, p. 20) put it, as a life he or she has largely "arranged." By virtue of this development, the analysand begins to be able both to view the analysis as a collaborative effort and to claim the analysis as his or her own. The analysand is less inclined to regard the analysis as another "it" that must be passively suffered or desperately manipulated. This change is, of course, always a matter of degree and always subject to some regressive repudiation (see also chapter 3).

Probably, the limits of human tolerance and the problems of verbalization being what they are, the analyst can at best only approximate a consistent rhetoric of action. And, as an ideal, absolute consistency in this regard would not be truly analytic. In addition to reasons I have already given for this, I mention that by adhering to this ideal one would certainly not help either oneself or the analysand to be relaxed and "free-floating" or "evenly hovering." But I do want to call attention to the fact that the interpretive possibilities of action language have not been explored systematically or technically. We are not very used to—because we are not very tolerant of—sustained action language. Not having assayed the resources of this language, we cannot know at this point what difference its consistent utilization would make in the analytic process. Would it in the long run clarify and more basically modify resistant actions, or would it obscure and confirm them? Would it, by frustrating them, throw into relief the gratifications obtained unconsciously through extensive use of disclaimers, or would such language merely promote even more careful disguises by the analysand, as, for example, through being compliantly and deliberately action-oriented in the use of language? Would it expose and resolve projections, denials, intellectualizations, and other defensive actions, or would it stimulate the analysand to contrive new modes of performing them?

Surely, the analyst's choice of words does not by itself determine everything that will happen during the attempt at analysis, but, just as surely, analytic progress depends on words; for understanding cannot be divorced from words, and some words are better manifestations than others of specifically psychoanalytic understanding. It is wrong to think of the choice of words as a part of the interpretive technique that follows understanding. In psychoanalysis the words *are* the understanding.

I hope it is clear that I have not been driving toward a Draconian judgment and prescription concerning clinical analysts' language. I have attempted to show the place in their interventions of locutions which claim and disclaim action, and to indicate the hazards and opportunities implied in their choice of language, which is to say implied in the way they think about analysis and their analysands.

9. AN APPLICATION

Before coming to my conclusion, I shall venture an application of my action-model analysis of interpretation. In today's therapeutic world, it is increasingly fashionable to be contemptuous of psychoanalysis as a passive and intellectual process, a sluggish if not cowardly and unethical approach to the real issues. Quick and intense aggressive and sexual confrontation or regression, or else thoughtless reconditioning, is becoming the order of the day. We analysts know that these therapies of consciousness, based as they are on transference manipulations, counterphobic gestures, expulsive fantasies, and manic dreams of self-transcendence, must be superficial and irrational. I suggest that we can also say of these therapies that they disclaim the personal activity inherent in what we call defense, inhibition, and avoidance, and in anxiety and guilt as

well; for they treat these features of life as hang-ups, anti-
actions rather than actions, something like sludge or misin-
formation or faintheartedness—definitely not the "real you" or
the "real self."

It follows from the arguments I have presented that these are
"therapies" that foster the disclaiming of action. They disclaim
defensive action rather than impulse, so-called. Or, to put it in
terms of psychoanalytic interpretation: interpretation defines
conflicts, symptoms, inhibitions, and anxieties as actions and
modes of action that are engaged in by people who have a
stake in them, however much they may deny that consciously;
it characterizes them as actions people do, and not as things
they have had implanted in them; it is based on the proposition
that there is no wish that is not an "I wish" or a "you wish," no
guilt feeling that is not an "I condemn" or a "you condemn,"
and no defense that is not an "I repudiate" or an "I contradict."
From this vantage point, we can say affirmatively of psychoanalytic interpretation that it confronts and works through the
most potentially explosive or nihilistic actions unconsciously
undertaken by analysands against the work of analysis itself.

10. Conclusion

I should like in conclusion to contrast the view I have been
taking with the traditional Freudian one. For this purpose I
shall comment briefly on a well-known statement by Freud
(1916b); it is one to which I alluded before in a different connection. Freud said:

> ...these two discoveries—that the life of our sexual instincts can-
> not be wholly tamed, and that mental processes are themselves
> unconscious and only reach the ego and come under its control
> through incomplete and untrustworthy perceptions—these two
> discoveries amount to a statement that *the ego is not master in
> its own house.* Together they represent the third blow to man's
> self love, what I call the *psychological* one. No wonder, then,
> that the ego does not look favorably upon psycho-analysis and
> obstinately refuses to believe in it (p. 143; Freud's italics).

The two earlier blows to man's narcissism that Freud was referring to are, of course, the "cosmological" blow delivered by
Copernicus and the "biological" blow delivered by Darwin.

Although much remains to be worked out about it, the action model of psychoanalytic conceptualization makes possible a different and complementary view of the widespread refusal to believe in psychoanalysis. In this view, the problem is not only a disagreeable *reduction* of people's conception of their personal scope and influence; it is also a threatening *expansion* of this conception. In a basic sense Freud extended people's narcissistic sense of themselves. He showed that people make their lives by what they do, and, for psychoanalysis, what they "do" includes all their mental operations and thereby all the circumstances they contrive and all the meanings they ascribe to their circumstances, whether contrived or imposed on them. People, thus, are far more creators and stand much closer to their gods than they can bear to recognize. I do not mean that most people consciously recognize this expanded idea of lives that is implied in psychoanalytic interpretation; but they fear it nonetheless.

It is Freud's commitment to mechanistic and organismic natural science theorizing and our continuing allegiance to him in this regard that have delayed our discovering this additional truth about the unpopularity of psychoanalysis. We have continued to think, with Freud, of energies, forces, structures, and so forth as *acting on the person* rather than as metaphoric approaches to *actions of a person*. It has been left to such searching thinkers as Binswanger and Sartre, working within the framework of existential analysis, to begin to formulate the relevant propositions. And yet the essential ideas have been at the center of Freudian psychoanalytic interpretation from its very beginning. What, after all, did Freud show in the *Studies on Hysteria* (Breuer and Freud 1893-95) but that a neurotic symptom is something a person *does* rather than *has* or has inflicted on him or her? It is a frightening truth that people make their own mental symptoms. It is an unwelcome insight that if neurosis is a disease at all, it is not like any other disease. It is an arrangement or a creation, an expression of many of an individual's most basic categories of understanding and vital interests.

Freud was to argue later, in his writings on society, that, according to psychoanalytic findings, neurosis now had to be seen as an aspect of living in relation to other people; this means, of course, that neurosis must be understood as an aspect of being human. Admittedly, the circumstances of life are often difficult, but it is not circumstances that create symptoms; it is mental activity in the face of circumstances. It is mental activity that establishes the precise significance of these circumstances and perhaps has been essential in bringing them about. And just as Freud showed people making their own neurotic symptoms, he showed them, to mention only a few points, making their own fantastic sexual theories, their own sexual prowess or pleasure or lack thereof, and, far more often than they dare to admit to themselves, their own unsatisfactory "destiny."

Consequently, the widespread rejection of psychoanalysis may be understood as a species of disclaimed action. It is a way of asserting: "Do not tell us how much we do and how much more we could do. Allow us our illusions of ignorance, passivity, and helplessness. We dare not acknowledge that we *are* masters in our own house." In the words of T.S. Eliot, people want to feel that they are "living and only partly living." This is the frightened, resistant, action-disclaiming stance with which, in part, each of our analysands greets us.

On our part, we analysts must dare to believe that being true to Freud's discoveries need not involve adhering to his metapsychology or to any psychobiological metatheory. We must be open to the idea that other psychological languages are not only possible, but also might even facilitate the achievement of a better understanding of the role of unconsciously carried on infantile sexuality and aggression in human existence. The action language is one such language model. It is, for psychoanalysis, an entirely new way of thinking systematically, though, as I have said, it has always been implicit, unsystematized, and essential in psychoanalytic thinking. As a language, as an avowed strategy or set of rules for systematizing, it is not yet finished, and there are, no doubt, other languages to come. Be that as it may, and contrary to what I think is a widespread feeling in the world of psychoanalysts, there does seem to be a future after all in Freudian theory.

8   Internalization: Process or Fantasy*

1. INTRODUCTION

When, speaking as psychoanalysts, we use the term "incorporation," we refer to a fantasy (ordinarily an unconscious fantasy) of taking part or all of a person, creature, or other substance into one's own body. When we use the term *internalization*, we refer not to a fantasy but to a psychological process, and we are saying that a shift of event, action, or situation in an inward direction or to an inner locale has occurred. For example, a boy imposes on himself prohibitions hitherto imposed on him by his parents: we think then of internality or inside-ness as having more or less replaced externality or outside-ness.

If, however, we ask, "Inside what?" we can provide no satisfactory answer. We do not mean inside the body or organism. Nor do we mean inside the brain, though we know the brain to be the necessary organ for all mental processes. Many of us would say we mean inside the mind or mental apparatus, or, more narrowly, inside the ego; in this usage, we are regarding mind, mental apparatus, and ego as places or locales. And yet this is not how we think of these terms when we define them formally. In our formal definitions we recognize them to be not places at all but concepts devised for descriptive and theoretical purposes; they refer to classes of events or actions. (I shall return to this point.) At the same time, however, many analysts would be loath to agree that when they speak of internalization they intend merely to include an event or action within a class; they would feel that something essential in the way of empirical reference had been lost. And so they might then turn to the empirical-sounding "inside the self" as a way out of this difficulty. But "the self" refers only to mental content; in Freudian theory, at any rate, it is a descriptive or phenomenological concept, and as such it cannot encompass the regulatory struc-

*This is a modified version of a paper that first appeared in *The Psychoanalytic Study of the Child*, 27: (1972), 411-36.

tures, functions, and relationships that are prime referents of the concept of internalization (Hartmann 1939b; Loewald 1960, 1962; Schafer 1968b). "Inside the self" proves to be no more than a bloodless statement of an incorporation fantasy.[1]

It does not help matters to claim, finally, that the idea of the inside is a metaphor, and then to go on to claim that, since science or at least the science of psychoanalysis is necessarily metaphoric, the metaphor of the inside is legitimate and useful. Not only is this set of claims mostly false or in any case not demonstrably true; it also neglects to show that the metaphor of the inside is needed, is the best one for the purpose, and is being used in a proper and consistent fashion. For instance, as I have just indicated, this metaphor cannot be satisfactorily completed; we cannot specify in a systematically useful way what anything mental is inside of. That Freud used spatial analogies to help formulate his theoretical propositions carries no weight at all in this connection; for preparatory phases of thought and visual aids to explanation are not theory proper.

As the notion of internality thus occupies an important but puzzling position in psychoanalytic propositions, I shall devote this chapter to an examination of the salient features of the language of internalization. First, I shall survey the *internalization words* we use. In this connection I shall also have something to say about *structure words,* for these presuppose the legitimacy of internalization words and so both imply them and seem to contribute to their legitimacy. To round off this part of the argument I shall propose alternative conceptualizations of the ideas in question. Second, I shall discuss two topics— *introjects* and *affects*—with respect to which both psychoanalytic observation and conceptualization have followed common usage on internalization and in doing so have suffered significantly. Third, I shall discuss a number of reasons for the prevalence of internalization concepts in our everyday language and, through that language, in our psychological theory. Fourth, I shall offer some suggestions concerning the framing of interpretations; these suggestions follow from my conceptual analysis, and in my view they should serve to increase the

1. Kohut (1971) has failed to provide a theoretical basis for his mixed structural-functional and phenomenological use of self concepts, and so has not helped resolve the difficulty with which we are here concerned (see chapter 5, section 3; see also chapter 9).

clarity of analytic interventions and thereby to facilitate the orderly and effective development of the traditional psychoanalytic process. Fifth and last, I shall review briefly the externalization words that are the counterparts of the internalization words; this should round out the critique of spatial designations of psychological activity. The entire discussion should demonstrate the advantages of shifting to action language.

2. INTERNALIZATION WORDS

Setting aside *incorporation*, which we know we use to refer to fantasy only, the chief internalization words are *internalization, internal, inner world, intrapsychic, introjection, introject,* and less clearly, *identification* (both the process and the end result of that process). I shall begin by concentrating on internalization itself.

I said before that by internalization we do not mean inside the body or organism. On this point I might be charged with neglecting Hartmann's (1939b) discussion of the topic in which he emphasized the progressive interiorization of reaction and regulation as the phylogenetic scale (and, by implication, the ontogenetic scale) is ascended. He said:

> In phylogenesis, evolution leads to an increased independence of the organism from its environment, so that reactions which originally occurred in relation to the external world are increasingly displaced into the interior of the organism. The development of thinking, of the superego, of the mastery of internal danger before it becomes external, and so forth, are examples of this process of internalization (p. 40).
> [He also said:] In the course of evolution, described here as a process of progressive "internalization," there arises a central regulating factor, usually called "the inner world" which is interpolated between the receptors and the effectors (p. 57).
> [And he said this, in a discussion of thinking:] It appears that in higher organisms, trial activity is increasingly displaced into the interior of the organism, and no longer appears in the form of motor action directed toward the external world (p. 59f.).

So far as the term internalization is concerned, Hartmann engaged in a certain amount of begging the question in these (and other such) formulations. He spoke of what is "central,"

"inner," and "between" as if these words were factual referents of and justifications for a concept like internalization. And
yet "central" makes sense only as conceptually central and
strategically central; "inner" makes sense only as a synonym
for mental or psychological; and "between" refers to the increasing size and complexity of the central nervous system—
the system which, though it does lie anatomically between re-
ceptors and effectors, has no bearing on the question of a
spatial location for mental processes. The terms of brain theory
cannot be the terms of psychological theory. Only by contamin-
ating the location of the brain with the location of ideas can one
create this misunderstanding. The contamination of the two
ideas is evident in the notion that thinking is trial activity
which has been displaced spatially into the "interior of the
organism." The correct way to put it, and the way that is in
accord with action language, is that thinking is activity *of a different kind* rather than *in a different place*.

Thus, even as a biological, evolutionary conception, internalization is faulty. It entails an illogical leap. The leap is from
greater organismic complexity, especially of the central
nervous system, and increasing organismic independence from
environmental stimulation, to some vague attribution of location to thought and subjective experience in general.

Conceptual difficulties are even greater when we turn from
phylogenesis to ontogenesis. In this regard there is not even a
fundamental change in physical makeup to point to, however
erroneously, as the spatial referent of internalization. The unreflective subject may ascribe internality to his or her own thinking on the basis of all kinds of "physical" fantasies about
mental processes. (Freud noted this factor particularly in his
paper on negation [1925b], where he described the subjective
link between early thinking and oral activity.) The subject may
also ascribe internality to the thinking of others, not only for
this reason but also because he or she is likely to infer illogi-
cally and concretistically that anything that cannot be perceived must be within, behind, or beneath something else. In
the role of psychological observer one must not repeat these
mistakes; one has no warrant to locate thinking anywhere.
Moreover, it is of the utmost importance that one cannot confuse one's own viewpoint with that of the unreflective subject;
one must maintain one's own criteria for applying or rejecting

notions concerning the designations inside and outside. With respect to mental processes, then, we are left with no answer at all to the question "Inside what?"

Actually, the evolutionary and especially the developmental propositions concerning internalization may be formulated in non-spatial ways that entail fewer assumptions and achieve more exactness than the spatial or pseudospatial. For example, with regard to phylogenesis, we may speak of increasing delay, selectivity, and modifiability of response; decreasing automaticity and stereotypy of action; less fixed dependence on specific environmental stimuli in the initiation or release, guidance, and stability of action; increasing self-stimulation; and so forth. Although Hartmann, like Freud before him, spoke in these very terms or terms like them, he thought it a scientific step forward to subsume these descriptions under some notion of increased interiorization; his theorizing was in this regard, as in so many others, predominantly biological rather than psychological (Schafer 1968a, 1968b; see especially chapter 4, above). I have already indicated that *even considered as a purely biological proposition,* this view of internalization is unsatisfactory.

Let us pursue the matter further. As I mentioned, Hartmann emphasized the evolution of thinking among the signs of increased interiorization. Although thinking is undoubtedly an advance in regulation of action and adaptational flexibility and accomplishment, what exactly is thinking inside of? Where is a thought? We can locate neural structures, glands, muscles, and chemicals in space, but where is a dream, a self-reproach, an introject? If one answers, "In the mind," one can be making a meaningful statement in only one sense of mind, namely, mind as an abstraction that includes thinking among its referents. In this sense, there is no question of spatial localization. To argue otherwise about "in the mind" is to be guilty of reification, that is, to be mistaking abstractions for things. For mind itself is not anywhere; logically, it is like liberty, truth, justice, and beauty in having no extension or habitation, requiring none and tolerating none. It is pure abstraction. The boundaries of mind are those of a concept, not of a place. Only certain referents of these abstractions may have place and substance.

Suppose that we have dispensed with the idea of the inside. Then, in describing human psychological development, we could, for example, say with greater parsimony and exactness that as one becomes an adult, one stops saying everything aloud; one thinks more often, more verbally, and with greater conceptual complexity and consistency than one did as a child; one uses words instead of motility far more often; more frequently than before, one anticipates (e.g., danger) and engages in mental experimentation concerning possible physical and verbal action; one's fantasies can be more detailed and organized; and so on. In all these ways the developing person becomes both more private and more elaborately mental. The observer, then, has increasingly to depend on the developing subject's reports in words to know what his or her subjective situation is, and often these reports are *of* words or *about* words, the words that make up unexpressed thoughts.

Additionally, dispensing with the idea of the inside enables us to recognize that a woman, let us say, is not keeping ideas or feelings *within* her when she keeps them to herself, that is, remains silent about them. In the same way we recognize that that woman does not have an *inner world* just because she has a *private world*. "Private" is a key concept here. It refers to what is not communicated, perhaps not yet formulated or even not unambiguously communicable; it includes what is unconsciously as well as consciously kept secret or passed over. "Private" is not just another word for "inner": it expresses an entirely different way of thinking about mental and other actions.

It follows from these considerations that *introjection* can only be a synonym of incorporation, which is to say that it must refer to the fantasy of taking something into one's body. In this light, it is redundant without appearing to be so, and if kept in use can only be confusing. *Introject* now becomes the thing that is fantasized as having been taken into one's body and as retaining in the fantasy some identity or some characteristic form of activity; it means the same as "the incorporated object," which is a more exact designation of the phenomenon in question. *Intrapsychic* now refers to what is private; in many instances, it pertains to the person's privately and to a large extent unconsciously remembering, imagining, planning, etc., and doing so more or less emotionally.

Identification, finally, is a bit more difficult to reconceptual-

ize. This is so because in psychoanalytic usage it has not been
used to imply internality directly. Traditionally, however,
psychoanalysts have assumed that identification goes on "in
the inner world," gets established "there," and may transform
its "internal" setting (e.g., in the case of superego identification). Once we dispense with the theoretical vocabulary of
internality, however, we are able to speak about identification
as a change in the way one conceives of oneself and perhaps a
corresponding change in the way one behaves publicly; as
before, the change would be modeled on personal and unconsciously elaborated versions of significant figures in real life or
imaginative life (e.g., fictional or historical characters). I have
discussed the full sense of identification at length elsewhere
(Schafer 1968b, esp. ch. 6).

Having mentioned identifications, I can pass right on to
structure words or *structural concepts* since they are so closely
intertwined with identification in psychoanalytic theory.
Though it may not be apparent at first, the idea of psychic
structure relies implicitly on a spatial metaphor—specifically,
the metaphor of mind as a place, an entity characterized by
extension. Thus, Freud positioned the superego ("Überich")
in some unspecified upper space—either directly ("über" as
"over") or indirectly ("über" as "higher," as in "higher
ideals"). And we all think of "levels" and "layers"; we all resort to "underlying" factors or causes; we all speak of "hierarchic" arrangements, "surfaces," and "depths." Indeed, who
would object to the idea that psychoanalysis is a "depth"
psychology or the idea that for Freudians, at any rate, interpretation must work from "the surface"? But, again, within
what space?

Despite this spatialization of mind, when pressed for a strict
metapsychological definition of psychic *structure,* we do not
resort to spatial metaphors. We refer instead to stability of
modes of function, slow rates of change, resistiveness to regressive transformations, and the like. In another respect, we
refer to certain similarities—of aims, of amenability to delay, of
relative degree of desomatization, and so forth. This is how we
customarily speak of id, ego, and superego—as functions
grouped together by the observer or theoretician on the basis of
such criteria as I have just listed. They are classes of events or

actions, and to include an event or action "within" a class, rather than being inherently and inescapably a spatial designation, is merely to say, "I consider *this* event or action a member of *that* class." Hartmann, Kris, and Loewenstein (1946) and Rapaport (1959, 1967) stand out among those who have established this mode of conceptualization of structure as the right one for traditional psychoanalytic theory (see also Hartmann 1964).

What does it mean, then, that identification is assigned so important a role in the development of psychic structure by Freud (see, e.g., 1923a) and others after him? It means that modeling change of ideas about oneself and change of one's public behavior on aspects of important real or imaginary people plays a decisive part in the progressive stabilization and integration of one's actions. It means that in order to develop as a specific person, one must have models; one cannot and does not have to create one's idea of being fully human by oneself. We know that the process of modeling oneself after another person is typically fantasied as an incorporation of that person and may even be undertaken for that very purpose (e.g., to preserve a sense of the presence of that person or of one of his or her qualities). But we realize too, that when we say "incorporation," we are speaking of the content of imagination or fantasy; we are not conceptualizing actions for systematic purposes.

It comes then to this: identification is or may be "structure-building" in the sense that it may make possible a high degree of consistency in certain modes of subjective experience and behavior; on the basis of identification, specific acts of desiring, thinking, and doing other things, along with specific emotional modes associated with these actions, may be in evidence much more regularly and readily than they would be otherwise. But we speak of psychic structure in this instance because, thinking metaphorically, we are picturing mind as a matter of places, currents, quantities, barriers, and interactions—in short, as a spatial entity containing other localizable entities and processes. This entire notion, once made explicit, can be seen to be the archaic invention it is.[2]

Not only invention, but convention: the spatial notion is so

2. The current "structuralist" conceptions of structure are not in question here.

well established in common usage, it has so many variations and so wide a range of application, that it seems the very stuff of thought. This usage is so powerful that if I were to say "John's internal standards," who, under ordinary circumstances, would think I was referring not to a fact but to a problematic metaphoric rendition of an observation? The observation itself, I suggest, would be stated more exactly in "John's standards" or "John's private standards," or perhaps "the standards John abides by unconsciously." And, if it was structure that was to be emphasized in this regard, the observation would not be rendered directly or exactly in "John's structuralized internal standards" but in "John acts pretty consistently, even when under stress, in abiding by his unconsciously maintained standards" or "John may be counted on to abide by certain standards he maintains privately even though he may do so conflictedly." One might even go so far as to disallow the word "standards" and then say, "John regularly criticizes certain of his actions and approves others, whether he does so consciously or otherwise."

It should be evident by now that the spatial metaphor comes between us and the potential fact, and that that fact is better rendered in action language. With which observation I shall go on to consider two sets of phenomena—usually subsumed under the headings *introjects* and *affects*—the observation and conceptualization of which have been seriously hampered by pseudospatial references to the inside and outside in mental functioning.

3. INTROJECTS

There is no topic to which the preceding considerations may be applied with more emphasis than traditional discussions of introjects (see also chapter 7, section 4). First of all, it is our custom to speak of introjects as though they were angels and demons with minds and powers of their own. We speak of them not as an analysand's construction and description of experience but as unqualified facts. This is the case, for example, when without qualification we say that introjects persecute, scold, comfort, etc., the person under consideration. In these instances we forget that an introject can only be a fantasy, that is, a special kind of daydream which, in a more or less clearly hallucinatory experience, the subject takes for a real-life event. We forget then that the introject can have no powers or motives of its own, and no perceptual and judgmental functions, except as, like a dream figure, it has these properties archaically ascribed to it by the imagining subject. The subject is, as it were, dreaming while ostensibly fully and consistently awake. The introject has the "reality" of a dream figure and is a "hallucination" in the same sense that a dream is.

In the second place, we designate as introjects many dream-like experiences of the nearness and influence of other persons or parts of persons when, according to the spontaneous reports of the analysand, he or she has either not localized them in subjective space at all or has indicated that they are "outside" (e.g., lurking behind). Why then "introject"? Is it not the result of reasoning that goes something like this: since the presence, as I call it, is objectively not outside the subject, and since thinking somehow goes on "in the head" because the mind is somehow "in the head," the presence must be inside the head, too, and so must be an introject? It is all quite crude, but there it is!

Thus, owing to the tenacity with which we hold on to our ideas about mind *in* space and mind *as* space, we do not always listen carefully to our analysands when they report these vivid imaginative experiences. We do not sort out the subject's experiential language and the observer's conceptual language. Consequently, the theory of introjects has always had the same spooky quality as the subjective experience it refers to; it has remained more a repetition or continuation of the problem than a clarification or explanation of it.

Obviously, this conceptual analysis may be applied to the related concept "internal objects" and all the pseudospatial words associated with it. And since, as I indicated earlier, incorporation is to be preferred to introjection, I think we shall achieve the greatest clarity in our discussions of these matters by speaking of some presences as "incorporated objects" while remembering that not all presences have been incorporated; some presences remain unlocalized in subjective space and perhaps, owing to the elusiveness of many of these phenomena, simply cannot be localized. I have discussed the "power" and the "locale" of introjects and other presences in greater detail elsewhere (1968b, esp. ch. 5).

4. AFFECTS

To take up affects in general would require me to consider issues that extend far beyond the scope of this chapter. This I shall do in part IV. For now, I shall single out *anger* as an example of an affect, the observation and conceptualization of which have been seriously hampered by our adhering to the notions of the inside and outside. In order to develop the implications and consequences of my critique, I shall go into some detail about spatial and non-spatial ways of talking about anger.

People speak of anger as being held in or suppressed, dammed up or pent up, exploding or erupting, consuming one or simmering. Similarly, they say that they express anger or let it out, that it spills out or spreads, and so on. It is as if anger were some kind of hot lava in a volcanic cone. In psychoanalytic parlance, we also speak of displacing anger, discharging it, and turning it around upon the self. In using these words we presuppose that anger has the properties not only of substance and quantity, but extension, place, or locale as well (these properties go together, necessarily). The vocabulary of anger thus depends on the legitimacy of assuming or referring to an inside and an outside—but, I ask again, inside or outside of what? Where? Is anger anywhere? And where does anger go when it is discharged or expressed? And what is left in the place occupied by anger before its purgation? A vacuum? A clean inside?

The questions are unanswerable, of course, because they cannot be asked in a logical inquiry. Anger is not the kind of word about which such questions may be asked, and we shall soon see what kind of word it is. Meanwhile, it follows from what I have said that, with respect to psychological theory, the spatial metaphor and the spatial (and substance-quantity) implications of our affect words are to be treated as unreal or not serious. It should be noted that affect theory and psychic energy theory are not independent in this respect, in that, according to the latter theory, affects are quantities, and, being quantities, they must therefore (we suppose) be somewhere, even if only within an ill-considered spatial metaphor.[3]

Much of the problem issues from the archaic notion, familiar to us from our studies of primary process thinking or unconscious fantasy, of affect as substance (see, e.g., Brierley 1937; Schafer 1964). Thus, when we speak of anger, we have the illusion that we are referring to something that may be designated by a concrete noun, that is, referring to a unit that can be pointed to, like a claw or a fang or a fecal mass. But that is not what anger is. The anger of common usage is really an abstract noun; it is a rubric for a set of referents, and it is the referents rather than anger that can be pointed to, at least in some instances. These referents include physiological arousal reactions, ideas of having been wronged and of doing something more or less violent about that, etc. These ideas or fantasies may be repressed altogether or replaced by "tamed" ideas or fantasies of some sort of retaliation against someone or other. I need not spell out all the variations in this regard.

There is, of course, a quantitative or quantifiable aspect of physiological arousal or muscular activity. Ordinarily, this quantity will correspond to the total situation as the subject defines it, especially unconsciously. But by itself this arousal and activity is not the affect "anger."

That the effect of anger is an abstract noun rather than an irreducible subjective experience, a "pure feeling," is evident from the fact that it makes perfect sense to ask people who claim to be angry, "How do you know you are?" It makes sense because they can then attempt to answer by surveying the referents of the term anger as they use it, which is to say by explaining how they work with the word anger in their vocabulary. They might, of course, protest that the question as to how they know they are angry makes no sense since this knowledge is given to them directly as experience; that is, they might claim to be experiencing what has been called "pure anger" as such. But this objection will not stand up to such further questions as "How can you tell that you are angry rather than

3. In his final major formulation of the matter (as translated by Strachey), Freud said that the ego was the "seat" of anxiety, and, by implication, of the affects in general (1926, p. 93). Freud's word was *"Angststätte"* which more literally would be translated "place (or locus) of anxiety." Being engrossed in establishing his implicitly spatial "structural theory," Freud understandably relied on the notion that affects have locales (see also chapter 15, section 6).

anxious?" "How can you tell that you are angry rather than irked?" and "How did you ever learn that the term anger was the one to apply to that 'pure feeling' you are feeling now?" For even if they were to say in response merely that each affect is a distinctive and immediately recognizable experience, they would be obliged in explaining how they use an affect word, to specify its distinguishing features—in which case they would have granted the legitimacy of the question to which they had initially objected. Additionally, the distinguishing features cited would prove to be equally applicable to others as well as themselves; it would become clear then that access to anger is not ultimately privileged.

For these reasons we can (and we do) on occasion point out sensibly (and usefully) in the course of our analytic work that an analysand, say a man, who claims to be angry is *not* angry, that he is only saying so, that he is in fact trying to obscure his acting unemotionally or his acting excitedly. Similarly, we can (and we do) on occasion say sensibly that an analysand is only pretending to be acting angrily, that despite his sounding irate and belligerent he is only trying to convince himself or us that he is acting angrily when he is not. On his part, the analysand whose anger we have called into question can ask us sensibly, "How do *you* know?" for we, too, base our judgments in this regard on criteria; that is to say, in referring to someone's acting angrily or not, we are following a language rule rather than reporting a direct perception of a pure something which is anger and which someone "has" or "doesn't have." That we need not engage in our appraisals consciously and that we may make them quickly, both contribute to the incorrect impression that there is something called anger that is directly experienced or perceived as a "pure feeling."

Being an abstract noun, anger is, of course, undischargeable. Moreover, the force of the word anger is not nominative but adverbial; it refers to a way of acting, though perhaps only to an inhibited, fantasied, or oblique way of acting—namely, *angrily* (see also chapter 13, section 3c). In clinical work, when we analyze "angry" fantasy and behavior, this is how we understand them—as thinking and behaving angrily. We may obscure this fact by using spatial metaphors ourselves; we use them because we think incorrectly that these metaphors describe something tangible and help us to understand the "angry" fantasy and behavior. In fact, however, by using the spatial metaphor we introduce primary process modes of thought into systematic thinking, and so, as we do in the spooky theory of introjects, we contaminate the explanation with what is to be explained. In this light we can see that "catharsis" expresses an anal-expulsive fantasy! The anger that is pent up, simmer, explodes, or spills over expresses a volcanic anal fantasy; it is psychological content to be explained, not psychological explanation. "Catharsis," thus, is peculiarly well suited for expressing in an aseptic fashion archaic ideas about anger as a spatially localizable, destructive substance of quantity; it cannot be a useful theoretical term.

If we give up the illusion that anger is a concrete noun in the sense I have discussed and think instead that *angrily* denotes a way of acting, we may proceed quite logically. We will state our propositions somewhat as follows. People act angrily. A number of ways of acting may be subsumed under *angrily*. Adjectival forms are easily transposed into adverbial: "an angry woman" refers to a woman acting angrily. Her acting angrily may or may not be done consciously. She may imagine herself to be filled with some sort of quantity of anger. She may try to avoid acting angrily or to avoid being aware that she is so acting, and she may succeed entirely or intermittently. She may act more angrily in certain situations than others. She may act angrily in different ways at different times. She may put on a show of behaving angrily.

Further, she is not likely to go on acting angrily if she has done something that signifies to her adequate revenge or retaliation, or adequate communciation and effectiveness of action with regard to her grievance, for then she will see her situation as having changed for the better, and she will no longer find provocation to think or behave angrily. Concurrently, her physiological arousal for vigorous action will subside, and she may begin to think of other, perhaps more pleasant matters. She will then be said to be "feeling better." This, in nonspatial, nonquantitative, nonsubstantial—and so, nonpurgative—terms is anger and diminution of anger, possibly cessation of anger as well. Nothing has gotten into or out of anyone's system except in fantasy. Objectively, there has been no anal event.

To anticipate a possible objection to my argument at this point, I want to emphasize that I am not advocating or slipping into a psychology of consciousness. The entire process I have described may—and often does—take place unconsciously. It is quite possible, as Freud demonstrated, to say "think," "believe," "conclude," "put on a show," and so forth, without implying "consciously" or "superficially." There is no opening here for the facile charge of superficiality—a charge which has too often hampered exploratory psychoanalytic discussion.

This, then, is the kind of word that anger is. Whenever we fail to realize or remember that this is so, we make the mistake of thinking of anger as an entity to which notions of substance, quantity, and place (inside and outside) are applicable. This is the mistake involved in using notions of discharging or abreacting anger. Also in error on this account is the assumption that some pure feeling of anger exists apart from language rules concerning observable or communicable characteristic features of action; in other words, that the subject has privileged access to this pure feeling of anger.

A few remarks regarding the so-called unconscious affects are in order here. According to the viewpoint I am developing, these unconscious affects must be understood always to be fully realized properties of action, that is, as unqualified verbal or adverbial characterizations; this is so provided that it is also understood that the person in question is successfully resisting being aware of performing some or all of these actions in these modes. Thus, it is quite common for the analyst to point out that the analysand is speaking angrily (or tearfully, etc.) while remaining defensively oblivious of the fact. This emotional mode is likely to become more vivid following the analysand's becoming consciously aware of it or following his or her refraining from overt action in this mode despite continued (subjective) provocation; but in neither instance does it follow that a potential affect has been actualized (which is one main sense of unconscious affect); nor does it follow that a dammed-up and unacknowledged affect has been released (the other main sense of unconscious affect): it does follow that the analysand has changed his or her attitude toward action in this emotional mode sufficiently to tolerate being consciously aware of it or to be no longer willing to abstain from action of this sort; and that this being so, he or she has defined a new situation in which it is appropriate and possible to behave in a more emphatic or demonstrative fashion and with more varied and elaborated ideas of grievance and retaliation. "Discharge" and "abreaction" are now seen to be emotional actions appropriate to changed subjective situations rather than movement of quantities of psychic energy.

It might be surmised—correctly!—that I am dispensing with the hypothesis of an instinctual drive of aggression whose psychic energy (also called "aggression") is accumulated and discharged in anger (among other responses). I, along with many others (e.g., Holt 1965, 1967; Applegarth 1971), have advanced at some length reasons for discarding "psychic energy" as a fundamental hypothesis in psychoanalytic theory (1968b, esp. ch. 3; 1970c; and see also chapters 4 and 10 of this book); I shall not repeat these arguments here.

Although I could extend this discussion to other affect words, such as joy, sadness, anxiety, and guilt, I shall not do so until part IV (see esp. chapter 13, section 3). My reason is that at this point I only want to make a methodological point in taking up anger (as well as introjects). This point is to expose a serious problem and suggest a possible solution. The problem is the confusion of observation and theory that results from our unwittingly applying the archaic notion of internality to mental actions. The solution is the elimination of words of the "inside" and "outside" variety from *theoretical* discourse. This change in our thinking will be one part of a general strategy for avoiding the concretistic error of ascribing substance and force (quantity, extension, momentum, etc.) to actions.

5. The Prevalence of the Idea of the Inside

Judging by its prevalence in our everyday language, the idea of the inside appears to be invested with profound significance in human experience. So much is this so that without our realizing it we have used the idea extensively in fashioning psychoanalytic theory. From among the factors contributing to the pervasiveness of the idea of the inside, I single out the following as being especially important.[4]

(1) The child seems to organize its earliest subjective experience around bodily sensations with their varying pleasure-pain

4. I am indebted to Dr. Ernst Prelinger for helping me to develop a number of the main propositions I shall set forth in this section—and also for his helpful suggestions regarding this paper as a whole.

properties. This early subjective experience is the "bodily ego" that, according to Freud (1923a), is the first ego. Thus, from its very beginnings, the organization of experience implies physical referents such as are later subjectively defined as being inside and outside.

(2) Throughout subsequent experience, the notion of the interiority of one's own being is supported by one's observing the often prominent physiological changes that are part aspects of the emotional side of significant activities, such as the sexual, the angry, and the frightened. With regard to the make-up and boundaries of the physical body, these physiological changes are indeed mostly "beneath the surface" or "inside," and in some instances "deep."

(3) Adding further to the idea of mental actions as occupying space and as moving in space are the crucial anatomical foci of psychosexual development—mouth, anus, genitalia—with their openings and closings, and the passage of substances in and out of them, all of which is associated with highly sensuous and emotional actions and events. So much of mental life concerns these places, spaces, substances, sensations, and fantasies that inevitably, when we begin to think about mind at all, we model it after the "bodily ego" and assume that it is somehow a substantial and sensitive entity with spatial characteristics.

(4) Early notions of self are strongly influenced by these archaic, concretistic factors. Self, too, is then thought of as being a place as well as being in places, e.g., within the physical boundaries of the body, though not necessarily filling it. As *a* place, self is thought to be like a body in having boundaries which contain processes or contents that "belong" to it. Sometimes the boundaries of self are thought to include possessions and other people we love, hate, or fear. And sometimes, as when we engage in projecting, these boundaries exclude features of our own being that we have repudiated. Other ways in which we spatialize self are by thinking of it as having parts, splits, layers, and levels. These pseudospatial metaphors are repeatedly emphasized in social discourse, a matter about which I shall say more under point 7. (More will be found on the idea of self in section 3 of chapter 5 and especially in chapter 9.)

(5) Our perceptions of others being, as we learn from experience, limited, fragmentary, and insufficient for predictive pur-

poses, we think from early on that the "more" that eludes us must be "behind" or "within" what we do perceive.

(6) Earlier in this chapter, I mentioned how we have contaminated the idea of the brain, which mediates mental actions and is inside the head, with the idea of mental actions themselves. The result of this conceptual contamination is that these actions, too, are thought to be somehow or other characterized by inside-ness.

(7) Finally, there is the factor of well-learned metaphysical assumptions. These assumptions are conveyed and perpetuated in the basic language of "experience." The child learns them from people in the environment and relies on them while learning to speak and to think in words. Moreover, and as one would expect from points 1-5 above, the child finds these assumptions congenial. That is to say, they match his or her own physical, sensuous, psychosexual categorial principles for comprehending and organizing ideas. I do not mean that children or even most adults realize that they entertain metaphysical assumptions, but, from the study of young children, dreams, and neurotic and psychotic symptoms, we know all too well the extent to which physical categorial principles constitute our understanding.[5]

6. Implications for the Language of Interpretation

In many instances analysts unwittingly encourage their analysands to use archaic (though also everyday) internalization language. They do so whenever they themselves use spatial metaphors to designate mental actions and do so not in the service of empathically verbalizing how an action seems or "feels" to an analysand but in the service of objectively describing how mental actions are performed. For example, the analyst might say "your internal standards," "your inner image," "your innermost conviction," "on another level," "the

5. Further consideration of this factor would require formulating fundamental doubts concerning the logical necessity and legitimacy of using *motivation words* to explain action. This is so because so often the term motive, for example, refers to a mover of action that is prior to it in time and "interior" to it as an inner or behind-the-scenes entity that is personlike in its comprehension and activity. I shall discuss motivation words in chapter 10 (see also chapter 1, section 2). For background, I refer the reader to Ryle's (1949) and Hampshire's (1959, 1962) discussions of mind, action, and dispositions. These discussions are an important part of the intellectual background of this chapter.

deepest meaning," and so on and so forth along the lines I laid down earlier. Of greater significance often is the analyst's use of internalization language in dealing with so-called introjects or internal objects and other presences, and also in dealing with affects and their disposition. Every time the analyst speaks of "the mother inside you," "the values you took in," "the structure you set up," "the boundaries between you and others," "the feelings you let out," etc., he or she reinforces the analysand's unconsciously fantasying that one's being a person is essentially an account of spatial locations rather than an account of the kinds of actions that one performs. Rendering these actions exclusively in the form of spatial metaphor can be done only at great expense to rational understanding. Objectively, "the mother inside you" is better said "the mother you think of whenever you thus and so," or "the mother you imagine inside you in order that you thus and so." I am here suggesting a nonspatial language as an alternative to our familiar one; actually, this alternative is one we do use at times, perhaps often or even regularly. And yet we do not altogether believe in it or appreciate it, for we lapse so readily into unacknowledged and unqualified spatial metaphor.

Certainly, there are many analytic contexts where it seems right for the analyst to use language that has the same archaic (though also everyday) implications as the analysand's language. Particularly is this so when the analysand is beginning to say new, significant, and difficult things in the analysis. But the analysand must have some steadily available sense, though not necessarily a steady conscious awareness, that at least the analyst is being metaphoric in his or her effort to help find the best words for hitherto unverbalized fantasies. That is to say, the analysand should increasingly appreciate that words are being used "as if" mind or being or ego were space and structure with objects moving into, out of, and through them. In making this point I am expanding and improving our interpretive options, not reducing them.

I want to mention here a matter I discussed at greater length in chapter 7, section 3. By joining in saying that things come to mind, or slip the mind, or are brought to mind, the analyst tends to confirm the idea of mind as place rather than as an abstract rubric which has expanse only in the sense of conceptual inclusiveness. These locutions also confirm the archaic, anthropomorphic belief that ideas are like animate beings that can "come," "slip away," and "bring" more like them.

Ultimately, the ideal language for interpretation that is aimed at objectifying mental actions would, according to my argument, no longer refer to inside or outside, structure and its variants (barriers, limits, boundaries, etc.), introjection and introject, and affects as moving or movable quantities that are implicitly objectlike or animate. References to inside and outside would be made along the way, of course, in the many appropriate comments by the analyst that express empathy, recognition, and articulation of archaic and obscure experiences. *In the main, the analyst would be working in that manner.* But when speaking strictly rationally, the analyst would avoid treating actions as spatial and personalized entities.

Here are a series of translations of the sort I mean. (Elsewhere in this chapter, I have indicated other translations—e.g., regarding introjects, affects, and mind.)

(1a) It was an old anger you finally got out.

(1b) You finally acted angrily after all this time.

(2a) You broke through the internal barriers against your feelings of love.

(2b) You finally did not refrain from acting lovingly.

(3a) Your chronic deep sense of worthlessness comes from the condemning inner voice of your mother.

(3b) You regularly imagine your mother's voice condemning you, and, agreeing with it, regard yourself as being essentially worthless.

(4a) Your underlying reason for being superficial is to avoid the shame about your past that haunts you.

(4b) The unacknowledged but crucial reason why you dwell on obvious or trivial matters is this: if you did not do so, you would be shaming yourself about your past, over and over again; your contrived obviousness and triviality is your alternative to doing so.

(5a) You are afraid of your impulse to throw caution to the winds.

(5b) You are afraid you might act extremely recklessly.

I offer these illustrative translations with the full realization that, like translations of the King James Bible into modern English, they seem to take the "body" and "soul" out of the language. But that is the point! A soulful language cannot help us understand all we wish to understand about "soul," "soulfulness," and, in Schreber's phrase, "soul-murder" (Freud 1911). And a language that is not "disembodied" cannot help us understand all we wish to understand about the fantastic concreteness and "embodiment" of unconsciously pursued or primary process thinking (Freud 1915c, 1925b). I mentioned earlier the actual disruption of habitual thought and speech and the sense of loss that accompany change in well-established modes of thought, and I argued then that these difficulties should not deter us from thinking through—and working through—chronic and crucial problems in psychoanalytic conceptualization. I must also mention again that the type of non-anthropomorphic, nonspatial locutions I am emphasizing are widely used anyway; my aim is to systematize them as an action language and to establish their value for systematic thinking in theory and practice.

7. EXTERNALIZATION WORDS

It is a necessary extension of my argument to survey *externalization words*. As I see no great problems in transposing the preceding conceptual analysis of internalization to the conceptual analysis of externalization, I shall be brief about it.

It must be said, first, that when it comes to psychological activity the idea of the *external* is as unsatisfactory as the idea of the internal. In the psychoanalytic literature, external has been used in three senses, and it has often been left unclear which meaning of it is intended. These meanings may be designated biological, psychological-observational, and psychological-subjective. The biological meaning of external is outside the physical boundaries of the organism; for this purpose the word environmental is clearer than the word external. The psychological-observational meaning of external is all the mental functioning that can be perceived by an independent observer; here, external refers to what is public rather than private. The psychological-subjective meaning of external is everything one does not include in one's idea of oneself; in this respect even one's entire body may be external to one subject, while possessions, love objects, home, and nation may be internal to another subject. The psychological-subjective meaning of external is the one that corresponds to the restricted usage of internal as fantasy which I have been urging in this chapter; for other purposes, environmental and public should be the preferred words. For purposes of psychoanalytic interpretation, *external world* and *external reality* must be understood in this subjective sense.

Projection should now be regarded as simply synonymous with fantasied expulsion from the body. The "projected" content expelled and then localized within the boundaries of someone else is typically a concretized (fecal, fetal, etc.) version of an act of wishing or a mode of behaving that one does not wish to recognize as one's own. *Reprojection* should refer to a second expulsion after an intermediate phase of re-incorporation; usage is unsatisfactory in this instance, however, in that reprojection is often used to mean simply the expulsion of something that has been incorporated.

Interpersonal, finally, refers to what the objective observer sees; that is to say, two or more people interacting. Insofar as one is thinking adaptively, one may be the objective observer of one's interpersonal situation. We know, however, that it is often the case that when the subject is ostensibly dealing with another real person, he or she is found on analytic examination to be dealing essentially with a fantasied version of that person; and we know, too, that that version is likely to include details of significant figures from the subject's childhood. We encounter the limits of "externality" of interpersonal relations most clearly in the analysis of the transference.

In making interpretations, we analysts often use externalization words as we use internalization words. We say, for example, "You projected your excitement into him," "You mistook an inner danger for an outer danger," "You finally got it out," "Your outward behavior covers up your inner feeling," etc. In this way, too, we confirm the analysand's use of archaic spatial metaphors in rendering and understanding his or her subjective experiences, both problematic and integrative. Sometimes it is useful to do so; sometimes not.

8. Conclusion

The gist of my argument is that internalization is a spatial metaphor that is so grossly incomplete and unworkable that we would do best to avoid it in psychoanalytic conceptualization.[6] Incorporation (and incorporated object or person) is the only term that has a real referent, namely, archaic fantasies of taking objects into the body. Logically, internalization cannot mean anything more than that: it refers to a fantasy, not to a process.

The unsatisfactoriness of "internalization" for *systematic purposes* is all the more apparent when, upon further reflection, we realize that a clear need for this metaphor has never been established in psychoanalytic theory. We realize, that is, that invalidly we have assumed a condition of conceptual need or impotence in this connection. After all, why do we have to add anything about localization once we have said that a girl, let us say, now reminds herself to do things when before it was her mother who did so; or that she imagines her father's commanding visage in her father's absence; or that she thinks of herself as looking after herself? Typically we have hastened to invoke internalization words to describe these phenomena. But why this haste or urgency? These simple (though not naive) accounts of phenomena do not confine us to a primitive, obstructed, or incomplete conceptual position. If we say that the girl "internalized" her mother's reminders or her reminding mother, that she "introjected" her father's authority or her authoritarian father, etc., have we understood or conveyed anything more? If anything, we are working with less. I maintain this for these reasons: we have complicated our theoretical thinking unnecessarily; we are using a spatial metaphor from which it is all too easy to slip into concreteness of thought; once embarked on metaphor, we tend to develop a sense of obligation to be metaphorically consistent and involve ourselves in

6. It is not so strange as it might seem at first that this sentence has been written by the author of a book on psychoanalytic theory entitled *Aspects of Internalization* (1968b). The reader of that book will find that to a great extent I was already redefining the central concepts in nonspatial terms. But, while writing that book, I did not yet realize the extent to which the very idea of internalization was part of a major problem in psychoanalytic theorizing.

extravagant niceties of formulation; and perhaps we even introduce still another assumption into theory where none is needed. The tortuous history of the pseudoquantitative energy metaphor in Freudian metapsychology demonstrates what I mean (see chapter 4, section 5).

I have indicated how our observations, understanding, and conceptualization of introjects, affects, and what we call psychic structure may be improved by our dispensing with notions of the inside and the outside in our theorizing. The terms organism and environment suffice for biological discussions; the terms inside and outside (and their variations) are suitable for verbalizing fantasies about mental actions, self, and human relations. But mental actions themselves—the referents of our theoretical propositions—are not localizable in any kind of space, for they are classes of nonsubstantial and therefore nonspatial psychological events. They do not exist anywhere and they do not move anywhere; we only—and fatefully! —think they do.

9 Concepts of Self and Identity in Relation to Separation-Individuation*

1. INTRODUCTION

For reasons I shall develop later in this chapter, the language of self and identity has in recent years been bidding to become the dominant language of Freudian theory. In chapter 5, section 3, I have already mentioned some of the principal features and problems of this language, especially as it appears in the work of Erikson and Kohut. There, I expressed my view that the development of this language represents a transitional phase of the conceptual revolution that is replacing natural science metapsychology with terms and explanatory propositions better suited to the methods and data of the psychoanalytic study of human beings. In the present chapter I shall review the issues in somewhat more detail and with special reference to another major figure of this transitional phase, Margaret Mahler (1968). Together with her co-workers, Mahler has been studying psychological development from the point of view of separation-individuation and has been presenting and elaborating concepts concerning the self and objects that are appropriate to that point of view. Although her studies have been focused on the first years of life, the application of her concepts has been extended to adolescence and the phenomena of the psychoanalytic process.

A discussion of separation-individuation centering on adolescence appears to be especially well suited to two tasks, that of establishing links between self and identity concepts and that of developing further my critique of these concepts from the standpoint of action language. With reference to Freud's views on adolescent "detachment" and a conceptual analysis of a brief clinical example, I shall undertake these two tasks in the following pages. I shall draw upon, though not follow exactly, the contributions of Anna Freud (1936, 1958), Helene Deutsch

*This is a modified version of an article that first appeared in *The Psychoanalytic Quarterly*, 42 (1973): 42-59.

(1944, 1945), Erikson (1950, 1956), and Blos (1962, 1967), to mention only a handful of notable investigators of adolescence. For the sake of conciseness, I shall here focus my remarks on the adolescent boy; the adolescent girl's development requires a significantly different, though not unrelated, discussion, and it would not serve my present purpose to deal with it.

2. Separation-Individuation

Mahler describes the process of separation-individuation as consisting of two sets of changes. There are changes in the degree and stability of the child's differentiation of its self-representations from its object representations; these changes we may call representational differentiation. And there are changes in the degree and flexibility of the child's independent activity in the social and physical world that surrounds it; these changes we may call behavioral differentiation. The two sets of changes are correlative; yet it is clear that representational differentiation is the core of the separation-individuation concept.

Self and identity serve as the superordinate terms for the self-representations that the child sorts out (separates, individuates) from its initially undifferentiated subjective experience of the mother-infant matrix. We must therefore be as clear as we can about these two terms.[1] In order to understand the uses to which the terms have been put, and in order to appraise their usefulness, we must also remain alert to context; for during the past several decades Freudian analysts have used self and identity concepts in a number of other contexts—specifically, in the study of adolescence (Erikson 1950, 1956; Spiegel 1958), psychosis (Winnicott 1958), narcissism (Kohut 1966, 1971; Levin 1970), and ego functions (Spiegel 1959). Since the relations of these contexts to each other have not been worked out, we may not assume that self and identity retain the same meaning from one to another. For example, with regard to self or identity during adolescence, representational cohesion seems to be at least as important a connotation of self and identity as representational differentiation from others.

---

1. My discussion overlaps earlier critiques by Glover (1966) and Leites (1971), though in ways too complicated to specify here it does not share many of their assumptions. See also Ryle (1949, pp. 186-98).

Before turning to the topic of adolescence, however, I must mention two special problems. First, although sometimes it is "the ego" that is referred to in metapsychological discussions of what it is that undergoes "separation-individuation," on close examination it appears that "the ego" is being used in the sense of self or identity rather than in its customary sense of a more or less neutrally energized organization of relatively homogeneous fuctions. Second, strictly speaking, the giving up of relations to infantile objects does not constitute "individuation." *Logically*, only an already individuated entity can be said to have "relations," however diffuse and unstable these relations may be; *psychologically* or *empirically*, only an already highly individuated person is capable of giving up infantile relations to others (more exactly, of modifying these relations greatly, as through personal analysis). One finds instances of confusion between "individuation" and "giving up infantile objects" in Jacobson (1964), Blos (1967), Mahler (1968), Kohut (1971), and other analysts who have recently contributed to the analytic literature on the phases of personal development.

3. ADOLESCENT "DETACHMENT"

In one of his most succinct and illuminating discussions of adolescent development Freud (1905b) wrote:

> At the same time as these plainly incestuous phantasies are overcome and repudiated, one of the most significant, but also one of the most painful, psychical achievements of the pubertal period is completed: detachment from parental authority, a process that alone makes possible the opposition, which is so important for the progress of civilization, between the new generation and the old. At every stage in the course of development...a certain number [of human beings] are held back; so there are some who have never got over their parents' authority and have withdrawn their affection from them either very incompletely or not at all (p. 227).

That Freud was not disposed to be so absolute about these distinctions and achievements as might appear from this discussion soon becomes clear; for after referring to the tendency of some young people to fall in love with older people who "reanimate pictures of their mother or father," he added, "There can be no doubt that every object-choice whatever is based, though less closely, on these prototypes" (p. 228). Which is to say that the detaching he spoke of cannot be completed. We know, too, that often there is another aspect—a fond, mutually supportive, and continuous aspect—of parent-adolescent relations. My concern here, however, is with the aspect of detachment rather than family solidarity. And it must be acknowledged that the process we are concerned with is more apparent in some adolescents than in others.

Let us now examine the adolescent boy's struggle for detachment. Perhaps the outstanding manifestation of his separation-individuation difficulties is his totalistic effort to "stamp out" his parents' influence on him. By means of his unconsciously projecting, which, ironically, only further limits his uncertain differentiation from his parents, he consciously locates the parental influence mainly in his actual parents as they are today. For this reason he avoids them, and when with them he acts aloof, indifferent, secretive, touchy, surly, and contemptuous.

Unconsciously, however, his situation is quite different. Unconsciously, he fears parental influence owing mainly to three factors: his anxiously and defensively regressing from intensified fantasies of incest, castration, and loss of love and of the people he loves; his persistently wishing to remain close to his parents, or even merged with them, which may be inferred from his imagining them in and around him as introjects or presences acting on him in a variety of ways and from his considering his very being as identical with theirs; and his inflated way of viewing his parents as omnipotent and omniscient, a way of viewing them that demonstrates his having unconsciously remained emotionally absorbed in his *infantile* idea of them.

Having unconsciously remained in this infantile situation, or regressed to it, the adolescent has no chance of solving his developmental problems by avoiding or overwhelming his actual contemporary parents, though to a degree and in some respects he may have to make such moves and may benefit from them; action in the present world is not irrelevant, of course. But what he needs most urgently is to transform his so-called inner world, particularly his archaic infantile world. Projective expulsion, fight and flight, and iron control do not accomplish this transformation: resort to these devices and slogans assumes a basically unchangeable predicament and serves to perpetuate it. Genuine emancipation seems to be built on revision, modulation, and selective acceptance as well as rejection; on flexible mastery; and on complex substitutions and other changes of aims, representations, and patterns of action. These changes are necessarily slow, subtle, ambivalent, limited, and fluctuating. I do not think we yet have extensive empirical knowledge of these representational and behavioral differentiations from the parents of infancy: we know that they occur, and something about why they occur and their consequences, but not so much about how they occur.

We understand the struggling adolescent's totalistic view of emancipation to be consistent with his fearing that which he most wishes for (wishing it and fearing it *unconsciously* for the most part). And we understand his alertness and over-responsiveness to "insidious influence" to be consistent with the same wishing-fearing conflict. His being so emotionally and conflictually engaged in this push-pull situation is what makes him so vulnerable and easily played upon—controlled, over-stimulated, put off, or put down by his elders and his contemporaries. Not only must he be on the alert against himself, it is himself that he must "stamp out," as in the asceticism described by Anna Freud (1936) and the radical experimentation with limits and with negative and strange "identities" described by Erikson (1950, 1956).

4. Primary Process Thinking About 'Detachment'

In carrying on this struggle, the adolescent unconsciously makes a number of fateful primitive psychological assumptions about the nature of feelings, self, identity, and his relations with other people. These assumptions exemplify primary process thinking; that is to say, the assumptions are the same as those that go into the making of dreams, neurotic and psychotic symptoms, slips, and symptomatic acts. They center around the idea that mental processes are substances, that they have such properties of matter as spatial extension and location, weight, quantity, and inertia (see also chapter 8). For example, feelings are substances, often fecal substances (Brierley 1937) which, accordingly, may be withheld or expelled and got rid of or destroyed; or they may fill one up and either explode or leak (or spill) out. Or perhaps they are oral substances (milk, poison, vomitus) or other psychosexual things (urine, semen, babies). Feelings for other persons are like ties that may be cut (like umbilical cords or like the sadist's chains) or the feelings for others and of others may be engulfing, suffocating, poisonous, paralyzing, and soul-murdering. The very idea of detachment is concretistic in this way. In primary process thinking, these are not metaphors but actualities (Freud 1915c, 1925b), though they are also the basis of corresponding metaphors in everyday language.

In his struggles to detach himself, the adolescent unconsciously works over these concretized feelings and "influences." Sometimes he hides, conserves, perhaps protects what he values by keeping it "inside." Often he unconsciously imagines that he is expelling threatening feelings and influences into his parents' minds and bodies; in his fight or flight, his blocked reincorporations, and his hypervigilance, he thinks of himself as guarding against the poisons, prisons, and other perilous spaces, places, and substances in the outer world. And, along with his fantasy of ridding himself of his dangerous substances, he will think of himself as being emptied out, disconnected, and perhaps as having lost or thrown away something called a self or identity.

Clearly, this way of thinking cannot be acceptable in any rational, secondary process appraisal of psychological situations and actions and of the changes they undergo. Even though such archaic thinking is widely used as metaphor in the adaptive communications of everyday life, it cannot be used for exact clinical description and interpretation or for rigorous theoretical conceptualization. Rationally, we do not (at least, we should not) ascribe substantiality to actions and situations. We work, or should work, instead to develop conceptions that describe changes in one or another aspect of actions and situations. In this regard, for example, we think of changes of aim and object, and of defensive restriction and revision of those actions that seem to bring about situations of danger.

5. A Clinical Example

Let us consider a clinical illustration of these archaic assumptions about personal action. Its usefulness is not diminished by the fact that chronologically the analysand is past
adolescence. The connection between this example and the
issues of self and identity will emerge shortly.

A young man began an analytic hour with some ruminations
about having exposed himself to a "rip off," owing to his
having left his car keys in the jacket he had left hanging in the
unattended waiting room of my office. He went on to talk about
his increased awareness that he had been blocking enthusiastic
feelings about recent accomplishments in his work, in his self-
awareness and self-regulation, and in his personal relationships. He said that he did not share his feelings, that he was not
really sharing them with the analyst right then and there, while
mentioning these accomplishments and good feelings.

He then reported the following fantasy: *he is standing in
front of a vault in which his feelings are stored; he opens the
door to take out a little and then locks it again to safeguard
them.*

This is an analysand whose infantile history is epitomized by
his having been toilet trained before the age of one. Particularly during his first year of life, he had been handled in such a
controlling way as to predispose him to develop convictions
later in childhood that he had been robbed of his motility,
affectivity, will, and initiative. Thus, especially during the
early years of his analysis, he could not experience desire as
his own action for very long; instead, soon after noting that he
desired something, he would be thinking of it angrily as a demand, usually as one coming from other people, such as the
analyst, but sometimes from the desire itself or from some
organ connected with the expression of the desire, such as his
penis. It appears that besides a relatively austere, over-con-
trolled, and physically undemonstrative mother, he had had
during his first year of life a harshly methodical nursemaid who
did the dirty work of prematurely "domesticating" the baby
boy in the privacy of the nursery.

Considering his fantasy of the vault together with his history, his preceding concern in the hour about being "ripped off," and his comments about enthusiasm, it appeared that he expected to be robbed of his feelings if he did not keep them safe in the vault; he was implying that the analyst would be the immediate robber. (He was implying something more—that he *wished* to be robbed of his feelings—which I shall pass over here.) One may say that in fashioning this fantasy he demonstrated particularly his having unconsciously equated feelings and feces (as money in the bank) and feelings and phallus (as car keys that will be "ripped off"). In effect, he was saying that feeling is substance—contents and organs of the body—and that as substance it can be shared or stolen, unless, of course, it is hidden or locked away inside. The "inside" pertains to the self, which is similarly substantialized as a place of limited access (a vault). But feeling is not substance; enthusiasm is not material; and self has no location and no locks. And so we must go on to consider how we may put into the secondary process language of action the ideas of shared or stolen feelings and of the self as a lockable container.

I suggest that what the analysand called not sharing a feeling or keeping it in a vault is best expressed as follows: he was making sure that he did not act emotionally, or did not act so beyond a certain point; and if he acted emotionally at all, he made sure (as much as he could) that he did so privately, unobservably. In many respects, he carried out these impoverishing, secretive actions unconsciously. Being robbed of a feeling can be stated in one of two ways: either others act so as to interrupt his acting emotionally or he interferes himself. If he acts enthusiastically, others may interfere for the reason that they see their defensive stability threatened by it. Or he may interfere for two reasons: that he would react guiltily to the triumphant oedipal significance of his acting enthusiastically and that he would react anxiously to the grandiose and manic potential of acting that way. In either case, to act enthusiastically would be to create a dangerous situation; consequently he must refrain from acting in that emotional mode. We recognize that ultimately it is he who is the robber and that he is robbing himself and others, including the analyst, not of substance but of opportunities to act and interact in certain ways. As for the vault, it refers to refraining, preventing, and acting secretively or privately rather than to containing and locking.

Our examination of the fantasy of the vault has illustrated the notions of substantiality of feeling and of self. Moreover, it has shown how these notions play an important part in one's misconstruing one's own actions and situation: they support the illusion that actions and their modes and occasions may be dealt with as though they are things or as though they have the properties of things. The illusion is culturally as well as ontogenetically ancient and pervasive, and it has been featured in many theories of mind, including the psychoanalytic, where it appears in a number of forms. In one form it appears as dammed up, bound, transformable, displaceable, and dis-chargeable quantities of psychic energy (see chapter 4, section 5). In another form—now mostly discredited though still quite prevalent—the concretistic illusion appears in the form of the personified psychic structures (id, ego, superego) interacting like the members of a close-knit and turbulent family. We speak not only of psychic energy and psychic structure in this way, but of self and identity as well.

6. Self and Identity: Substances or Abstractions?

These considerations help us understand better the adolescent's experience of emptiness, deadness, and desolation. Almost inevitably, this experience accompanies the adolescent's struggle against emotionality, against identification (Greenson 1954), and against relations with certain people who have become and have remained both emotionally significant to him (constant objects in Mahler's sense) and practically important (especially the contemporary parents with their real powers). Thinking unconsciously that feelings, identifications, and relationships are substances, the adolescent attempts to smash, cut, befoul, shrink, and obliterate them, certainly to expel them by means of real as well as imagined separation; and so, with his feelings and identifications and relationships cast out and destroyed, he comes to think of himself as empty and dead and of the world as desolate, and to feel and behave accordingly; that is, he adopts the dropping-out, rock-bottom, non-negotiable mode of action.

Similarly and concurrently substantialized and placed somewhere in space is the adolescent's notion of who he is—what we and he might call his self, his identity. Thus, he may lose or be searching for an identity; boundaries may dissolve; and one self (a false self) may cover another (a real self) that has been stunted, fragmented, and concealed. Erikson (1950, 1956), Laing (1969a, 1969b), and others will seem to the sensitive and thoughtful adolescent to be talking specifically about him, if not to him.

All of this is subjective experience that has been shaped by primary process thinking and conventional metaphor based on it. It is of the greatest clinical importance to explore these adolescent phenomena, and it is of theoretical importance to conceptualize them. But surely the exploration should not validate the substantialization of actions and situations, and the theory should not use in the explanation itself the experiential terms that are to be explained. Self and identity are not things with boundaries, contents, locations, sizes, forces, and degrees of brittleness. And yet these terms have been used in theoretical discussions as if they refer to things with these properties. Consider for example the following quotations from some recent publications: "during the quasi-prehistoric phase of magic hallucinatory omnipotence, the breast or the bottle belongs to the self" (Mahler 1968, p. 12); "The modification of the archaic idealizing cathexes (their taming, neutralization, and differentiation) is achieved by their passage through the idealized self-objects" (Kohut 1971, p. 43); "The self...is a very individual and originally a very narcissistic structure, whose boundaries can expand and contract more or less at will" (Levin 1970, p. 175); and "the lifelong struggle for dominance between ego and self" (Levin 1970, p. 176).

With the help of discussions by Hartmann, Kris, and Loewenstein (1964), Rapaport (1959, 1967), Gill (1963), Holt (1967), and others, we have learned not to reify id, ego, and superego. But it seems we are reluctant to stop reifying our abstractions. One might go so far as to paraphrase Freud in this regard: where "the ego" was, there shall "the self" or "identity" be.

Does it make sense for us as observers and conceptualizers to use formulations like these, or to say that someone "has" a self or an identity, as if each is a thing that may be had or possessed? Is either self or identity even a consistent phenomenological datum? Is either a fact that may be discovered? My answer to each of these questions is, "No." Self and identity are not facts about people; they are technical ways of thinking about people; and they have become ways in which many people think about themselves. Still they are not outside of and above the realm of self-representation and object representation; each is merely one type of representation or one way of representing. For example, the sense of self-sameness that Erikson emphasizes in connection with identity formation is, in this view, a certain kind of representation, an idea one has about one's being, a way of organizing and giving more meaning to one's subjectivity, a conception of continuity based on recognition or familiarity—and yet empirically self-sameness is usually a rather inconstant experience in that it can change markedly in form and content with a significant change in mood and circumstance. There is, I submit, a claim to unity and stability of self-representation in the way terms of this sort are used or understood that is not supported by observation (cf. Spiegel 1959, esp. pp. 85-88, on self and self-feeling).

Self and identity themselves are changeable. This changeability consists, however, not of alteration of an empirically encountered entity; rather, it consists of the observer's changeable purposes in using these terms. It is the kind of changeability that derives from the fact that self and identity are not names of identifiable homogeneous or monolithic entities; they are classes of self-representations that exist only in the vocabulary of the observer. The self-representations in this class are quite varied in scope, time of origin, and objectivity; many are maintained unconsciously (for example, self as phallus and self as turd), and many remain forever uncoordinated, if not contradictory. When I speak of the changeable observer, I include the changeable self-observer, for at different times one may speak of one's self or identity for different reasons, which means from different vantage points and so with different referents.

Also to be considered in this regard are the many different senses in which "self" words are used to define experience. For example: I hit myself; I hate myself; I'm self-conscious; I'm self-sufficient; I feel like my old self; I'm selfish; my humiliation was self-inflicted; and I couldn't contain myself. Self does not mean exactly the same thing from one of these sentences to the next. It means my body, my personality, my actions, my competence, my continuity, my needs, my agency, and my subjective space. Self is thus a diffuse, multipurpose word; like the pronouns "I" and "me," of which it is after all a variant, self is a way of pointing. In other words, it is a way of saying this or that feature of my being. Consequently, one has always to decide, on the basis of the situational and the verbal context in which the word self is being used at any moment, which aspect of a person is being pointed to; it may, of course, be a comprehensive and complex aspect and it may be *relatively* stable.

We must also note that whatever the situation and context, many people use self to refer essentially to ideas they do not experience as threatening, which is to say ideas they maintain consciously or preconsciously—and comfortably. The case is the same with identity. I think that Hartmann was correct to avoid using self and identity as metapsychological concepts. (For him "the self" meant the organism.) Neither logical analysis nor careful psychoanalytic observation supports or comfortably includes their use as unambiguously systematic terms.

7. SEPARATION-INDIVIDUATION AS A MATTER OF REPRESENTATIONS

If we dispense with self and identity, we can still talk about separation-individuation. With regard to representational differentiation, we can say that, as normal development proceeds, the person (child, adolescent, adult) differentiates self-representations more often, more sharply, and more stably than before. And we can say that the person may organize these differentiated representations into groups and may give them more or less abstract names, such as trait names or even person names. The person may consider some of these groupings in intensely emotional ways—lovingly, hatefully, disgustedly; and the person may endow them with more or less stability of organization and content. Of course, the person effects many of these changes unconsciously, and there is always much that he or she will leave unchanged.

If we restrict ourselves to formulations of this type, that is to say, formulations at some remove from the primary process, we remain both logical and close to observation and practice. We do not use primary process to observe, explain, and formulate propositions about primary process. We do not, for example, use anal theories to explain anal fantasies. And we do not foster those illusions of natural, rightful, and conscious unity of being that tend to be suggested by the terms self and identity. These illusions are precious to many adolescents; in some ways they may even be useful to the adolescent in reordering his or her psychosexual priorities and in exchanging the persons of psychosexual significance. But they are not the terms of sound theory.

8. SELF AND IDENTITY IN FREUDIAN THEORY

Why have self and identity become so popular of late among Freudian analysts?[2]

(1) There has always been a tendency toward reification and personification of terms in Freudian theorizing. With the curb on treating id, ego, and superego in this way, this tendency has been reasserted, like a return of the repressed, in self and identity concepts.

(2) The emphasis on self and identity is a logical development within psychoanalytic ego psychology in that ego psychology has brought the concept of representation to new prominence and importance. It has done so in the investigation of child development and psychosis, and, more generally, in the study of object relations (personal relationships) and the new regard for "external" reality and narcissism entailed by the careful conceptualization of those object relations.

(3) With self-representation and object representation legitimized and ensconced in theory along with considerations of ego autonomy and such ego functions as aim setting and rank ordering (Hartmann 1939b, 1950, 1964; see also chapter 4), a need developed for some concept that would serve two purposes: it would stand for the adaptive, executive, undriven regulating of one's being, and, at the same time, it would not reintroduce the personified ego of earlier theoretical times.

(4) In recent decades particularly, many psychoanalysts have become increasingly dissatisfied with the apparent remoteness, impersonality, and austerity, as well as inordinate complexity, of modern ego psychology. As a result they have developed a heightened and insufficiently critical readiness to

2. I am not referring to the place of these terms in the broad history of ideas and culture, a topic that deserves a long discussion in its own right.

accept and use theoretical concepts that seem to be closer to the subjective experience that is the stuff of actual clinical work. Self and identity appear to be such concepts.

(5) There are now available a number of worthy attempts to introduce self and identity concepts into metapsychology. Identity is prominent, for example, in Jacobson's (1964) *The Self and the Object World,* and self is central to Kohut's (1966, 1971) studies of narcissism. These are attempts by analysts not associated with the overextended psychosocial and ego-autonomous emphases of Erikson and the many authors who outdo him in this respect. But these more orthodox Freudian authors seem not to recognize that once they go beyond self-representation and object representation; once they begin to speak of self or identity as a structure, as a dynamic or forceful psychic organization, as a determinant of behavior and fantasy and feeling: once they make these changes, they are in theoretical trouble. Either they are being redundant in that they should be making only the traditional psychic structures and the principle of multiple function (Waelder 1930) do the work they are also assigning to self and identity, or they are entering a new realm of discourse in which they will have to abandon the particular natural science model of psychoanalytic theory.[3] In the latter regard, the natural science model will have to give way to an altogether different model—a historical, experiential, intentionalistic model; a model in which concepts like force, energy, function, structure, and apparatus will no longer be useful or appropriate; a model that is established through the use of action language.

What I am suggesting comes to this: the popularity of concepts of self and identity is symptomatic of a fundamental shift toward a modern conception of theory making and a modern psychological concern with specifically human phenomenology and with concepts intrinsically related to the psychoanalytic method. Freudian analysis can only benefit from such a shift.

9. Summary and Conclusions

The terms self and identity are quite ambiguous owing to their having been used variously by different authors. Never-

3. Kohut (1971) does show some awareness of this problem but so far has not attempted to deal with it head on.

theless, these two terms now play a large role in general theoretical discussion of interpersonal relations and self-representations, and in specific discussions of separation-individuation. In these discussions, rather than their being viewed as types of representations, self and identity are commonly treated as motivational-structural entities on the order of "the ego," in which regard they suffer the same reification that has afflicted Freud's concepts of psychic structure. Thus, self and identity have been spoken of as though they are spaces, places, substances, agencies, independent minds, forces, and so forth.

In connection with separation-individuation during adolescence—what Freud called detachment from parental authority—and with the help of a clinical example, I argue that adolescents think about self and identity, and the emotions and relationships they imply, in infantile, concretistic, substantialized, or primary process forms. To some extent under the heading of self or identity, psychoanalysts on their part have imported these archaic experiential reports into their general theory, and this has been to the detriment of both their explanatory propositions and their descriptive or phenomenological endeavors. With reference to recent psychoanalytic enthusiasts of self and identity concepts, I contend that they are responding to a serious problem: more and more the particular natural science model of traditional psychoanalytic theoretizing—its metapsychology—seems to be inadequate to deal with contemporary theoretical and empirical concerns. Other models must be developed in its stead. The current usage of self and identity concepts marks a transitional phase in the development of psychoanalytic conceptualization. Action language appears to be a promising next step in this development.

10   The Explanation of Actions*

1. INTRODUCTION

A distinguishing feature of Freud's commitment to conceptualize and explain phenomena in the terms of natural science
is his invoking Newtonian forces to explain the workings of the
psychic apparatus. For Freud, forces move the mind as they
move physical bodies in the environment. He gave formal
recognition to this feature of his thinking by setting up the
psychodynamic point of view, along with the economic and the
structural, as an indispensible constituent of psychoanalytic
explanation.[1]

The psychodynamic point of view has always occupied a
special place in clinical discussion owing to its speaking directly (so it has seemed) to the phenomenon of psychological conflict. This way of thinking seems to capture analysands' reports
of their distressing subjective experiences and behaviors. It
seems so natural, inevitable, and fully warranted as to be hardly a theoretical matter at all.

Beyond doubt, an important place must be given to conflict
in any psychoanalytic language—in action language as in metapsychology. But the assumption that conflict implies or necessi-
tates psychodynamic formulations is another matter entirely and
one that it is my purpose to reject in this chapter. As there is a
family of words more or less closely related to psychodynamics, I
shall review them critically in this connection. This family includes, in addition to psychodynamics, drives, impulses, wishes,
and the id; it also includes motives, dispositions, and intentions,
which can, however, be used in ways that follow the rules of
action language. I shall also point to the relation of these terms
to reasons, meanings, and goal-directedness, the latter being
essential constituents of the idea of action.

*This chapter is a modified version of one portion of "Psychoanalysis without Psy-
chodynamics," which first appeared in the *International Journal of Psycho-analysis*,
55 (1975): 41-55.
1. In "The Ego and the Id" (Freud 1923a), the structural point of view (id, ego, and
superego) replaced the topographic point of view (unconscious, preconscious, and
conscious) for defining the constituent mental systems.

Relying on these discussions as my immediate foundation, I shall then take the stand that references to casuality are inconsistent with psychoanalytic explanation; for logically the ideas cause and psychodynamics imply each other, both of them following from a precommitment to explanation along Newtonian lines. The idea of action is free of these implications. As this part of my argument has obvious crucial consequences for the idea we are to hold of psychoanalysis, I shall return to it and amplify it in chapter 11. This argument's general background has already been presented throughout the preceding chapters, though perhaps especially in chapter 3 on the psychoanalytic vision of reality and chapter 4 on Hartmann's contributions to psychoanalysis; its specific background will be found in chapter 1 in my discussion of rule 1d of action language.

2. Psychodynamic Terms

Psychodynamics means just what it says: the interaction of mental forces. From the psychodynamic point of view, thoughts, feelings, and behavior are to be considered the manifestations and the resultants of these interacting forces. But force is one of those terms that we must now disallow owing to: its being a substantive; its being implicitly personified through having aim and intensity imputed to it; its having a place in theory only on the assumption that phenomena, in order to occur at all, have to be propelled in some way by the forces that are their causes; and its being one kind of entity that eventuates—who knows how?—in another kind of entity,. such as a thought or some other psychological item. In disallowing forces, we also disallow psychodynamics.

In discarding the term psychodynamics, we also disallow such closely related terms as instinctual drive, impulse, psychic energy, discharge, and resultant. And so we seem to be emptying the concept of the id of all its content. However, following a suggestion of Hayman's (1969), which is consistent with the rules of action language, we can retain the important adverbial sense of id (see also Gillespie 1971 on aggression). Specifically, we can understand id to refer to a way of acting: it is a way of acting erotically or aggressively that is more or less infantile in its being irrational, unmodulated, unrestrained, heedless of consequences and contradiction, thoroughly egocentric, and more than likely associated with those vivid and diffuse physiological processes that fall under the common heading of excitement or arousal.

We shall of course, continue to note and emphasize the fact that many of the actions involved in the id mode of behaving are usually performed unconsciously. We shall also continue to emphasize the ways in which people attend to, intensify, define, and adapt to pleasurable and painful bodily stimuli, above all to those stimuli issuing from, or based on, the anatomy and physiology of the erogenous zones and musculature as well as those associated with acting emotionally in certain respects. Additionally, we shall continue to be concerned steadily with the history of each person's dealings with these stimuli and with any irrational repetitiveness he or she displays in this regard.

The idea of the wish is a crucial referent of the more general idea of the id, although as I have argued elsewhere (1968a), to be consistently metapsychological, we must attribute wishes to each of the psychic structures. In the present scheme, we shall retain the ideas *to wish* and *wishing*, for they refer to a most important kind of action. But we shall not speak of *the* wish as an active, propulsive entity of force; nor shall we say that a person *has* a wish. We shall say simply, just as we often say in our informal discussions, that the analysand wished this or that, and that he or she did or did not engage in further actions to realize what was wished for.

My continuing concern with preserving and enhancing Freud's fundamental discoveries should be plain from my having said just this much about wishing, about action in the infantile and unconscious modes, and about the experiential history of bodily stimuli. In no way does it follow that, in abandoning the Newtonian idea of psychodynamics and the terms it implies, we are bound to neglect the person's preoccupation with, and experiencing of, bodily happenings. But now we are required to view the preoccupation and experiencing as yet other forms of action, though indeed crucial ones.

3. "Motive" and Motivation Terms

Motive. Generally speaking, the term motive is taken to be a dynamic concept. Like instinctual drive, motive is used to imply an agent-like propulsive entity existing and acting in some kind of mental space. For we do speak of *a* motive, *the* motive, *underlying* motives, *having* or *lacking* a motive, *weak* motives, and *hierarchies* of motives. Motive is also used to imply a force whose application eventuates inexplicably in manifestations or resultants that are qualitatively different from it, such as thoughts, emotions, and performances. When we use motive in these ways, we impose three conditions on our thinking about the relevant phenomena: that we must speak in terms of substantives (thought, emotion, behavior), that we must treat each of these substantives as an entity distinct from the others, and that we must understand these entities to exist only as expressions or consequences of underlying motives. The motive is set up as a necessary influential entity that exists apart from and prior to thoughts, emotions and deeds. However, there are a number of other senses in which motive is used. The following are outstanding examples of these.

Resolutions. Motive is sometimes used in the sense of resolution. Certainly, people do frequently resolve consciously, preconsciously, or unconsciously to think only certain thoughts, feel only certain emotions, and perform only certain deeds. But to say this is merely to designate a type of action people may perform and a way in which they think about action; it does not establish the point that a resolution or set of resolutions is a necessary instigator of every action. To accept resolutions as this set of motivational preconditions of action is to commit oneself to the mechanistic language we are seeking to reject. To resolve to do something is not yet to do it; it is to decide to do it, to plan it, to make some sort of promise to oneself to carry it out. Thus, the action of resolving is distinct from the action of performing that which one has resolved to do, and its predictive value, as we know so well, remains uncertain.

Reasons. Sometimes, however, motive is used to mean the reason for an action, which is to say the meaning or goal by which an action may be defined. Then, motive is not set apart and viewed as a propulsive agency. With this use of motive one would not now need to quarrel; for it is consistent with the rules of action language. But motive is not the best word for the purpose in that, being a substantive itself, it lends itself all too easily to psychodynamic types of propositions. The danger of poor usage is not a strong argument, but neither is it without merit; for what is poor usage from a systematic standpoint is a commonplace of the everyday language of dynamic explanation, the result being that it is especially difficult to use motive only as a technical word. And we do have the words, reasons, meanings, and goals, words that are relatively free of these unacceptable connotations and consequences of mechanistic assumptions, both popular and metapsychological. Though they, too, are substantives, we commonly use them to refer to the actions of people viewed as agents; in line with this usage they do not suggest influences on action that are distinct from them, prior to them, and propelling them from behind or below.

Dispositions and Inclinations. Another use of motive is one that conveys the idea of disposition. In its narrowest sense, disposition refers only to a noteworthy degree of regularity in a person's actions. It is a way of saying, "Given this situation, this person may be expected to do this or that, or to do it in this or that way." Disposition is an observational term, available also to the person as self-observer. Far from designating actions and modes of action, it merely specifies their regularity. It is better, therefore, to say disposition when that's what we mean and to reserve motive, if we do so at all, for descriptive and explanatory purposes. Understood in its narrow sense, disposition is easily accommodated within action language. It is, however, not uncommon to encounter disposition used as a motivation term, with conceptual confusion as the result.

In many instances, what goes for disposition also goes for inclination: "He has this disposition" and "He is inclined that way" say essentially the same thing. In other instances, however, inclination refers only to a momentary readiness to act a certain way.

Functions and Mechanisms. In metapsychology, definite functions have been assigned to each of the psychic structures, above all to the ego. These functions are designated on varied levels of abstractness and from varied points of view. Relatively specific cognitive functions (perceiving, remembering) are referred to along with very general ones (reality-testing, synthesis). Some functions, such as defense, have a more definite psychodynamic ring to them. It is my contention that each function word is a psychodynamic word in biological (adaptational) clothing; for each is referred to as an agent-like influence on behavior, as when the ego's synthetic function is said to determine certain mental performances; also, some functions are referred to as parties to conflict, as when ego functions are said to stand in opposition to id impulses (e.g., drive-defense conflicts). It is metapsychologically inconsistent not to ascribe wishing to the ego and superego structures, the result being logically confused propositions to the effect that *functions* of these structures oppose the *wishes* of the id. And especially in chapter 4 of the present book, I pointed out the disadvantages for psychoanalytic conceptualization that reside in the biological adaptation language.

In connection with the function of defense, the term mechanism also appears as a disguised motivation term. For however formalistically we may define the mechanisms of defense, we somehow present them anthropomorphically as motivational agencies that stand guard, oppose, repel, succumb, etc. In this we seem to be relying on a vague analogy to homeostatic mechanisms being triggered by somatic signals of various kinds; but this resort merely obscures rather than eliminates the psychodynamic presuppositions that inhere in the idea of mechanism. And if it is "the ego" that is said to oppose "the drives," the problem of psychodynamic language has merely been shifted to another ground.

Both functions and mechanisms are easily restated as actions: for example, to perceive, to remember, to synthesize, to test reality, and to defend. Adverbial forms of these ideas are, of course, also available to us: for example, to perceive realistically and to remember defensively.

Intention and Intentionality. Some authors invoke intention and intentionality as nonmechanistic, nonorganismic, purely psychological motivation terms. Intention presents no problem for action language when it is used to designate consciously formulating resolutions or reasons for, or goals of, action. In these instances it is clear that one is referring not to propulsive entities but to meaningful actions. "She intended to get there on time" is a way of saying, "She planned and was ready to take pains to get there on time." "His intentions were honorable" is a way of saying, "He acted honorably." In this connection we can easily use the verb *to intend* and the adverb *intentionally*. (This is the sense in which Hartmann appeared to use "intentionality" as one of the ego's functions: see chapter 4, section 5). Like disposition, however, intention often gets to be used as a propulsive motivation term, that is, as some influence that is distinct from the action and prior to it. Usually, the intention is already implied in the designation of the action in question. For example, "She spoke intelligently," would ordinarily state her intention well enough; to insist that she *had to* intend to speak intelligently before she *could* do so, would amount to practicing another form of psychodynamic explanation. In some instances, however, one might first decide to speak in a certain way before doing so; then we can properly say the intending preceded the speaking intelligently or emphatically or whatever.

When we turn to intentionality, however, the case is different and far more difficult. Intentionality does get to be used as the general term for specific actions of intending to do this or that, in which respect it seems unobjectionable. But this is confusing in that the term intentionality has a long and complex history within philosophical psychology and phenomenology, and its role within this history has little or nothing to do with specific actions of intending to do one thing or another, as discussed above. Suffice it to say that intentionality, interpreted philosophically, implies the proposition that every mental act "intends" an object, by which is meant that a mental act must necessarily be directed toward (or onto) something other than itself and so requires a specific "intentional" object (not in the sense of a thing) for it to be what it is. For Brentano (1874), intentionality was a way of defining mental phenomena as distinct from physical phenomena. It is not a casual framework for explaining actions in general; it is a priori or definitional rather than empirical. The project of discovering the motive of an action, which has been an essential aspect of psychoanalysis as an empirical psychology, can have little to do with this established sense of intentionality.

With this I conclude my brief survey of key motivation terms and psychodynamic terms. For the most part these terms are either inherently inconsistent with the rules of action language or are so in usual discourse. Although some are compatible with these rules, they are either too narrow (intention) or not within the same frame of reference (disposition); and some of them are essentially irrelevant and confusing when used as motivation words (intentionality, function).

We are left with a hard question. If we give up the idea of psychodynamic causes or motivational preconditions of actions, what happens to explanation? Is it enough simply to name actions and their modes through the right selection of verbs and adverbs? Is this selection really simple? Or, to put it differently, how shall we now usefully answer psychological why-questions? Why this action and not that, or this mode and not that? To these questions we shall now turn.

4. WHY-QUESTIONS AND THE EXPLANATION OF ACTIONS

In what sense have we used traditional motivation words to tell us why? The answer, contrary to all appearances, is that we have not used them to designate causes. Instead, we have used them to restate psychological observations in the terms of a particular set or system of language rules; that is to say, we have used them for technical or systematic translation. The traditional motivation words (psychodynamics, underlying motives) have enabled us to constitute data within a particular philosophical universe. They have served as tools in our effort to make human phenomena more comprehensible because more ordered, internally consistent, and comparable in their rendition.

Freud thought it was necessarily a matter of translating phenomena into the language of the laboratory science of his day; this is how we must understand his statement of theoretical objectives that I quoted in the opening section of chapter 1. But, strictly speaking, as I have already argued, there are no phenomena accessible to us in which the subject has not already played a part. The very statement of these phenomena must already subscribe to some language rules, rules that establish the kind of reality within which phenomena may be stated. Ordinarily, we fail to realize that this is so. One main reason for this failure is this: in our everyday speech, which is the speech we use to designate so-called phenomena, we are so eclectic, vague, and ambiguous in our philosophical assumptions that we confuse ourselves and seem to be seeing phenomena as though they were accessible without mediation, that is, as prior to and independent of some rendition of them, and which therefore seem to stand there innocently open to multiple approaches. But this is illusion. There are no virginal phenomena.

The language rules for which the traditional motivation words are peculiarly well suited are those of a mechanical universe governed by casual interplays of forces, as described in Newtonian physics, and of a subhuman universe governed by the biological struggle for survival, as described in Darwinian biology. According to the Newtonian view, nothing would change were it not for the application of forces (inertia: what moves will continue moving; what is at rest will remain so); it presents the person as machine. According to the Darwinian, it is the survival value of drives, functions, adaptations, and suchlike that is of paramount causal importance; it presents the person as brute organism. In earlier chapters, I have already suggested other reasons for the extraordinary appeal of these problematic conceptions—which, anyway, are nowadays recognized to be fruitful only in connection with certain aspects of mechanical systems and organic life.

Consequently, to say that we have used motivation words to tell us why, is to say that we have stated actions and their modes in terms of a physicochemical and biological system of some kind. It has been merely one (eclectic) way of going about the job of making actions intelligible or more intelligible than they have been. There are other ways. One might, for example, state these same actions and modes dispositionally. Thus, instead of saying, "His motive for cheating on his tax return was greed," one might say, "He is disposed to acquire wealth even if it means cheating, as in the instance of his tax return." In the latter form, instead of any underlying propulsive motive-entity, reference is made only to a certain observed and anticipated regularity of action. There is a gain in intelligibility, though it is a modest one. It is, for example, a piece of an explanation to answer the question, "Why did he take offense?" with "That's the way he is"; people do often settle for just this much of an explanation.

Action language is yet another alternative to the use of traditional motivation terms. In its terms one might say, "He cheated greedily in making out his tax return." Now, simply stating the mode of the action, *greedily*, gives its reason at least as well as the word *greed* names a motive or determinant. (In this case, the question of disposition is left open.) Adopting these alternatives, one does not give up trying to understand and explain human activity systematically. The only question is how one is to do it, that is, what rules one is to follow and how.

The two sets of rules with which we are most concerned here are those that center around causes and those that center around reasons. One must ask, therefore, how the ideas of causes and reasons differ from one another and how, if at all, they are related to one another. I shall deal with these questions, which have been discussed and debated at great length by philosophers and social scientists, only in terms of action language.

In saying why, one is restating particular actions and their corresponding situations so as to make the events in question *Wittgenstein* more comprehensible to the questioner, who may be oneself. By asking why-questions, people indicate that they want the action in question to be restated in line with another set of interests than that which dictated the initial statement of the action and situation. They may be not yet satisfied with the vantage point from which they are viewing the action and its situation; they may be not yet satisfied with the statement of the action and situation relative to the vantage point they already occupy; or they may be not yet satisfied that the matter is being defined on the proper or most useful level of abstractness. As a rule, the answer wanted entails a shift of conceptual organization such that the action to be explained is subsumed under some other term; but that other term need not be a more abstract term; thus an apparently aggressive action may be explained as a sexual one with no change in level of abstractness. Corresponding to the wide range of interests in terms of which one may raise why-questions, there are many ways— perhaps innumerable ways—of stating any action and its situation. Elsewhere (1968b, pp. 161-70), I have shown how this is the case for traditional designations of motives, too.

Consider, for example, the following schematic sequence of statement(S), question as to reason(Q), and answer(A):

S: The boy made fun of the girl when she sat down to urinate.

Q: Why did he do that?

A: Upon being confronted by the genital difference between himself and the girl, he thought anxiously of his being castrated, and by ridiculing the girl as defective, he avoided thinking consciously, fearfully, and excitedly of this frightening eventuality. That is why.

Here, the answer to the why-question restates what the boy was doing from the vantage point of "castration anxiety" as a reason. The questioner might just as well ask, "What is that boy doing, laughing at the girl like that?" or, what does the same job, "What reason has that boy to laugh like that at the girl?"—to which the answer is, "He is avoiding thinking consciously, fearfully, and excitedly of his being castrated himself. That is what he is doing, or that is his reason."

Here is a second example:

S: He was impotent when he attempted sexual intercourse.

Q: Why?

A: Unconsciously, he viewed intercourse as a filthy and destructive invasion of his mother's womb, and still unconsciously, he anticipated that he would react in a most painfully guilty and self-destructive way to his performing that action; not being in a predominantly genital sexual situation and intimate personal relationship, and not being engaged in sexual actions in a predominantly unthreatened, exciting, and pleasurable mode, he did not perform potently. That is why. These are his reasons.

Here, the reasons for his impotence are established by restating the action and situation as being unconsciously incestuous in an anal-sadistic and guilt-provoking mode. The reasons given state what we might designate, in our loose way of speaking, as what he was "really" doing, in which case we are using the word "really" to indicate that, as psychoanalysts, we are satisfied with the type and degree of intelligibility we have achieved through this restatement of the action and situation in question. Degrees of reality or all-or-none conclusions about reality are not in question; at least, they need not be.

In this approach, we rely on reasons—reasons that are, in essence, redescriptions that make actions comprehensible. We do not rely on causes—causes that are the conditions regularly antecedent to the actions in question. Causes are the conditions in the absence of which the specific action would not be performed and in the presence of which it must be performed. Moreover, the idea of cause makes sense only with respect to the description of antecedent conditions *by an independent, objective observer engaged in a particular project.* In contrast, in a psychology of action, these "causes" can exist only as the agent's reasons, which are features of his or her personal world of meaning and goals. To put it in terms closer to metapsychology: it is how the person represents these "causes" unconsciously, as well as preconsciously and consciously, that is the decisive consideration for psychoanalytic understanding and explanation; in other words, what counts in psychoanalysis are the causes as they appear in an individual's world. To seek the causes of these representations only leads to further issues of individual representation, so that causes forever elude one's grasp while reasons of every kind fill one's hands.

reasons

As if this infinite regress of causes were not enough, there is the additional and equally conclusive consideration that we psychoanalysts cannot rightly claim to establish casuality through our investigations in any rigorous and untrivial sense of that term. Control, prediction, mathematical precision are beyond our reach, for we are not engaged in the kind of investigation that can yield these results; fundamentally, we are always looking backward, not forward. Under the banner of "scientific psychoanalysis," we have devoted ourselves to untenable casual language when all the while we have been manifesting our unexceptionable commitment to understand as fully as possible the course and problems of individual human development. In this latter endeavor we set a splendid example for all psychological investigators of these matters.

5. Translating Psychodynamics into Action Language

In the next chapter I shall return to the fundamental issues of casuality and determinism in relation to action language. For the present, however, I want to present some further translations, with running commentary, of psychodynamic language into action language. My doing so expresses both my appreciation of how much is at stake in revising the terms of psychodynamic propositions and my recognition that seemingly simple psychodynamic statements imply or entail a heavy commitment to the traditional modes of thought that are now in question. It is especially important to make clear the consequences of these revisions for our thinking in the clinical psychoanalytic situation. The few exercises in translation that follow are intended to make explicit the complex nature of the changes that I am proposing.

(1) "His repression of this dangerous impulse was too weak to prevent it from gaining consciousness." To effect a translation, we have to speak of repression as an action in a certain mode rather than as a mechanism with structural and energic attributes (see chapter 11 for an extended discussion of the issues involved). Also, we have to speak of the impulse as a would-be or conditional action, that is, an action that the person is refraining from taking and would take under other circumstances. We can no longer attribute to the impulse the power of gaining consciousness or, indeed, of gaining anything at all. And we have to speak of consciousness as a mode of engaging in the action of thinking, i.e., consciously. Thus, the translation might read, "By failing to be sufficiently on guard about not doing so, he thought consciously of the action that he wished to perform and would have performed had he not deemed it too dangerous to do so."

(2) "The conflict between her id and ego was so evenly balanced as to cause a paralysis of thought, affect, and behavior." This translation we must work out slowly and carefully. First, we have to understand the id to be a term for a class of actions and modes of action. Next, we have to understand the ego to be a term for another such class, one that is not characterized, as the id class is, by acting erotically and aggressively in the excited, diffusely physical, impulsive, egocentric, irrational, self-contradictory, and hazardous manner in which young children often act. Further, we must realize that older children and especially adults do not ordinarily think about or perform the id class of actions and modes of action either consciously or preconsciously. I need not detail the characteristics of the ego class or review the ways in which these and other classes co-constitute actions. This co-constituting of actions is Waelder's "principle of multiple function" (1930) stated in nonstructural

terms. Finally, we have to translate into action terms the substantives *paralysis, thought, affect,* and *behavior.*

Thus, the translation might read, "She behaved in a mentally paralyzed fashion; she did not think or perform any other actions in any other mode. (Putting it this way implies that behaving as though paralyzed is necessarily an action in a certain mode.) She behaved neither in terms of her already personally defined id class nor in terms of her already defined ego class of actions and modes of action. (Both classes could be detailed according to her specific psychological situation.) Having accepted neither class of actions alone and having recognized no satisfactory way of integrating or compromising them, she resorted to a new action: she remained utterly immobile."

Then, in a necessary clinical extension of this set of points, we should, so far as possible, go on to define the id-type and ego-type of reasons for her new action—her behaving as though paralyzed. We should do so because it is a logical consequence of using action language to do so; for now every action must be located within the realm of reasons. In this we would be proceeding in parallel with our use of traditional metapsychology; for it is a logical consequence of that language that every psychological process or phenomenon must be located within the realm of psychic determinism or psychodynamics. In both cases, we are properly concerned with following the rules of a language; we are not concerned with observations that are simply given.

(3) "He can't control his sexual drive." First, we have to undo the isolation of the idea of sexual drive from the idea of the person. This isolation results from our conceiving of sexuality as a propulsive entity which, though it is somehow "his," is not his doing in the same sense that his controlling efforts are his doing. In action language, we must state both of them as his doing. (This is just what we do in good clinical interpretations, whatever the words we use.) In chapter 7, I discussed a variety of isolations of this sort under the heading *disclaimed actions.* We commonly encounter disclaimed actions in such familiar utterances of analysands as "The impulse overwhelmed me" and "I have this compulsion." Next, we have to recognize that the idea of control follows from our having accepted this dis-

claimed version of sexuality; for in this instance control can only mean performing the action of refraining from taking certain sexual actions. That the person is implicated in both types of action—the sexual and the refraining—is obscured by the customary use of the word control. Additionally, we must appreciate that "can't" is a hypothetical inability-word that is often used carelessly or defensively in place of the more exact and simple descriptive words "don't" and sometimes "won't" (see chapter 11, section 2). The idea that one is powerless is a common variation of the inexact word "can't."

Thus, the translation of this psychodynamic sentence might read as follows: "He continues to act sexually even though he also wishes he did not do so (or rebukes himself for doing so)." Or it might read like this: "He acts sexually (e.g., by fantasying, masturbating, seducing) despite his also engaging in refraining counteractions in that very regard (e.g., by taking cold showers, praying, punishing himself)." Or it might read: "He readily engages in sexual actions even when he knows it would be wise not to do so."

(4) "In the resolution of the oedipus complex, the child's incestuous wishes must be renounced." First, we must reject the isolation of the idea of the oedipus complex or the idea of incestuous wishes from the idea of the child's actions. Also we must change the passive voice to the active in order not to leave the agent of renunciation indefinite; for it is only by using the active voice that we unquestionably require there to be a specific author of the action in question. This translation might then read, "In ceasing to act oedipally, the child no longer regards its parents in an intensely sexual and rivalrous way." We might then go on to detail how the child accomplishes this remarkable feat, for example, by repressing, identifying, reversing, and displacing, and by consistently condemning any overt act or conditional act through which he or she might regard the parents in this now frightening and objectionable light.

So much for illustrations. I have not presented them as final, all-purpose translations of key formulations. I have used them to suggest the kinds of critical considerations and alternatives with which one would be concerned in attempting to work within the rules of action language. It is perhaps needless to mention that no translation can be exact; translation is also transformation, and something must be given up in the process of transformation, as analysts know all too well. But this is not to imply that translation necessarily entails devastating and irremediable loss or discontinuity. Translation may also be extension of significance through exploration and discovery.

6. COSMOGONY AND PHENOMENOLOGY IN FREUD'S EXPLANATIONS

It would be remiss to conclude my discussion of the explanation of actions without mentioning two additional significant and problematic types of answers to which Freud resorted in this connection (see also G.S. Klein, 1969 and Holt 1972). In this I shall be brief, though the ideas deserve extended discussion. I mention them chiefly to indicate that there is more to Freud's mode of theorizing than relying explicitly on his esteemed physicochemical and biological language—for mind in general, for motivation or psychodynamics in particular. The two approaches in question have remained neither well integrated with his basic (eclectic) language nor adequately developed in their own proper terms.

One approach may be called cosmogonic. According to it, in the beginning all is chaos, and only some remarkable transformation of primal chaotic "stuff" into more advanced "stuff," and even into enduring structure, brings progress, order, and stability into mental life. This cosmogonic view is tangential to the biological, evolutionary view. That Freud always valued it highly is implied in his basic proposition that mental life starts with instinctual drives, the id and the primary process. In this context, to explain why is to invoke the unstable emergence from primal chaos. Freud's few suggestive remarks about congenital ego variations, significant though they are, are incompatible with his cosmogony and hardly have a place in his general theory, though subsequently much has been made of them by certain theoreticians, notably the Hartmann-Kris-Loewenstein group and Rapaport. It is doubtful that Freud could have systematically developed this cosmogonic approach as such. Chaos cannot "experience" or "learn." In recent years, however, some Freudian analysts have instructively revised and refined this approach and incorporated it within one or

another type of developmental and interpersonal perspective
on the mother-infant relationship (e.g., Winnicott 1958, 1965;
Loewald 1960; Mahler 1968).

The other approach may be called phenomenological. It is
evident in Freud's basic ideas about psychic reality and danger
situations. In this context, to explain why is to invoke as full a
picture as possible of one's subjective version of one's life situation and one's actions in it. Here, mind is distinctively human
mind, and, on that account, psychoanalytic authors are inclined to subsume it under "Freud's clinical theory," in contrast to his "scientific metapsychology." It should be clear by
now that this designation is hasty, confused, and utterly misleading; for tacitly the word clinical is being used as a synonym
of human. "Clinical theory" means the terms suitable for making interpretations to human beings about what they are doing.
Freud never recognized and developed this potentially fruitful
phenomenological alternative as far as it would have been
possible to do so. In his evocative but unsystematic way, Winnicott is one of those Freudian analysts who have made notable
and illuminating attempts along this line. Like Erikson, he
humanizes psychoanalytic explanation; he keeps his theory
close to his clinical interpretations. The action language I have
been presenting is, in one of its main aspects, a further development of this alternative, though in other terms.

7. CONCLUSION

Using action language, one no longer explains behavior and
mental processes in terms of the forces of psychodynamics or
the influence of underlying motives. Instead, one answers why-
questions in terms of reasons. Essentially, in giving reasons for
particular actions, that is, in explaining them, one restates
these actions in a way that makes them more comprehensible.
A reason is either another vantage point from which to view
and define an action and its context or a statement more consistent with an existing vantage point. It may involve a shift to
another level of abstraction for the designation of actions. The
new designation serves interests other than those which dictated the initial version of the action in question. This kind of
explanation continues to set forth significant features of the
analysand's psychic reality. *In this view, the traditional distinc-*

tion between description and explanation is discarded.

This alternative language does the same type of explanatory job that psychic determinism and other physicochemical and biological language rules are supposed to do. It establishes an orderly universe of propositions concerning the definition, description, and interrelationships of psychological phenomena or "psychic reality," now viewed as actions in various modes. Consequently, to urge a psychoanalysis without psychodynamics is not to promote chaos in the sense of an end to understanding and explanation; it is to develop an alternative mode of understanding and explanation. This mode is, in fact, the true mode of psychoanalytic interpretation, what I call its native tongue (see especially chapters 3 and 16). In clinical analysis, it is the interpretation of development, present experience, and disturbance of functioning as action, especially action performed unconsciously, that makes transformative and remedial action both conceivable and possible for the analysand. By definition, the impersonal forces of psychodynamics would have to remain forever beyond the human analysand's reach; indeed, the idea of these forces establishes a world in which there never could be an analysand.

11   The Idea of Resistance*

> The resistance accompanies the treatment step by step. Every single association, every act of the person under treatment must reckon with the resistance and represents a compromise between the forces that are striving toward recovery and the opposing ones which I have described. Freud (1912, p. 103).

1. INTRODUCTION

There is no part of clinical analytic work that is more exacting than the analysis of resistance and no part of giving training in analytic technique with respect to which one has to be more vigilant. It is a hotbed of concealed hostility and, as such, stimulates much negative countertransference. It bars the way to the analysis of significant life-historical material and even to its own analysis (the resistance against the analysis of resistance). Further, resistance cancels out the emotional impact, the sense of relevance, and the potentially lasting consequences of the most penetrating, well-founded, and historically integrative interpretations of transference. On top of which the resistance stops the analysand from putting into practice the understanding he or she has gained through analytic work, tending instead to foster repetitive acting out.

Yet what exactly is the resistance? The idea of resistance seems to include so much—the defenses, drives, character traits, ego attitudes of defiance and desperate opposition to change, even transference—that it seems hardly distinguishable from the totality of the analysis itself. Wilhelm Reich's great work on character-analysis (1933), which centers on the analysis of character resistance, must leave one with exactly this impression: once the character resistances have been analyzed, what *really* remains to be analyzed? We should insist that a technical concept that takes in everything is no concept at all.

The present chapter is an attempt to clarify and in some use-

*This chapter is a modified version of an article first published in *The International Journal of Psycho-Analysis*, 54 (1973): 259-85.

ful way delimit the concept of resistance. If successful, it can only further our comprehension of the clinical process of analysis generally as well as sharpen our technique for analyzing resistance. But, though this chapter implies a great deal about the process and technique of analysis, it is primarily an essay on the idea of resistance.

I venture to add that, at this point in the history of our discipline, there may no longer be much sense in the goal of a definitive, unitary treatment of any major psychoanalytic topic as it stands at any one time. A linear, synthesized exposition of what it is all about may be suitable for certain mathematical proofs and physical experiments. And while it has been the psychoanalytic tradition to write as if that kind of exposition were also suitable for our discussions and reports, the fact is that our writings, both clinical and theoretical, have always really been presentations of one or more ways of getting to know about something in a useful psychoanalytic way; or else they have been review articles summarizing a number of such ways. We have lived with heterogeneity for a long time. The justification for my venturing to make these remarks lies in the diversity of impressive discussions of many single topics in the psychoanalytic literature, and in there being for me, at least, no evidence that a final, static synthesis of this diversity is conceivable, let alone desirable.

Let me therefore say that, in exploring the idea of resistance, I shall be taking four approaches to it. They are the only ones I presently feel able to discuss profitably in relation to action language, and though they are interrelated in various ways and are harmonious in spirit, they are not conceptual coordinates. I allow that other approaches might add whole new perspectives and perhaps even present the entire reconceptualization in a new light.

I present the four parts of this lengthy study under these headings: a logical and linguistic approach to the concept of resistance; the concept of self-deception; resisting maternal authority; and negative and affirmative language in psychoanalytic propositions. In the first I shall argue that resistance refers to an action that is best described in action language. In the second I shall argue that the concept of self-deception is the key to understanding all defensive activity, of which resistance is a major instance, and that it is best conceptualized as faultily observing one's own actual or conditional actions. In the third I shall argue that Freud approached resistance in a patriarchal manner, which is the way he approached model building in general, and that we have yet to develop systematically the place of the mother in the concept of resistance (see also Schafer 1974a). In the last part I shall attempt to advance the under-standing of resistance beyond its predominantly negative sense of defiance and omission on to a number of affirmative senses; I shall try to show that these affirmations must be understood and interpreted before we can have a sound action theory of resistance and a firm base for its most productive clinical application.

2. A Logical and Linguistic Approach to Resistance

I am going to present a series of logical and linguistic argu-ments concerning the concept of resistance. In particular, I shall examine certain assumptions associated with this concept and certain uses to which it has been put. Although in the course of setting forth these arguments I shall refer to the method and data of clinical psychoanalysis, I shall focus pri-marily on logical and linguistic considerations. In this way I shall progressively delineate certain fundamental and unre-solved problems in the traditional Freudian mode of concep-tualization, and I shall be able to present the outlines of an-other specific mode that seems to be less problematic. As has been the case in preceding chapters, this alternative mode is organized around the concept of action, and I shall set forth its nature while clarifying the concept of resistance; the two jobs must be done together.

(1) *"The resistance."* Freud frequently referred to "the re-sistance," and he spoke of it as doing this or that (1912, 1913a, 1914). For purposes of systematic thinking, we may set aside this substantive approach to what is, after all, an activity of a person. To do otherwise is to include a personifying or reifying metaphorical mode of thinking within what can be a more directly stated theory. This is so because to say that "the re-sistance" does anything at all is to imply the existence of an independent agency or entity with aims, strategies, cognitive functions, and meanings of its own; thus it is to set up a mind within the mind—and an oppositional mind at that! It must be

noted that thinking of resistance in this reified way carries over modes of thought concerning instinctual drives, defenses, and the major psychic structures, which, though generally accepted, prove on examination to be based on fundamentally archaic metaphors. Certainly we shall have to speak of conflict one way or another, but would it not be well to have an alternative to reification? I shall return to this point soon.

It is logical and direct to approach the concept of resistance through its verb form: to resist. This is to say that there is an action which may be approached under the heading "resisting." This action approach avoids the implicit archaisms of the substantive approach. Immediately, however, one must attempt to say who or what might be the subject of this verb and who or what might be its object.

Let us consider its object first. Is the object of "to resist" the analyst's pressure? In psychic reality, of course, it is the analyst's pressure that is resisted; but it is not only that, as we also take into account the resister's opposing much of what he or she wishes unconsciously. And yet, objectively, the analyst is not making demands or exerting pressure. That the analysand has entered into an agreement with the analyst from the first to abide by the fundamental rule does not, strictly speaking, amount to yielding to a demand or submitting to pressure. Consequently, the analyst's activity is not the appropriate object of the verb "to resist." We understand that, in seeming to resist the analyst, the analysand is acting fearfully, wishfully, defiantly, in identification with others, or what have you, and so in our work we press our inquiry beyond the answer that subjectively, even if not objectively, the analysand is resisting the analyst's pressure.

In developing this thesis, it is permissible to ignore both countertransference demands and the many psychoanalytic views of the analyst's proper objective position that differ from the classical Freudian ones. When countertransference is carried into interventions, it constitutes a departure from the psychoanalytic method; consequently, for systematic purposes, we may ignore it. In the Freudian situation, as systematically defined, the analyst and the analysand have agreed on the procedure as a method of therapy. They both understand that this therapy has been requested by the analysand and that this procedure requires of the analyst only that he or she listen and interpret in the interest of helping the analysand achieve increased comprehension of his or her life history, and especially of his or her psychological difficulties in this life-historical context. They expect that, on the strength of that increased comprehension, the analysand will be able to live in a more beneficial and less painful and hampered manner than before. Moreover, as the analysis proceeds, the analysand increasingly realizes that there is a reciprocal influence between increasing one's comprehension and changing oneself psychologically. The analysand also realizes that, as there are many areas with which the analytic work deals, one may not expect thoroughgoing coordination of the processes of comprehension and change. In contrast, when the analyst introduces other methods into the analytic situation, he or she is likely to be introducing implicit, if not explicit, demands on the analysand. For example, exuberant friendliness on the analyst's part will introduce such demands (not really or not simply "transference gratifications"). Thus, in the terms of the traditional systematic definition of the psychoanalytic method, one may say this: that since objectively the analyst makes no demands on the analysand, therefore the analyst's pressure cannot be the actual object of the verb "to resist," except when he or she departs from the proper technical position, as in manifest countertransference activity or unanalytic technical innovations.

Sometimes one encounters the proposition that it is the analytic process that the analysand is resisting. Freud spoke of analysis as a process that is set going by the analyst and then takes its own course (1913a, p. 130). But this is only a manner of speaking, for, in using it, one is personifying the abstract concept of process in much the same way that one might personify other abstractions, say fate, love, or history, and in the same way that one might speak of "the resistance," as I mentioned earlier. Logically, the analysand can only resist specific pressures that are among the complex and extended series of interactions that constitute the analytic process. One cannot resist the process itself. To say that one can do so is to commit what Ryle (1949) called a category mistake, i.e., it would be equivalent to saying of a college student that he or she is "taking college" rather than certain specific courses the taking of which constitutes the more abstract category "going to college."

And so, having ruled out the analyst and the process, we nominate next the drive as the object of the verb "to resist." Again, however, we must contend with the hazard of personification, for only by personifying the idea of drive do we give it any sense in *human* psychology. I mean that, before drive can be what we assert it to be, we must attribute mind to it. This is so because we cannot think of a drive without imputing an aim to it, and, in any useful sense of the term "aim," it means both cognitive activity and cognitive content of some complexity. This is so even in the case of the simplest so-called drive and its expression or gratification; for to speak at all of the expression or gratification of a drive, in the sense of an empowered aim, is necessarily to imply that drive activity is constituted in essential ways by consideration of occasions, circumstances, and other interests and methods. However, without personification, it cannot be the aim that sets itself, maintains itself, expresses itself or estimates its own gratification, even in the sense of reduction of the intensity or so-called energy with which it is "charged" or "invested"; nor can these operations be carried out by the drive's quantitative or empowering aspect. And yet aim and quantity are the two identifying characteristics of drive. One arrives at the conclusion that, for an action language, such words as "drive" and "impulse" will not do as the objects of the verb "to resist" (see also chapter 7, section 4, and chapter 10).

I propose, finally, the person as the object of the verb "to resist." We would then say that it is the person who is the aim-setter, aim-holder, context-grasper, gratification-estimator, etc. By "the person" I mean no more than is designated by such pronouns as I, she, and you. Although I realize that many philosophical problems concerning personal identity remain to be dealt with in this regard, as a matter of procedure I think it permissable to set "the person" as one of the unquestioned starting-points of my discussion.

At this point, however, metapsychologists might object that the proper term to use in this regard is "the ego" rather than the person. But to assert this is to remove all sense from the concept of drive (which it is *my* purpose to do, not *theirs*), and so the objection defeats itself. That is to say, the objection would attribute the meaning of the drive to the ego, at which point everything would be ego, and, in order to make sense,

we would have to acknowledge that ego and person mean the
same thing. (In a roundabout and problematical way, Fairbairn
[1952] came to this pass when he populated the mind with his
personified types of ego only.)

There is still another basic difficulty entailed by invoking
"the ego," and it is one that has troubled Freudian theoreticians for a long time. It is that, with the exception of formalistic
sentences in which it is being defined, "the ego," like "the resistance," is inherently a reified or personified concept. This is
so because all strict theoretical definitions of the ego specify
that it is an abstract term we use to subsume or refer to a number of functions that usually resemble each other in certain
respects (Hartmann 1950). These resemblances might include
their dealing with reality relations or their usually operating
on the same side of conflicts, i.e., on behalf of adaptation and
synthesis. Granted for the moment that this type of definition
makes sense (it does personify functions!), it also makes it
perfectly plain that there can be no "the" about ego, for ego is
not a unified and irreducible agency, a fixed and homogeneous
entity that engages in action. Ego refers rather to certain kinds
of action or action in a certain mode. (For a similar examination of how we reify "the id," see Hayman 1969; see also
chapter 4). Rightly understood, the term ego refers to pursuing
certain human aims in certain ways, e.g., through perceiving,
remembering, reasoning, repressing, projecting, and synthesiz-
ing. (Though we may call these activities "functions," can we,
without personifying them or being redundant, say that *they*
do anything? A psychological function, unlike a biological one,
is at best implied in the doing of something *by an agent.*) As to
who or what it is that does this pursuing of aims, one must
again conclude that it is the person. There is no other term for
it really, except unrecognized synonyms of the person, such as
"the self" and "the self-system" (see in this regard chapter 5).
I shall soon mention some other synonyms of this sort.

In this light, one sees that Hartmann was merely deferring
acceptance of this alternative when, to deal with this problem,
he invoked the idea of higher-order ego functions which regulate other ego functions (1939b). This is so because there must
be a point at which one gets to the highest-order functions,
the functions which, by definition, govern all regulatory activity; and at that point one would be merely and transparently

speaking about the person without acknowledging it. In doing so, one would be putting terminological consistency before good sense. Hartmann stopped short of the consideration that higher- and highest-order functions are synonymous with the person.

A similar last-ditch or rearguard attempt is encountered in the theoretical arguments which speak of id-ego levels, configurations, or hierarchic arrangements (Gill 1963; myself 1968b). In these, the traditional sense of id and ego is gone, though the words linger on. The "hierarchy" and the "configuration" are other unacknowledged synonyms of the person.

To add only one more telling point against "the ego," I shall mention the relativity of ego activity that is implied in certain widely accepted formulations concerning ego functions. One is Fenichel's (1941), which is to the effect that what is defense on one level may be that which is defended against on the next level. Another such formulation is that by Hartmann et al (1946), to the effect that what makes a function an *ego* function is that *usually* it is found on the same side of conflict as other so-called ego functions. But once it is acknowledged that what is to be called ego depends on context and is therefore relative to circumstances and objectives, it is being granted, in effect, that when one says "the ego," one means something like the person as agent. The person as agent is someone who does certain things in certain ways in what amounts to the pursuit of certain aims, rather than doing other things in other ways, perhaps in connection with other aims.

The foregoing arguments lead as well to a second conclusion, namely that we may also designate the person as the *subject* of the verb "to resist."

What point has now been reached in this effort to comprehend the idea of resistance? Once we have barred all recourse to "the resistance," "the drive," and "the ego," we may formulate the concept in this way: *in resisting, the person is engaged in two paradoxical or contradictory actions at once.* The person opposes analysis while also collaborating with it as constituted by both the analyst's actions and his or her own. We see that one of these actions might be done more insistently, explicitly, or effectively than the other: speaking traditionally we might say in one case that the resistance is stronger and in the next case that the collaboration is stronger; but, once we stop personifying and begin to work with the rules of the action language, we realize that, in speaking traditionally, we are saying something absurd, namely that the person is stronger than himself or herself. The case is the same when we say that the id is stronger than the ego or vice versa. These propositions say—what is impossible—that the person is stronger than himself or herself. In contrast, it is entirely logical to say that the person does one action more completely or conspicuously than another or even to the exclusion of effective or recognizable manifestations of the other.

(2) *"Can't," "won't," and "don't."* Resistance is often talked about as a force or entity which renders the person *unable* to proceed with the work of analysis. Consequently, the next step for us to take is to consider the idea of inability under the heading "can't," as it occurs, for example, in the statements, "I can't think of anything to say" and "I can't bear to think of my sinfulness." There is no question that inability—sometimes called weakness—is a frequent, emotionally significant feature of the way people customarily render their subjective experience. But to grant this is not yet to understand the idea of inability. Like "passivity," it must be analyzed in each instance (Schafer 1968c), and invariably it is instructive to do so.

We note, first of all, that people make such statements when they do not *do* the action (to think, to bear, etc.) of which they are speaking. Yet they seem to be saying more than that; they seem to be saying that, though they try, they *can't*. But, again, this statement still refers to the fact that they do not *do* the action in question, i.e., the full statement of their meaning is this, that though they try, they still do not *do* the action. In this developed form, the statement has two parts, each of which asserts something that is describable and, by the same token, falsifiable. Each therefore is a legitimate empirical proposition. There are various acceptable manifestations of *trying to do something*, such as spending time at it, visibly straining in some way, doing the action repeatedly in an incomplete or otherwise unsatisfactory way, dreaming about it, applying oneself emotionally or at some expense or in a way that convincingly indicates concern or chagrin, and so forth. And, with respect to the second part of the full statement, in most instances we can ascertain through the proper use of the psychoanalytic method whether in fact one does or does not *do* the action in question. This is so as much for the actions of thinking as for the actions involving motor behavior.

To link just this much of the argument to clinical work, I would say this: that very often when analysands say they cannot do something, think something, or feel something, they are referring mainly to the fact that they do not do it and hardly at all to convincing effort. Their speaking of futile efforts is likely to refer less to application and more to something else, such as wishing that they did do it or had done it, or regretting that they have not done it, or thinking exasperatedly that they do not understand why they have not done it; or they might be referring only to the fact that, although they stayed at the right place and in the right posture to do the action (e.g., writing an essay for a college course), they did not really apply themselves to doing the action itself; in other words, they might be conveying that they did try to get busy with the action in question, not that they were unsuccessfully engaged in doing it. Obsessional analysands teach us a great deal in this regard.

Being "unable" to overcome the so-called resistance is often a statement of this sort. Analysands will sometimes say that they know they are somehow resisting the analysis but are unable to do otherwise. What this means, however, is that though they have formulated some good reasons to stop resisting, they do not stop, and though they have not as yet formulated good reasons for continuing to resist, they do so anyway. Meanwhile, it remains unclear *how* they are trying to do otherwise.

In this context "unable" usually implies not prevailing against a force or entity that has the property of otherness and so is a species of what I have called "disclaimed action" (see chapter 7). It is as if on the one hand there is the somehow straining person and on the other hand the somehow unyielding resistance. In other words, it is as if we are to think that the resistance is not really the person's own activity, which it is, of course. (Cf. Fenichel's [1941] discussion of defense and my [1968b] discussion of the alleged power of the introject.) Disclaiming action is itself a form of resisting, and, when it is the very action of resisting that is being disclaimed, we have an instance of the so-called resistance against the analysis of resistance.

At this point the objection might be raised that some actions are beyond the person's range of skill or physical strength. One may accept this objection while continuing to hold the main ground of the present argument. To do so, one would make the following rejoinder. While there are bound to be borderline cases in this connection, most statements about psychological inability have nothing whatever to do with physical strength or with skill. "Thinking of anything" or "tolerating the idea" are statements about actions and not about abilities or skills. One does them or one does not do them. With respect to these actions, "I don't" has meaning; "I can't" has none.

In making this argument, I seem ominously to be implying "won't" when saying "don't," and, with regard to people in distress, such as analysands, I might seem both harsh and incurious. Consequently, I must go on to spend a few moments on the place of the idea "won't" in the proposed action language. It is always more or less true that people are eager to take a morally superior, condemning, and accusatory attitude toward others who do not meet some standard, and thus to charge them with being wilful, defiant, or obstinate. The person accused is likely to plead, "I can't," while the accuser is likely to insist, "You won't!" I submit that usually both statements are meaningless, the meaningful statements being, "I don't" and "You don't." On the basis of these statements, one may go on to offer reasons, ask for reasons, or search for reasons why one does not. Reasons are what make it more or less comprehensible that one does not or did not do the action in question (see chapter 10). Sound analysis of resistance proceeds in just this way. It is not judgmental at all, though it is often taken that way by the analysand. In a matter-of-fact way, analysis of resistance is, like all analysis, an inquiry into present and past psychological activity, including deliberate inactivity.

In contrast to those who analyze resisting in this way, some analysts use the term to imply "won't," even though they might have observed only that the analysand has not done a certain action, say has not told an embarrassing dream. Did the analyst demand that the dream be told? If so, should he or she have made this demand? Should not the analyst rather have raised questions about the reasons for the omission of the dream report? Then he or she would have been following the invaluable rules about taking up resistance first and not making value judgments in the usual sense of the phrase.

Of course, one of the actions people sometimes take is to resolve, consciously or otherwise, that they will disappoint certain expectations, fail to meet certain standards, or refuse to perform certain tasks. Resolving, too, is an action; it is an action taken with regard to certain actions one might carry out in the near or distant future. Whether or not one's later actions conform to this act of resolving is another matter. To resolve in this oppositional way amounts to formulating a reason for not doing those future actions; it makes their future omissions at least partly understandable. The constituting of this reason marks the occasions when it makes some sense to say, "You won't" and "I won't." But it is essential to realize that, when this later time for action comes, words like resolution and intention can only refer to specific actions or modes of action; they are not substantives and do not impel actions. That is to say, they are verbs and adverbs that designate the actions in question. Thus one could say, "You did not tell me the embarrassing dream deliberately," or "You intended to direct my attention away from a sore point." Also, one might mean doing these actions consciously, preconsciously, or unconsciously. I shall return to this last point later in this section and again in section 3.

It is not to be assumed, however, that all actions must be done in this way, i.e., must be done resolutely or intentionally. Otherwise, it would make no sense to mention resolving or intending at all, in that to do so would be to speak redundantly; acting and intending would mean very much the same thing. And yet to say that some actions are simply done or performed is to seem to throw out the assumption of thoroughgoing or exceptionless determinism in mental life that has been the hallmark of metapsychology; however, the matter is far more complicated than this, as I shall try to show shortly (see also chapter 10).

At the beginning of this subsection, working within the framework of the demythologized action language, I was setting forth some different implications of, or some rules guiding the use of, the words *can't, don't,* and *won't*. After sorting out considerations of skill and physical strength, and allowing for difficult borderline instances, I attempted to show that: saying *can't* in relation to psychological processes is likely to be meaningless; in its proper analytic sense, saying *won't* specifies a

particular way of acting or not acting; and saying *don't* establishes the proper basic designation of actions not carried out;
this designation has the advantage of being open to many
kinds of descriptive qualification. Focusing on "don't" is to
the advantage of description and technique, and is quite consistent with the emphasis on affirmative propositions in section
5 below.

It follows that, with appropriate changes being made, these
remarks apply to *can, will,* and *do* (considered as independent
verbs, not as auxiliaries). I shall discuss one aspect of the important cases of *would* and *wouldn't* in the fifth part of section
3, which is on the dynamic unconscious.

Returning now to the subject of resisting, I draw the following conclusions: resisting is not an inability; resisting does not
produce an inability; and resisting may or may not entail refusal to engage in certain actions considered appropriate,
helpful, or essential for the progress of an analysis. Tying these
ideas in with the earlier discussions, I propose that *resisting is
engaging in actions contrary to analysis while also engaging in
analysis itself; it is the analysand as analysand contradicting
himself or herself in action; it is analytic counteraction.* According to the action language, resisting is neither an affliction
by some autonomous entity called "the resistance," understood
as something one "has," nor an inability based on the strength
or weakness of inexorable mechanistic factors; rather resisting
("resistance") is something one does, and one might do it more
resolutely or effectively than one does the work of collaborating in any ordinary sense of that word. Many issues of resisting
in clinical work are approachable only through *don't* and *do.*

(3) *Determinism.* As I indicated earlier, arriving at the conclusions just presented has involved us in further problems.
There is the problem of determinism I mentioned in connection
with my assumption that each action need not be based on resolving or intending; and along with that problem goes the
problem of responsibility. And there is the problem of how we
are to understand instances of resisting that are not based on
acts of resolving and are not carried out resolutely.

Let us first consider resisting that is not being done resolutely. Freud faced this problem in the sixth section of "Analysis Terminable and Interminable" (1937a). There, in a loose
way, he differentiated five types of resistance, of which he said

that, far from being expressions of conflict, they are characteristics of the mental apparatus of some people. These resistances are loss of plasticity, adhesiveness of the libido, mobility of the libido, defusion of instincts, and an excess of free
aggression. By these designations Freud more or less clearly
referred to a certain inertia, unresponsiveness, or agitation that
is insusceptible to change, and thus to a resistance different
from that attributable to such active principles of mental functioning as specific defense or wishful transference-repetition.
Freud was referring to what in everyday speech we might call
being set in one's ways or might sum up by saying, "You can't
teach an old dog new tricks" and "You can't make a silk purse
out of a sow's ear."

Resistances such as these can have no essential relationship
to the defiance of paternal authority that Freud often cited as
the prototypical dynamic of resistance; for to call anything
defiant is to imply that it is being enacted deliberately or intentionally. Defiance and related actions are understood to be
actions of a certain sort or in a certain mode. However, with
regard to the other resistances, Freud implied that they ob-
struct certain changes during the analytic process without
having been conceived or planned as obstructions; they do not
constitute resisting resolutely. This is not to say that once their
resistant potentialities have been noted, they might not be
resolutely exploited in a secondary way.

My thesis in this connection may be stated simply, though it
has been distilled from the complex philosophical discussions
of Wittgenstein (1934-35, 1945-49), Ryle (1949), Austin
(1956), Hampshire (1959, 1962) and others. It is that it is not
necessary to assume that an action, in the sense of whatever is
carried out behaviorally, spoken, or thought, must have been
prepared by some immediately preceding mental activity that
sets the stage for that action. It is common to assume that
specific mental activity must be based on a preparatory phase.
Freud and analysts after him have assumed that mental activity is first carried out unconsciously or preconsciously and is
raised to consciousness or invested with conscious quality only
by a special additional act—the direction toward it of attention
cathexis. We all assume that we could not perform a motoric
action without first intending it and thinking what to do, and
that we could not remember a fact or a tune without first

having a motive to do so and also having been carrying it around with us somehow and somewhere "in mind." These assumptions have been convincingly disputed by Ryle. Ryle has demonstrated as well their being derivatives of the Cartesian model of mind.

Of the many telling arguments advanced by Ryle, I will mention one, which is to the effect that these assumptions entail an infinite regress and so render the entire model unserviceable: for if a thought spoken aloud or to oneself requires its own preparation, then the preparation itself, being mental in some aspect, also requires its own preparation—and the infinite regress is launched. Or, to come at it another way, there must also be a thought as to when the preparation of a thought is complete, and that thought would require preparation, and so on ad infinitum. In Freud's terms, the directing of attention cathexis is not indiscriminate: except when it is somehow compelled (as we say) by a vivid stimulus, it is the consequence of some kind of judgment, and, if this is so, that judgment must also require review and acceptance before being acted upon, with the proviso, however, that this cathexis, and this review and acceptance, would also require cathexis prior to an act of judgment. There is no escaping this consequence of the infinite regress when working with the Cartesian model. I shall add to this point later.

Things appear in a different and, I think, clearer light when we say simply that a person has thought, said, or motorically performed something, and perhaps specify further that either he or she did or didn't do it knowingly or heedfully or consciously. "Consciously" now becomes a way of doing things; the word "conscious" is understood to refer, not to a system, an organ of the mind, or a quality of a thought, but to a mode of doing the action of thinking or some other action. Similarly, "preconscious" refers to the unreflective mode, the unknowing or unheedful mode of thinking or doing some other action, so long as this mode can be easily altered to the mode of doing that action attentively or consciously. In action terms, "preconscious," like "conscious," is not a quality of mental content. According to the action language being set forth here, neither conscious nor preconscious requires any conceptualization or explanation in terms of deployment of cathexis. That explanation is required by a different model—the mechanistic one. *It is all a question of the rules of the language being used, not of the facts.* The subject of *the dynamic unconscious* is a thornier one than *the conscious* and *the preconscious;* I shall come to it in my discussion of self-deception in section 3, part 5. Here, however, I want to make the point that it is logical to think of actions purely as such, without necessarily invoking the ideas about resolve, intention, or thoughts that prepare actions. In taking this position, I am in no way rejecting the historical aspect of psychoanalytic understanding and interpretation. Life-historical considerations are indispensable in psychoanalysis.

To come now to the first problem I mentioned—determinism—I want to go on to point out that the concept of determinism did double duty in Freud's thinking. One duty was to carry through the nineteenth century conception of natural science theory to which Freud had sworn allegiance. In particular, this duty was to develop the mechanistic conceptions of mind that Freud called his "metapsychology." These conceptions required Freud to explain psychological events in terms of forces, forces being causes or determinants that are necessary in a mechanical or Newtonian universe. In this approach, subjective experience, meaning, action, and so forth are merely phenomena which require translation into mechanistic terms in order to be endowed with theoretical significance. For example, Freud said:

> We seek not merely to describe and to clarify phenomena, but to understand them as signs of an interplay of forces in the mind, as a manifestation of purposeful intentions working concurrently or in mutual opposition. We are concerned with a *dynamic view* of mental phenomena. On our view the phenomena that are perceived must yield in importance to trends which are only hypothetical (1916b, p. 67).

According to its other duty, however, the concept of determinism stood for the idea of intelligibility, meaningfulness, interpretability, or translatability. One finds relatively more emphasis put on words of this sort in Freud's earlier writings. For example:

> Obsessional ideas, as is well known, have an appearance of being either without motive or without meaning, just as dreams have.

The first problem is how to give them a sense and a status in the subject's mental life, so as to make them comprehensible and even obvious. The problem of translating them may seem insoluble; but we must never let ourselves to misled by that illusion (1909b, p. 186).

It was only as time went on that Freud used these "intelligibility" words, first, as equivalent to force, determinant, and cause, and, then, as inessential or atheoretical words whose importance now resided in the underlying force, determinant, and cause, as in the first of these quotations. But to affirm the principle of determinism in line with this second duty is to say that one must always seek to establish the *reasons* of human activity—the *reasons* why people do the things they do behaviorally, verbally, or purely in thought, and the *reasons* why they do them in the ways that they do, e.g., unconsciously, emotionally, or only in fantasy. Determinism in this sense is a way of putting questions to action; it is a principle of inquiry. It is the way of clinical analysis. It is explanation through redescription (see chapter 10).

It is the second sense of determinism that is essential to the psychoanalytic method and the explanations of the data it elicits. If one throws out determinism in that sense, one does indeed throw out psychoanalysis. Psychoanalysts always ask, "Why?" and again "Why?" and again and again, striving toward the ideal of the finest particularity of understanding. Psychoanalysts do not accept the proposition that human behavior may occur without meaning, hence without reasons. This much has to be affirmed by every psychoanalyst. This is how human behavior is defined; it is not an empirical finding. Behavior without meaning may be a reflex activity or other biological activity; it cannot be psychological activity.

But a psychoanalyst may set aside the Newtonian and Cartesian models of the human mind and of explanation. In fact, psychoanalysts have not really used these models outside of their formal theorizing and the spill-overs of their theorizing into their clinical discourse. In their actual work, which is the clinical method of psychoanalytic interpretation, analysts have always dealt with meanings and reasons. They have sought to establish the intelligibility of seemingly senseless or unintelligible actions, such as neurotic symptoms, neurotic anxiety attacks, dreams, delusions—and resistance! But the psycho-analytic commitment has been maintained under the wrong banner. As we see plainly in clinical work, the analyst's real commitment is not to determinism in a universe of mechanical causes, but to intelligibility in a universe of actions with reasons. The action language is the native, but neglected, tongue of psychoanalysis. Approaches to this position have been made, implied, or anticipated by a number of other psycho-analytic authors, as mentioned in my introduction.

(4) *A note on causes and reasons.* Before proceeding directly with my discussion of resisting, I must resume the discussion I began in chapter 10, section 4, of that most important—and difficult—distinction between causes and reasons; for on it depends not only our grasp of the idea of resisting but our grasp of the essence of all psychoanalytic interpretation.

Wittgenstein (1934-35, 1945-49; see also Pears 1969) dis-tinguished sharply between causes and reasons: causes are the conditions under which one will perform a certain action, while reasons are the statements one makes in answer to the question why one has performed a certain action. In order for Witt-genstein's distinction to work, however, the idea of conditions must be understood within a purely behavioristic framework. That is to say, conditions are those public circumstances, de-fined by the independent observer, that are regularly followed by the subject's engaging in some public behavior again de-fined by the independent observer. In speaking of conditions behavioristically, one excludes from consideration the subject's definition or experience of both circumstances and reactive behavior, as well as the entire realm of private circumstances and private reactions that can be made public (e.g., telling one's dreams to one's analyst). This is so because in order to take into account psychic reality or the world as experienced, which is the world of meaning and private activity, one must shift to explanation in terms of reasons rather than causes or conditions.

Why is this shift to reasons entailed by reference to psychic reality? Let us assume that there are certain scientifically well-established conditions of certain public behaviors. For the conditions to be operative in psychological life, which is life above the level of reflex response, they must be present as components of experience, whether or not their presence is consciously apprehended by the subject or not. That the subject, in giving reasons for a certain action, might not refer to the behavioristically established conditions as such does not invalidate the point I have just made, for it follows from this omission only that, through inattention or misunderstanding, the subject inadequately recognizes or expresses his or her experience of those conditions. The subject gives poor reasons for the actions he or she is explaining. And just how are these inadequacies to be understood? By now the realm of public conditions has already been left behind for the most part, and the inadequacies are understandable only in terms of additional reasons. None of which implies that it is simple to arrive at a sense of closure and conviction about the reasons for a certain action or for certain inadequacies of action. In addition to difficulties stemming from the inevitable complexity of reasons for major and complex life actions, there are all those additional difficulties introduced by one's intricate and consequential reasons for not faithfully recognizing or acknowledging all of one's reasons to oneself as well as to others.

Not only because of its methodologically prescribed narrowness of data and definition, but because it is an attempt to work without any concept of mind whatsoever, which is what establishes its narrowness, the behavioristic method is at best *pre*-psychological. Such conditions as it establishes have value for psychology only insofar as they suggest psychological questions; at least this is so with respect to human beings. These are the questions about reasons and the person's problems with achieving accuracy and adequacy in knowing and giving reasons. Psychoanalysis is the study of both the person's reasons and the person's problems with reasons. For example, Little Hans's phobia of horses (Freud 1909a) was understandable in terms of reasons which were definable only in terms of the world as he experienced it: as he saw it, he was in a dangerous family situation, which had its reasons, and he presented it to himself and others as his being in a different danger situation—the prospect of being bitten by a horse—which transformation also had its reasons, both as to the point of there being *some* transformation and the choice of *this* transformation; and by a further action, which also had its reasons, he blurred this transformed danger situation and response, thereby obscuring the details of his symptom.

To abandon the idea of conditions or causes in the psychology of human beings would seem to be accepting a principle of chaos in human affairs. Exactly the reverse is true. It is still to think in terms of order, though not the same type of order. Explanation remains on the agenda. There is a fundamental assumption on which we base explanation in terms of reasons. This assumption is that whenever one sees oneself as being in the same situation, one will react in the same way. (As I shall argue at greater length in part IV on "the emotions," it is entailed by this assumption that, in specific instances, we cannot absolutely separate the definition of a situation and the definition of a reaction to it, for the two are correlative.) To make any other assumption would be to argue for a chaotic universe, or, more exactly, a chaotic approach to the universe. The seeking of psychological explanations presupposes an orderly universe, or an orderly approach to it, and to say this is to say that *there cannot be more than one reaction to one situation* and that *there cannot be more than a relatively narrow range of similar reactions to a group of relatively similar situations.* Clearly different actions must imply clearly different situations. The concept of situation is the same as the concept of psychic reality, and so expresses an important aspect of the sense of psychoanalytic interpretation. Freud's great revision of his anxiety theory implies this proposition (1926).

It must be recognized that there can be no absolute distinction drawn between reasons for an action and the definition of the action itself. An action is called that by virtue of our attributing meaning to it, and to state its reasons is one way of stating what that meaning is, just as to state its meaning is one way of stating what its reasons are. In this light it can be seen that, when Wittgenstein argued that a person might act without giving himself reasons, he was using the word "reasons" in a behavioristic sense, and, psychologically, this is no sense at all (but see below for an acceptable part of his meaning). If it is an action that is in question, it has reasons; these reasons may not be formulated consciously or reflectively, and their report may be distorted in some way, but none of these eventualities corresponds to acting without reasons. Only reflexes and physiological processes and suchlike have no reasons, and we do not call them actions. When we call something an action, we mean that it has reasons, though we imply nothing about self-consciousness with respect to reasons. And when we state reasons, we mean that we are talking about human activity.

Thus the four terms—meaning, action, reason, and situation —are aspects of the psychological mode of considering human activity, and they co-define or co-constitute each other. In contrast, the other four terms—cause, condition, determinant, and force—when used in psychology, express a subhumanizing or dehumanizing mode of considering human activity as though it were the workings of a machine. I know that Sartre (1943) equates psychology and mechanistic thinking and sets them off from humanistic, phenomenological approaches to human beings; I think it better, however, to reclaim the word psychology from the mechanists. On behalf of this mechanistic mode, however, one may grant that it can serve as a *pre*psychological search for those regularities in human activity that warrant a search for psychological explanation. One wishes it did serve so more often.

We need not assume that each action must be triggered by something. We view actions historically, that is, as following one another in a sequence that is intelligible in a number of related ways; the sequence is more than a chaotic chronicle whose only organizing principle is the passage of time. In this respect psychoanalysis is an historical approach to lives (see chapter 3). But historical background is not to be confused with the ideas of preparatory phases of thought and of causal motives that somehow precede, underlie, trigger, and guide action.

(5) *Responsibility.* To conclude this part of my discussion, I shall discuss the concept of responsibility in the language of action. For how we understand responsibility deeply influences how we think of resistance, and how we think of both is closely related to how we see the place of determinism or intelligibility in psychoanalytic explanation.

In their everyday thinking, people recognize that actions may be performed without conscious resolve, deliberation, or intention, and they are inclined to waive or reduce attributions of responsibility whenever they are satisfied that the actions in question have been performed in that way. However, when they make these judgments, they do not quite mean what I mean; for they seem to mean merely that something exceptional has happened, that there has been some odd departure from a norm or from the rules of the game of social existence, whereas I mean more than this. I mean that, as a rule, we may say that *people just do what they do* and that we need not qualify this statement with suggestions of prior reflective activity. (This is the acceptable part of Wittgenstein's meaning; see above.) Action performed reflectively, while not rare or exceptional, is still only action in one of its modes; it is a more complex mode. Unreflective action does not lose the name of action. Consequently, attribution of responsibility may be carried out on the basis of *whether* one has done the action or on the basis of *how* one has done the action, or both. *How* includes the notions "deliberately," "impulsively," "accidentally," "vengefully," and so forth, and thus takes in situations and reasons or the "why" of the action. Be that as it may, *that* and *how* should not be confused, and, in any case, the decision to waive responsibility is a separate matter to be settled in the terms of personal or societal rules adopted for that purpose.

Responsibility is not a trait or a possession. The use of this word may, however, point to a way, or one of several ways, of doing an action. In this respect its force is adverbial: it says *how* something was done. Of the action itself we can say only that it was done or not done. Viewing it under its adverbial aspect—"responsibly"—we see that using the word presupposes that we have adopted one or another convention which states the criteria of what it is to act responsibly. The person acting responsibly acts in accord with these criteria. My earlier remarks on the relations between *can't, won't,* and *don't* in the second part of this section should also be consulted in this connection.

Surely it does not go very far with the concept of responsibility to say only this much, but this much is, I believe, essential for a right understanding of it. At any rate, even at this early stage we are closer to a psychoanalytic understanding of responsibility than we have ever been when using the mechanistic and organismic language of metapsychology: for by its nature that language excludes concepts like responsibility from explanation; it deals instead in resultants of forces and interacting functions, even after having the equivocal concept of relative autonomy added to it (see chapters 4 and 5).

When Freud said about dreams that they are the dreamer's responsibility (1925a), he based this assertion not on his metapsychology but on an implicit action model of responsibility. For his argument was this, simply that the dreamer dreamt the dream, i.e., that it was his or her action. He did not mean that the dreamer dreamt the dream *responsibly*. Many of Freud's propositions have this form; they derive from the side of his thinking that he regarded as *merely* describing phenomena and that I regard as the essence of psychoanalytic explanation.

Resisting, like dreaming, may be said to be the analysand's doing or deed. But we would be wrong to infer that to say this is to make a moral judgment or an accusation. Freud taught us that the analysand is continuously disposed to resist. This is not only a well-founded empirical generalization. It is also an inevitable consequence of accepting Freud's fundamental discoveries about the unconsciously continued infantile modes of wishing and fantasying along erotic and aggressive lines and the paradoxical actions in which people engage in this regard. And for this latter reason, the analysis of resisting rivals the analysis of transference in value and is thoroughly intertwined with it. Thus Freud's paper, "The Dynamics of Transference" (1912), says as much about resisting as about transference.

3. SELF-DECEPTION

(1) *The problem.* By resisting, the analysand somehow continues to keep many truths from himself or herself. This is to be self-deceiving. But what does it mean, what can it mean to say this?

Traditionally, Freudian psychoanalysts have not addressed the problem of self-deception under that name. For the most part, they have dealt with it as unconscious defense, mechanisms of defense, censorship, or resistance. Nevertheless, each such name must imply some theory of self-deception. By a theory of self-deception I refer to some account of what it means to say the following: one does not know that one knows something, wishes something, considers something emotionally, or is doing or has done some other action; one keeps oneself from discovering *what* one does not know, etc., thus deceiving oneself once; and one keeps oneself from discovering *that* and *how* one is deceiving oneself in this way ("unconscious defense"), thus deceiving oneself a second time or in a second respect.

But, one may ask, doesn't a person have to know what he or she is doing in order to do it? In other words, doesn't one have special access as an "insider" to these deceptions? How can one not know, refuse to know, and not know *that* and *how* one is refusing to know, when each of these is an action that one is carrying out? Can one person be in two conditions at one time? That is to say, can one be, as it were, more than one individual so that one can deceive oneself just as one can deceive someone else? This is the problem of self-deception (cf. Sartre's discussion of "bad faith," 1943).

(2) *Metapsychology*. Before we proceed any further with this attempt to understand the idea of self-deception, we must undertake a brief review of a few pertinent aspects of Freudian metapsychology.

As metapsychologists, we seem to imply, though we would not openly avow, that the person is always more than one individual. We imply this multiplicity of individuals constituting one person in this way: we set up a number of agencies or divisions within the person's co-called mental apparatus and speak as though each of them functions in the manner of an individual in that it has a circumscribed set of objectives, a certain type and amount of energy, and a strategy and influence. Further, we speak of each agency or division as relating to the others as one person might relate to other persons. We engage in this manner of speaking, for example, when we say, with Freud, that the superego takes the rest of the ego as its object. As metapsychologists we also speak of separate agencies or divisions *within* each agency. We engage in this manner of speaking, for example, when we refer to the activity of the different parts of the ego agency, such as the defensive ego and the adaptive ego, and say of each that it includes different functions or impulses, each of which may at times act on its own, as in the instance of the ego agency's synthetic function; and we do the same with respect to the id when we speak of the independent activity of a particular sexual impulse. Thereby, for each instance of action, we provide a designer, a mover, and an executor; implicitly we view the action as a manifestation of that "agency." Mental activity being viewed in this way, the number of possible agencies within agencies approaches infinity. At least, mind is being dealt with as a potential or actual multitude of more or less single-minded, more or less unruly, and more or less regulated and regulating individuals.

This metaphorical way of dividing up mind while keeping it operative is inelegant and anthropomorphic in the extreme. I propose that it is clearer and more suggestive of connections and explanations, and that it entails no loss of significance, to speak of one person's doing a large number of actions, each of which may be looked at from many points of view, i.e., may be defined variously as an action. Each action may be defined variously by the agent as well as by independent observers. One would have to allow for the facts, still to be explained, that the person: does not know about all of his or her actions; gives signs of not wanting to know about all of them; and is successful in actively preventing his or her knowing all that might be known in this regard. But at least a formulation in terms of action, unlike the traditional metapsychological formulation, would not attribute substance, space, and autonomous mind to particular mental operations.

And yet, to give it its due, the anthromorphism we analysts have been resorting to is a crude way of recognizing that fundamentally we have been trying to understand actions. We have been trying to retain some sense of human action while using a mechanistic and organismic model of mind. Actually, like Freud, we have been using two types of explanatory models: one is the person as agent and the other is a mechanical and biological system moved by forces and energies. One of the ways in which we have skirted or masked this confusion of languages is so common in analytic writing as to be almost its hallmark, namely falling back on the non-committal passive voice and on implicit variations of it when dealing with awkward or insoluble theoretical problems, which is to say language problems. We construct or encounter such formulations as, "There was an increase in aggression," "As the self and object representations are differentiated," "A shift of cathexis took place," "The ego, now grown stronger," "His defenses having been undermined," and "The depression had run its course."

(3) *"Self-."* Let us return once more to the concept of self-deception, viewed as a fundamental component of the idea of resisting, and ask this question: How might one understand self-deception within the framework of an action psychology? For reasons already given, it is essential not to create a multiplicity of minds within the mind or individuals within the person.

The approach I shall take is through an examination of the "self-" part of "self-deception" (see also chapter 9). Let me begin by picking up one point I made in part 2 of this chapter. It is to the effect that, in attempting to go beyond traditional metapsychology, we do not now assume that actions, including silent and uttered thoughts, require preparatory phases. I argued then that to assume that they require these phases is to begin an infinite regress of preparations of preparations of preparations, and so on ad infinitum. In action language, we need only say that someone does this or that action. We do not have to say that one thinks it first or that one thinks it as one does it. For instance, some actions are merely thinking, and of these it makes no sense to say that one has first to think before one can think; in another case, actions of any sort might or might not have these preplanned or self-observing features. It is true that we sometimes notice with surprise or incredulity that we have acted without thinking either beforehand or concurrently, but that fact does not prove that usually we do think before we act or while we act; emphasizing that we acted "unthinkingly" has to do only with naive expectations about doing everything attentively that were not fulfilled.

As metapsychologists, we would say in this regard that, when one seems simply to act, one has already thought, and presently is thinking, about one's action *preconsciously* or *unconsciously*. We would reason in the common way that, unless one had thought and was thinking about what one was doing, one could not act. As evidence for preconscious and unconscious preparatory phases of thought, we might cite post-hypnotic suggestion or creative solutions to problems that seem to come "out of the blue." But in presenting these ideas, we would not be advancing a compelling argument, in the sense of leading up to an inescapable conclusion; we would merely be saying that our hypothesis gives one account—a very cumbersome metaphorical one—of how such things might be; it is a way of talking about such things. Moreover, having said this much, we would have to fall silent, for thereby we would neither have presented or constructed new facts nor diminished our ignorance as to how such actions are done; additionally, to go further than this would be to launch ourselves into the infinite regress entailed by that language.

Well, what about "self-"? It is a sign that the speaker is saying something about reflective activity, i.e., is talking about acting with regard to his or her own actions and modes of action. (Remember that these include thinking or speaking in various ways as well as performing motoric actions in various ways.) For example, "self-improvement" says the person is acting to increase the skilfulness with which he or she does things, or something along that line, and "self-abasement" says the person is acting to minimize or discredit the worth of his or her actions. In this light, we can see that "self-actualization" says nothing at all in that it confuses predicted, wished-for, merely contemplated, or actual future actions with present actions or existents; it is a prediction that is either empty or after the fact.

Does "self-deception" refer to a type of reflective activity? We do not assume that there is a substantive self that may be deceived; there is no one and nothing distinct from the deceiver to deceive (see chapter 9). Nor does it make sense to speak of deceiving one's actions. So we must consider self-deception to be a misnomer. It is no kind of reflective activity at all. It is something else. I suggest that it is an incorrect or faulty way of observing one's own actions. Whatever the differences, one may, after all, observe one's own actions just as one may observe the action of others; in doing so, one would employ the usual combination of remembering, anticipating, describing, relating, and judging events, contexts, implications, alternatives, and so forth. I believe this is how one would have to put it in action language.

Using "self-" in this way, we do not necessarily propose some kind of "split" in the mind; implications of that concretistic metaphor are entailed only by adopting the mechanistic idea of a mental apparatus. In action language, in contrast to mechanistic language, "self-" implies only a different object of action. The subject or agent is the same; it is the person. But "self-" says, diffusely, that the person is now the object, too; to put it more exactly, it says that the object is specific actions done by the person who is observing them. In principle, just because one is able to observe what anyone does, one is able to observe what one does, too. The faultiness of faulty self-observation is a matter of bias in some instances and ignorance in others; or it may be a mixture of these, as when ignorance or unreadiness is itself a constituent of bias, or when a specific bias is a constituent of not confronting an incapacity. I am using the word bias to refer to every variety of defensive distortion, including sheer omission or deletion (repression).

(4) *Observation.* Yet before we can really know what to make of the idea of faulty self-observation, we must have some developed conception of observation itself. The position I am taking is that initial observation is not necessarily veridical and then, perhaps, distorted by biased or defensive action. Developmental psychologies (Freud and Piaget), experimental psychology (G.S. Klein 1970; see also Schafer 1972a), certain trends in modern philosophy (Casey 1972), and common sense, all converge on a pluralistic conception of reality. There *is* a reality in the sense of there being some inescapable limits to possibility, which means some necessity that is being encountered, interpreted, and allowed for. But there is no single right way in which this reality must be observed, even though there are many irrational ways. In other words, there are versions of necessity or "visions of reality" (see chapter 3). *How* we observe *what* we observe will depend on whether we are acting needfully, desperately, submissively, etc.; on our level of cognitive development and our task orientation; on factors of context and figure-ground relations; on the linguistic traditions that we have learned; and the implicit or explicit theoretical model we are using. Nothing is being implied here about the factors mentioned being in the conscious, preconscious, or unconscious modes; anything one might say in that regard would have to be established in individual cases after suitable study. What we can properly call *distorted* observation must be idiosyncratic to the point of either grossly violating the rules of observation that are generally accepted in a particular culture at a particular time in its history or, since we must allow for fresh perceptions, the rules that are appropriate to a particular new task-context.

But the main point I want to make in this regard is this: logically, we may speak of distorted observation without assuming that, to begin with, there was only veridical observation, distortion being introduced later: for to make the assumption of primary or naive veridicality is to fall into the trap of granting the necessity of preparatory phases of thought before and behind each action. Although we analysts do frequently encounter instances in which originally accurate observation has been distorted, we may not on that ground take veridical observation as the starting point or model of observation; for the fact is that we also encounter many instances of other kinds. Moreover, once we distinguish, as we should, action plain and action observed, we realize that there are four possibilities in this regard: faulty action that is accurately observed (catching oneself making a mistake), faulty observation of action that is just right (seeing a success as a failure), faulty observation of faulty action (failing to notice a mistake upon review), and accurate observation of action that is just right (adaptive actions viewed as such). In practice, we encounter instances of all four possibilities as well as a wide range of doubtful or mixed cases.

Also, by avoiding the assumption of naive veridicality, we do not have to deal with the tricky question, how a person might carry out two actions at once or be in two conditions at once. If we follow Ryle's (1949) reasoning, we may say of those acts that the agent is observing as he or she does them that they are being done attentively. It is better to say attentively than self-observantly because attentively does not invoke the ambiguous "self-"; to say attentively is simply to say something about the mode of action. (Ryle's word for it is "heedful.")

It is no mere verbal trick to switch from "act of self-observation" to "attentively"; nor do I recommend this switch from a noun to an adverb simply for the sake of superficial verbal consistency. Rather, I think we should make this switch because we recognize that, according to the rules of action language, we are wrong to speak as if there could be an independent and complete act of self-observation or of taking heed. That there can be no such act is evident from the fact that it makes no sense simply to tell someone, "Be heedful!" One would have to ask, "Of what?" (Of course, one's knowing the command's context would enable one to "fill in" its verbalization and so be in no doubt as to what is wanted—but that is another matter.) Similarly, to say, "Be self-observant," unless it is a Kafkaesque assignment, is to invite the question, "In which respect?" These considerations support the proposal that the adverb "attentively," which describes the mode of an action, is the best word to use when dealing with matters traditionally dealt with under self-observation.

Returning now to the idea of faulty self-observation, we can see that it means acting unheedfully, inattentively, unobservantly, or inaccurately, or else remembering an action in one of these "inadequate" modes. Once having said this about an instance of action, we may go on to state in which respects the mode of doing the action or of remembering it is inadequate, and we may also inquire into the reasons why this is so. But on the strength of a pluralistic conception of reality, we would not have assumed that every known departure from veridicality was based on a specific motive or intent to distort. We shall have to clarify further the place of motivation in self-deception, now understood as faulty self-observation. We are obliged to do so also because it remains for us to arrive at an at least provisionally satisfactory conception of "the dynamic unconscious" in the language of action. Background for the ensuing discussion will found especially in chapter 10.

(5) *The dynamic unconscious.* The dynamic unconscious refers to two classes of actions. One class includes those actions and modes of action in which one is engaged, but which, for reasons of personal comfort, one observes faultily as something else—as another action, another mode of action, no action at all (an accident or not even an event), not one's own action, or not one's own choice of action or mode of action. (See also my discussion of disclaimed action in chapter 7.) For instance, a man who has acted in a sadistically hurtful manner might observe it as his having done a kindness; or he might observe it as a slip, a non-event (i.e., he might repress it), a misfortune the victim brought on himself, an action he was compelled to do by circumstances or as a duty, or an action that was not so hurtful or sadistic after all. There are still other variations on this theme. By "reasons of comfort" I refer either to one's avoiding experiencing one's actions anxiously, guiltily, ashamedly, or in some other painful emotional way, or to one's avoiding recognizing one's being in what is, subjectively, some typical danger situation.

There is a second major referent of the dynamic unconscious, in addition to unacknowledged actions in which the person is engaged. It is the class of actions in which one *would be* engaged were one not refraining from doing so by engaging in counteractions. There are the so-called impulses one is repressing or otherwise defending against; i.e., *in mechanistic lan-*

guage, they are impulses while, in action language, they are would-be actions. This means that one's thinking of them ("experiencing" them) as impulses is a matter of obeying a convention of language, for one could just as well follow the action convention and say that, more or less effortfully, one is refraining from initiating certain actions; one might be conscious of these would-be actions or might conclude, on the basis of one's apprehensive sense of effort, that one is about to engage in them. Through so-called free association in analysis, one frequently discovers that one is acting just this way.

Of course, the person could be mistaken in thinking that he or she would do something were it not for specific refrainings or counteractions. Actually, a would-be action is a prediction in one of its aspects, and as such it might be right or wrong. The clinical analyst banks on this fact, for in his or her view the would-be actions that are most alarming and consequential to the analysand are those that have been maintained unconsciously since childhood and that have never been assessed in the context of the analysand's adult values, resources, opportunities, relationships, understanding, and judgment. Freud repeatedly made this point in terms of reducing anxiety through making conscious the infantile unconscious impulses that the adult person will then reject as outmoded or inappropriate.

The actions one might do without acknowledging the fact include remembering, anticipating, and connecting; and the modes in which one might do them without acknowledging that fact include all the infantile and all the emotional ways in which people do act. I stipulate this to stress again that I am not using action merely in the sense of visible motoric action or conscious, orderly behavior. Thus it is permissable to say that one remembers something but faultily fails to observe that one does remember it ("acting out"), and it is permissible to say that one thinks of something angrily but faultily observes that one is thinking about it purely sadly ("reversal of affect"). And one may say that a person *would be* devouring or murderous were it not for his or her rigidly persisting in acting generously ("reaction formation"). And so forth.

The question of unconscious affect, which has plagued psychoanalytic theory for many years, might find an answer once we have accepted the following three propositions. First, affect is not a substantive; it is an action or a mode of action, and so its force is verbal or adverbial (I have been using it this way). Second, unconscious is not a state, a quality, or a place; it is a mode of action, and so its force is adverbial ("unconsciously"). Third, one might do an action in a certain emotional way and consciously observe that way of acting faultily, while unconsciously observing it accurately. Thus it makes perfect sense for an analyst to maintain in the face of denials, that, unconsciously, an analysand is reacting angrily or would be reacting angrily were it not for this or that—it makes perfect sense, that is, once it has been accepted in principle that the analyst should be able to state criteria for saying "unconsciously," "would be," and "angrily," and there is no reason why he or she could not try to do so—for theoretical purposes at least.

I shall mention only briefly one more problem in the use of emotion words. There are adjectival forms of these emotion words, as when one says, "His angry reaction to the way he was treated was unconscious." These adjectival forms presuppose the use of substantives in a way that is ruled out in action language. But the nouns are easily translated into verbs (reaction→he reacted) and the adjectives into verbs or adverbs (unconscious→unconsciously and angry→angrily; or he reacted angrily→he resented it or hated it or whatever): "Unconsciously, he reacted to it angrily," "Unconsciously, he resented it," etc. (See part IV for an extended discussion of these problems and proposals.)

(6) *Self-deception, "the unconscious," and resisting.* To sum up this discussion of self-deception: I have argued that self-deception is a misnomer for attending faultily to one's actions; and I have further argued that, in turn, attending faultily is a rough way of referring to one of two possibilities: either one is carrying out actions inattentively when it is maladaptive to do so or one is remaining ignorant of actions one would do were one not engaged in effective counteractions of some sort. To put the matter this way is to invite investigation of both the reasons why people do only some things maladaptively because they are inattentive, and the reasons why people insist on remaining ignorant of the actions they would do under other circumstances. Putting the concept of self-deception this way also invites investigation of the modes of action by means of which people can act in selectively inattentive and selectively

ignorant modes, especially with regard to personal matters of great moment. *The investigation of these reasons and of these actions and their modes is what the metapsychologist would call the investigation of "the dynamic unconscious."* All the infantile psychosexual actions ("impulses" and "drives") and counteractions ("defenses," "reversals," "superego prohibitions," etc.), and all the later, modified versions of them singly and in combination ("derivatives," "symptoms," etc.) *remain* the subject-matter of clinical psychoanalysis, and, *as before,* they are performed unconsciously, preconsciously, or consciously. But now, at least in a beginning way, we are systematically using a language that suits our clinical method and data better than the traditional mechanistic and organismic language.

In view of the central theoretical position occupied by the idea of "the unconscious," my proposed restatement of it calls for a fuller treatment than I have given it here. I can, however, add two more points about it now. First, in the course of developing these formulations I have presented arguments for working with the idea of the unconscious, as with the ideas of the conscious and preconscious, in adverbial form ("unconsciously"). The adverbial form reflects our recognizing it to be a mode of action. We are not bound to regard it as a quality of thought content, for now thought content itself may be regarded as an action; it is thinking something, and so one might be doing it in any number of ways—consciously, preconsciously, unconsciously, recklessly, passionately, fearfully, etc. But not all acting unconsciously need be thinking. Secondly, there are many vital instances in which people do all they can to make sure that the mode of action will remain an unconscious one. It takes certain actions, some of them done unconsciously, too, to guarantee the continuation of the primary action's unconscious mode. The primary action may be only a conditional one, a would-be action; still, that it is what one *would do* might have to be maintained unconsciously. *It is both the factual actions and conditional actions that are the referents of the word dynamic in the concept of the dynamic unconscious.*

I conclude that: resisting is action that may be taken either knowingly or inattentively and inaccurately (resisting consciously or preconsciously and resisting unconsciously, respectively) or some combination of these if it is a complex action;

we may seek to establish reasons why this action is taken and we may seek to describe the modes of this action; and the resisting person might also take action against investigation of the reasons, the actions, and the modes of these actions, and in doing so he or she would be engaging in what Freud (1923a, 1937a) called resistance against the analysis of resistance.

There is a point at which the self-deceiving of attending faultily stops. This is the point where one says such things as, "I do not want to think I could do such a terrible thing" and "I will not believe I could feel that toward my own child!" Here we are explicitly in the realm of the "unthinkable." Sooner or later during psychoanalysis, resisting unconsciously becomes resisting consciously: the person avowedly draws some boundary line that he or she will not cross. The investigation of "the resistance" and of "the resistance against the analysis of resistance" does not confront an infinite regress. Analysis of "the resistance" begins where resisting is consciously affirmed, though this is not to say that this effort at analysis will always get very far. But the clinical analyst counts on this manifest resisting, and he or she is never disappointed. Here begins the investigation that is psychoanalysis.

The boundary line that is drawn also divides the analysand from the analyst, in that it signifies the analysand's taking a stand against the analyst, too, whatever and whomever the latter stands for at the time. For the analysand resisting is very much of an interpersonal action, too. It is to the question of what and whom the analyst stands for that we shall turn next, for the idea of resistance requires further clarification and development in this regard also.

4. Resisting Maternal Authority

(1) *The patriarchal perspective.* In his general propositions Freud almost always presented the analytic relationship in terms of the relationship with the father. He showed the many guises in which acute, unresolved ambivalence toward the father appeared in the transference and resistance. And usually Freud presented the other party to the analytic relationship as the son. In this respect he used his preferred explanatory model of the father-son relationship in its positive oedipal aspect. Although he frequently took account of the son's fear of the

father and his "feminine" wishes toward him, he centered on
the son's rivalry with and defiance of this patriarchal figure
and his fear of the consequences (castration in all its forms). It
was as though, for Freud, the analyst could only stand for the
powerful and frightening oedipal father. Although he presented resistance as internal opposition to becoming conscious
of dynamically unconscious material of all kinds, he also
showed how resistance operated in the analysand's defiance of
the analyst's authority, as in violating the fundamental rule,
and he discussed it in a way that shaded it over into the concept
of negative transference. He was viewing resistance in both its
intrapsychic and interpersonal aspects.

As for the female analysand, Freud usually presented her in
a narrow way as simply struggling intrapsychically and inter-
personally with *her* positive oedipal wishes. These are sexual
and possessive wishes directed toward the father and his representative in the transference, the analyst. And so Freud urged
repeatedly in this connection that the analyst must remain
aloof from the ultimately incestuous heterosexual passions of
the female analysand. But in this role the analyst is still like the
patriarchal father—and *really* like him—in warding off the
"daughter's" seductions and educating her toward renunciation. In Freud's discussion, her hostility is reactive to the
father's spurning of her love. Thus it is that Freud conceived
the analyst as the real and imagined anti-instinctual patriarch
coping primarily with the various aspects of the male and
female positive Oedipus complexes.

I am well aware that, in some of his late papers (1931, 1933),
Freud was groping toward a revised view of female development which included new ideas about the role and importance
of the mother, and so represented a modification of his primarily patriarchal orientation. Yet nowhere is this partiarchal
orientation more conspicuous than in these papers, perhaps
just because he was initiating fundamental changes. Only in
recent years have the implications of these changes begun to be
fully recognized and appreciated by Freudian analysts. In what
follows I shall not center on these late, inconclusive papers in
which anyway Freud still clung to his primary "masculine"
model. I have presented a more general critique of this feature
of Freud's theorizing elsewhere (1974a).

Freud regularly viewed relationships in terms of struggle

with patriarchal authority. For the most part, he saw reality as a harsh paternal reality and society as patriarchically at war with the rebellious instinctual boy and man, demanding renunciation of him, and threatening severe reprisals. This view of relations with the world remains even after we allow, with Freud, for the large measure of fantasied exaggeration introduced by the sexually rivalrous son and sexually ambitious daughter.

We cannot question the heuristic value of viewing reality and relationships within this anti-instinctual patriarchal perspective. Many profound psychological truths have been established as a result of our following Freud in doing so. Yet we must realize that this is only one perspective on relations with the world, and that other perspectives have been regularly employed by psychoanalysts (Freud among them *at times*) and have also yielded significant benefits. For example, Hartmann (1939b) and Erikson (1950): each in his own way has provided us with another major and more or less systematic way of viewing the person in the world. Each has helped us see the world as *also* sustaining and enhancing personal development, and as doing so both by providing guidance, opportunity, reward, articulation, and confirmation, and by manifesting a more or less reliable readiness for a long series of mutual adaptations. These modes of relationship suggest rather the loving mother or loving parents than the forbidding patriarch. And what reason could there be in this respect simply to be resisting these figures in the sense of defying them?

(2) *The negative view of resisting.* One way in which these considerations are relevant to the concept of resistance is this: viewing relationships mainly or only from the vantage point of struggle with authority commits us to modes of conceptualization in which negative terminology occupies an especially strategic place. Ultimately, these modes are detrimental to the progress of theory and observation. The question of modes is important because the terms we learn to think in are the terms we learn to observe by, and thereby they become the key terms in the development of our psychology, which should not be simply negative. Resistance is one such negative term; negative therapeutic reaction is another. There are more. Freud's view of the embattled son, and of the embattled child in civilization, does not help us see what is affirmative in resisting, which is to say what resisting is for or what it accomplishes. (I know that,

in his discussion of adolescent development [1905b], Freud spoke differently of the adolescent's defiance of authority. There he saw it as an aspect of the adolescent's emancipating himself from his parents, and he said that defiance is necessary for the progress of civilization. But this is an isolated comment, and anyway it would be hard to establish what would count as "progress of civilization" within Freud's general psychoanalytic theory or theories.) The "embattled son" view also overlooks the place of paternal love and pride in the son's development. I shall return to the problem of negative and affirmative language in section 5 of this chapter. For now I want to develop another consequence of the patriarchal slant of Freud's theorizing.

Speaking only with regard to the subject of resisting, though the implications of the remarks to follow are far broader than this, I call to your attention that Freud left the child's relationship to the mother entirely out of account and saw the girl's activity in too limited a way. We must therefore go on to ask about the girl's defiant resisting and about the mother's authority.

(3) *The daughter's resisting.* Who is defied by the little girl? And who is being defied by the grown woman on the analytic couch? Her father? One does often get the impression that Freud might have said, "Her father," in answer to these questions; he never did develop a comprehensive theory of female superego development. Moreover, in viewing the female superego as relatively weak in comparison to the male, he was implicitly using a patriarchal model of the superego for both sexes; he seemed to be suggesting that, having accepted her castrated status and taken the father as a love-object, the girl has neither a lost love-object with respect to which she might establish a moral identification, nor very much incentive to become moral *in that patriarchal way.* It is a clear case of arrested development—as viewed in relation to the father.

It will not help us here to resort to the argument that the Oedipus complex is bisexual and that both father and mother are given up, identified with, enter into superego formation, etc.; nor will it help to argue in terms of constitutional differences in the strength of masculine and feminine tendencies. Freud resorted to these two arguments in "The Ego and the Id" to help him through the difficulties I am discussing (1923a). As for constitutional differences, invoking them to explain anything about the psychoneuroses is always an after the fact explanation which is in any case inverifiable through the analysis of individual adult neurotics. Furthermore, Freud's resort to constitutional differences applies more to "feminine" boys than "manly" boys and so does not serve the purpose for which it was intended. And, as for the psychological bisexual argument, Freud did not systematically develop it; if he had, he would have developed a theory of a bisexual superego in the male, even if he went on mostly ignoring women in his formal theorizing. And this he did not do. His principal explanatory tool remained the positive Oedipus complex of the boy, and he viewed the negative or inverse side of this complex as a problematic reversal inspired by defensive needs in the face of castration anxiety, though constructed out of the boy's love of his father (e.g., in the case of the Rat Man [1909b]). And today, we still do not have a detailed, systematic, and generally accepted Freudian *theory* of bisexual superego activity in both sexes, though *clinically* Freudian analysts do regularly analyze as much as they can the mother's real and fantastic influence in the development of superego activity in both sexes.

(4) *Freud's view of mothers.* This is not the place to develop an extended critique of Freud's psychology of women, valuable though that would be. The specific points I want to make are, first, that Freud's relative neglect of the girl's interpersonal defiance is closely related to his neglect of the mother and her authority and, second, that this neglect is consistent with the curious fact of Freud's diffidence with regard to the details of preoedipal-pregenital development. The diffidence is already strongly suggested by the prefix "pre" in the words preoedipal and pregenital, as if there is only one real psychoanalytic vantage point, which is the boy's castration anxiety in his sexually rivalrous, fantastically exaggerated, and frightening, *oedipal* and *genital* struggle with his father.

One must approach this topic also with the awareness that, in a few essentially informal comments, Freud indicated his having an extremely restricted conception of the mother's typical emotional position in the mother-son relationship. This is a position of love that is virtually free of the ambivalence that haunts all other human relationships. For example, he said:

> A mother is only brought unlimited satisfaction by her relation to a son; this is altogether the most perfect, the most free from ambivalence of all human relationships. A mother can transfer to her son the ambition which she has been obliged to suppress in herself, and she can expect from him the satisfaction of all that has been left over in her of her masculinity complex (1933, p. 133).

Here we may disregard the question of what personal reasons Freud had for idealizing the mother-son relationship in this way, for we are concerned with the logic of his systematic thinking and not with speculative psychohistory.

For present purposes, I would stress that this conception of the mother's love for her son is perfectly consistent with, and easily predictable from, Freud's using the boy's positive Oedipus complex as his fundamental developmental model; for it was this model that established the centrality of castration anxiety in the mental development of the boy and of penis envy in that of the girl. According to Freud, the girl (the mother-to-be) resolves her penis envy by wanting to be loved by the father as a woman, and, through sexual relations with him, to have his penis and his baby as consolation for her own penisless state; and best of all to receive a boy from her father or his surrogate as the closest possible symbolic equivalent of having a penis herself. In order to develop his beatific view of the son as the realization of the mother's dreams, Freud had to be viewing mothers as little girls whose penis envy culminates in these dreams. The evidence in our culture does show that this maternal bias is extremely common and that its manifestations are often extremely vivid. Clinical analysts must constantly deal with these factors in their work. Nevertheless, they also find that this is not the only major maternal bias, and these are not the only vivid phenomena in typical mother-son relationships; they also find that there is more to being and becoming a mother than penis envy and its derivatives just as there is more to being a child than being a son in opposition to his father. Furthermore, it does not seem that the son is spared his mother's envy and hostility, altogether; her love is not that unambivalent especially when, as is so often the case, her relationship with her husband is troubled and her relationship with her own mother still turbulent, manifestly or unconsciously.

(5) *The mother's authority.* But what of the mother simply as mother? Is she without authority? Neither in objective reality nor in psychic reality; especially not in the latter! The mother of pregenital life is a powerful, controlling, threatening figure against whom the child continually struggles actually and in fantasy, often with much dread. (I may leave aside the benevolent side of the mother in this connection.) We know from the record Freud left of his self-analysis that he knew personally and in some painful detail what it is to struggle against the archaic father; and I daresay he also knew in the same intimate way what it is still to succumb to that incorporated figure even in one's prime, for as much as anything else he developed our sense of endless struggle toward adulthood generally and manhood (though not womanhood) specifically. But he taught us virtually nothing directly about what it is to struggle endlessly with the archaic mother. He mostly neglected the real transactional aspects of particular mother-child relationships; he treated the preoedipal mother—and also the oedipal mother— as some combination of a warm milieu for hatching children, so to say, an almost iconic prop for the child's fantasies, and an impersonal force or agency busy with such necessities as nursing, weaning, toilet training, and getting busy with the next baby. Although he showed her to be a constant figure in the child's progression through the psychosexual stages of development, Freud ignored the individuality of particular mothers, the phenomenology of particular mother-child relationships, and the fantasied incorporation of the mother.

As I argued in section 2 of this chapter, Freud's ignoring these phenomena is also a consequence of his attempting to develop a mechanistic and organismic psychology. It is true that one finds in Freud's writings allusions to real mothers with their babies, as when Freud mentioned how the mother introduces her baby to sexuality and object love through her bodily ministrations (1905b); but these allusions are scattered and anyway not developed into theoretical statements.

Freud did teach us to appreciate the fundamental developmental importance of the infant's prolonged helplessness and of the early danger situations corresponding to this helplessness, especially of loss of the love-object and loss of love (1926).

These realizations establish, of course, the basis for the mother's great authority. Clinical analysts know that this mother's authority stays with her children throughout their subsequent lives. For her children, the prospect of being abandoned by her physically and emotionally, really or in fantasy, never loses its painful, if not terrifying aspect. If anxiety over castration at the father's hand threatens to undermine the boy's narcissistic integrity and his present and future masculine sexuality, anxiety over losing the mother or her love threatens to undermine the boy's and the girl's very sense of worth or right to exist, and for both she is even a castrating figure of some consequence as well! And, to mention only two more considerations: psychoanalytic investigators of early mother-child relations and of early ego development now put great emphasis on the appeal and dread of merging with this mother, whether that be through incorporating her or being incorporated by her; and they also emphasize the infant's wishing to attack and damage her body and the babies inside it, and its consequent fear of her taking revenge in these very ways.

I am not arguing that the preoedipal-pregenital phases of development are *more* important in the neuroses than the oedipal. I do not even know how one might measure these factors. I am arguing for a developmental theory of resisting that is more complex and complete and *closer to our actual clinical work* than the one Freud left us. For this we must correct the patriarchal bias of Freudian theory.

(6) *Freud's attitude to early mental activity.* To complete this argument for establishing the mother, along with the father, in the center of the theory of resisting, I should attempt to set forth at least some of the reasons for Freud's curious diffidence with regard to these preoedipal matters. I think Freud's diffidence may be attributed in part to a methodological wisdom according to which one should attempt few definite formulations about mental life during the earliest years of life (see, e.g., 1931). Basing his propositions, as always, mainly on the clinical analysis of adults, he knew that the requisite memories are rarely available, even after significant reduction of infantile amnesia, and that reconstructions of very early infantile history from transference repetitions are too fragmentary and speculative to rely on confidently. In this regard he put to good use the scientific training and experience he had gathered before he

started the clinical work that was to result in his creating psychoanalysis. Yet I think more was within his reach than he grasped in this area of his developmental theory. There is reason to think that, using the clinical data available to him, he might well have arrived at some of the propositions about pregenital development that today are commonplaces. It would have been as central to his general theory and his clinical method to have undertaken this work as any other. Abraham, for one, was making the attempt and having noteworthy success with it (1924). But Freud chose to do otherwise.

In the main, however, the issue was not methodology. I think it was Freud's commitment to developing the systematic implications and applications of his discovery of the profoundly influential Oedipus complex and its associated castration fantasies. For Freud, this discovery was the foundation stone of his entire theory; after all, he said it was the nuclear complex of the neuroses! And he tried to protect this estimate of it. One way he tried to preserve this discovery's special place was by paying relatively little attention to mental development before the time of the Oedipus complex. One may say this of Freud despite his having written such papers as "Instincts and their Vicissitudes" (1915b) and "Negation" (1925b); for either these are merely fragments of a real theory of very early mental development ("Negation") or they are instances of his trying to allow for some mentation in the earliest period of life through the concept of instinctual aims and objects ("Instincts and their Vicissitudes"); and in section 2 of this chapter I argued that, by taking this latter step, Freud introduced many problems of personification and reification into his theorizing (see also Grossman and Simon 1969).

For the most part, however, Freud was content to refer to a preoedipal nucleus of ego development in the ill-defined system *Pcpt.-Cs.* (1923a). In Freud's view (and terms) real ego development—which means real cognitive development and object relations that are really represented as such—begins with the Oedipus complex, or, to be more exact, with the passing of the Oedipus complex, for only then is there an ego with the desexualized energies, the parental identifications, and the sublimations necessary for stable mental processes. And the Oedipus complex whose passing was foremost in Freud's mind was the boy's positive Oedipus complex. Elsewhere (1968b, ch. 7), I have tried to show that his oedipal theory of ego development presupposes much of the ego development that it is supposed to explain, and so, in that form, does not work in the way Freud proposed or to the extent that he assumed.

If it is granted now that Freud's approach to the place of parental authority in resisting was, relatively speaking, fragmentary and one-sided, as well as incorrect in certain important respects, it is possible to add these considerations to our other reasons for rethinking every important aspect of his concept of resistance. For some time now we have been encountering in our literature the same kind of fundamental rethinking of the role of preoedipal-pregenital development in the type, severity, and degree of resolvability of the Oedipus complexes of all children. We modern psychoanalysts see the Oedipus complex in a broader perspective than Freud did. I think that, not having discovered it and built psychoanalysis on it as a foundation, we can never value it as much as Freud did, and so, without really slighting the importance of the Oedipus complex, we are free to take a broader view than Freud in this respect. After all, we are standing on his shoulders!

If we think of the analysand as defying the archaic mother's authority, too, we will think as well of the growing importance to the child of differentiating itself from its mother; some of the defiance of her will be to this very end inasmuch as unvarying identity of aims or values perpetuates one's being merged with her. By dint of these strivings, the child establishes and maintains differentiation and wards off both its wishing to merge with its mother through incorporation and its mother's seductions to merge and her devouring approaches. These strivings are repeated in the analytic resisting in such forms as blocking the influence of interpretations (not "swallowing" and "digesting" them) and maintaining a detached, aloof, "bitter," mistrustful attitude to the analyst. From among many other instances of preoedipal resisting, I will mention only the "constipated" anal way of disappointing the analyst-mother of toilet-training. But, in taking account of these strivings toward differentiation and autonomy, we are characterizing defiance as an instrument of growth, too, and so are verging on the final topic of this chapter, negative and affirmative language in psychoanalytic propositions.

5. Negative and Affirmative Language in
Psychoanalytic Propositions

(1) *The search for affirmations.* In any theoretical or empirical investigation, everything depends on the way in which we
frame our questions. For as the questions go, so go the concepts
and the criteria of relevance and coherence of the investigation, and it is these that establish both what shall count as
observations and what the relationships among them shall be.
For example, by framing the right questions, Freud was able to
explore and understand infantile psychosexuality. It was not
just there to be worked over. Of course, the very framing of a
question involves the selection of concepts of a certain sort, a
step which already begins to limit the direction and the boundaries of further considerations.

There is a set of terms that makes up a negative language
and an incomplete and thereby potentially unanalytic perspective within psychoanalysis. Among these terms are resistance,
defense, negative therapeutic reaction, negativism, and defiance. These words refer to what the observer (who may be a
self-observer) regards as not doing something—something expected, usual, direct, realistic, comprehensive, satisfying, or
otherwise desirable. Left in their negative and incomplete
forms, these words are pejoratively tinged. This is so because
they direct attention only to what the analysand is *against,* or
what he or she is *not,* or *should be* or *should be doing;* they do
not direct attention to what he or she *is* and *is doing* as well. To
be cast in their complete, neutral, nonpatriarchal, and truly
analytic form, the propositions built around these words must
be developed into affirmations, too.

It is not that the negative terms are wrong, in the sense of
being descriptively inapplicable, for they do describe oppositional aspects of certain actions and modes of action. They are
centered on what someone is *against;* what they have in common is their *anti-aim* feature. One way or another, they all
block, cancel out, spoil, befoul, or destroy. But the unqualified
use of these negative terms does often indicate neglect of another and more essential aspect of the person's activities, that
is, they counter-suggest the goals one sets, the aims one maintains, and the successes one achieves. In the case of so-called
resistance or negativism, for example, these goals and suc-

cesses may include enjoying sadomasochistic excitement, maintaining emotional composure and self-esteem, getting "justified" revenge, keeping a friend or a lover, "hanging on" to sanity, or preserving a sense of differentiation and integrity. The goals are wish-fulfilments relevant to what we call, in metapsychological terms, id drives, ego interests, and superego dictates.

Here is a simple clinical example of what I mean. An analysand was dispiritedly reporting that lately he had just been "drifting," letting slide his work and some important applications he had to complete and send off. I commented that what he called drifting must be accomplishing something indirectly that he could not do openly, perhaps undermining his job and his future prospects for some reason as yet undefined. He responded by revealing a wishful daydream of chucking his present projects altogether, going to another city, starting all over again, perhaps finally doing the very things he would have rejected, but now with the conviction that he was freely choosing to do them and not, as he feared, submitting to the will and manipulations of his parents. Soon, however, he minimized this possibility and this daydream. In effect, then, his response to my affirmation-oriented comment was to say that he did have another program but was keeping it secret and inactivated. Thus, his negatively conceived "drifting" both concealed and indicated a threatening affirmation.

Looking at it from the analysand's standpoint, even the intention to be negativistic to the analyst is an affirmation of a certain kind; for example, it might affirm, "I have a mind of my own," "I will be manly rather than feminine in relation to you," or "I invite your sadistic attack." Furthermore, the terms "resistance" and "defense" are abstractions from specific actions of the analysand, each of which necessarily has its indicative designation, such as talking about trivia, over-emphasizing affectionate feelings, keeping secrets, or shifting blame. Ideally, the analyst as investigator will not be bound by the potentially evaluative and demanding negative terms; he or she will think also of implied affirmations and their explanations. And the analyst's thinking in this affirmative way will be entirely in accord with Freud's (1915c) conception of the system *Ucs.* as being altogether wishful and affirmative; he said that there are no No's in the *Ucs.* Analysis is a search for affirmations.

(2) *Health values.* In this perspective, health values and the terms they inspire, such as disease, symptom, cure, impairment, disorganization, and negative therapeutic reaction, are, at best, beside the point in *analytic* work and, at worst, obstructions to truly *analytic* understanding. The questions that the analyst steadily asks, implicitly if not explicitly, are these: "What is this person doing? What is this person aiming at? Why is he or she doing it? How are we to understand his or her living in just this way, producing just these symptoms, suffering in just this way, effecting just these relationships, experiencing just these feelings, interfering with further understanding in just this way and at just this time? How are these actions wish-fulfilling?" It is in this sense that clinical analysis eventuates in investigation of affirmations ("wish-fulfilments"). This is what is meant finally by analysis of resistance and defense. What are they *for*? What is this person *for*?

In this inquiry it is the person who is taken as the object of investigation, not his or her "affliction." And the goal of the inquiry is personal change through understanding, not "cure" through "treatment." The idea of curing affliction through treatment isolates or splits off the problems, the analysis, and the analyst from the analysand's conception of his or her being, a splitting off that is progressively reduced as the analysis proceeds. I recognize, however, that there is nothing to gain, and perhaps much to lose, by the analyst's initially insisting on an explicit mutual understanding that analysis will not be a "cure of affliction through treatment," for it is almost certain that, to a considerable extent, beginning analysands do not dare to see it any other way, just as they have not dared to view their troubled lives in an unsplit or undisclaimed way beforehand.

But lest it seem that I am proclaiming "the power of positive thinking," let me stress that, as I am using it, the idea of affirmation has nothing to do with conventional ideas of conscious goodness. As well as undertakings conventionally regarded as constructive, the notion of acting affirmatively includes acting greedily, exhibitionistically, enviously, expulsively, incestuously, and so on, and doing so unconsciously as well as preconsciously and consciously. And, as I said, during psychoanalysis the negative connotations of resisting must be focused on, too; "don't" and "won't" count as well as "do" and "will." Whatever it is, everything depends on our looking at it in more than one way (cf. the concept of *over*determination and the principle of *multiple* function).

(3) *Pregenital resisting and analyzability.* Not ever looking at things in more than one way is easily the most powerful "resistance" of all. There are people who, on attempting to be analysands, never take more than one really consequential view of their life situation. It is as though for all practical purposes they are continuously in one "danger situation" (e.g., fear of loss of love) or one "instinctual situation" (e.g., the anal stage of psychosexual development). However wide-ranging their conscious perspective and words might be, they react routinely as if life amounted to no more than being in this one situation.

In analysis such people soon reveal that unconsciously, they take a steady and exclusive view of the analytic situation as that one "danger situation" or "instinctual situation." To illustrate the latter possibility specifically, the would-be analysand might view analysis from the perspective of a two-year-old being toilet trained: for this analysand, associations (thoughts, feelings, physical movements) will be feces being extorted by the analyst; analysis will be designed to enforce cleanliness and submissiveness; resistance will be being constipated or, in the case of "acting out," being indiscriminately anally expulsive. And when the analyst interprets this anal perspective on the analytic situation itself, this analysand will take the interpretation as merely another fecal manipulation—a scolding for being dirty or disorderly, an anal seduction or rape, an enema, or some other assault on his or her autonomy and worth. Clearly, there will be no hearing the interpretation in terms other than the very terms that constitute the problem being interpreted. And, equally clearly, "cure" or "successful termination" of the treatment will be viewed by the analysand exclusively in the same terms. This means, of course, that for this analysand there is no conceiving of change in the future just because there is no envisaging any variety of experience, and so there is only living timelessly in a closed phenomenal world. Interpretation gets into an infinite regress; then there can be no analytic situation.

Let me refer schematically to a few more instances of this sort. Certain depressively inclined people envisage termination of analysis only as another devastating object loss; the immediate object being lost in the analyst who, in an extreme of transference reaction, is not recognized as such. Then there are certain masochistically orientated people who think of any "therapeutic cure" or "success" as being finally rejected after all, which is to say that they never fundamentally think of the analysis in terms other than those of sexualized suffering. In fact, all analysands reveal that they live in these unipolar worlds to a considerable extent; still, its not being their *only* world is what makes effective analysis possible in their cases. Freud emphasized how "cure" could be viewed as dangerous by the analysand in such ways as these (1937a).

I have drawn my examples from pregenital life, and this is the crux of the matter. When, speaking in traditional terms, we say that a person has powerful pregenital fixations or severe preoedipal pathology and add, as we are likely to do, that the person's ego is weak and that there is not enough observing ego to work with analytically, and then conclude that classical analysis or an approximation of it is contraindicated—when we say all this, are we not saying that, analyze as we may, we have no reason to count on this person's ever really being an analysand? To exist reliably as an analysand is to retain, even under great stress, some understanding of the rationale of analysis, and more or less to follow the analytic method, and to do so in terms that are relatively distinct from those of the burdensome, disruptive "fixations" or "pathology." Before a predominantly anal person will understand what analysis means, he or she must think about it with some degree of conviction *also* in other than anal terms, specifically, and other than "instinctual" terms, generally. A predominantly oral person must give comparable signs of not being limited to his or her oral orientation. And the person with "a severe superego" must somehow or other question the tyranny of "guilt" in the analytic situation.

Thus, when we say, as we do, that analysis is best-suited to people who have developed somewhat beyond the oedipalphallic phase of their childhood, despite their having established major "fixation points" along the way and their having "regressed" to these points in some respects, we imply, perhaps without realizing it consciously, that we expect them relatively reliably to view analysis unerotically and unsadistically, neutrally, and objectively, *however else they may also view it*. This means that, by virtue of their having developed somewhat beyond the oedipal-phallic phases, they do establish stable affectionate relationships with others ("capacity for good object relations"), and they do function more or less responsibly and rationally in the face of stress, anxiety, and guilt ("integrity," "maturity," and "good reality-testing").

One might view the severe pregenital fixations in traditional terms as involving questions of arrested ego development and ego deformation. Or one might view them phenomenologically as the person's seeming to exist in only one situation or to be in only one world—a narrow context of infantile danger, deprivation, and gratification. Alternatively, one might view these narrow pregenital orientations in quasi-Kantian epistemological terms as instances of the observer's being in principle unable to abstract himself or herself out of the very categories of knowing by which he or she constitutes knowing anything at all. Again, one might think of them in the terms of Wittgenstein's thesis that there can be no philosophical standpoint outside any given set of linguistic rules that constitutes a language.

In action terms, the action of seeing cannot simultaneously be the object of seeing. We do reflect on some of our actions after performing them, but that is to review past actions and so is another action altogether. And we do perform some of our actions observantly or attentively, but that is to perform them in a manner that is different enough from just performing them to qualify them as different, though related, actions. In either case, action language abolishes the tension between doing and observing the doing; it recognizes only—and significantly— different actions and different modes of action. Ryle (1949) dealt with this problem under the heading of the systematic elusiveness of the first-person pronoun, nominative singular "I." I remind you also of my critique, in section 3 of this chapter, of Freud's idea that the ego takes itself as object. These systematic formulations may be summed up figuratively in the idea that the eye cannot see itself directly.

Let us return to the analyzable person, the one who does reliably see the world in more than one way, including the somehow objective way. We can appreciate now what some of the main questions to be asked in this person's analysis will be: why is this person's situation or world of one kind at certain times and not others; and on which occasions does this person switch from one orientation to another, or fluctuate between two or more orientations, or, as if often the case and to every-one's confusion, mix several orientations?

(4) *"Resistance" as a perspective on the total person.* Final-ly, we come to realize what being in analysis means: not seek-ing "to be cured," but striving toward personal change through collaborative psychoanalytic understanding. And we under-stand this personal change to be constituted by the analysand's developing expanded versions of his or her past and present worlds, and by objectively defining and accepting his or her living in a context of social relationships which includes a variety of future options. To put it another way, the analysand gets to appreciate the complex cognitive-affective implications of his or her past, present, and future actions in the world.

In drawing these conclusions about analytic change, I am restating Freud's description of analysis as a method of ex-panding the scope of the ego at the expense of the id and superego, and also as a method of expanding the scope of the conscious, rational ego at the expense of the unconscious, infantile, defensive ego. But, however one puts it, it is clear that analysis has nothing to do with the idea of "becoming my old self again": that is the way of behavior therapy. As Freud put it, "The neurotic who is cured has really become another man, though at bottom, of course, he has remained the same . . . he has become what he might have become at best under the most favorable conditions" (1917b, p. 435). (One wishes he had said, "another man *or woman*.")

In this light we can see that what we have called analyzing resistance is analyzing one's opposing any change in the phe-nomenal world that one has constructed, especially any change that increases the scope and variety of that world and one's actions in it. But, as I have just argued, such an analysis means also getting to understand the affirmative reasons for the analysand's mounting this opposition. While mounting this op-position has its negative aspects, such as defiance, avoidance, dread, disclaimed action, and primitive reductionism in under-standing, it also has its affirmative, even constructive aspects, such as protecting relationships, being faithful to ideals, main-taining pride and autonomy, and achieving mastery. I men-tioned other, archaic affirmations earlier. In analysis it is the affirmative aspects above all that must be consciously defined and critically appraised. This takes time and patience, of course.

By thinking along these lines we can give more content to the traditional concept "ego-syntonic," especially as it is applied to so-called pathological or pathogenic factors (symptoms, perversions, character resistances, etc.). The term "ego-syntonic" hints at the concealed affirmations in apparently negative action. (See also Reich's discussion of character armor [1933].) We can also give more content to such ideas as "controlling" and "manipulating" other people and being "inhibited" and "defensive" in relation to oneself.

The so-called analysis of resistance has become for us the analysis of the total person. By analyzing all that the person does not wish to be or do, we analyze, too, everything that he or she is for. Together, these two aspects make up a total psychoanalytic view of a person. According to the conceptual approach I have been developing, the so-called analysis of transference would also become the analysis of the total person. This consequence implies that the terms resistance and transference are not the names of specific phenomena, problems, or dynamics of the analytic process. The relevant phenomena, problems, and dynamics are merely the occasions of our putting these terms to use. Ultimately, resistance and transference are *methodological* terms; they are the names the analyst gives to one or another slant he or she is taking on those features of a life that are currently prominent in the analysis. Understood in this way, all transference "is" resistance, all resistance "is" transference, and both "are" repetition, which is yet another analytic slant on lives. Other such equations are possible, too. Briefly, the idea of resistance is the idea of analysis, though it is not the only idea of analysis. And it is the idea of technique, too, though not the only idea of technique. Resistance is not everything, though it is a way of looking at everything.

6. SUMMARY

In the present chapter, I applied action language to the idea of resistance, using four approaches.

The first approach was a logical and linguistic analysis of the concept of resistance. I expounded the value of regarding resistance as an action—"to resist" or "resisting"—and developed

somewhat the implications of this approach for our understanding of such key concepts as psychic structure, the dynamic unconscious, determinism, and responsibility. Also, I
discussed the interrelated words, "can't," "won't," and
"don't," which present fundamental conceptual and technical
problems and possibilities for psychoanalysis.

The second approach was an analysis of the concept of self-
deception, a concept implied in all propositions concerning
resistance, defense, and unconscious mental processes. I revised Freud's final idea of conscious, preconscious, and unconscious as mental qualities, proposing instead that they refer to
modes of action and hence are best expressed adverbially (e.g.,
"unconsciously"). The dynamic unconscious was then reinter-
preted in action terms.

The third approach questioned the absence of the mother
from Freud's major discussions of resisting. Freud's one-sided
patriarchal model of mental development—the father-son relationship considered mainly in the light of the positive Oedipus
complex—is the key to his preferred clinical view that resisting
is defiance of paternal authority. With the help of action language, I discussed the resisting of girls and women, the boy's
and girl's resisting the mother's authority, and also took up
Freud's *relative* neglect, in his major systematic propositions
concerning mental development, of the pregenital mother-
child relationship and of early mental processes in general.

The fourth and final approach was a discussion of negative
and affirmative language in psychoanalytic propositions, in the
course of which I argued that, unless we also identify the affirmations implied by apparently negative behavior, we are
committed to using the idea of resisting pejoratively. Achieving
this balanced understanding has considerable technical significance and modifies our conception of psychoanalysis as a therapy. Also it paves the way toward our recognizing that resisting
is primarily a methodological term and only secondarily a technical problem; that is to say, what we call analyzing resistance
refers principally to our adopting a certain slant on the total
psychoanalytic process and thus on a total life. The same may
be said of "transference," repetition, and certain other basic
terms.

Part IV

The Emotions and Action

12 The Problem of the Emotions*

So many links have been forged between the idea of emotion and other key ideas about human existence that the prospect of discussing the emotions seems as forbidding as the prospect of discussing life in its entirety. This prospect becomes all the more formidable once it is realized how readily almost any reader might become emotional in response to what is being said about the emotions, as if he or she necessarily had a large personal stake in how I am handling the topic, indeed, as if I would somehow be tampering with, if not endangering, his or her own feelings. And the reader would be right about this; for how one thinks of the emotions establishes what they will be, not to speak of the esteem in which they will be held. I shall be arguing in the following pages that what we call our emotions, far from being simply "there" as entities of some sort to be thought about, are "there" only by virtue of a certain kind of thinking; additionally, I shall be arguing that each kind of thinking implies and implements values. I have already forecast this approach to the emotions in some of the preceding chapters, especially in section 4 of chapter 8.

I cannot expect many psychoanalysts to welcome my recommendation that they give up the infinite possibilities of literary device which, in keeping with our present unsystematized approach to the emotions, continue to remain available to all of us, for the seemingly lifeless possibilities of systematic discourse on this topic. Nevertheless, since I am attempting to establish an action language in the major areas of personal psychology, I must also discuss the emotions in its terms. However, in undertaking this project I am not required to present an empirical psychology of specific emotions; rather, I must define and work out the principal problems involved in using action language consistently in discussing emotions. I shall, of course, necessarily refer to specific emotions many times in this connection, but that is another matter.

*This chapter is a revised version of the introduction to "Emotion in the Language of Action," in *Psychological Issues*, Monograph No. 36 (1975). Other portions of that article are included, in revised form, in chapters 13 and 14 as well.

Even within the limits I just mentioned, it would be tedious to consider in detail the problems associated with every type of emotion-proposition. Because my project is methodological and my chief concern is with knowing how to use action language, it should suffice to discuss those ideas about emotion that seem to be strategically the most significant.

In the next three chapters I shall be considering such questions as the following. Is it consistent with the rules of action language to say that we "express" emotion or that we carry with us "old" or "deep" or "pent-up" emotion? When, if ever, are the words "feel" and "feeling" precise and useful in an action-vocabulary of emotions? May one ever speak of "the emotions" substantively, that is, as nouns? Is it not always a requirement of action language to view what we call emotions under the aspect of actions and modes of action rather than as some more or less abstractly designated things or events we experience? In other words, are not verbs and adverbs more suitable than nouns and adjectives for speaking of the emotions? If so, shouldn't we then disallow all the other ways in which we attribute substance and spatial location to emotion, such as those implied when we speak of emotional withdrawal, displacement, layering, state, locus, and mixture? Further, what can it mean to speak of sincere, deep, and real emotion as opposed to artificial, shallow, and pretended emotion? What of preverbal emotions? Nonverbal empathy? And, especially, what of "unconscious emotion," that chronically vexing question that I touched on earlier (chapter 11, section 3 [5])?

Other questions I shall be considering refer in one way or another to the fundamental idea of passivity in emotional life. The assumption that passivity characterizes the coming about of emotions so pervades our thinking, as in the notion that people struggle with their emotions—after the fact, as it were—that in psychoanalysis at any rate it has never been systematically examined, let alone thoroughly revised. In philosophy, however, Langer (1967) has developed an approach which places great emphasis on emotion as action; although her approach differs from mine in ways too complex to review here, her wide-ranging discussion does provide considerable support for my undertaking.

The problem of passivity is this: if adopting an action language entails our no longer using such mechanistic, substantializing conceptions as impulse, force, energy, threshold, and discharge, how, if at all, are we to construe and use the term passivity when speaking of emotion? To ask this question is to ask whether in the terms of action language we can ever *suffer* emotions or must always be *making* and *choosing* them through the performances in which we engage, including observing and labeling our own actions and bodily happenings. If the latter, what can it mean to say that we make and choose emotions, and what effect does our answer to this question have on our ideas of situation, stimulus, reaction, and experience? Are even those emotions that are felt in extreme situations or under duress to be viewed as made and chosen rather than caused and suffered? If so, what place would we then give to the physiological changes that are involved in so many emotions? For these at least seem to qualify as happenings that people could struggle with. And what significance, if any, would be retained by "the conflict theory of emotions" and "the signal theory of emotions" that have been assigned so large a part in psychoanalytic thinking. The questions are plentiful and difficult (see in this regard Rapaport [1953] and Schafer [1964, 1968c]).

One can hardly present any discussion of the emotions in which the problem of passivity is not implicated. Whether it is the control of emotion, the experience of emotion or whatever, the viewpoints with which we are familiar presuppose some definite separation of the person from his or her emotions and imply some independent activity of the emotions with which the person must cope, hence, in relation to which he or she stands in some initial posture of passivity. Consequently, there can be no way of discussing by itself the problem of emotional passivity that is not arbitrary in some measure. Nevertheless, I have reserved my most explicit and sustained discussion of this problem for chapter 15, "Emotion Undergone or Emotion Enacted?", on the assumption that the two chapters preceding it will have established the general foundations for this concluding and culminating discussion. By the same token, although chapter 14 is entitled "Reworking the Language of Emotion," in chapter 15, I will be found to be continuing that reworking; and in fact I will have begun that job already in chapter 13, "Defining Emotion as Action." It is the unity of these three chapters that justifies my segregating them in part IV, even though they are a continuation of the essays on action language presented in part III.

13 Defining Emotion as Action

1. VERBS AND ADVERBS

The idea of action language implies as the correct approach to
the emotions foregoing the use of substantives in making emotion-statements and employing for this purpose only verbs and
adverbs or adverbial locutions. That is to say, emotions are now
to be rendered as actions or modes of action. Thus, one is not to
speak of *an* emotion (or *an* affect or *a* feeling); one is to speak
of doing an emotion-action or doing an action in an emotion-
mode. This is the correct approach because it implements the
principle that one is to speak of people only as agents, that is,
as the performers of actions. What we call emotion is one of the
things people do or one of the ways in which they do things.

Verbs specify the emotion-actions; for example, to enjoy, to
hate, to fear, and to grieve.

Adverbs specify the emotion-modes of action; for example,
lovingly, hatefully, and fearfully. They modify any number of
verbs that may be intrinsically neutral, such as to walk, to talk,
and to think. We speak of walking fearfully, talking hatefully,
thinking lovingly, and so forth.

People frequently use verbs and adverbs in just these ways.
Clearly, I am far from proposing altogether new usage or new
words. I am proposing only that we limit ourselves to just these
familiar ways and that we forego the equally familiar but problematic abstract nouns or substantives such as love, jealousy,
and sorrow, which, typically, people concretize and personify.
In connection with love, for example, they speak of what *it* is
and what *it* does, of *its* properties and *its* tendencies, of *its*
source and *its* influence. In contrast, we would now speak of
those actions a person must perform in order to love and of
what acting lovingly entails.

In such a verbal shifting of gears, one is almost bound to
object to the idea that only verbs and adverbs may now be used
as emotion-words. It is worth repeating here the point I emphasized in chapter 6, that one is bound to view reluctantly, to say

the least, any proposal that one must adopt a revised language, thereby committing oneself to a changed mode of thought; for in doing so, even though one would still be using easily understandable and familiar English locutions, one would be giving up many familiar, tried and true conventions and presuppositions. One would then be moving into a world of being that is different enough to be, as different worlds always are, alarming. In the present connection, we are all used to and secure in the world in which we treat emotion as an *it*, an entity with a name of its own and adjectivally designated properties of its own. We are used to personifying emotions and "coping with them" as with people or creatures or spirits. Equally, we are used to and secure in the idea that emotions have ineffable or ultimately inaccessible aspects that can only be suggested or approximated by more or less witty, earthy, or fanciful metaphors and other devices of colorful speech and the arts. Now, however, there would be nothing to which one could in any sense at all gain access; there is only something one does. In the comparable case of imagining, my imaginings are not in any sense *mine* even though someone else can only learn about them from me; that is to say, my imagining is not something to which I have access, but something I do, and I may, in a further action, go on to convey something about it to someone else. In the same sense, upon moving into the modified world of action language, emotion becomes a *how* or a *thus* rather than an *it*.

To say that emotion would be fully and necessarily designated by verbs and adverbs is to imply that the notion of residuals would become superfluous. One's maintaining that there are residuals could only mean that one is dissatisfied with an existing statement and wants to search for alternative or additional verbs and adverbs in order to develop one's rendition more fully, exactly, or vividly. For these verbs and adverbs are not *about* emotion; they are emotion conceived. What cannot be stated at all with verbs and adverbs, what seems to be ineffable or forever limited to private access, cannot be emotion; for to claim that it can be emotion in this sense is also to say that it cannot be experienced. On the other hand, to think of something smilingly without smiling is a defined and communicable experience and qualifies as an instance of emotion— one that cannot be accommodated in behaviorist psychology.

Once some supposed residual is stated in appropriate terms—

should this become possible upon further thought or other action—the conception and experience of the emotion in question will be changed, if only by being further defined. Otherwise, the "residual" must remain emotion unconceived, no more than a potential, an action that can exist only in the conditional mode (what one would feel if . . .). To accept these formulations is to allow a radical assault on the many modes of thinking by which, unconsciously, we shape our observations of human existence and our theoretical discourse about it.

However, objection to this action thesis might also be grounded elsewhere than in the effort to beat back a challenge to accustomed modes of thinking or being. It might be argued that to follow the action rules would be to eliminate any basis for deciding on the truth value of propositions concerning emotion. One might insist that, before one can legitimately say of any emotion-proposition that it is objective or true, one must be able to point to some *it* to which the emotion-words correspond. Just what would one be talking about otherwise? The answer to this objection is this: certainly, our empirical statements about emotions have to be falsifiable; otherwise, one could say anything concerning emotion regardless of its emptiness or absurdity. But vacuousness and arbitrariness are not logical consequences of my thesis. For the rules according to which we use the verbs and adverbs in question or, if one prefers, the implicit criteria we use in attempting to apply these words correctly, are well known and generally regarded as useful, even when they are not universally agreed upon in every respect. We do know what it is to make a mistake in referring to emotion or to disagree about an emotion and to muster proof for one point of view or another. For example, what in the ordinary way we call (substantively) love or grief or hatred is the performing of certain more or less conventional emotion-actions and emotion-modes, and nothing other than that. The *it* to which the verbs and adverbs correspond is the set of actions and modes in question; establishing these, we establish what the emotion is. This has always been the case. How else have we ever established knowledge about emotions? To be persuaded of this point about the rules of emotion language, one has only to listen to two people arguing over whether one "really" loves the other or hates the other, or to listen to one person, who may be oneself, ruminating over questions of that sort. I shall develop this counterargument more fully as I continue.

To make it clear that this is not a behaviorist argument, I must emphasize that these actions and modes include private "feeling tones" that are potentially reportable in addition to the "feeling tone" of public actions.

Another ground on which my thesis seems open to criticism is the redundancy entailed by retaining both verbs and adverbs as emotion-words. To hate and to act hatefully; to fear and to act fearfully; and so forth: each pair seems to consist of two ways of saying the same thing. Consequently, it might be argued that, in the interest of clarity and economy, we should settle on just one form, the verb or the adverb. In response to this criticism, it must be pointed out that we do not have such pairs in every instance. For example, we have no verb that is equivalent to the adverb anxiously (and the noun anxiety); we use such verbs as to fear, to dread, and to worry, to do somewhat different jobs, and, for reasons given elsewhere in this chapter, it would be consistent with the rules of action language to avoid locutions built around the verb to be, as in "to be anxious." Similar considerations apply to angrily, anger, and to be angry.

It might be possible to reduce all adverbs to verbs on the idea that a mode of action must be a set of actions with a certain kind of internal consistency. I think it likely, however, that any such reductionistic effort would be endless owing, first, to how invaluable we find adverbs to be for the scope, versatility, and precision of our descriptions of action and, secondly, to the virtual inevitability of our using adverbs in our very efforts to reduce adverbs to verbs. Similar considerations apply to reducing everything to adverbs. On the assumption that it is logically permissible and useful to retain both verbs and adverbs in the present version of action language, I shall not attempt to settle this question here.

Finally, if it is objected that emotion-verbs and emotion-adverbs are themselves abstractions and so are in some sense entities like the nouns they are replacing, I must reply with this reminder: it has already been accepted that actions may be designated on every conceivable level of generality or abstractness, so that on this account they do not lose the name of action. The same is true of modes. For example, the verb to fear

is no less an action because it subsumes a number of more concrete actions and modes, such as to flee, to avoid, to act timidly
or placatingly, to have a sinking feeling or a clutching feeling,
and so forth. It is not at all abstractness that is in question here,
but rather nominative designations.

2. "HEART" AND THE BODILY METAPHORS OF EMOTION

It is characteristic of infantile thinking, as it is of everyday
speech, to represent emotion-actions and emotion-modes in
bodily terms. In ordinary language, we so take for granted the
bodily figures of speech that they seem natural, true, or inevitable rather than imaginative constructions. Upon reflection,
however, it is not difficult to realize that in this way we are
using and suggesting common irrational, animistic fantasies
about the anatomy, physiology, life-cycle, and social context of
the body. So it is that casually, even unthinkingly, we invoke
the intestines ("guts"), the liver ("lily-livered"), the spine
("spineless"), and the testicles ("no balls"), and we go on in this
way about the stomach, spleen, buttocks, feces, urine, blood,
senses, birth, death, contact, and, time and time again, the
heart. In order to illustrate in an introductory way some of the
principal consequences of these essentially archaic, though
conventionalized, body-centered metaphors of emotion, I shall
center my remarks in this section on the idea of heart.

Obviously, I have taken the locutions in question not from
the language of theoretical psychoanalysis but from ordinary
language. Why then should we even pause briefly to consider
them? My answer is this: through ordinary language the world
supplies all of the mind-formative locutions encountered by the
young, language-learning child; the physical or material metaphors and implications of ordinary language are among its
dominant features; and unwittingly, we theorize with biases
and constraints corresponding to the structure and logic of
these body-oriented locutions. The result is that, far more than
we have dared to realize, our psychoanalytic propositions concerning the emotions have been no more than technical, scientific, or professional versions of this ordinary bodily language
(see also chapter 8, esp. section 5).

What, then, of heart? In everyday speech we refer to the
heart as the source and container of emotions. Usually, we re-

serve heart for positively valued emotions or emotional conduct, as when, with more or less clear meaning, we say hearty, heart-felt, big-hearted, a full heart, a broken heart, have a heart, and heavy heart. In such instances we seem to mean loving, compassionate, generous, tender, vigorous, courageous, concerned, responsible, and other such "good things." But heart is ambiguous enough to require qualification in many instances; it does not always denote a warm, lively quality of emotions. For instance, we also say chicken-hearted as well as stouthearted, coldhearted as well as warmhearted, and, equally for hate and love, we say with all one's heart and from the bottom of one's heart.

The logical problems posed by these locutions are obvious. The heart is being put in place of the person, which is to say that the speaker is either personifying an organ or portraying a way of acting as a substance or a quantity of energy of a certain kind. Moreover, this substance or energy, if it is not presented as being dispensed by a heart of a certain disposition, is at least held to emanate from the heart. In comparable synechdoches, people reduce themselves to brain or mind when they say such things as "scatterbrained" or "a logical mind" (see also chapter 7, section 3). Depending on the psychoanalyst's context of goals and concepts, this substitution of part for whole may be viewed as a splitting of self or ego, a projection into an organ of an attribute of self or ego or id, magical thinking, a disclaimer of responsibility, a fantasy of being invaded or controlled by some foreign agency (as by a god, e.g., Cupid), etc. In any case one must acknowledge that the implied substantializing and personifying of emotion-actions and emotion-modes are major structural features of the way people ordinarily think and communicate about themselves and others.

How might we translate heart-metaphors into the action language of verbs and adverbs? A warmhearted person is someone who deals affectionately and generously with others. A chicken-hearted person is one who fearfully avoids dealing with ordinary dangers. A hearty person is one who does a variety of things vigorously, zestfully, and good-humoredly. When people have a heart-to-heart talk, they are making known to each other certain emotional ways in which they have been thinking about and dealing with each other; it is implied that hitherto they have kept these ways private, indirect, vague, or even mostly unformulated or incoherently formulated.

I propose these few translations casually. In the next section I shall consider at greater length the complex issues involved in translating ordinary emotion-words into action language. Before doing so, I want to emphasize again that translation is necessarily both approximate and transformative, so that it is unwarranted to reject a translation merely because it seems inexact. The world must change with the translation, if ever so slightly. One cannot have it both ways.

3. FIVE EMOTIONS: HAPPINESS, LOVE, ANGER, GUILT, AND FEAR

This section contains brief essays on five specific emotions. It is my purpose in presenting these essays to illustrate the differences between using, in the case of our emotion-words, nouns on the one hand and verbs and adverbs on the other. In this connection I shall have occasion to demonstrate how the apparently fundamental theoretical ideas of pleasure principle, aggression, and libido simply repeat the logically problematic modes of ordinary language.

(1) *Happiness and happily.* In daily life we speak of being filled with happiness, of seeking and finding happiness ("the pursuit of happiness"), and of the destruction of happiness. In each instance we are speaking of happiness as an entity. Having given it a noun name, we have apparently legitimized a concretistic way of thinking about the topic. Through similar locutions, we have made an animated *it* of joy, pleasure, hope, trust, serenity, bliss, and other such desirables.

Using action language, we replace the idea of happiness by the idea of doing actions happily. As a first approximation, to do actions happily is to be likely, while doing them, to smile, laugh, sing, and dance; to embrace oneself and others; to speak favorably of oneself and one's situation and of other persons as well; perhaps to undergo some physiological sexual arousal; and to believe that one has what one wants and has it securely and to be potentially able to say so. When we observe others acting in some or all of these ways, we infer that they are happy, which is to say that we realize that whatever it is they are doing, they are doing it happily; it is not that they "have" or "have found" any entity happiness.

One of those whom one might observe doing things happily is oneself. To say this is to say that one's acting happily is something one may come to realize. In this instance one will be making much the same type of observations and drawing much the same type of conclusions as one would when observing others. One would not be relying on any privileged access to some entity called happiness that is forever unobservable by others. Whatever the reasons, sometimes one's readiness to sing and dance, for example, might not be visible to others, owing perhaps to one's taking care effectively to present oneself to others in a different guise; at these times one will just be observing more of one's actions than others can, for the time being anyway. Keeping secrets from others is also an action. On the other hand, one might be more biased than others in observing one's own actions. Keeping secrets *from oneself* is yet another kind of action one might take (see the discussion of self-deception in chapter 11, section 3). The result is that others might discover some of one's own secrets of which one is consciously ignorant. An obvious instance is the manic person's effectively redefining depressive situations in order to avoid consciously experiencing things depressively, and overtly behaving accordingly; this is a course of public and private action that usually is transparent to the trained clinical examiner.

Apart from keeping secrets from oneself, one might just be observing one's actions intermittently, carelessly, ignorantly, or crudely, and so coming to correspondingly inaccurate conclusions. Equally, one may observe faultily one's own actions and the actions of others. Especially in connection with "heightened emotion" do we expect people to observe their actions and modes of action faultily.

In no case can it be legitimately implied that, after all these other factors have been taken into account, some residual pure emotion exists which in principle can be reached only by the "introspecting" subject looking somewhere "inside" (see chapter 8). We cannot, in this sense, ask *what* happiness is or *where* it is. And with so large and varied a family of actions and modes embraced by the idea happily, could there ever be even a specific physiology of happiness to point to? Need there even be physiological concomitants in each and every instance of happiness?

On the same grounds, we can argue the necessity and usefulness of the adverbial designations joyfully, trustfully, hopefully, serenely, blissfully, and so forth. In some instances we also have available to us proper and useful emotion-verbs, such as to enjoy, to hope, and to trust.

In his *Ethics,* especially in Book X, Aristotle argued that pleasure should be regarded as an attribute of action rather that as an entity or process. The possibility and desirability of an action language for the emotions is, I think, derivable from that discussion, particularly with the further guidance provided by Ryle (1949) and Austin (1946, 1956). The point has consequences for Freud's pleasure principle: even though that principle is now generally understood to refer to certain degrees and rates in the rise and fall of psychic tension that people experience pleasurably, though not necessarily only pleasurably and not necessarily consciously, still it depicts people as basically pleasure-seeking; whereas in action terms one would now say that they seek to do things pleasurably (and to avoid doing things painfully). The adverbial designation, pleasurably, entails no denial or minimization of the facts that people do consistently act in this way, that certain actions of a psychosexual nature are especially well suited for the pleasurable mode, and that these actions in these modes are often and significantly performed unconsciously.

(2) *Love, to love, and lovingly.* To love and to act lovingly are the proper forms for rendering the idea of love in action language. Having thereby lost its status as an entity in this language, love can no longer make the world go round; it can no longer glow, grow, or wither; and it can no longer be lost or found, cherished, poisoned, or destroyed. We are to regard those kinds of concretistic and personified ideas as referring to our actions, including thought-actions, and the modes in which we perform them, including modes of thinking. It is we who regard the world as going round, in that excited sense of the image; it is we who glow, love more or love less, love at all or stop loving, or imagine wildly and perhaps unconsciously that our hearts or minds have been poisoned; it is we who write or enjoy reading the poetry in which love is allegorized in many shapes and with many powers.

The metapsychological idea of libido should be reviewed in connection with this analysis of love-words. I contend that in speaking of libido, we are merely giving the appearance of endowing discussions of sex, pleasure, and love with the (presumed) scientific "dignity" of mechanics, hydraulics, or electrostatics. One has only to inspect how we use the idea of libido to realize that this hypothetical energy is no more than a poetic condensation of many concretistic, personified ideas. In our theoretical propositions, we present libido as an energy that waxes and wanes, as one that accumulates and is discharged, as one that attaches itself tenaciously to ideas of people and things but may also abruptly and totally withdraw itself from them in response to the vicissitudes of gratification; we present it as an energy that may be controlled, even ruthlessly suppressed, by a cohesive agency, the ego, that has itself been constituted by this very energy since it is the nature of this energy to bind all mental things together (libido as Eros). Additionally, we maintain that the primary urgency or peremptoriness of libido is only partly modifiable and that its modification ("neutralization") is frequently difficult to sustain. In its biologically based pure state, this libido is imperious in its demands, and, in the extreme, in its uncompromising drive toward pleasure at any cost, it may even overwhelm and demolish what it has also established—the ego (or self) and its world. With this status, libido also seems to stand as the theoretical link between body and mind; Freud presented it just that way.

It should be obvious what lurks barely concealed behind the physicochemical and biological language of libido: primarily, ideas of hot blood coursing through one's veins, clinging lovers, rapists, unrestrained masturbators, orgastic ecstasy, and ejaculate substance, together with erect penises, warm and moist vaginas, drooling mouths and incontinent sphincters; and, secondarily, ideas about the many superficially nonsensual forms of self-satisfaction and satisfaction in others that may also be thrilling in their own way, as, for example, the forms of vanity, triumph, devotion, and awe. I suggest, therefore, that the popularity of the term libido rests on its serving so well as a pseudoscientific poetic metaphor for all the psychosexual actions people do or imagine doing, often unconsciously, and all the excited, tenacious, fluid, and pleasurable ways in which they might perform any action at all; and to its serving in the same way to allude to the parts, substances, and changes of the body and its sensations that may be involved in these actions and modes of action. Again, there is no denying or minimizing bodily processes and psychoanalytic observations and interpretations; only the language is in question— but that is a lot.

The theme of this subsection is love. It is because psychoanalysts generally speak of libido in connection with sex and pleasure as well as love that I have not attempted to sort out these uses in the preceding paragraphs.

(3) *Anger and angrily.* I return here to a topic I took up in chapter 8, section 4; for the most part these two discussions complement rather than duplicate each other, and here I shall have occasion to take up aggression as the other type of psychic energy.

In daily life, we have created an emotional entity that we call anger. We have done so by giving it a name in noun form. We think of this entity as being a substance or quantity of energy that behaves somehow like a person in its being insistent, devious, emphatic, destructive, and so forth. As one analysand said, "It's bad if I let anger do to me what it did—overwhelm me." Speaking of a third person, another analysand said, "If his emotions of anger are aroused, they make him violent."

As a substance, the entity anger may be implicitly liquid (when it is said to spill over), solid (when it is said to crush or penetrate), gaseous (when it is said that one must keep the lid on it), or some combination of the three. Unconsciously, we usually represent this entity as excrement: feces (firm or loose), urine (flooding or burning), or flatus (explosive or poisonous). Further, this excremental stuff is personified or conceived animistically so that it seems to exhibit such properties of agency as being furtive, persecutory, or recalcitrant. Then it may appear as ratty, swinish, predatory, monstrous, and so forth. We allude to these excremental representations consciously in our figurative language (e.g., to take shit from someone).

In thinking this way about anger, one necessarily thinks of oneself as having to contend with this inspirited stuff. That is to say, one thinks that, though this entity is *in* the self, it is not *of* the self; thus, the self must still act in relation to it or deal with it. One makes of anger (and thereby also of one's excremental substances, organs, and urges and their personified presentations) one's demon, though sometimes one thinks of it (and them) as one's ally or valuable weapon. We accept a basic and fateful split in our ideas of ourselves as persons.

I shall make a leap here (not a huge one, really) to the metapsychology of aggression. Following Freud, we have accepted aggression as a quite general instinctual impulsion. We define aggression as an energy whose quality is destructive. It is destructive in the sense that its potential is restricted to those processes that bring about fragmenting, oppositional, hurtful, eliminative, sullying, or alienating effects. If not inevitably literally destructive, this energy is at least oppositional and divisive, perhaps useful in setting boundaries and asserting rights, privileges, and responsibilities. But in any case it is destined for and limited to some version of fight or attack. Further, according to metapsychology, when one feels anger or expresses it, one is experiencing the increase or discharge of a quantity of the energy aggression.

It should be obvious that, in using this theory, one is speaking of aggression as though it were the creature, spirit, substance, or quantity encountered in everyday speech, as described above. It does not go too far to suggest that, however austerely this conceptualization may be expressed, it implies an archaic, animistic, usually excremental model of aggression.

In action language, we avoid setting up this kind of entity or *it*. Consequently, we no longer accept and use this conception of aggression and such nominative variations on it as anger, hostility, and hate. We replace aggression with "acting aggressively," anger with "acting angrily," etc. (see also Hayman 1969 and Gillespie 1971). Our rules for using the suitable verbs and adverbs remain those we have always used, and we may make them explicit in order to justify our employing aggression-words once a question is raised about our terms. It is not so much a matter of one's inferring that someone is angry as a matter of explaining how one uses the word angry; sometimes, however, as in the case of the analyst's work, inferring is involved. These rules apply to a family of actions and modes of actions only some members of which, and not always the same ones, need be present before the verbs and adverbs in question may be used aptly or justified.

To return to anger: the mode of acting angrily includes tensing muscles, clenching teeth, biting fiercely, hitting, soiling, thinking of attack, and subjectively defining it as vengeance or defense or even pleasure, and so on and so forth. Acting angrily, even if only by fantasying, tends to be accompanied by certain kinds of appropriately speeded-up physiological processes; these, however, though they support the designation "angrily," are not themselves actions in the sense of personal projects.

The person who is acting angrily and the others who may be witnesses of the relevant actions and modes may not realize consciously that he or she is acting that way. In principle, however, one and all *could* infer it. This is so because, as there is in action language no entity emotion but only emotion-actions and emotion-modes, there can be no ultimately privileged access to anger: there can only be observation, reasoning, and communication made more or less consciously and knowledgeably by people.

Among the observers of acting angrily may be one who is possibly, but not necessarily, in an especially favorable position as observer; this is the one who performs the actions and modes in question—the agent. In his essay, "Other Minds," J.L. Austin (1946) presented a similar discussion of emotion in general and anger in particular.

(4) *Guilt and guiltily.* Guilt is another of the emotional entities that we have created by giving it a name in noun form. Sometimes this entity is material, as when we speak of it as a crushing load or a burden to be cast off; sometimes it is ghostly, as when we say it haunts or torments one. We often personify guilt as an inner tyrant, a judge, or a policeman demanding that we be exposed and punished. It was in connection with these versions of guilt that Freud said he preferred the idea of need for punishment to the idea of guilt feelings. In any event, when we are so to speak seeking to evade guilt, to repress it, or to atone for our "sins," we are maneuvering in relation to this harsh authority.

The concept of superego comes into question in this regard. In its individual rather than social aspect, one thinks that it is oneself who is doing the scolding or punishing, perhaps unconsciously. Metapsychologically, we call this individual aspect by the name Freud gave it, the superego, and we say it is an intrapsychic agency. But by resorting to this language, we no longer say (what is perfectly adequate to the occasion) that sometimes one judges one's own actions in an irrational, infantile, severely moralistic, or punitive manner, and especially that one does so even unbeknown to oneself, that is, unconsciously; we say instead that it is one's superego that (or who) judges one's ego (or one's self) in these ways. Thereby we set up superego as a personified entity of another sort: a so-called psychic structure that sets standards, prohibits, judges, and punishes cruelly just as the parents of one's childhood once did or, with the help of exaggeration, seemed to do or seemed ready to do. The obsessional neurotic is our best example in this connection.

Like the noun anger, however, the noun guilt is, within the framework of action language, an unsatisfactory designation of the phenomena to which it pertains. The phenomena now must be rendered as ways of acting, namely guiltily. These ways of acting include behaving as though one expects some deserved and perhaps severe punishment, thinks of oneself as an immoral wretch, and in many instances either consciously or unconsciously tries to bring about a "punishing" by some person or agency in one's environment or else punishes oneself through self-imposed deprivation, humiliation, pain, or injury. Both as characteristics of thinking or as features of publicly observable deeds, these ways of acting constitute the meaning of guiltily: they are its referents, the members of the family of guilt-words, the phenomena that we define and organize by using the adverb "guiltily."

As I mentioned, one may act guiltily without recognizing that one is doing so. In this case we might speak of one's unconsciously acting guiltily or unconsciously desiring or bringing about "punishing" misfortune. Other people who are observing one's actions of this sort may not realize consciously that one is acting guiltily; this may be the result of their ignorance, their careless observing, their being deceived, or their behaving repressively with respect to the very idea. In principle, however, anyone, including oneself, may get to realize consciously that one is acting guiltily; for this way of acting, like acting angrily, is a knowable even though not presently known mode of action. It is not inescapably privileged. Psychoanalytic interpretion presupposes this proposition.

We shall have to choose other words with dysphoric meaning in the same way in order to use action language systematically; for example, sadly rather than sadness, miserably rather than misery, depressively rather than depression, and the same for suspiciously, despairingly, agitatedly, etc. In some instances, suitable verb forms are directly available; for example, to suspect, to despair, and to regret.

(5) *Fear, to fear, and fearfully.* Along with the entities happiness, love, anger, and guilt, we have created the entity fear and endowed it with the properties of agency. We say of fear that it grips us, strikes us, betrays us, paralyzes us, and overwhelms us. Fear may lurk, hide, creep, loom, and attack. It may be a wave, a flood, a spasm, a twinge, or a fit. As if reactively, the self or ego may yield to it, suppress it, nip it in the bud, or use it as a signal, as a tool of interpersonal relation, or as a mode of erotic gratification ("libidinization of anxiety").

In contrast, we render fear in action terms through the adverb fearfully and the verb to fear. In both of these instances we should be able to specify, whenever necessary, at least some of the bodily changes, public behavior, and thought-actions that are the referents, and so the occasions, of these terms. To fear is, among other things, to engage in fantasies of harm coming to one from some source of danger; to develop ideas of fleeing from that danger or else attacking its source; to make incipient movements of attack or escape, both of which involve setting off physiological and muscular changes that enable the anticipated exertions to be performed; to be restless; and either to be hypervigilant and jumpy or to avoid representing the danger consciously (denial, repression, counterphobic activity). It is when we see people doing these actions in these ways that we say in action language that they fear something or that they are acting fearfully, whereas, when we are employing the substantive language, we say that they are filled with fear, dominated by fear, striken with fear, or something of that sort.

It should be noted that in neither language are we implying that the person has correctly and consciously recognized even one objective danger. So-called phobias and anxiety attacks illustrate this independence of fear-propositions from consciously and correctly ascertained dangers. Freud favored the designation "fear" in relation to conscious and objective dangers and "anxiety" in relation to dangers that are set up irrationally, unconsciously, and in disguised form. We may adhere to this verbal convention without violating the rules concerning the words fear, to fear, and fearfully; for the fact is that in this subsection we might just as well have used as our key words anxiety and anxiously, and, in the same way, seen how, *without loss of clinical understanding and range,* the noun anxiety is both inadmissible in action language and easily dispensed with. The word anxiously should suffice (see also sections 6 and 8 of chapter 15).

4. To Feel and Feelings

Among the most popular of all emotion-words is the verb to feel. Its popularity is, however, matched by its great ambiguity, which is to say the many different ways in which it is used, and so also by the problems to which its uses give rise. These uses include to feel some emotional state (thrilled or despondent), to feel some interpersonal situation (rejected or intimate), to feel that something is so (true or about to happen), to feel like doing something (playing tennis or keeping quiet), to feel as if something is happening (as if one is being pried into or the world is crumbling), and to feel some emotionally toned bodily state (tired or hungry). Although these uses more or less overlap one another, they may not be reduced to just one meaning. Consequently, in order to develop further an action language for the emotions, I shall have to discuss typical or strategically significant uses of to feel. My doing so should make it possible to decide finally on how, if at all, one might still be able to use to feel as an emotion-verb. The important place we give to "to feel" in our language warrants a lengthy review of the problem (cf. Langer 1967).

Two things I shall not do. First, I shall not discuss the verbal noun feelings. I base this decision on a conclusion I have come to which I shall merely state and not argue. There has not been one successful attempt to show that the word feelings can be used systematically and profitably to mean something other than emotions. I take the same view of the emotion-word most favored in the metapsychological language, namely affects. That nevertheless each of these two words retains its own penumbra of ambiguities does not require me to alter my conclusion. Accordingly, I present this entire chapter as a discussion of feelings and affects as well as (because equivalent to) emotions.

The second thing I shall not do is discuss the use of to feel in its physical or sensory meaning. In this use, to feel is not an emotion-word at all. Tactile actions can, of course, be performed emotionally or in an emotional context; for example, we speak of feeling a lover's body passionately. But the action itself is like walking and talking in its not being inherently an emotion-action. Recognizing, however, that sensory thresholds and qualities do have their psychosomatic aspects, in that they vary somewhat with the agent's beliefs, attitudes, and situations, I shall say a bit more about these phenomena later on. The sensory meaning of *to feel* is implied in the tactile metaphors that confer upon emotion-words the spurious authority of bodily substantiality; for example, the ideas of "gut feeling" and of "having a feel" for one or another kind of nonsubstantial activity or subject matter, such as human relationships, suggest that emotion is after all an affair of the body, especially of its sensory equipment. When we use these tactile metaphors, we obscure conceptual problems of emotion in relation to action.

I shall now review ten common ways in which we use *to feel* as an emotion-word.

(1) One might use *to feel* to indicate indefinitely that one is thinking in some emotional mode. The thinking might be in the nature of assuming, comparing, remembering, anticipating, and so on. For example, one might say, "I feel that he is honest," when one means something more than "I judge that he is honest" or "I guess that he is honest" or something of that sort; for by using *to feel* in this way, one would be indicating something about the emotional mode in which one is judging or guessing or whatever. For example, one might be speaking *ambivalently* (is overriding some doubt to say so), *hopefully* (would be pleased if it were so), *anxiously* (would not dare to assert it flatly), *frustratedly* (has not established the point as convincingly as one hoped), or *insecurely* (is asking the listener not to press too hard for proofs). Upon encountering any one of these uses of *to feel*, the listener must rely on context plus nonverbal cues in order to establish just which emotion-mode is being used. On the other hand, sometimes one says, "I feel," in order to establish this very ambiguity as a loophole in case it should become necessary to escape taxing criticisms or insistent demands that one justify one's statement: "Well," one might then say, "it was just my feeling."

(2) One might speak of feeling an emotion either in its specific sensory meaning of *to touch* or in its general meaning of

to grasp through the senses. For example, one male analysand said, "I felt my anger; I got in touch with it finally." Often, of course, one does feel the bodily changes that are concomitants of some kinds of acting emotionally. But it would be incorrect to conclude on the basis of such locutions that these perceived bodily changes *are* the emotion, let alone that the speaker has literally got in sensory touch with an emotion. To have put his idea more accurately, and the assumptions on which it was based more explicitly, the analysand I just mentioned might have said (of course, in his own words), "I realize that I am angry not only by knowingly thinking of taking revenge for what was done to me; I am also taking account of the fact that I am as physically aroused as I am and in the way I am"; further, "I think of my anger as a substance that may be touched and simultaneously as something that is an aspect of my psychological self that is within reach of my body"; and, finally, "I am often unsure whether I am responding angrily or not; this time, using this evidence, I am sure." In this instance it is evident that the appropriate use of emotion-words may be arrived at (realized) rather than given; it is also evident that each such observation of one's own actions, as of the actions of others, may be presented as an inference and cannot be taken only or simply as an instance of naive, unmediated perception. Observation implies potential accountability. This is so even though the observation might be made, as it often is, "in a flash" and unreflectively.

With respect to the use of emotion-words, it always makes sense, even if it is unusual, to ask, "How do you know?" or "How do I know?" Again, there are no pure feelings to which only the subject-observer can have access. In another context, it would have been more accurate, instead of saying, "I felt my anger; I got in touch with it finally," if the aforementioned analysand had said something like this: "I imagine my anger to be a cold, knifelike blade, and it was as if I could feel it in my gut right then." In other instances, analysands indicate that they imagine anger to be venom, fangs, projectile feces, or other such concrete aggression-substances; typically, they imagine all this unconsciously, though common speech is pervaded by the deliverate use of these ideas as metaphors.

(3) One might use to feel to suggest that one is doing an action in that complex way that is more exactly designated by

the adverbs attentively, heedfully, observantly, even self-consciously in the sense of seeming to see oneself through the eyes of real or imagined others. In the case of an emotion-action, the "felt" action is more complex than just doing it; in the case of a "felt" emotion-mode, it is more complex than just doing it in that specific emotional way. (To some extent, I implied this idea of complex actions and modes of action under (1) and (2) above.) For example, to say, "I feel that I care" or "I feel mistrustful of him" is to allude to the idea that, at least for the moment, one is caring or mistrusting in a certain complex, self-scrutinizing way, and that, accordingly, one's experience is not quite what it would be were one to be simply or spontaneously just caring or mistrusting. In these uses of to feel, one is not referring only and directly to emotion; one is referring to a cognitive complication of an emotion-action or emotion-mode such that the simple performance of it is no longer in question.

(4) One might use to feel as part of a simile that suggests some fantasy content. This is the *as if* use of to feel. For example, "I feel like my anger is rising," "I feel like I'm being pried into," "It feels as if I'm walking on air," and "I feel like a worm." In each such instance one is using the verb to feel very much in the sense of to imagine, though in some of these instances one might also be alluding as well to actual bodily sensations (e.g., sensations of muscular stiffening in reaction to intimate questions).

(5) One might use the verb to feel to refer to one's being disposed to do something or at least to one's thinking that one is so disposed. For example, in saying, "I feel like playing tennis," one is likely to mean, "I would do a lot to play," "It would please me to play," "I'm eager to play," "I'm looking for a chance to play," "I hope I'll get a chance to play," or, finally, by indirection, "Would *you* like to play?"

(6) To feel might be used in the sense of to be about to do something, to be on the verge of doing it, to be beginning to do it, perhaps even to be barely refraining from doing it, or else to be taking care not to do it. For example, "I feel like crying" usually carries one or more of these virtually-but-not-quite-doing-it meanings.

(7) To feel might be used as part of an implicit conditional statement—this overlaps the uses just described under (5) and

(6). For example, in certain contexts one says, "I feel like crying," when one means, "But for the consideration that this or that problem would arise if I cried, I would cry." It is a way of saying what one would do or how one would do it if only one felt freer, safer, or otherwise readier to do so.

(8) One might use to feel to allude to one's recognizing that one is in conceptual border territory, namely, where one is alluding simultaneously to attitude, physical feelings, and inferences. For example, "I feel tired" and "I feel hungry" are usually weaker in force than "I am tired" and "I am hungry"; for by throwing in "I feel," one is suggesting that one is having to decide about the matter rather than simply knowing or affirming it. (I know that we do not always choose our border territory language precisely; nevertheless, we do often make these distinctions by emphatically or repeatedly using these familiar qualifiers.) Here we arrive at the psychosomatic issue: it is well known that the so-called sensory and sensorimotor thresholds and qualities vary with attitude, involvement, sheer level of activity, and other psychological variables; for instance, it is often the case that the threshold of feeling consciously hungry or tired is lower when one is "in a low mood," and that the taste of food may be significantly dulled in the same circumstances.

(9) To feel might be used to allude to a conceptual border territory of another sort than that just described. In this case it is the territory that lies between sensation and commentary on it. This is where we begin using such words as perturbations and agitations; here we encounter the qualms, tickles, throbs, aches, pricks, clutches, and so on that make up a sizable portion of our emotion-language (see Ryle 1949). Although sometimes we use these words to refer mainly to actual sensations associated with altered physiological functioning, often we use them simply to refer to fantasy content. For example, there are differences between the "pricking of conscience," which implies something like a pure pitchfork fantasy, and the "throes of despair," which strongly suggests, among other things, the acutely felt physiological changes and inhibited muscular activity associated with privatized agitation. Although the entire expression is not always given explicitly, perturbation words are parts of idiomatic expressions of the form "to feel a perturbation of X about Y," e.g., "to feel qualms about cheat-

ing." Accordingly, we should not attempt to dislodge these words from their contexts. Ultimately, the idioms of which they are parts have been designed, more or less intelligibly, to liken acting emotionally to sensation-felt. It follows from this that, in those instances where we regard the idiom as unsatisfactory, we would be well advised to avoid using it rather than to begin tampering with it. We encounter no principle problem with the verb to feel in this connection.

(10) Finally, one might use to feel when one is speaking defensively about one's acting emotionally. It is a case of one's defensively relying on verbal diffuseness, formlessness, or incompleteness (see (1) above). For example, "That's just the way I feel about it," "Each to his own feelings," and "I get no feeling in reaction to that." In these instances one is disclaiming action by saying either that one is inactive and just undergoing feeling or that, though active, one cannot be expected to determine the nature of the activity, especially not its emotional aspects, or simply that there can be no useful communicating about feelings. In another defensive context, one might first acknowledge a feeling, then say, "I have no reason to feel this way," and go on arbitratily but nonetheless emphatically to deny that one is feeling that way *just because* one has no good reason to feel so. Analysands often deny that they are acting guiltily or anxiously, for example, by insisting that there is no reason to be guilty or anxious. (I am assuming here, as throughout this discussion, that knowingly withholding information is not a factor in these instances; in other words, that one is acknowledging the action or mode of action neither to oneself nor to others.)

This completes my sorting out and discussion of the common uses of to feel. I believe that we are now in a position to agree on the inadvisability of using the verb to feel in systematic action language propositions concerning the emotions. So great are the ambiguities, confusions, and unacceptable logical consequences of using to feel as an emotion-word, that its employment greatly reduces the precision and explicitness of emotion-propositions. I repeat that I am concerned only with systematic statements. Although I have drawn my examples from the language of everyday life, I am not concerned with that language as such. I am concerned with the wide-scale im-

porting of this ordinary language into the metapsychological
language of "affects" and into interpretations, and the logical
difficulties that result.

On these grounds it may seem advisable also to avoid using
the verb to think, owing to the many ambiguities with which it
is imbued. It might seem better, that is to say, always to specify
which constituent of "thinking" we mean—remembering, cal-
culating, anticipating, etc. But in view of the complex mingling
of constituent actions that characterizes ordinary thinking, it
would get cumbersome in the extreme to oblige oneself always
to specify constituents and never to use to think.

I know how awkward it will sometimes feel to do without the
verb to feel, even if one is doing so only in one's systematic
discourse; but, in time, one should get the feel of doing so and
should even be able to do so with feeling.

5. To Be Emotional

When we say, "I am pleased," "He was sad," or "They'll be
sorry," we are using to be as a linking verb between the subject
and an emotion-adjective. We might thereby seem to be dealing adequately with problems entailed by using the verb to feel
that I just discussed. That is to say, for the design of an action
language, it might now seem to be an improvement to say "I
am pleased" rather than "I feel pleased." But upon thinking
further we realize these "to be" sentences suggest something
static and vaguely passive about emotion. In particular, they
do not say that there is some action being performed. Consequently, emotion-sentences built around the verb to be often
amount to shorthand statements that conceal at least as much
as they reveal. For example, one might say, "She was unhappy," as shorthand for saying, "She was unhappy about the
way he was neglecting her." An even fuller statement might be
this: "She was thinking unhappily of the way he was neglecting her, but (therefore?) saying nothing about it." This last
way of putting the matter clearly indicates that one could then
get to give information about just how this woman has been
thinking unhappily (for example, imagining herself all alone in
the world); one could also go on to inquire why, in this situation, she was thinking but not saying. She might volunteer this
information herself or she might disclose it only upon being

questioned. Utilizing some of the verbal and nonverbal cues people customarily rely on in such situations, the observer might just infer correctly and with relative confidence that this is the emotional state of affairs. In a different instance, "She was unhappy" might refer directly to some obvious public actions in which the woman was engaged, such as weeping and wailing.

In the main, the emotion-adjectives in these "to be" statements can be translated into verbs or adverbs and then placed in systematic action-propositions. In everyday speech, however, it is clear that the ambiguity of the shorthand statement using emotion-adjectives is in no way fatal to its usefulness. This is the usefulness of giving a quick approximation, of indicating the general kind of activity that is in question, of deliberately saying only so much and no more, or of maintaining a certain rhythm or style of speech. In general, sacrifice of precision is not even necessarily costly, and often it is desirable. Many messages must be blurred, muted, or incomplete in order to be heard at all—a consideration that enters into skill in analytic interpretation.

6. Conclusion

Using verbs and adverbs, it is possible to make emotion-statements suitable for an action language. It is inconsistent with action language either to speak substantively about *the* emotions and *their* activity or to render emotion-actions and emotion-modes through the use of bodily or other metaphors, the ideas feel and feeling, and the linking verb to be when it connects subjects with emotion-adjectives.

14 Reworking the Language of Emotion

1. THE CONTROL OF EMOTION

Just what is it that one controls when, as we say, one controls one's emotions? And just what is it that one does in exercising this control? These two questions are among the most critical to be answered in developing any action theory of the emotions; for the way we answer them will define essential aspects of what we mean by emotion and, further, will show how we may speak of emotion consistently in the terms of action.

As it is usually used, the idea of control of emotion is a good example of the way we concretize and personify or otherwise animate personal actions; for this customary usage implies that during the period of control, some emotion entity is "there," inside and unchanged, like a caged wild animal striving to break out and run wild. This is also Freud's "affect" as instinctual energy or force, which, while it may achieve or be allowed some degree of display and "discharge" while under control, continues to retain the identity it would have were it to achieve or be allowed its true and full expression.

This idea of continuous identity of emotion has always appeared to be supported by direct observation, including self-observation. That is to say, it has seemed to be the case that once people stop exercising control, they are likely to act passionately as they did, or almost did, before they instituted control; at least they will act more passionately than they have just been doing. It is noteworthy, though not essential to my argument, that this is not always the case: counting to ten can make a difference, as can other enforced delays. The important issue, however, is the kind of conceptualizing that we are engaged in when we speak of control in this connection; for what we call our observations are shaped by this conceptualizing, which is to say that one must be begging the question when one refers to the observation of emotional control in support of the idea of control itself. The idea of control makes sense only in the conceptual universe established by the mechanistic-organismic model of mind that is the basis of Freud's metapsychology. In the conceptual universe of action, there are no forceful entities to be controlled; there are only actions and modes of action to be performed or changed.

Control of emotion takes in three classes of referents: (1) refraining from performing some or all of the emotive actions one wishes to perform in a certain situation; (2) engaging in cognitive actions by which one transforms one's situation, hence one's occasions for acting emotionally; and (3) taking action socially and physically to change one's position in one's given environment or else to change the environment itself (cf. Hartmann 1947).

(1) *Emotive actions* are those instances of acting emotionally that are done publicly. They include frank statements, facial expressions, gestures, exclamations, tones of voice, postures, and movements in space relative to other people, objects in the environment, and parts of one's body. In controlling these actions, one is limiting the visibility to others of the fact that one is acting emotionally.

These emotive actions are not simply signals of, or statements about, one's acting emotionally; they are constitutive aspects of acting emotionally. Logically, any change in the actions implies a change in the emotion; for once we understand emotion to mean some emotion-action or some way of acting emotionally, we cannot say that an emotion remains entirely unchanged despite the person's having refrained from performing one or more of the constitutive actions and modes. Things seem different, of course, when we employ the metapsychological idea of emotion or affect; for then we have committed ourselves to thinking that the inhibited affect remains the same and that it is only a question of blockage or delay and resulting pressure toward discharge. In contrast, when we use action language, we commit ourselves to thinking that by refraining from performing certain actions in certain modes, the person will be acting differently than would be the case were he or she simply, unconcernedly, and visibly acting emotionally.

Let us take grieving as an example. Although holding back tears in this context overlaps outright weeping in the grieving action it implies, the action of holding back tears also implies that the person is busy with more than grieving at the moment. Perhaps that person is grieving ashamedly or, with respect to the prospect of being "overwhelmed by despair," apprehensively. But in any case that person's grieving, including the way he or she represents it and values or condemns it, is more complex in this respect than the freely tearful grieving. On this basis, it makes sense to say that the emotion is different in the two cases; for even though we might disregard their differences and call both of them instances of grieving, we would know that we are dealing with different kinds of grieving, one of them more qualified and complex than the other.

The distinction I am making bears on an important principle of clinical psychoanalytic interpretation, namely interpreting tactfully or empathically. For if the analysand is grieving apprehensively and the analyst decides to comment in this regard, the analyst should say so (in whatever words seem fitting at the time). Were the analyst simply to remark on the grieving or "the grief," it would be a case of what we ordinarily call tactlessly breaking through or circumventing the resistance or defensiveness instead of analyzing it. ("Breaking through or circumventing the resistance" is a fine example of thinking concretistically about both the analysand's actions and one's own interpretations.)

(2) *Cognitive action* is the second class of referents of control of emotion. These actions include perceiving, comprehending, isolating, integrating, repressing, attending, and anticipating (metapsychology's "ego functions" and "mechanisms"). By taking these cognitive actions, one develops one's situations, thereby establishing the occasions and significances of one's emotions. More than developing and establishing situations, however, one may take these actions to transform situations. With regard to the issue of control, one may use transformational cognitive action to greatly reduce or even eliminate the possibility of acting emotionally in a particular way or in general. For example, one might review one's previous impressions, gather more information, take stock of one's prospects, admonish oneself to be resigned or detached, unconsciously overlook or reverse certain salient features of one's situation—all to the point where one would no longer "feel the same way" or "feel it as strongly as before" or indeed "feel anything at all." One

would just have less reason or no reason to be emotional in the way or to the extent one has judged undesirable. Psychoanalysts understand the process of mourning in this way, though in following Freud (1917a), they usually "explain" it psychoeconomically.

Earlier I said that controlling emotive actions refers not so much to inhibition of an unchanging entity as to a modification of the emotional activity in question. The same is true of the cognitive transformation of situations: rather than blocking the expression of a fixed emotion or moderating it only quantitatively, the transformation of situations also transforms the person's emotion-actions and emotion-modes. However, of the two types of "control," the cognitive transformation of situations has the greater potential for bringing about emotional change. Analysts assume that this is so every time they make an interpretation. Clinically, analysts have always viewed affects in cognitive as well as emotive terms, their metapsychological language notwithstanding.

(3) The third class of referents of the idea of control of emotion embraces the *social* and *physical actions* one takes to alter one's position in the environment, if not to alter the environment itself. This class includes leaving the scene, confronting an antagonist overtly, offering or demanding an explanation, and finding a friend or a shelter or a weapon. It also includes some of the same actions as the class of emotive actions in that the emotive actions one performs or leaves off performing, such as smiling, crying, or snarling, might affect the actions of others in the environment; but the two classes are mostly different in that the class of social and physical action in and on the environment takes in a great range of things that cannot be called emotive actions.

As for the distinction between cognitive transformation and environmental transformation, it is not one that is difficult to draw either in everyday life or in clinical work. It is the difference between "I realized he was a troublemaker" and "I got rid of that troublemaker" and the difference between "I considered her a friend" and "I looked up a friend." Also, the three classes of referents are not mutually exclusive; for example, in grieving apprehensively (fearing the action of despairing), a person might simultaneously refrain from crying, try to look only at the bright side of things, and search eagerly for a new person to love. And finally, the three classes of referents exhaust the implications of the idea of control of emotion; at least, I can identify no residuals.

By making environmental changes, one might very well control (modify) one's acting emotionally. In this, making environmental changes is like cognitively transforming one's view of a given situation: one is seeing to it that one no longer defines a sufficient reason or indeed any reason to begin or continue acting in a certain emotional way.

Repeatedly we have had to view the control of emotion as a matter of change in emotion-actions and emotion-modes. Seeming merely to keep control of an emotion, one may go so far as to eliminate it (except in its conditional mode) or transform it into its opposite, as, for example, the paranoiac does in transforming homosexual love to hate and then fleeing or provoking persecution by others, and as the obsessional neurotic does in finding or constructing situations that call for acting kindly when otherwise he or she would be "filled with rage." But never is it really a matter of transforming an entity, emotion, by one's actions: the *it* that is transformed refers to a situation and the actions appropriate to it.

Just what is it that one does in controlling one's emotions? This is the second question about the idea of control that I raised at the beginning of this section. But I have already answered this second question in the course of answering the first, namely what it is that is controlled. The essential point to grasp here is this: in seeming to exercise control, one is not manipulating emotions in any sense that is analogous to, or identical with, manipulating objects in nature; for emotions are not entities of any kind. In action terms, the idea of methods of control refers to what one does in establishing other ways of engaging or not engaging in specific emotive actions and cognitive actions and what one does to effect changes in one's environment or in one's position in it. For the psychoanalyst, not just any description of these actions and modes of action will do, however; nor will just any description of situations do: the interpreting psychoanalyst occupies a special vantage point for describing transformational (controlling) actions as for describing all other actions (see chapters 7, 10, and 11, particularly; see also Schafer 1974b).

Before concluding this section, it remains to consider this

one objection to my line of argument: that the action language provides no way to account for the possibility of reinstating, reviving, or resuming an earlier mode of acting emotionally. People do seem to be able to do just that. Suppose it is accepted that a person has changed situation and action twice, the first time in order to refrain from acting in a visibly and emphatically emotional way, and the second time in order to resume the initial actions that were suspended or "nipped in the bud": how, the objection might run, could one ever pick up where one had left off in the absence of some kind of enduring structure that amounted to an organized continuation of the earlier moment, and some retention of the initial affect-charge or affect-quantity? There must be something that insures a faithful reinstatement, revival, or release of what had first been "controlled" and now has been "decontrolled."

This is not a strong challenge to my thesis. These questions presuppose that apparent psychological continuity must be explained metaphorically in terms of material and quantitative continuity. They imply that there must be some static form of mental entity "there" to be reactivated, some fixed amount of energy "there" to be discharged, and some mental channels "there" for the psychic energies to flow through once again. It is as if the questions hold up these materialistic metaphors as bulwarks against mental chaos; in fact, however, the metaphors are merely mechanistic-materialistic restatements of observed continuity or repetition of action. One's faith in these metaphors often rests on a serious confusion between, on the one hand, the continuous identity and intactness of the central nervous system, which is not at all in question here, which has functional laws of its own, and which is an empirical matter, and, on the other hand, the philosophical problems of conceptualizing personal identity over time. The latter problems concern language rules, as Ryle (1949), for example, has shown in his discussion of what constitutes knowing something over time: does, for example, knowing a tune imply that one is imaginatively playing it in one's mind continuously? Knowing a tune is not that kind of proposition; neither is resuming acting emotionally that kind of proposition: both are matters of language rules for describing actual human actions.

In conclusion: using action language instead of the familiar materialistic-mechanistic metaphors to deal with the concep-

tual issues posed by the idea of control of emotion, we gain
some important advantages. No longer do we have to split off
emotion from the controlling person or agent. No longer are we
committed to substantializing and animating either the emotions or the controls (or defenses). We are able to discontinue
our colluding unwittingly with the analysand in perpetuating
the existence of a large class of disclaimers in the realm of
emotional activity (see also chapter 7). And we stop impeding
our making further and finer observations in the emotional
sphere of life.

To sum up my argument briefly: in the final analysis, although much may be changed and the consequences experienced in intensely pleasurable or painful ways, there is nothing
one loses in one's "loss of control."

2. The Expression of Emotion

The idea of expressing emotion is based on two interrelated
presuppositions: that emotion is (or may be usefully spoken of
as) a substance or quantity of energy and that self or person is
(or may be usefully spoken of as) a place, a container, or a set
of channels (see chapters 8 and 9). This is so because to refer in
any way to expressing emotion is to imply both that there is an
entity to be "pressed" and that it is pressed from the "inside"
to the "outside." The excremental prototype of this idea is
familiar to psychoanalysts and is strongly suggested by the
cathartic or purgative figures of speech that are commonly
used in this connection. (See in this regard Brierly's [1937]
discussion of affects.) Once we have repudiated theoretical
presuppositions of substance, quantity, and place, we would be
wrong to go on speaking of expressing emotion.

Fully rejecting the idea of expressing emotion entails also
rejecting "give vent to," "pour out," "get out," "release," "discharge," "unpack," and other expulsive metaphors; it further
entails rejecting those locutions referring to *not* expressing
emotion, such as "stifle," "hide," "store up," "put the lid on,"
"bottle up," and "subdue."

There is a more subtle way in which emotion is conceived as
an entity to be expressed rather than as an action to be done or
as a mode of such action. We encounter it in locutions that refer
in one way or another to "putting feelings into words" or "giv-

ing voice to feelings." The idea of expressing emotion often implies putting feelings into words. This is especially so in the context of clinical psychoanalysis and other "talking treatments." Briefly, the critical argument against this usage is the following: to say that one is putting a feeling into words is to imply, what is no longer admissible, both that there is an independently existing emotion-entity and that this entity remains unchanged by being verbalized; that is to say, it is to imply that an emotion is what it is apart from the actions by which we bring it into the world, such as naming, choosing words, gesturing, and observing one's actions. If one makes of emotion an entity or *it*, one establishes the idea that it is something one may have and about which one may do this, that, or the other thing. Consequently, it seems that one may speak of an emotion in the same way that one may speak of fecal matter, that is, as a thing that is what it is whether one calls it by that name or by any name. (There are even limits to the correctness of this idea about material things and their names: is shit exactly the same as feces?) In the next section I shall deal further with the idea that emotion is a thing.

There are alternative ways in which we can convey the sense of expressing emotion or putting feelings into words; we can speak, for example, of saying something emotionally and aloud, saying it despite misgivings, saying it more clearly and fully than before, saying it demonstratively, and ceasing merely to imagine it and beginning to describe it or communicate it or confess it. In using any of these alternatives, one is just specifying actions or modes of action or both.

3. The Subjective Experience of Emotion

Emotion cannot be the object of the transitive verb to experience. Having already settled on the language rule that, in action language, the only proper emotion-words are verbs and adverbs, we must reject the idea that there is some entity called emotion to be experienced. The idea of subjective experience of emotion can refer only to one or both of two things: *actions*, including the action of thinking about emotion-actions and action-modes, and *modes of action*, including the mode of engaging in emotion-actions attentively and so performing a complex, potentially reportorial action.

Consider the following situation. While in company I think of
a friend fondly. No one knows this since I do not mention it. It
is possible that someone in the company might infer it from the
momentary context, the look on my face, previous conversa-
tions, and other cues and pieces of information. The possibility
of this inference implies that thinking of someone fondly can be
a public action, though it does not require it to be intentionally
public, entirely public, or public at all. At a certain moment I
mention my thinking of that friend fondly. Then, this crucial
question may be asked: is there now any residual of pure emotion that I have not communicated, indeed, could not communicate owing to its being forever privileged? Within the rules
of action language, the answer to this question is, No. What is
correct to say is this: once having announced this action, it
remains possible for me to try to say more about it, either vol-
untarily or in response to such questions as "Why do you say
fondly rather than passionately or enthusiastically?" Although
it is unusual, it is not odd to give reasons for saying fondly or
other things of that kind; in the psychoanalytic situation or in
response to jealous challenges, it has a special importance. In
explaining my choice of fondly, I might then refer to characterizations and estimates of my own physiological arousal,
anticipated or remembered or fantasied actions with respect to
this friend, the way these observations differ from those connected with thoughts of other friends or other moments, and so
on—all of which is to say that ordinarily I would be prepared to
back up my using just this emotion-adverb. If I were not so prepared, I could not assert it as a fact that that is the way I am
thinking of the friend; all I could say is that "fondly" is the
word that I am thinking and that I am simply assuming that my
thinking it is not a random, accidental, false, or meaningless
action. Still I would have to acknowledge that under these conditions the truth value of "fondly" remains indeterminate. In
other words, I can only back up my claim to be thinking of the
friend fondly by saying how I use the word fondly. Not that I
have to marshall my reasons beforehand, but that I imply that
I am using the word responsibly in the present context. The
truth as to whether in daily life I do actually engage fondly with
this friend is another matter, of course, one that can be established through observations of my actions with respect to that

friend; at least this is so under ordinary circumstances and if we exclude any intent to deceive others.

I just referred in passing to the factor of physiological arousal. Physiological arousal includes muscular tensions, visceral and genital sensations and changes, pulse, temperature, respiration, and the like. This factor is important because it is cited as one of the major supports for the idea that emotion is an internal entity and that, on that account, it is ultimately privileged. This support is, however, flimsy. Granted that others cannot have my sensations, nevertheless they can understand my saying that I feel hot and bothered, cold and clammy, stiff and put off, or pained and crushed, for they are likely to have been using these words more or less according to the same rules as I have. Thus far there is nothing privileged about the physiological concomitants of my emotions.

Beyond the unshared aspects of physiological arousal, the idea of privileged internal emotional experience seems to gain support from the more or less singular metaphors and implied fantasies by means of which people represent arousal. People use or devise these metaphors and fantasies unconsciously as well as consciously and preconsciously. A person might well think that his or her renderings of arousal are, always have been, and always will be closely guarded secrets, hence, unknowable by others. But it does not follow that they are inevitably unknowable. Perhaps all one means is that one intends never to disclose these matters to anyone else; perhaps one means that one never thinks clearly about them and so seems fated to remain a relative stranger to certain aspects of arousal; and perhaps one means both of these at once.

The idea that subjective emotional experience is not privileged is further supported by the fact that many emotion-actions and emotion-modes appear to involve no physiological arousal or at least no distinctive and consistent signs of arousal.

Furthermore, others may independently observe certain aspects of one's arousal. Not every feature of arousal is interior to the organism. Some may be discerned with the naked eye or with other sense organs (think how much one can tell by touch), and many or most may be discerned through the use of technical instruments.

The claim of privileged subjective experience of emotion

reduces to one or more of the following propositions. First, others cannot have one's own sensations; but this is merely an assertion of the identity of persons, i.e., that a person is either this one or that one but not both. Secondly, others cannot know what one is thinking so long as one has not communicated it clearly or at all, even to oneself (repression); but far from being universally true, this proposition is true only in some instances or only to some degree. Thirdly, others cannot understand what one has not yet said or otherwise formed into some kind of private or public statement; but this is true by definition, for under these inchoate conditions that which is to be understood has not yet been performed as a thought-action.

Let us now consider a specific example of the use of the word experience in relation to the emotions. A woman says, "That is my emotional experience of it." What does she mean? She could mean that she knows she has performed a certain emotion-action or an action in a certain emotion-mode. Alternatively, she could mean that she knows that thinking about certain actions is the action she is now performing in a certain emotion-mode. (For "knows," one could substitute remembers, realizes, admits to herself, etc.) However, the *it* she claims to experience might not be actions she is performing; *it* might refer to the actions of others or to events in which personal action is not even in question (e.g., an earthquake). Were she to spell out her statement, she might, for example, say, "I remember the earthquake anxiously" or "I realize sadly how I missed my chance" or "I view my daughter's present life situation happily, for it seems to realize her fondest hopes." But suppose she means that she thinks there are some emotional aspects of certain actions or events which she cannot put into words; she might even be implying (speaking naively as a Cartesian) that they can never be put into words because *in principle* there is necessarily some residual, some "feel" of the event, which remains the subjective core of it, inviolate, virginal to the end. In this she would be concluding that just because there is much she has not said or just because she remains dissatisfied with what she has managed to say, we are compelled to accept the idea that *in principle* there must be any such ultimate emotional residuals. This is a mistaken conclusion; more exactly, it is a presupposition being misrepresented as a conclusion, that is, a begging of the question. The logical conclusion is simply this: with reference to that which she thinks she has left unsaid, she would do best to add such qualifiers as "thus far," "under these conditions," "in the light of what I presently understand," "I don't like the way I put it" or "I realize that other accounts (other verbs, adverbs, metaphors, whatever) might be preferable."

The idea that one's utterances concerning emotion are inadequate to one's purpose is a variant of thinking that there is a real action consisting of "putting emotions into words" or simply "expressing emotions," a matter which I discussed critically in section 2, above.

It is not part of my argument to deny that a person's actions may possess unique features. I agree that they may possess such features, especially when the actions in question are complex. In principle, however, there ought to be a number of ways of stating these features, none of which will, however, convey exactly what any other will convey. While there is often considerable ambiguity in the contents and modes of any one person's thought-actions, this ambiguity and the correlated prospect of multiple versions is not the same as inaccessibility or inexpressibility. I further stress that it would amount to using words obsessionally to try to "say it all" each time we spoke; for, consistent with our interest in getting specific jobs done and getting them done expeditiously, we deliberately barely approximate conveying many details relevant to our performances, if we do not omit them altogether. Especially is this so when it comes to emotion-statements.

It is a part of my argument, and a central one, too, to defend the claim that, in one or more respects, one might know others better than they know themselves. In the present context, my argument is that it is never absurd to make this claim with respect to the emotions of other people. That one may be wrong in specific instances is another matter. Far more than psychoanalytic practice, I am thinking of daily life where we frequently and correctly act as though it is entirely appropriate to make this claim. There, we are not constrained by preconceptions concerning ultimately privileged access to emotional experience. If necessary, we are prepared to back up our claims by citing instances, amassing evidence, justifying inferences, and establishing connections and correlations. Explicitly or implicitly, we say to others such things as these: "Of course

you care! It's no use denying it!" "You are angry! Anyone can
see that!" "Despite what you say, I do frighten you! Look how
you tremble when I speak!" Of course, the recipients of these
statements might argue with us and even prove that we are
wrong. Alternatively, we might later discover by ourselves that
we were wrong. Unless one were desperately defensive, however, one would not maintain for long that it is absurd to claim
to know better in this sense.

As observers of others, we do not invariably encounter dis-
agreement or disproof in this connection. The person being
observed might readily agree with our views or conclusions.
Two people might compare notes and come to realize that they
have both been "having the same feelings" about something:
for example, both have been stifling sobs, anticipating the
future gloomily, and enacting "pulling into themselves" by
their postures, expressive movements, and fantasies; having
established that this is so, they might then agree that both have
been behaving sadly. Also, with the help of tactful and balanced comments, one person might help another "experience
emotions" that the other has more or less defensively been
keeping relatively undefined or repressed. Psychoanalysts at
work and in their daily lives count on the possibility of all these
kinds of agreement.

Because the verb to experience, like the verb to feel, is ex-
cessively ambiguous owing to its referring to too many different actions and modes of action, and because it generally is
used to imply meaningful phenomena that are prior to and free
from personal action, it must be viewed as an impediment to
the formulation of systematic propositions. That it will continue to be used frequently in both ordinary and clinical thinking and discourse is another matter altogether.

Although we should reject the idea that there must always be
a crucial residue of inaccessible or uncommunicable subjective
experience, we must acknowledge that in principle any actions
and modes of actions that we have designated in one way may
be approached from other points of view, in line with other
goals and by other methods, and so may be designated in other
ways. The possibility of multiple versions is an alternative to
the idea of the forever private residue. The alternative versions
I mean include: finer description or more global rendering; an
account that isolates for study or develops connections and im-

plications more fully; a presentation that provides a more retrospective (historical) context or a more prospective or predictive one; and one that stresses irrational resisting and transference or validates reality testing. I suggest that it is partly because we know of all these possibilities that, in specific instances, we so readily believe in the idea of uncommunicable residues of emotion. As psychoanalysts, however, we also know that a large share of people's believing in residues is contributed by their knowing, however much they might deny it consciously, that in their daily lives they engage in a great deal of defensive nonrecognition of actual and conditional emotion.

Against all this it might be argued that I have not acknowledged the reality of emotional *states*, whether they be transient moods or lasting attitudes or orientations to life, and that thereby I have invalidly dismissed the claim of privileged subjective experience of these states. Thus, the argument might continue, we do speak of states of happiness, confusion, despair, frenzy, hypomania, and so on, and who can know these states better than the subject, and how can anyone else know anything about them except through the subject's own but secondary account? In response to this argument, we should ask whether by using these ideas of emotional states one is referring to anything other than certain overt and covert actions carried out in certain modes over some period of time by the same person. Those who are inclined to think materialistically of enduring entities as prerequisites of organized mental functioning will think of those states as more or less fixed and somehow localized structures that act as agencies of the mind and are acted upon by other agencies of the mind. In action language, however, we would simply speak of certain actual or conditional, overt or covert emotion-actions and emotion-modes that may be observed or inferred repeatedly, continuously, regularly, predictably, or something of that sort. We would not introduce the assumption, now to be regarded as unnecessary and burdensome, that every action must be a derivative or expression of an underlying state of mind. Nor would we regard the subject's report as anything other than one more action we must include in our considerations before arriving at any conclusions concerning his or her emotional activity; certainly, that report might be a particularly significant or revealing action, but that does not affect the argument.

According to this analysis, one cannot make a good case for retaining the idea that there exists some kind of subjective experience of emotion which *as experience* remains privileged and beyond the reach of an action language. For it is always possible to say that people engage in emotion-actions and emotion-modes, and that the manner of their doing so is more or less public, more or less complex, more or less conscious, more or less clearly definable, more or less accurately perceived or justifiably inferred by them and by others who are their witnesses, and more or less amenable to multiple versions of the emotional *it* that is said to be experienced. Once all such features have been specified, the notion of a purely private, experiential remainder becomes superfluous; there can only be features of action that have remained unrecognized or unstated and possibly some critical contemplation of this state of affairs by the subject or some other observer. This is so, finally, because the adoption of action language entails an agreement to live in that kind of world.

4. EMOTIONS AND MENTAL TOPOGRAPHY

The ideas conscious, preconscious, and unconscious will no longer appear as such in action language. Now they are rendered as modes of action, that is, in adverbial form. We change them to consciously, preconsciously, and unconsciously. Because I have already discussed at some length the translation of the topographic qualities into modes of action (see especially chapter 11), I shall limit myself here to specifying and discussing a few propositions that bear particularly on our taken-for-granted ways of discussing the emotions in relation to consciousness.

One may consciously recognize that one is engaged in an emotion-action or emotion-made, or one may remain more or less unaware that this is the case—unconsciously and preconsciously, respectively. The same may be said both of other people's witnessing one's actions and modes of action and of one's own witnessing the actions of others and their modes. When more fixedly and insistently unaware, one is acting resistantly or defensively; in this instance it is not just the emotion-actions and emotion-modes themselves that are in question but also the fact that one is acting resistantly or defensively at all ("unconscious defense").

Remaining unaware may be a manifestation of the person's engaging in some other action very attentively. For example, concentrating on solving an intellectual problem, on may for a time "forget one's troubles." In this instance, it may not be correct to emphasize defensive or resistant reasons implicit in the emotional obliviousness; whether or not it would be correct to impose that emphasis would depend on how easily and comfortably the person in question could engage attentively in the emotion-actions and emotion-modes once he or she has set the other problem aside. That one may cling to "absorbing" projects defensively is, of course, a familiar observation, but it is not one that we can make in all relevant instances.

Remaining unaware may be a manifestation of one's not yet having established vantage points from which to define the relevant emotion-actions and emotion-modes clearly or at all. Especially useful with regard to the psychoanalytic vantage points is knowing the right or the best designations for the prevailing emotion-contexts. Although it is often true that defensiveness or resistiveness has played a part in one's not yet having established good vantage points of this sort, it need not be always true or all that is true. We see that this is so on those occasions when analysands readily and fruitfully put to use the relevant psychoanalytic designations supplied by the analyst through interpretation: then, although we might speak of the analysand's having continued up to that point resisting preconsciously, we would be wrong to dismiss the idea that the analysand is also learning new connections and achieving and applying new perspectives. To take a comparable instance, it would be sheer and foolish psychoanalytic dogmatism to insist that the scope and complexity of emotional-cognitive life achieved through writing and reading poetry are simply matters of "overcoming defenses," even though at the same time it would be irrationally anti-psychoanalytic to insist that, in principle, involving oneself in poetry or any other art can have no bearing on one's defensiveness and thereby on one's emotional-cognitive actions and one's knowledge of them.

The emotions we successfully resist attending to may exist only in the conditional mode, that is, as some emotion-action

we *would* perform or some emotional way of acting in which
we *would* engage were it not for some circumstances, consequences, or objectives that we regard as being more important,
such as the dangers of losing gratification and security. These
conditional actions and modes correspond to Freud's idea of
"potential affect," the idea he came to favor over "unconscious
affect" (1915c). And while he gave good reasons for rejecting
the latter idea, he merely equivocated in recommending the
former; for by "potential affect" he was saying that an affect
may be influential in its own right even though it does not exist.
Logically and unequivocally, a potential affect can only be one
which *would be* experienced consciously were the situation
different in some crucial respect (e.g., less threatening). The
conditional mode is psychologically real in its cognitive aspect,
that is, in connection with the person's preconsciously or consciously *anticipating* situations, such as the prototypical danger situations. By using action language, we escape Freud's
dilemma in this connection. Understanding affect to be action
and mode of action and taking these now as the essential emo-
tion-content of our psychoanalytic propositions, we need not
hesitate to say that any of these actions and modes may be performed unconsciously, preconsciously, or consciously. Additionally, we may readily say of the conditional action or mode
that it may be known in any one of these three modes of
consciousness.

Using action language, we can state the modes of consciousness of past and future actions and conditional actions in the
same way that we state these modes in connection with the
present. Thus, that one has performed an emotion-action or
could have performed it is a fact that one may remember unconsciously, preconsciously, or consciously; and that one will
do it or might do it in the future is a fact that one may anticipate in any one of these three modes. We are used to speaking
this way in everyday life; with respect to love, for example, we
make such statements as these: "You don't want to admit to
yourself how much you once loved her: that's why you never
even think of her," and "You know you steer clear of him because you're afraid you'll fall in love with him."

Rejecting the idea of unconscious or preconscious emotion
often appears in another guise, that is, in the assertion that
experiencing or knowing anything can only be done con-

sciously. However, as I argued in section 4 and also elsewhere in this book, we have committed ourselves to the view that experiencing and knowing the emotions are versions of action and not authoritative records to be consulted through introspection; they are versions of observed, remembered, and imagined emotive actions, thought-actions, and actions relative to environmental circumstances. Consequently, there is no longer any reason to insist that they, unlike all other actions, can only be performed consciously.

It must be granted that one cannot perform consciously what one has thus far performed only unconsciously without changing the action or mode of action in question; for thinking consciously is not like turning on a light in a dark room in order to see an object which remains unchanged by the change in illumination. Sometimes Freud did theorize as though this were the case; he did so, for instance, in his basic explanation of consciousness as being a result of one's directing attention cathexis toward an idea. Thinking consciously does often show such primary process features as distortion, logical contradiction, and fluidity, so that when one observes these features of one's own thinking or the thinking of others, one gets the impression, so to speak, of looking directly "into the depths." At other (and better) times, Freud stressed the point that thinking consciously is thinking according to the requirements of the secondary process; by definition, this is to think in a mode very different from that of the primary process, the one that ordinarily characterizes thinking unconsciously. As a rule, to think something consciously is to be better prepared to consider it in terms of factual and hypothetical relationships that are more or less orderly, rational, conventionally realistic, interactive, and, with respect to infantile danger situations, safe. This is why Freud concluded that thinking consciously ordinarily transforms the inferred "unconscious idea"—specifically that it transcends its "thing" quality (1915c). He recognized similar transformation in the instance of someone's actually speaking emotionally to another person instead of remaining emotionally private, that is, "keeping one's feelings to oneself"; here, however, Freud usually dealt with these transformations in the now inadmissible terms of discharge of psychic energy.

Transformation and enhanced transformability of emotion-actions and emotion-modes is central to Freud's theory of the therapeutic effect of interpretation; these changes are implied in what he called making the unconscious conscious or establishing ego where id and archaic superego were. But in action terms we would say that the analysand begins doing different emotion-actions and doing actions in different emotion-modes; for example, welcoming friends rather than putting them off or acting less moodily. These different actions and modes include new versions of old actions and modes; for example, new versions of loving (genitally rather more than anally) and new versions of acting tenderly (with appropriate concern for the other rather more than being egoistically and reactively concerned with one's anticipated or implied sadistic actions and modes).

In any case, once a person consciously considers and performs emotion-actions and emotion-modes that previously he or she only performed unconsciously, that person is necessarily engaging in actions and modes that are qualitatively different in essential respects. In the following sections on the ideas of old and accumulated feelings, this point will be developed further.

Repressing an emotion-action or emotion-mode is a comparable transformation of situations and performances—in the reverse direction, of course.

Both experientially and therapeutically, one cannot exaggerate the significance and consequences of differentiating these three modes—consciously, preconsciously, and unconsciously. Logically, however, these modes are merely attributes of action on a par with such modes of action as carelessly, conscientiously, hastily, and grudgingly. This is to say that, as adverbs, they merely indicate yet other ways in which actions may be carried out.

I have been referring to the modes consciously, preconsciously, and unconsciously as though they correspond to three altogether distinct, discontinuous ways of action emotionally. My doing so should not be construed to mean that one is to overlook or rule out consideration of the graduated, complex, and concurrent versions of any one or more of them. The variety, subtlety, and complexity of the emotions; their apparent ineffability, delicacy, and evanescence; the sense in which we claim that we may have them and know them and communicate them wordlessly—all these attributes and claims correspond as much to modal transitions and ambiguities as they do to the large number of ways in which we set up groups and sequences of emotion-actions and emotion-modes. My being decisive about the right or best language in which to speak of these things should not be understood as a proclamation that now all things emotional stand revealed once and for all; it is just that ambiguity and subtlety must, for systematic purposes, be discussed in terms of the same set of rules as clarity and simplicity.

5. OLD FEELING

Having disallowed the idea of emotion as a substantial and quantifiable entity, we must also disallow the idea of storage and preservation of emotion. There can be no "old feelings." Emotion-actions and emotion-modes are performed only in their own situations, that is, during the doing of them under specific subjective circumstances. Those that have been done in the past may be remembered or else continued into the present; those to be done in the future, anticipated; those being considered, imagined. The remembering, continuing, anticipating, and imagining are themselves thought-actions that may be carried out in various emotion-modes; for example, one may imagine or continue to imagine an action longingly, anticipate it eagerly, remember it mournfully, or one may do any of these actions indifferently.

On what have we based our idea of old feelings? To answer this, I must first recur to the fact that, mostly unconsciously, people tend to conceive of all mental events or phenomena concretistically, that is, as objects. Typically, they render them as bodily objects (organs, substances) that are more or less animated or personified. In this form, they imply ideas of storage and preservation. Cases in point are the personified fecal emotions of the obsessive and the paranoiac. Yet when an idea is as well established as that of old feelings, it must also have its seeming justification in rational, conscious, useful considerations. The outstanding consideration in this regard is the frequent resemblance, and the occasional apparent exact likeness, between one's remembered emotionality in some situation and one's perceived or subjectively experienced emotionality upon thinking of it in the present. It seems in this regard as if the emotion has survived agelessly. Accordingly, one may well think it a simple statement of fact to say, "I got in touch with that old feeling," "That old feeling has resurfaced," or something of that sort. In contrast, when using action language, one would say, "I am thinking of some previous situation in more or less the same emotional way as I remember having acted within that situation in its time." In saying this, one would be implying that, despite the passage of time, one judges that one has not changed significantly in this regard; often one would be implying as well that one seems to have changed less than one had thought. Thus, we favor the idea of old feelings because of the importance we ascribe to ideas of personal continuity or identity. But we can talk about continuity and identity in the terms of action and so serve the same purpose logically and nonconcretistically.

Sometimes we use the idea of old feelings to refer to a certain contrast between past and present performance of emotion-actions and emotion-modes. The contrast is that between having done them before and mostly unconsciously, because defensively, and doing them now and more consciously, because ready to acknowledge these performances as such. In these instances, the essential idea is that one has been waiting a long time both to acknowledge (confront, experience) more frankly and consciously the existence of a certain situation and to do so in a more emotional manner than one has done before. But it is the situation, not the feeling, that is old in the sense that it has been defined in the same way for a long time.

At other times, we use the idea of old feelings to say that we are presently in an actual situation that seems so similar to the old one or is so evocative of it that we necessarily react in it and to it in the way we did in the past. For example, we might form this impression upon revisiting scenes of our childhood. This use conforms closely to the rules of action language. Significant though differently conceptualized discussions of this use will be found in "Constructions in Analysis" (Freud 1937b) and "The Recovery of Childhood Memories" (Kris 1956b).

One may, of course, misremember the past, and so may be judging both differences and similarities inaccurately. Also, one may know that one is now remembering a past action in an emotional mode that differs significantly from that which had characterized the original action; for example, one may remember regretfully an action one had initially carried out enthusiastically. How often we do so! In these instances, the original action or mode of action is necessarily being viewed under another aspect or in a more complex way. However, neither misremembering nor remembering differently bears on the inadmissibility of the idea of old feelings; for the force of that idea depends on its being assumed that in fact the very emotions of the past are being "felt" or could be "felt" in the present or that they could be "felt" in the future should conditions change in the right way, and it is just this assumption that makes no sense under the rules of action language.

6. Accumulated Feelings

The idea that feelings or emotions may accumulate is implied in such locutions as "pent-up emotion," "emotions welling up," "emotions filling one up," "giving vent to emotions," and the like. Especially to be singled out in this connection are the terms discharge and catharsis.

The idea of accumulated feelings is a cousin of the idea of old feelings, both being descended from the assumption that emotions are quantifiable entities and from unconsciously held ideas about emotions as more or less personified and durable substances. But again we must look for those presumably factual, rational, and utilitarian considerations that seem to warrant the belief that feelings do accumulate, and what we find is this: as a rule, people do perform emotion-actions and emotion-modes more vigorously, emphatically, lengthily, insistently, stirringly, appealingly, etc., whenever they delay these performances in a context that combines continued provocation and certain restraints on action. It is then that we think of emotion building up, like the straws on the camel's back accumulating until the back breaks or like steam pressure rising in the boiler until the inevitable explosion takes place; it is then that we say, "This is too much!" and say of ourselves that we·"blow up," "let off steam," "cry it out," or, in the fortunate instances, "jump for joy," "break into song," and the like.

But are we compelled to think and speak in these terms? Must we regard the emotions in question as cumulative in nature? Can we ever justify theoretical propositions that presuppose this idea? Certainly, people may speak louder, hit harder, jump higher, or sing longer under these conditions, but does it follow that these actions are simply magnified but otherwise unaltered versions of the deferred actions? It cannot be correct to think so: for example, it is not the same "only more so" to yell at someone after having long deferred speaking to that person irritably; the two responses are set in different phenomenological worlds, in that the yelling response is enacted in something of a dehumanized world or in one that seems further away or more hopeless than the still interpersonal and responsive world of the irritable response. Thus, even though one may "see red" in the world of yelling, it does not follow, and it is not said, that one "sees pink" in the less extreme world of irritability; the very question of color makes sense only in the first of these two worlds.

We do have at our disposal conventionalized criteria for making quantitative judgments of emphasis, subtlety, rigidity, etc. These criteria includes duration, frequency, and degrees of physical force of various kinds (vocal, muscular, etc.). We say of those actions and modes of action that meet relatively more of these criteria and meet them to a higher degree that they are more intense or stronger. But have we in these instances measured an emotion on a single scale? We seem rather to have made a global quantitative statement as a way of conveying something about the kinds of actions and modes of action in question. It can only be our unquestioned prior commitment to view emotion as a quantifiable entity that accounts for our readiness to accept and use unqualified quantitative statements about the emotions, among them statements about accumulated feelings. Furthermore, in making estimates of emphasis, subtlety, rigidity, etc., we necessarily use such *qualitative* criteria as complexity, coherence, and relevance. The result is that our seemingly simple quantitative judgments are intrinsically impure as well as misrepresented in the sense discussed above. That the idea of accumulated feelings may be put forward by the agent as his or her subjective experience and, as such, beyond the reach of our questions, criticisms, and revisions, is, for reasons given in section 3, an idea we are not obliged to accept.

It is only superficially that the idea of cumulative feeling imparts dramatic intensity to certain descriptive statements about the emotions. Fundamentally, the idea postulates a universe of emotion that is so like a universe of static objects that it cannot convey the flux and the wonder of emotional experience. In using quantitative conceptualizations, we tend to obscure the very phenomena we are trying to say something about; for we presuppose a constant or unchanging stimulus and situation as well as type of action, and as a result we may not realize that (ordinarily within certain limits) the agent might be continuously redefining the stimulus in terms of his or her changing situation. For example, continued tickling might get to be viewed as an assault even though nothing in its objective nature has changed except its duration. Similarly, continued complaining might, beyond a certain point, get to be viewed as a form of torture and a lingering kiss viewed as a seduction.

In some situations, one may deem it inadvisable to respond overtly in a certain way or even to respond overtly at all. Then, upon realizing that one is continuously in that situation, one might redefine the significance of refraining from overt action as well as the nature of both the stimulus and the situation. For example, after a while one might view the same refraining from action that one initially viewed as an exercise of patience or tolerance, as failed masculinity or castratedness. The agent might redefine everything—stimulus, situation, action, and self. As I shall develop in more detail later, it is the nature of the action universe that: these four terms be understood as correlative, that is, as defining each other; all of them be understood or described from the vantage point of the agent; and static definitions of variables be suspect. Consider in this last regard how often it occurs that subjectively the same sexual behavior with the same partner changes radically and in many fundamental respects once the context changes from premarital sex to marital sex.

7. MIXED EMOTIONS

What we are used to calling mixed emotions, we must now render as complex emotion-actions. Using our familiar substantializing and animating locutions, we are used to saying such things as that certain mixed emotions can tear one apart; in our revised formulations, we would speak of these as complex emotion-actions that one may execute only with great difficulty and painfully. In action terms, the "experience of being torn apart" is the action of imagining animated and hostile emotion-entities attacking a corporeal self. This common and clinically very important type of imagining is an action, too; among other things it may be a way of portraying the muscular tension engendered by the incipient incompatible movements one may be making in connection with irreconcilable aspects of the complex emotion-action in question. For example, there are the incompatible movements of fighting and fleeing in danger situations and those of loving and hating (ambivalence) in relations between lovers.

We may understand a complex action better by sorting out its constitutive features and speaking of them separately. We do so regularly in clinical psychoanalysis. To take an obvious example, an adolescent boy's masturbating is an action the complexity of which is rendered most systematically as a family of actions, each in its own mode, rather than as one action carried on "with mixed emotions." Upon analysis, the masturbating may prove to include the following actions and modes: pridefully manifesting sexual potency; self-reassuringly manifesting sexual intactness; guiltily violating moral precepts; defiantly disregarding parental prohibitions; miserably failing to "get the real thing;" and in the safety of merely imagining them, enjoying situations that seem dangerously uncontrollable in "real life." Viewing the masturbatory activity as this family of actions makes it possible to comprehend it more easily and clearly than defining it as one action. Then, we are describing and interrelating in a more exact way the situations in which it is done, the modes of its doing, and its sequelae. At the least we are stating the action more simply and informatively as a family of actions even if we use more words to do it. The idea of a family of actions is the equivalent of "overdetermination" in the mechanistic-causal aspect of Freud's language and of "multiple function" in the organismic aspect of that language.

8. Emotional Withdrawal

The idea of emotional withdrawal is based on certain implicit assumptions or fantasies as to the nature of a person's being emotionally engaged with anything or anyone. The assumptions or fantasies are these: emotion is *radiation* directed through space onto its object in the manner of radiant energy or light; emotion is *touch* in the manner of an embrace, a blow, a push, or a shove; emotion is *investment* in the manner of money sunk into a business or purchase or pulled out and distributed to one's creditors or dependents; some sort of *spiritual presence* inheres in the radiation, touch, or investment of emotion, such that two people may be joined together by emotion or may interact emotionally despite their being separated from one another in physical space ("Feeling your love, I am not alone"; "I am burdened in everything I do by your contempt"; "You get under my skin"; etc.)

In large part, these ideas are culturally supported residues of the young child's undifferentiated concretistic and magical thinking, especially as it concerns the interpersonal actions that are so crucial in its life and development. Loving and embracing; hating and hitting; fearing and running away; cuddling and flashing smiles affectionately across breasts, bottles, teddy bears, tables, or rooms; being present though absent (the loving or disapproving parent): these and many more emotion-actions and emotion-modes characterize much of the spatial, motoric, and interpersonal world of the early years. Young children frequently think of influences acting magically through space in all kinds of ways. But not only young children: adults, too, continue these infantile actions and modes in their thinking; they do so unconsciously (especially in connection with the literally concrete and magical aspects) and they do so preconsciously and consciously (especially in their favoring material, spatial, and energic emotion-metaphors). Because emotion is regarded as an inspirited ray, touch, or investment, it seems warranted to say that it may be withdrawn or that it may withdraw itself. And so we speak of it: if it is the subject who does the withdrawing, then the subject no longer reaches, feels, or possesses the object; if it is an imagined presence or an actual person who withdraws from the subject, then the subject no longer is reached, felt, or possessed by that presence or person; and in either case, if the withdrawal is prolonged, the person is said to be "out of touch," or "out of contact," or "unreachable."

In metapsychology, the various spatial and spiritual fantasies of emotional approach, contact, and withdrawal have

been given the appearance of scientific "dignity" and legitimacy through their being translated into the terms of psychoeconomics, especially the variants of cathexis. Consequently,
we must pause at the idea of cathexis which has figured so
prominently in metapsychology.

The idea of cathexis allegedly refers to something like an
electrostatic charge of libidinal and/or aggressive energy that
is extended toward, placed on, or invested in some representation of self or object. As this process is designated *cathecting*,
and as the cathectic charge may be removed from that representation by withdrawal (and displacement), there is an anti-
thetical process designated *decathecting*. Basically, this type
of thinking merely implements a theoretical commitment one
has already made, a commitment to the proposition that it is
necessary to hypothesize psychic energy in order that there be
something to make the psychic apparatus work, much as elec-
tricity "makes" a light turn on or as gasoline "makes" an auto-
mobile engine go. As I have presented my criticisms of the
psychoeconomic commitment elsewhere in this volume (see
chapters 4 and 5) and in other publications (1968b, 1970c), I
shall say no more about it here.

We can easily translate emotional withdrawal into action
language. To withdraw emotionally from someone is to engage
in fewer emotion-actions than before in relation to that person
and to perform any actions in that relation in calmer or more
indifferent emotion-modes. This means actually taking and
showing less interest in that person or, in other words, valuing
that person less. Unconsciously as well as preconsciously and
consciously, one does not concern oneself so much with that
person. It is necessary to specify that this is so unconsciously,
for it is wrong to speak of emotional withdrawal when there is
only defensive minimization or conscious pretense of de-
creased interest.

Consider grieving. Usually, we say that the grieving person
has withdrawn emotionally from the surrounding world and
has centered all of his or her feeling on some experience of loss
or on some lost object (Freud 1917a). In this way we concretize
feelings, for we imply that feelings may be moved, centered,
recentered, etc. What we are referring to, however, is a set of
performed and avoided actions and modes of action that constitute that person's grieving. This set includes thinking sadly

and longingly of the lost person or of one's past and hoped for relationship with him or her; refraining from taking interest in other people; refraining from engaging in other actions in emotionally pleasurable ways; maintaining this manner of living by devaluing other people, other actions, and other modes of action, and perhaps even the idea of the present and the future, thereby centering on what is impossible to the exclusion of what may be possible and what certainly is conceivable. Undoubtedly, the grieving person acts differently, but only in fantasy can it be thought that this person is acting *from a different distance, deploying spiritualized rays, touches, and investments differently* or *simply witnessing these rays, touches, and investments behave differently.*

What does it mean to say that certain actions "constitute" grieving or other emotion-actions? In formulating emotion-propositions this way, I am simply following the rules of action language. These formulations indicate that there is no grief apart from a set of grieving actions and modes of action. In each case, the constitutents of actions are not to be understood as signifying something else; nor are they to be characterized as derivatives, representatives, or manifestations of something else: they are the thing itself, the actions in question, the grieving in this case. Furthermore, it is when most of the actions and modes that make up the set are discernible at one time that the ambiguity of the action or mode in question is greatly reduced; for example, this clustering will make it plain in a certain instance that a person is crying sadly and therefore is simply grieving rather than crying happily and therefore rejoicing in a complex fashion or crying angrily and therefore acting aggressively in a complex fashion.

9. DISPLACEMENT OF EMOTION

What is displaced in displacement? And what place is it displaced from or displaced to? In metapsychology, displacement refers to the shifting of psychic energy or cathexis onto a substitute for the self-representation or object representation toward which the energy is truly directed or in which it is truly invested. Accordingly, loving or hating one person is a matter of directing libido or aggression toward the representation of that person, while displacement means that the subject now directs that libido or aggression onto the representation of another person or thing instead. In thinking of it this way, one assumes that the alternative has been chosen because it will serve well as a disguised substitute for, and representative of, the true object and that consequently the displacement will provide some relatively unanxious gratification of the true unconscious wish (e.g., the familiar "displacement upward"). However, once one stops using the idea of a psychic energy that may be distributed through some kind of space, nothing remains to displace and no places remain to displace anything from or to. As a theoretical term, displacement is another one of those that illustrate how psychological conceptualization may be modeled too closely on archaic fantasy.

There is a compromise theoretical move that is apparently more acceptable. We might say that it is the feeling, the accent, or the emphasis that the subject displaces rather than psychic energy or cathexis. But we gain nothing by making this compromise in that we are still using inadmissible ideas of places and quantities while simply being less forthright about our doing so.

In action terms, one does not think of displacement at all. Such phrases as "instead of" or "as a substitute for" will do the required explanatory job perfectly well. Even though we may discern etymological implications of place in the words "instead" and "substitute"—so many words and phrases may be traced back to ideas of place, substance, quantity and movement!—these implications are inconsequential in these instances; for systematizing purposes, they entail no troublesome reliance on blatantly materialistic and mechanistic preconceptions, metaphors, and rules.

To love or hate one person instead of, or as a substitute for, another: this specification of an action facilitates our investigating it; having simply referred to the activities in question, we might then go on to ask why the agent made a substitution and why he or she chose that particular substitute (for example, the reasons why he or she chose Tom rather than Harry to be the substitute for Dick). We might also ask in which respects the "displacer" has carried out the substitution unconsciously and how insistently he or she has continued to do so. In answering these questions, we would arrive at such familiar forms of clinical interpretation as the following: "It was safer

to get mad at him instead of me," and "You had to find someone to love who less obviously resembled your mother." In fact,
this is just how clinical psychoanalysts work.

10. EMOTION AS DEFENSE

Generally speaking, we psychoanalysts accept and use the
idea that one emotion may be used as a defense against another; for example, we believe that love may defend against
hate, rage against fear, and euphoria against depression. When
we think of the defending emotion as a wall, a facade, or a
screen, we are envisioning the defense as being somehow verti-
cal in space; when we think of the defending emotion as a
layer, on the order of a blanket, a lid, or some other cover, we
are envisioning it as being horizontal; and when we think of it
as a coating or wrapping, perhaps as atmosphere, we are envisioning it as some kind of surrounding or medium the nature
of which may be thermal, oral, oceanic, etc. A notable instance
of this kind of spatial thinking will be found in the classic and
illuminating paper on affects by Ernest Jones (1929) where he
based his argument on the spatial metaphor that affects may
constitute defensive layers in relation to each other.

Again, we must find a way of doing without the conception
of emotions as entities in space. When discussing the idea of
accumulated feeling in section 6, I developed the idea that defense is constituted by the agent's revised and correlative conceptions of actions, modes, and situations. It is these revised
conceptions that reduce, if they do not eliminate, the apparent
dangerousness of the agent's situation; thereby, they make it
possible for the person to act, even to act emotionally, without
risking such intolerable real or imagined consequences as utter
loss of love or castration. It is not implied that the person
fashions or maintains these redefinitions consciously. In taking
hypomanic action, for example, the person unconsciously substitutes for a depressive mode a euphoric mode of conceiving
of situations and actions; and it is a major feature of taking
depressive action that the person unconsciously substitutes a
depressive mode for an angry mode. Similarly, as Jones
pointed out in other terms, the person may substitute loving
modes for hateful ones, hateful ones for fearful or guilty
ones, etc.

At this point, the approach to emotion-as-defense in action terms may seem vulnerable to the charge that it tacitly substitutes one kind of wall or layer for another, in that the revised defensive conception must still imply some blocking or covering up of the initial, intolerably dangerous conception. Surely, it will be argued in this vein, the initial conception does not go out of existence once it is defended against; for if it did, it would no longer make sense to speak of the revision as defensive, the idea of defense necessarily implying the continued existence of that which is to be defended against. (Freud's defensive cathexes are "counter" or "anti"-cathexes.) Having already dealt in some detail with this challenge in chapter 11 on the idea of resistance, I shall only review two of my main points here: in action terms, defense is to be viewed partly as the agent's refraining from engaging in certain desired actions, such as exhibiting or looking, or refraining from performing them in certain modes, such as consciously or passionately; and defense is to be viewed partly as the agent's arranging things so that the dangerous actions and modes that would be performed under other circumstances are not performed and instead remain in the conditional mode, that is, as that which the agent would do under other circumstances. These actions and modes that are simply not performed or remain conditional cannot have the concretistic, archaic implications of Freud's metapsychological impulses, fantasies, memories, or even wishful situations that autonomously insist on continuing to exist and continuously lurk behind and press against some sort of structural-energic defensive disguises, walls, layers, and other barriers.

11. SINCERE AND PRETENDED EMOTION

We speak of some emotions as being sincere. In variations on this theme we use the words genuine, authentic, and really felt. Other emotions we know or surmise to be pretended. In variations on this theme we use the words insincere, artificial, false, and feigned. In transitional cases we speak of shallow and deep feelings. There are numerous other words, each with its own nuances, for the distinctions I am making here; the ones I have cited constitute only a small though representative sample of the vocabulary of sincerity and pretense. I shall center the first part of my discussion on the word sincere.

One dictionary has it that sincere "stresses a revelation of just what one feels, thinks, or sees, and no more, and an unwillingness to embellish or exaggerate" (Webster's New Collegiate Dictionary 1953). With respect to this definition, the translation of sincere emotion into action language presents no special problem. A sincere emotion is an emotion-action or an emotion-mode that is performed sincerely, that is, frankly and not in some showy or affected way. In any case, it will be actions and modes, not emotion-entities, that will be sincere.

Sincerity words play a special role in ordinary language. There, it is usually redundant to specify that an action is being performed sincerely. It is enough simply to state what the action is. When it is not redundant to do so, one uses the specification "sincerely" to put an end to a person's doubting whether someone—it may be oneself—is acting sincerely. In this instance, sincerely means about the same as "undoubtedly," "you may count on it," or "with no secret reservations or qualifications." Just because such doubting is both widespread and, more than one likes to admit, often justified, our vocabulary includes so many sincerity words.

It is important to take note of a reductionist fallacy that is commonly implied in the way sincerity words are used. This fallacy tends to appear in the context of statements about "true feelings" or "real feelings." This usage is endemic in romanticist thinking and in "psychoanalyse," the latter being the simplistic psychoanalytic language often used by the lay public and sometimes unthinkingly and overeagerly by analysts themselves. We are most likely to encounter this fallacy when emotion-actions and emotion-modes, hitherto defensively repudiated, are being discovered, disclosed, hinted at, or inferred. For example, when someone makes an error in speaking and says "I want to go" instead of the consciously intended "I don't want to go," the observer might say, "Oh ho! So that's what you *really* feel! You *do* want to go!" But the only thing that is real here is the observer's non sequitur! For while it might be argued that the slip indicates what the speaker *also* "feels" but would rather not admit, it cannot be argued that the error negates the "feeling" that the speaker consciously intended and expected to convey in the first place. (I am assuming, of course, that there is no issue of conscious dissimulation here.)

The non sequitur is based on two preconceptions: first, that at any one time it is not possible to "feel" more than one way about something, and second, that whatever "feeling" one keeps secret must be one's true and only feeling. These preconceptions are as widespread as they are contradicted by the evidence of everyday life (see also my discussion of slips as actions in section 2 of chapter 7). Insofar as we crave simple explanations and uncomplicated emotions, we carelessly accept, or ourselves commit, the reductionist fallacy. We do not even stop to consider that keeping secrets is a kind of action one would hardly carry out emotionlessly. Thereby we both mistake simplemindedness for simplicity and introduce considerable confusion into our ideas about sincerity. Every emotion-action and emotion-mode must be taken as real in the sense of that which is performed or would be performed under certain circumstances. Whether or not the person consciously notes and acknowledges the actions and modes is another matter entirely. Consequently, there is no place in action language for the reductionist idea of "the real feeling." At best that idea conveys the proposition that someone has taken too limited an initial view of an emotion-situation and in that sense made a mistake and that he or she made this mistake for defensive reasons.

Turning now to the ideas of pretending and insincerity, it must be said first that they are exceedingly complex; that this is so is evident from the intricate, extended, and controversial discussions of them undertaken by Sartre (1943), Ryle (1949), Austin (1957-8), Anscombe (1958), and other modern philosophers. Here I shall do no more than present some introductory statements about these difficult ideas. I shall do so by concentrating particularly on histrionic behavior in the clinical psychoanalytic situation. As its name already makes plain, this is the behavior that so often seems to oblige us to use such words as pretending and insincerity.

Pretending emotionally is deceiving others knowingly or oneself unconsciously, or both, as to "how one feels." It is possible to deceive others this way. At least, a person might often be successfully deceptive, especially if that person is talented at dissimulation and if the others are, for whatever reason, not observing perceptively in this connection.

In the instance of histrionics, the analyst must ask what the pretender is affirming or accomplishing in pretending. In this way, the analyst may hope to construct a context for understanding the histrionic actions. If the analyst were to approach feigned emotions as *mere* histrionics, self-dramatization, a smoke-screen, or a put on, he or she would miss most of the interpretation. For example, after analyzing a particular instance of a man's acting histrionically, I concluded, "His pretending to be friendly, or more friendly than is in fact the case, is an instance of his defensively ingratiating himself with others in order not to realize that he believes himself to be unloveable." So construed, his pretending was as real as that which it obscured or replaced. For it can really be the case that one is feigning acting emotionally. Creating a false impression is really an action. This kind of pretense is one kind of real action.

In this light, an analysand's behaving histrionically is not something the analyst must try to "break through," "circumvent," or otherwise devalue and attack. The analyst must see the histrionic, not see through it; understand it, not fight it or dismiss it. Thinking affirmatively, the analyst approaches acting histrionically as an action to be defined in its own right. So far as possible, the analyst should, of course, also try to establish just what it is that acting histrionically obscures or replaces. First, however, he or she must attend carefully to the action of obscuring or substituting and the particular modes of doing so that the analysand is employing; otherwise it may never be possible to develop a satisfactory understanding of what is "behind the histrionics." This principle is identical with that generally accepted in analyzing "defenses" and "resistances" (see section 5 of chapter 11). Of course, the analyst will have to pay attention to that aspect of the histrionics that is plain lying.

In addition to, or instead of, knowingly deceiving others by pretending, one may deceive oneself as to one's own emotion-actions and emotion-modes. In everyday life we take it for granted that this is so, and in psychoanalysis it is deliberately made a matter of continuing concern. Unlike deception of others, which may be done consciously, self-deception can only be accomplished unconsciously. The conceptualization of self-deception is complex and problematical, and I refer the reader to my extended discussion of it in section 3 of chapter 11 on the

idea of resistance. Here, I shall say only that we may apply the
preceding analysis of pretending as much in the realm of one's
observing one's own actions as in the realm of others observing one's actions and one's observing the actions of others. One
may pretend to oneself, more or less successfully, that one does
not care or does care, does not hurt or does hurt, does not rejoice or does rejoice, and so on. On occasion, one may finally
recognize an instance of this sort and say, for example, "I was
kidding myself" or, still with some disclaiming, "How could I
have been so blind!"

One pretense commonly reported or discovered during psychoanalytic work is that of "faking" desire, excitement, and
gratification in connection with sexual intercourse. This is an
instance of pretending to be engaged in exciting sexual activity
with one's partner, perhaps as a means of maintaining his or
her interest, potency, or good will. Here, however, we are concerned not with deceptions of others but with *self*-deceptions,
which must be carried out unconsciously. In another case, then,
further investigation of the sexual "faking" might establish
that the analysand is unconsciously defending against consciously enjoying sexual activity and is doing so in order to
avoid reacting anxiously and guiltily to copulating pleasurably.
In yet another case the pretending might finally be understood
as the analysand's acting out a fantasy of personal omnipotence. In a third it might amount to a self-deceiving effort to
prove that one is not so emotionally dead as one fears. These
are only some of the possibilities, and they are not mutually
exclusive. Each strategy thus defined will have its history, and
the analysis of that history will constitute an essential part of
the so-called analysis of the ego, especially of its defensive aspects. This part of the analytic work should not be undertaken
with the coercive attitude of unmasking the analysand; rather,
it should be undertaken patiently as the necessary analysis of
masks, of which there are always so many, whether or not the
analysand is someone we would ordinarily call histrionic. Far
from being unreal, unrecognizable, indescribable, mere ob-
stacles, or of negligible importance, masks (maskings) are
among the real, fundamental, and analyzable aspects of human
action that must be dealt with thoroughly during psychoanalysis, for nothing exceeds them in strategic importance.

At the beginning of this section I mentioned the ideas of deep and shallow in relation to sincere and pretended emotions. By using the words deep and shallow, we perpetuate the spatializing of emotion-language in particular and of psychological language in general. Deep and shallow are typical instances of the large group of words and word usages that I discussed in chapter 8 on internalization. But there are pairs of words of other kinds to take note of in this connection. For instance, we say of certain emotions that they are either fleeting or enduring: by introducing these time-indices into emotion-language, we continue to make entities out of emotion-actions and emotion-modes and to disclaim them as actions, which are performed briefly or over long stretches of time. In other instances, we say of specific emotions that they are light or heavy, bright or dark, subtle or gross (crude, primitive), delicate or sturdy (robust), or noble or base. All now are to be translated into contrasting characterizations of actions and modes of action. It should be unnecessary to continue to spell out how this translating might be done in each instance.

15   Emotion Undergone or
Emotion Enacted?

1. Introduction

By now I have considered critically a number of important forms in which emotion is rendered as passive experience. In each of these forms emotion is presented as an experience *undergone*, though perhaps subject to regulation, rather than as a kind of action that is *undertaken, fashioned,* or *enacted.* In this chapter I shall be taking up some strategically significant issues, both general and specific, that are involved in first rendering emotion as passivity and then seeming to encounter it as such.

To do this job, I shall have to extend my theoretical base, and this I shall do in the following fashion. First, I shall review the confused and confusing uses of the terms active and passive (see also Schafer 1968c). Next, I shall examine the lawfulness that seems to characterize the appearance or experience of emotions. In this connection I shall discuss four important topics: the predictability of emotion; the emotions appropriate to extreme environmental circumstances and duress; the significance of the absence of expected emotions; and the regular physiological and sensory concomitants of emotion. Then I shall develop further the proposition that the concepts of emotion, situation, and action are correlative or co-constitutive of one another.

With this as my extended base, I shall go on to review and revise a number of key terms and propositions that embody the idea of emotion as passive experience. Specifically, I shall take up the conflict theory of emotions, the signal theory of emotions, and the notions of thresholds, tolerances, moods, empathy, preverbal emotions, and pathological states of emotion such as depression. In conclusion, I shall attempt to state the idea of emotion in a form that is free of faulty attributions of passivity.

Because it is easy to be misunderstood in this connection, I must append a few words of clarification to these introductory remarks. I am not minimizing or otherwise disparaging the important place people give to ideas of passivity in the way they represent and experience their lives in general and their emotions in particular. Nor am I arguing on behalf of an insistently active orientation to existence or emotion. I am attempting to work out a consistent action language for what we are used to calling the emotions. Just because "passive emotional experience" is so pervasive and important in ideas about human existence, and its scope so subject to reduction and its nature so subject to change in the course of a personal psychoanalysis, we are obliged to discuss this notion as systematically as we can. If I am being prescriptive at all it is to urge this consistency in theoretical discourse. And if being consistent entails that passivity be regarded as no more than an idea about action and no longer as an alternative to action, then so be it.

2. Active and Passive

Discussions of the notions active and passive, ordinarily conducted under the headings activity and passivity, present five types of confusion: the point of view of the subject confused with the point of view of the independent observer; passivity confused with refraining from taking overt action; action as an abstract term pertaining to every kind of performance confused with specific ideas about concrete actions; the pejorative use of the terms passive and passivity confused with description and explanation; and nonaction confused in retrospect with passivity.

In the first type of confusion, it is often overlooked that what is activity to the independent observer may be passivity to the subject and vice versa. For example, an independent observer might view a busy housewife and mother as being continuously active while the woman herself might view it all as her enforced subservient passivity in a male-centered society.

In the second type, it is often overlooked that refraining from moving about and talking is most usefully defined as one form of activity, while hypermotility and much talking is best understood as just another form of activity, one that may not even be characterized as greater activity except in the crude sense of activity as motility. For example, the psychoanalyst's refraining much of the time from talking is a central aspect of actively fulfilling his or her professional role; to a naive observer—or a bitter analysand—the analyst may seem almost entirely passive.

In the third type, actions described by the subject are confused with the idea of action itself. For example, when, in the course of excusing an act of indiscretion, someone says, "The impulse seized me," the listener might mistakenly classify as passivity what has to be some kind of activity, however it was brought about. Here we are in the realm of disclaimed actions (see chapter 7).

In the fourth type of confusion, people often use the terms passive and passivity pejoratively, implying condemnation of someone who has failed to do an action deemed desirable under the circumstances. For example, someone refusing to get entangled in a political, occupational, or domestic struggle might very well be charged with "just standing by passively instead of doing something about it." An unfortunately common clinical instance of this confusion is the judgmental use of the clinical designation "passive aggressive." Although it is true that any description implies some aim, hence, some valuations that are being used as selective and organizing principles, that sense of valuation is not close to the blatantly pejorative usage being considered here.

The fifth type, in which nonaction is confused with passivity, is exemplified by people's holding themselves accountable in retrospect for not having behaved differently at some earlier time even though there is no sensible reason for them to do so. It is a case of accountability after the fact. For example, some people blame themselves for not having been present at the deathbed of a relative even though they could not have anticipated the event or done anything about it if they had; others blame themselves for not having previously concerned themselves more solicitously with someone who has only now become acutely depressed or suicidal even though they had no good grounds for expecting these morbid developments. These confusions of nonaction with culpable passivity are, of course, indications that *unconsciously* the self-blamer is acting guiltily, and we have every reason to accept Freud's conclusion that seemingly senseless self-recriminations are potentially fully intelligible once we take into account all the things that people perceive, wish, do, or neglect to do *unconsciously*. Because it involves the pejorative use of the term passivity, this type of confusion overlaps the confusion of description with blatant valuation.

In viewing thinking of every sort as action or mode of action, we must include among the forms and modes of action the different ways of thinking oneself or others passive. We must regard passivity as one kind of content of thought-actions and not as one of the possible properties of actions or an alternative to action.

3. LAWFUL ASPECTS OF THE EMOTIONS

Although we know we can sometimes fool others and fool ourselves about our emotions, and although we sometimes strain to make emotion happen, as when we work ourselves "into a lather," in the main we do not believe that we can directly make ourselves feel one way or another. Even when we hold ourselves accountable for our emotions (e.g., "I hate myself for feeling so envious!"), we usually go on believing that we are in fact finding or encountering our own emotions, thereby taking the paradoxical position of being responsible for what we cannot help feeling. For most people, the idea that emotion is or can be simply some form or mode of action remains beyond belief.

We know, however, that we can actively bring on certain emotions or facilitate our undergoing them. We know that we can seek out situations and engage in certain actions that bring on or facilitate fear, depression, thrills, etc. For example, we go to the comic theater, listen to mournful music, play exciting games, and decorate with flowers for the joyous, sentimental, or reverential feelings we say they evoke in us. Though we know all this, still we do not think that by performing these actions we are *creating* emotions in the same sense that we sometimes think we are creating new ideas or new opportunities. Customarily, we just think that we undertake these actions in certain situations on the expectation that upon our doing so we will encounter certain emotions. As psychoanalysts, we are especially concerned in this connection with unconsciously performed, repetitive activity that tends to produce certain painful emotions, as in the instance of the moral masochist's maneuverings and manipulations through which he or she then constantly encounters unhappy feelings. But we think that a person's choice is limited to a choice of action and situation and that once the choice is made, the emotions will come of themselves; the emotions are predictable and one undergoes them passively.

In taking this view of emotion, we presuppose some lawlike or lawful relation between action and situation on the one hand and emotion on the other. Often, we just know that if we were to perform a specific action or enter into a specific set of circumstances, we would react in an equally specific emotional way; for example, fearfully, if it is speaking to a hostile audience, or cheerfully, if it is going on a long-awaited vacation. Thus, we seem to take for granted the existence of some invariant or lawful relation between our emotions and our actions in certain situations. That this is so is further evident from this consideration, that when our expectations or predictions of emotional experience are not confirmed, we do not challenge the assumption of lawfulness but rather set about looking for complicating factors in the actions and situations; once having found them, we then say that we failed to take them sufficiently into account before the fact, and we say, "If only we had known!"

Should this apparently lawlike behavior of emotion stand up under examination, we should have to accept a passive conception of emotional experience; for then we could attribute activity legitimately only to a person's getting into, staying in, or putting an end to those situations that *must* engender one emotion or another.

We make other general assumptions about people's emotions that, like predictability of emotion, imply this attribution of lawfulness. For one thing, we assume that in extreme situations and under duress all people will react in the same emotional way: with respect to these circumstances we ask, rhetorically, who would not be terrified or enraged or despairing, and we regard those people whose emotions do not conform to our expectations as odd, emotionally disturbed, defensively rigid or dishonest; we are usually quite confident of these expectations. For another thing, people generally (and analysts especially) regard the absence of expected emotion as an interpretable phenomenon on the assumption that it is clear what the lawful emotional reaction would have been. In this connection, for example, Anna Freud (1936) pointed out that in child analytic work, where the free association method cannot be used, the analyst can use the absence of expected affect as an indicator of specific unconscious conflicts, to which I would add that on many occasions the analyst of adults, too, interprets just this absence of predictable emotion. Finally, the idea of lawfulness is assumed in connection with the regularity with which certain physiological changes and corresponding sensations are featured in emotional responses.

We must now examine in turn these interrelated lawlike features of emotional life: predictability, uniform response to extreme situations and under duress, interpretability of the absence of expected emotion, and regularity in the physiological and sensory features of emotion.

(1) *Predictability.* Observation does not validate any claim of perfect or near-perfect predictability of emotion. The impression of this predictability is an artifact of certain of our (usually) unrecognized presuppositions. In making our predictions, we presuppose that we are talking about a normal person (however we define that) viewing his or her situation in the right way (however we define that). When a person reacts in a way that we did not predict, we are likely to say in explanation that we had formed the wrong idea of that person or that, owing to conditions as yet unknown to us, that person must have been viewing the situation in a way we could not have anticipated, or perhaps that both are true in some measure. For example, if someone does not mourn the death of a friend, we might decide on further thought or after further investigation that he or she did not regard the deceased as a friend. "You thought I like him? I hated him! I did try never to show how I really felt, and so I suppose I misled you": this could be a convincing statement; it need not be a defensive avoidance of mourning or indeed of melancholia, the latter being more in question when we observe someone acting insistently defensive in this regard. Thus, it seems that predictability of emotions depends on a number of usually unspecified conditions being met, all of them being versions of action and its modes. And the emotions no longer appear as logically independent variables; they seem to be aspects of the situations themselves. In other words, the lawlike propositions about emotion seem to involve a noteworthy degree of circularity.

(2) *Extreme situations and duress.* It is said of extreme environmental circumstances or great duress that they eliminate the possibility of choice or activity ("I had no choice," "I was compelled," etc.). The entire proof of this assertion is held to be the regularity with which people engage in the same emotion-actions when placed in these circumstances. Even those circumstances that are not quite extreme are said to elicit uniform responses from the most varied people; for example, being startled usually leads to one's acting irritably or angrily. But empirically, these claims of uniformity are greatly exaggerated, and logically, as we have seen repeatedly, circumstance—even extreme circumstance—must imply action, for there are many ways of seeking out a particular set of circumstances, creating them, maintaining them, exaggerating them, and defining and redefining them. Some people are more adventurous, more counterphobic, more unconsciously suicidal, or simply more steadfast than others, and so are the more likely to be "exposed" to extreme situations and duress and to the emotions corresponding to them. And among those exposed to these stresses purely by chance, some will view their circumstances heroically, as occasions for courage, resourcefulness, and endurance, while others will view them helplessly, as occasions for resignation, submission, and apathy. We know that some but not others have died as a result of exposure, illness, and starvation because they would not cheat, betray, organize, or cannibalize fellow sufferers; we know that some but not others have died before they would break under torture; and we know that some react to abuse with pride and rage, while others react to it with mortification and despondency. Think of the variety of responses to the extreme circumstances that the Nazis created for their victims.

About certain of these people under duress (it is not always the survivors), we say that they have or show more ego strength than the others. What do we mean by this estimate? Are we not saying that in circumstances that seem identical to us as independent observers, some people conduct themselves more reasonably, resourcefully, patiently, boldly, or decently than others, and are we not implying that at least in some important respects the "stronger" ones have defined their stressful circumstances differently, perhaps in a broader and more forthright and selfless manner, that being a large part of what we mean by ego strength? For us, the idea of situation is necessarily subjective and so it must include some estimate of oneself relative to the threats and opportunities in the environment as well as some estimate of these threats and opportunities relative to oneself. One must be viewing a situation as frightening in order to act frightened in it; one must be viewing it as infuriating in order to act furiously in it. The circularity of these statements indicates again that there is no way of treating action and situation as distinct or logically independent variables; at least this is the case so long as one is considering these matters from the standpoint of an agent or subject, which is the psychoanalytic standpoint.

People do, of course, generally define common environmental circumstances in similar ways. This is to be expected when (it is what we mean by saying that) people are members of the same culture; that they speak similar languages; that they share similar developmental backgrounds; and that they hold similar values concerning objectivity, self-preservation, concern for others, etc. On this account we are right to expect that, throughout our culture, people will usually construct similar situations out of the same environmental circumstances, go on to perform similar or unconsciously interrelated actions in these situations, and experience these situations and actions in similar emotional ways. But we are wrong to conclude from our confident expectations in this regard that one of the scientifically demonstrable features of nature is lawfulness of emotional response.

I do not include among the emotions the conditioned approach-avoidance responses of the infant. According to the rules of action language, emotion implies situation, and both imply the actions, not yet available to the infant, of anticipating, remembering, judging, interpreting, and so on. I am concerned here with a language for psychology. I shall return to this topic in section 12.

It is important to realize how much we tacitly presuppose in our propositions concerning the emotions. As a rule, we explicate these presuppositions only when our customary expectations are not borne out or when we are challenged. Because so much remains tacit, we are inclined to make the mistake of thinking that the emotions are governed by some simple and conventionally conceived lawfulness.

(3) *Interpretability of the absence of expected emotion.* This heading refers to unexpected and effective defensiveness in relation to an emotion, and the chief proposition it implies is this: not that something is being hidden, but that the person and situation are different from what we thought. The person's views and estimates of self relative to circumstance as well as the person's definition of emotional response must be different in this way; if not, why would he or she have undertaken to be rigidly and uncompromisingly defensive in relation to the expected emotion? A short while ago I mentioned that acting in a desperately defensive way with respect to mourning often indicates that one dreads "falling into melancholia": when that is the case, the correlative factors of person, situation, and emotion must be of quite another sort than what they are in the case of unhampered mourning. We can often interpret deviations from the norm of emotional action; but a norm is not a cause-effect law, and if instead we view it in these correlative action terms, we can see that norms and deviations from them, though potentially understandable, can have nothing to do with lawful relations, that is, relations between logically independent stimuli and responses that have been defined by independent observers.

(4) *Regularities of physiological change and sensation.* Upon empirical inspection, the physiological regularities prove to be not nearly as impressive as we are wont to think. They are discernible only in certain instances of emotion and even then they are not specific to single emotions. For instance, we do not know of any physiology of regret, bittersweet reminiscence, or awe; nor can we distinguish exactly the physiologies of fear, anxiety, and rage. True, we do make metaphoric references to the bodily states allegedly associated with the various emotions: in everyday language we speak of feeling empty, driven, shattered, flattened, upended, charged up, turned on, etc. But in speaking so, we are alluding to fantasies, many of them quite conventionalized infantile fantasies: we are not referring directly or exclusively to sensations; nor are we directly describing physiological changes, though we may be conveying fantastic interpretations we have made of actual changes and sensations. Also to be considered in this regard are the perturbations and agitations that I discussed in connection with the problematic verb "to feel" (see chapter 13, section 4);

these, too, refer to mixtures of pure fantasy and fantastic interpretations of the physiological and sensory concomitants of some emotional responses.

It seems, therefore, that we must state the idea of lawlike behavior of the emotions in the following fashion: Under certain conditions, people perform certain emotion-actions or act in certain emotion-modes. The conditions include the person's own actions of one sort or another, among them the actions of defining and estimating environmental circumstances as threats, opportunities, etc., and of estimating oneself relative to these. In a general sense, the conditions refer to the personal action of constructing and maintaining situations of certain sorts. This action need not be carried out realistically, according to certain prevailing norms of what it is to be realistic; but because by definition most members of a culture try to construct their situations in line with the conventional criteria of being realistic, they will construct similar situations and act emotionally in similar or interrelated ways, and will do so to a high degree. The entire affair will then seem natural and lawful in the manner of natural science law. But only seem, for in the action approach, lawful is the wrong word for it. Emotion, that is to say, pertains to what one will do and how one will do it and not to anything that must befall one or be simply encountered and passively experienced as effects of the unmediated casual influence of circumstances and actions that are logically independent factors.

4. The Correlative Concepts of Action, Situation and Emotion

Action, situation, and emotion are all aspects of one description or explanation. This is the logical import of the preceding discussion of the apparently lawful aspects of the emotions. Consequently, to say something about one of these aspects is to go far toward specifying the others; at least it is greatly to limit the ways in which the others may be stated. For this reason we cannot ordinarily say both that someone is acting angrily and that his or her situation and actions are peaceful or loving.

Similarly, we cannot ordinarily call someone's action flight without implying that he or she is acting fearfully in a threatening situation. And we cannot ordinarily say that a person's situation is gratifying and at the same time emphasize that he or she is waiting longingly.

This interpenetration or co-definition of action, situation, and emotion is not empirical; it is conceptual, logical, a priori. Consequently, the assumption of invariant connections or lawful connections must be rejected *in principle*. The separation of emotional experience from action and situation is untenable. Making this separation implies that we are treating emotion as an independent entity that may or may not be added on to behavior or included in it; it implies as well that the presence or absence of emotion has no bearing on our definition of action and situation. Both implications are to be rejected; for this separation is inconsistent with our actual ways of arriving at such definitions. In practice, we define, or may define, both actions and situations in part by the emotional way in which the person is doing something, just as we define, or may define, a person's emotion-action, and emotion-modes by stating his or her situation in a certain way.

Let us take as an example a male student studying very anxiously. We will define his situation as being somehow or other threatening, and we will define his action in terms of his being threatened. In action terms, we could not satisfactorily describe the student as engaged in studying *plus* his doing it very anxiously; for describing it that way would miss the mark entirely. Perhaps we will say that in a situation that seems to threaten failure, disgrace, and loss of love and self-esteem, the student is warding off these threats as best he can, in this instance by studying worriedly or desperately. I am not implying that we will limit ourselves, as the naive behaviorist might do, to observation of the student's nonverbal deeds. I mean that, as observers, we can establish that the student is working very anxiously by what we see, what we hear from the student, and what we can legitimately infer from both of these observations and from other knowledge of him as well. I also mean that the observer might be the student himself, who might just discover upon reflection that he or she *is* studying very anxiously. But in any case, action, emotion, and situation form an interpretive circle.

5. THE CONFLICT THEORY OF EMOTIONS

An old, though never fully integrated feature of psycho-analytic theorizing is the idea that emotions arise only at points of intrapsychic conflict, so-called. It is said that emotion discharges some of the energy of the drive that has been blocked by opposing forces from its full and direct expression; were there to be full and direct expression, there would be no residue of psychic energy pressing for discharge and so no affect. At this point in the argument, we need not linger over the problems inherent in this mechanistic approach to drive, conflict, and emotion. Although there are related traditional psycho-analytic views of emotions and their occasions, it would be possible to show that they, too, are conceived in terms of the unsatisfactory mechanistic model.

Psychoanalysis has demonstrated the usefulness of searching for conflict in all significant human actions and situations. This search for conflict has become an essential methodological principle of psychoanalytic work. The dynamic point of view of metapsychology is one version of this principle. The principle of multiple function is another version of it: according to it, psychoanalytic investigators must examine all psychological events from the standpoint of id, ego, and superego influences and the necessarily, even though not totally, conflictful interrelations of these influences. Putting this principle of conflict in the terms of action language, we could say something like this: we would always be well advised to inquire whether the prospect of performing paradoxical actions or acting in paradoxical modes was the occasion of the person's initiating the emotion-actions and emotion-modes we are trying to understand, and to inquire further whether the subject has performed those emotion-actions and emotion-modes in order to resolve, heighten, or avoid acting in any such contradictory fashion.

It is unnecessary to take any empirical position on the question of whether conflict is necessarily and importantly involved in every instance of acting emotionally. Considering the complexity of human existence, that empirical generalization could be "shown" to be supported by innumerable specific cases; it would not be a falsifiable generalization and so would be useless in psychoanalytic theory. The methodological value of seeking conflict or paradoxical features in every emotional action is, however, here not in question.

6. SIGNAL ANXIETY AND OTHER AFFECTS

Freud said that the ego was the seat of anxiety (1926). *Angststätte* was the word he used in the German original: translated literally, *Angststätte* means place or locus of anxiety. His designating the ego as this seat was not and could not have been an empirical observation; rather, it was a logical consequence of the way he had just recently defined the id, the ego, and the superego in his structural theory (1923a). Freud had assigned cognitive functions to the ego; in the present regard we must note that this assignment included perception, memory, and anticipation. Then, in the revision of anxiety theory which he undertook within a few years of "The Ego and the Id," Freud said that anxiety was the ego's response to perceiving a danger situation and anticipating a repetition of a somehow remembered early infantile traumatic situation. Consequently, it could only be the ego that could generate anxiety and perceive it. And since Freud's definition of the ego also included the function of protecting the entire psychic apparatus from disturbance, it would have to be this same ego that would use the appearance of anxiety as a signal to engage in some protective or defensive response. In this way the ego would be fulfilling its function as the organ of adaptation, as Hartmann was to call it later (1939b).

But in speaking of the ego's fulfilling its function, the metapsychologist is merely using conceptualizations consistently; the locution says nothing empirical about the behavior of an entity, the ego. The metapsychologist's strategy is this: if it should prove necessary to speak of the ego as signaling itself to do something, rather on the order of one person signaling another, then so be it, for there is no other structure to devise and send signals, no other to receive them, and no other to do anything in response to them. The functions assigned to the structures id and superego are of quite another sort and could not do the job. Consequently, *Angststätte* means that anxiety is an intrasystemic event—specifically, one within the ego. Following Freud's introducing this idea, general as well as specific theories of emotion as an intrasystemic event have been put forward by such outstanding theoreticians as Rapaport (1953), Bibring (1953), and Jacobson (1964).

In action language, however, there are neither mental places nor emotion-entities to localize and so there can be no *Angststätte.* There may be a person acting defensively or adaptively or both in order to avert dangers and suffering that he or she anticipates. Should that person fail in these efforts, he or she might indeed begin acting panicky and suffering in the anticipated way. It is, however, always possible to find that one anticipated incorrectly, as is the case when one finds that the world has not come crashing down following the success or failure of a particular sexual overture or hostile response. As to why the person should have begun acting defensively or adaptively in a particular instance, we need only remain aware of two things: people do keep on the lookout for danger, that being one of the actions they perform, some more assiduously and self-protectively than others; and when people discern or anticipate danger, whether correctly or not, they can only do so uncomfortably in the way we call anxiously or apprehensively, perhaps undergoing in that connection the well-known, though not entirely specific, physiological concomitants of anxiety.

As it presents no great problem to develop comparable formulations concerning other "signal affects," I shall say no more about the matter here.

7. Emotional Thresholds

The idea of emotional thresholds presupposes emotion to be an entity that may accumulate in unnoticeable increments until it reaches a certain intensity, at which point it must be noticed, expressed, or warded off by the person in whom this process takes place. In the terms of action, this idea is inadmissible (see chapter 14, section 6). What is admissible is the idea of *sensory* thresholds: there is a sensory or psychophysical point (actually a range of points) that divides the subliminal from the supraliminal; it is a point determined jointly by bodily conditions and stimulus conditions, though within limits it may shift in either direction in keeping with exaggerated or fluctuating attitudes. Because some sensations are aspects of the physiological concomitants of emotion-actions and emotion-modes,

their achieving sufficient intensity to cross the threshold may
alert one to the fact that one *is* responding emotionally or *is* in
an emotion-situation or may make it difficult for one to remain
defensively oblivious to this fact; thereupon one may perform
any kind of expressive, defensive, or corrective action. That
these events seem literally to constitute the crossing of an emotional threshold, that is to say, of an emotion crossing *its*
threshold, is no more than a manifestation of the spatial material, and quantitative preconceptions concerning psychological
activity that I have been identifying and criticizing. These preconceptions rejected, it can only be sensory or psychophysical
processes to which these quantitative and liminal propositions
apply.

The significant *psychological* event in this connection is
one's defining an emotion-situation at all. There is a point in
time (actually a range of points) when one makes this definition, in part by initiating the co-constitutive emotion-actions
and emotion-modes. For defensive reasons, however, one
might have remained oblivious to one's performing any of
these actions in any of these modes; only subsequently might
one begin consciously to recognize the relevant situation,
actions, and modes, and then one might well be inclined to
think that an emotion has spilled over its threshold. It makes a
lot more sense, however, to think that one has just made a significant discovery or rediscovery. Instead of oneself, it may, of
course, be others who perceive one's actions insightfully in
this connection.

8. Tolerance of Emotion

Because the question of tolerance comes up most often in
connection with the so-called unpleasant or painful emotions, I
shall use anxiety and depression as my examples in this section. I realize, however, that some people, such as severely
depressive people, may barely tolerate pleasant emotions.

In a general way, we sort people out as having high, medium,
or low anxiety tolerance. We also say of children and hypomanic people that they have little or no tolerance for mourning
or depression, and that defensively they either seal off these
emotional reactions by massive repression or reverse them by
massive denial. Looking at these propositions from the stand-

point of action, what may we say they mean? One's response to this question will depend on one's grasp of the issues involved in the idea of emotional passivity and the separation of emotion and action that is associated with that idea.

When we speak of emotions in the sense of independently acting entities that impinge on us and with which we must contend, we implicitly define tolerance as a set limit with respect to which we can only be observers, hence, passive. We speak, that is to say, as if we are disengaged witnesses of a force (the emotion) hitting a barrier (the level of tolerance) and either being withstood or breaking through (or spilling over). Accordingly, we speak of tolerance as something one *has* and *experiences* rather than as an action one *performs*, that is, the action of tolerating. However, we are not consistent in this regard in that we also assume that the limits of tolerance can be modified; for example, we believe that interpretation, encouragement, reassurance, enticement, exhortation and threats can alter the level of a person's tolerance of emotion. In this respect we seem to recognize that at least to some extent we are dealing with attitudes people take toward their performances rather than with static traits that they "have," and we go part way toward recognizing that the word tolerance refers to the correlatives action, situation, and emotion, as discussed earlier.

To translate anxiety tolerance into action language, we must speak of one's tolerating one's own acting anxiously. One might be acting slightly anxiously, moderately anxiously, or very anxiously; and one might tolerate no more than acting slightly anxiously or one might tolerate acting anxiously in the extreme. According to the translation, anxiety tolerance is neither a strength nor a capacity: it is an action—specifically, the action of tolerating acting anxiously.

This action may be stated affirmatively as a matter of doing something or negatively as a matter of refraining from doing something. Stated affirmatively, anxiety tolerance means continuing to do whatever one is doing despite the fact that one is doing it anxiously. Stated negatively, anxiety tolerance means refraining from engaging in certain actions such as fleeing, however much one might wish to engage in them, because it is more important to go on with what one is doing, however anxiously. Affirmatively, for instance, one goes on fighting for one's rights in a situation despite one's doing so fearfully (being worried about reprisals, etc.). Negatively, one refrains from falling silent about one's rights, from running away, or from redefining one's rights in such a way as to eliminate conflicting points of view even though one's speaking frankly about these rights is something one does anxiously. Thus, to say that a person's anxiety tolerance is high is to confirm and predict a noteworthy regularity and continuity of his or her actions and modes of action in danger situations; specifically, it is to assert that we may count on that person to persevere in actions even though he or she does them very anxiously. We are referring to what is also called a disposition.

So-called tolerance of depression, to switch briefly to my other example, refers to the person's persevering in actions which will be performed depressively if they are performed at all. In this instance, to do something depressively includes to consider or imagine painfully the harm one has done, the deprivation one has suffered, the reproaches one directs toward oneself, the apparent helplessness and hopelessness of one's present position, and so on, and especially to do so unconsciously and in archaic (especially oral) terms (see also section 10, below).

Thus, to tolerate emotion is to persevere in acting emotionally when acting that way is experienced in a disagreeable, threatening, or painful fashion. One addendum is necessary: when we speak of high tolerance, we usually imply the comparative judgment that some or many other people would not persevere to that extent, and when we speak of low tolerance we usually refer to persevering that is below the average in its extent; and the idea of the norm or average varies considerably from person to person or from mood to mood.

9. Moods

According to the common conception of moods, we experience them passively. Like weather, a mood comes over one, and like an autonomous adversary, it grips one. To be in the mood to do something is to find oneself in that mood; it is not to choose it, bring it about, and sustain it. At the same time, moods are thought to operate like powerful motives in that they drive one to act along certain lines and to seek out or create the situations in which to act that way; at least they constrain one to put certain self-justifying, moody constructions on events and circumstances. For example, a good mood is thought to compel one to view everything in an agreeable light and to minimize and avoid whatever would threaten to interfere with its continuation.

So conceived, moods share essential features with self-fulfilling prophesies. In a circular fashion, moods are both the causes and the effects of the same phenomena: one is in a good mood just because it is a good world and simultaneously one's being in that mood amounts to one's being disposed to expect, construct, and insist on only a good world; consequently, it is a good mood that impels one to be in a good mood. We mean all of this when we speak of a good mood.

To say that one is in the mood to do something is to imply that one has adopted a view of one's future activity as passivity. As if observing someone else, one predicts that one will continue to be disposed to act along the lines of that mood. Thereby one disclaims any sense of primary initiative; for one implies that one's later activity can only be secondary to the present tone or direction of one's emotions, which is the mood to act only along certain lines. Thus, in the customary idea of mood, activity presupposes passivity.

Consider a grouchy mood. Ordinarily we think of it as a state in which one finds oneself or as a disposition with which one is afflicted. One says, "I woke up on the wrong side of the bed this morning" or "I fell into this bad mood." And even when we attribute the mood to frustrating environmental circumstances, we still imply that, once it has settled in, the grouchy mood is both autonomous and discontinuous with other experience. The mood "calls the shots." Grouchy activity presupposes this passivity. One presents oneself both as compelled by the grouchy mood to see things in a disagreeable light and as justifying the mood by pointing to a disagreeable world. Correspondingly, when one is grouchy, one may take two positions simultaneously: one may warn others that one is in a grouchy mood, that is, warn them to expect one to be easily provoked to anger, discontent, and the like—in so doing one will be stressing one's activity on a premise of passivity; and one may plead the inevitability of grouchiness in so disagreeable a world—in so doing one will be stressing one's passivity without qualification.

Using action language consistently, we may hope to eliminate at least some of the conceptual mud puddles we usually encounter in discussions of these matters. We disallow both the notion of passive mental processes and the notion of emotion-entities characterized by discontinuity and autonomy. We speak only of what a person is doing and how he or she is doing it. In the case of grouchiness, we say that one is readily and consistently taking irritated and discontented positions with respect to past, present, and future events and situations; that in order not to be swayed from one's grouchy course, one is both resisting the efforts of others and denying observations of one's own that could have this effect; that one has been acting this way only from a certain time onward ("mood" ordinarily implies transiency); that it may not be easy or possible for anyone to define one's reasons for acting this way; and that, in thinking of the grouchiness as a mood that surrounds or seizes one and runs its own course, one is both disclaiming one's own responsibility for acting grouchily and defensively avoiding establishing one's reasons for acting this way.

In the terms of action, we may not speak of the passing of a mood as if it were an event on the order of a passing rainstorm; for in doing so we would be supporting disclaimers of activity, responsibility, and personal continuity. It is enough to say merely that the person in question now thinks of himself or herself as being in a changed emotional situation and that there must be reasons for this actual or imagined change.

Here, for example, is the beginning of an action-oriented, psychoanalytic formulation of the grouchy mood of a man I shall call John. "Whenever John thinks he has been slighted by a man to whom he has turned for paternal approval, he persistently engages in acting grouchily (grouchy mood). He does so by dwelling on related past events and relationships that he has experienced disagreeably and also by consistently thinking of present and future situations from the standpoint of their disappointing and irritating potentialities. Unremittingly, he creates a disagreeable world. He does so in order to avoid questioning his own worth; for were he not to begin acting grouchily, as described, he would doubt his worth in response to being slighted. Thus, damning the world is his alternative to damning himself. Unconsciously, John conceives of these events and responses as castrations, maternal deprivations, revenge on the paternal phallus and maternal breast, reversible sadomasochistic positions, and moral punishments." I could develop this formulation of John's grouchy mood further, both developmentally and cross-sectionally; in so doing I would be saying more fully and precisely what John is *doing* by "being in a grouchy mood" and how he has come to be doing just that.

To summarize: moods are temporarily emphasized, historically understandable dispositions to do everything in a certain emotional way; they are characterized by a distinctive organization of ideas about what this emotional disposition entails in the way of activity and passivity, continuity and discontinuity, and responsibility and disclaimed responsibility; and the alleged comings, lingerings, and passings of moods are as amenable as any other performance to being stated in the terms of action.

10. PATHOLOGICAL EMOTIONAL STATES: THE EXAMPLE OF DEPRESSION

Freud took up depression under the heading of melancholia (1917a). He dealt with it in two ways. One way, consistent with his mechanistic theory of mental functioning, is cast in the terms of psychoeconomics and psychodynamics: depression is the energic resultant of the play of instinctual and other forces within the mental apparatus; in this account, which occupies the latter part of Freud's essay, mind is portrayed as the arena in which mental forces struggle against each other. Freud's other account of depression is cast in terms of action, though not explicitly and systematically so: depression is a complex way of simultaneously acting angrily, fearfully, self-punitively, even protectively or lovingly; in this account, depression is something one does, not something one has or something that has happened to one. Because Freud's idea of scientific explanation was so thoroughly mechanistic, he regarded the latter account of depression as mere description of phenomena rather than as legitimate explanation.

From the vantage point of action, however, we may say that the valuable part of Freud's account is his unsystematized presentation of depression as action. Here, the central figure is not the pathological emotional state of depression: it is the depressive agent; the one who is continuously and desperately acting egocentrically, guiltily, reproachfully, etc.; the one who

is deviously, fantastically, and unconsciously attacking others
while ostensibly being only self-attacking; the one who is in
fact protecting loved ones from directly destructive actions;
and the one who is attempting in these and other ways to regulate both self-esteem and relationships with others. By presenting depression as intelligible activity, as a wishfulfilling
creation or arrangement, however consciously anguished its
experience may be, Freud was rejecting the passive implications of the idea that one may "be depressed" or "get depressed." Like a mood, with which it shares many features,
depression is now seen to be a certain way of acting emotionally.

In the same paper, Freud also presented mania as activity,
though again he explained it mechanistically in terms of psychoeconomic and systemic (topographic) processes; he accorded no theoretical status to his recognition of the manic
agent.

Returning to the depressive person as agent, and without
attempting to be complete about it or to present a distinctive
configuration of the factors involved, I suggest that in acting
depressively one is unconsciously engaged in affirming or enacting the following propositions: I hate those I love (ambivalence); I interact with them lovingly insofar as they support
my precarious self-esteem by being loving, admiring, attentive,
and steadily available to me (narcissism), and I interact with
them hatefully, even to the extent of wishing them dead, insofar as they do not relate to me in the ways I desire (ruthless
destructiveness); because I cannot altogether control how they
actually behave (hopelessness), and because I think of being
loved as being fed (oral fixation and regression), I imagine that
I eat them in order to get them inside me where, fantastically,
I can control them, punish them, protect them, and feed off
them endlessly (oral aggression or cannibalism); when I feel I
must be rid of them, I imagine that I excrete them (anal-expul-
sion); however, I must soon take them back into me in order to
reassert control and to feel full again (reincorporation); I seem
to be reproaching only myself when in fact I am simultaneously
reproaching these others as well, so that secretly it is my esteem for them as well as self-esteem that is at stake (self-punishment and latent persecution of others); I defeat them by
remaining despondent no matter how patiently they try to

reassure me and cheer me up (masochistic triumph); I execute my policy of thinking of myself hopelessly, helplessly, and unhappily by construing everything negatively (depression as a complex action or project); it is crucial to disclaim my following this strategy, and so, overtly, I insistently suffer pathetically (defensive and manipulative aspects of depression); in short, far from getting depressed, I depress myself and others, which I could not do were I simply the miserable wretch the world encounters (the depressive agent revealed).

However much genetic and neurophysiological factors may be necessary conditions of severe and recurrent depressions, there is no evidence that they are also the sufficient conditions of these depressions, and there is evidence that in any case it is descriptively and therapeutically useful to view depression nonjudgmentally as an action and mode of action.

Other so-called pathological emotional states may be restated as actions and modes of action in the same way.

11. EMPATHY

We have surrounded the idea of empathy with a mystique of passivity. We say that empathy just happens or is something one "has" either through being born "with it" or through "acquiring it" by experience. Women, it is often said, have "more of it" than men, usually on the assumption that it is a natural feature of femininity. These conceptions seem to be supported by the following three observations: it helps little to strain to be empathic; it is mostly, if not entirely, unavailing to try to teach empathy as a skill; and at least overtly and often dramatically, women in our culture do frequently claim and perform empathic actions. Because empathy is one of a group of terms that affirm some primary and essential passivity in emotion, and because of its significance in theories of therapy, it will be useful to examine carefully the preconceptions that govern its use and to attempt to reformulate it as action.

We have assigned to intuition a key role in our maintaining the mystique of passive empathy. Our conception of intuition implies that many instances of emotional sensitivity, understanding, and tact are based on an unknowable something that happens rather than on actions which as yet remain unknown or insufficiently known. Thus do we make a virtue of a deficiency of understanding; indeed, some even base a credo on this insufficient understanding when they proclaim intuition to be sacrosanct and not to be violated by coarse and insensitive investigators.

We further support the mystique of passive empathy by referring to the phenomenon of emotional contagion. But emotional contagion is not a fact; it is a social psychological metaphor. In its conceptual orientation, the idea of contagion is transparently passive; metaphorically, it implies that, like an illness, emotions may be "caught" by "contact." As there are no emotional bacteria or viruses, and no physical contact necessary in emotional influence, contagion seems to imply that there are ghostly carriers that may be caught by ghostly contact. As an expression of the archaic fantasies with which psychoanalysts regularly and necessarily deal, the metaphor makes sense and is important to take account of, but as a systematic statement, it stands revealed as nonsense. Contagion is a cousin of intuition, and both terms should be excluded from systematic statements of psychological phenomena.

Yet we do after all use contagion to refer to something we actually observe, and so we should try to ascertain what that something is. We seem to be referring to this: unexpectedly and uncomprehendingly one may begin to do actions in the emotional way they are being done by others in one's proximity; for example, listening to an evangelist ecstatically, regarding a school lunch with disgust, or marching with patriotic pride to the beat of a drum in a parade. But it is not contagion of ecstasy, disgust, and pride that is being observed; rather it is the unexpectedness, the lack of comprehension, and the similarity of the actions being performed in the social setting in question.

Setting aside preconceptions about emotion-entities, intuitions, and contagions, how shall we now speak of empathy in the language of action? To begin with, we shall have to say that empathy is an action or a mode of action, something one does or a way of doing things in social situations: one empathizes or one acts (listens, anticipates, responds) empathically. In the form of a verb or adverb, empathy may be suitably modified by other words; for example, we may say that some people empathize more often, more keenly, more broadly or more subtly than others; and we may say that some people anticipate or respond emphathically more readily, more passionately, or more trustingly than others. Despite our having long used this verb and this adverb, we have tended to regard the noun, empathy, as the primary term.

It does seem to be the case that the actions constituting empathizing or acting empathically are not easily defined. Psychoanalysts have tended to attribute this fact to empathy's being arrived at preconsciously or unconsciously, which is to say by mental activity that is not carried out in focal awareness and that may even involve processes and ideas which the empathizer resists noting consciously. Additionally, it seems to be the case that we do our empathizing most sensitively when we do it preconsciously and unconsciously; for when we empathize self-consciously, as when we strive conscientiously to be empathic, we seem to be less exact, expressive, evocative, and effective than we are when we do it unself-consciously. But this is true by definition in that acting self-consciously implies a situation, actions, and modes of relationship with others that differ from those implied by acting unself-consciously: in the case of empathy, the fact that one is acting self-consciously means that one cannot be simply observing the other person empathically; rather, one can only be observing oneself observing the other person empathically. Like ostentatious sincerity, self-conscious empathy is logically problematic; and, empirically, its being seriously compromised means only that it is not plain empathy that is in question. Empathizing is like playing and joking in that it is best conceived as that which is done artlessly, hence, largely preconsciously and unconsciously.

Empathizing seems to be a passive phenomenon because the "topographic" modes, preconsciously and unconsciously, figure so strategically in its effective execution. On account of our acting in these modes, we are not likely to know *that* we are doing it or *how* we are doing it; for we are not consciously representing it as a project that we have undertaken. We know empathizing by its result. Consequently, it just seems to happen.

In action terms we may say of empathizing that it is a complex action and mode of action in which, preconsciously and unconsciously, and with some significant accuracy, one imagines and in a limited way shares another person's experience of his or her situation, actions, and emotions. To say this is not to imply that the other person fully and consciously comprehends and experiences his or her situation; for one may empathize with what the other person would comprehend and experience consciously were it not for his or her defensive activities and the effects of other limiting conditions such as the inarticulateness of early childhood.

According to psychoanalytic study, the following statements about emphathizing seem to hold: it requires free use of the imaginative actions we call projecting, introjecting, and identifying; one's readiness to take these facilitating actions and to bring about these results seems to be associated particularly with a moderated but characteristic mode of responding depressively; this readiness also seems to be associated with relative nondefensiveness as regards both the *content* and the regressive aspects of the *modes* of empathizing; and in its fully developed form, empathizing means thinking keenly, comprehensively, and feelingly about the complexities of another person's experience and doing so in terms of many interrelated actual and conditional emotion-actions and emotion-modes (Schafer 1959).

12. PREVERBAL EMOTIONS

Among the advances traced by observers of the psychological development of infants are the beginnings of emotion-actions and emotion-modes. However much these observers may disagree among themselves as to when it is proper to speak of the infant's beginning to act emotionally, it will be acting emotionally that is in question and not the infant's passively experiencing autonomous emotion-entities. In the action scheme, the infant will be viewed as being not so much passive as inactive or uncomprehending of its bodily and social circumstances. Slowly and unstably, the infant will begin to perform actions; however rudimentary these actions may be, it will become possible for the observers to agree that at some point the infant is comprehending, defining situations, setting projects, or pursuing goals and doing so in certain emotional ways.

Actions and modes need not be verbal or verbalized. For example, the infant need not be using the words love and anger in order to be loving or to be acting angrily. In the case of acting angrily, it will suffice if the infant tries to attack or acts as if responding to attack, yells, kicks, bites, displays the physiological arousal needed for vigorous action, and engages in any of the other nonverbal performances that will satisfy the agreed-upon criteria of acting angrily. In the case of loving, it will suffice if the infant smiles, gurgles, reaches out, relaxes, attends, and does whatever else will satisfy the agreed-upon criteria of loving. It is no different from how it would be in the case of the nonverbal emotion-actions and emotion-modes of the adult ("expressive movements"); for even though as an adult one may not, even to oneself, speak of acting angrily or lovingly, perhaps on account of being unconsciously defensive in this connection, an observer may be able to judge correctly that angrily or lovingly is the very word for what one is doing.

But without the words for it, people in fact remain unprepared to experience much that we ordinarily regard as essential to adult emotional life; in many instances, suitable words or names are needed to make the relevant actions, modes, and situations conceivable and thus possible. However, it does not follow from this that words or names are indispensable to every instance of acting emotionally. What does follow in the case of the preverbal infant is that it will act emotionally only in the most rudimentary way and with a small and unstable repertoire of emotion-actions and emotion-modes. In acquiring and using language as part of its development, the child will be expanding its emotional life. The extent of this expansion will, however, be subject to the defensive restrictions on thinking, including verbalizing, that the child imposes in connection with the developmental conflicts it must both enact and attempt to resolve.

We must be careful not to equate the infant's acting emotionally with the adult's acting emotionally along the same line. Although we may use the same name for both in a specific pair of instances, say the action of loving, we should remain aware that we are referring to opposite ends of a series of actions in that an adult's acting lovingly comprises far more constituent actions done in far more ways than a child's. No matter how childlike the adult, he or she cannot act happily in the very way an actual child does and vice versa. The accuracy with which a psychoanalyst empathizes depends in part on his or her alertness to these differences, just as it depends in part on his or her alertness to the significant continuation into adult life of infantile modes of action. Yet, as analysts, we do well to remember that these continuities and analogies are not identities.

According to the rules of action language, the idea that the beginning of emotional life is passive is inadmissible. It is correct to say that the infant manifests little or no comprehension of its circumstances, that it takes little or no action to influence them, and that it seems hardly to remember and anticipate them. And it is correct to say that physiological reactivity during infancy and childhood is far less differentiated and modulated than it is likely to be later on and that primitive conditioned responses make up much of the infant's repertoire of reactivity. But it is incorrect to draw from any such observations the conclusion that infantile emotionality is passive; for to do so would be to violate the working definitions of action language. The actions and modes that constitute the infant's emotionality are correlatives of the infant's creation of projects and situations. On this account they cannot *be* passive though observers may *think of them* as passive. Accordingly, the observation of preverbal emotion presents no principle problem for an action theory of the emotions. The problem is where to set the psychological vanishing point for action, looking backward toward infancy, and how much of a gray area to allow between bodily and social happening and personal action.

13. CONCLUSION: EMOTION ENACTED

Emotion is not: an entity; a quantity of psychic energy; the discharge of some or all of that energy; the resultant of conflicting forces; an instinctual presentation; a physiological response; a sensation; a phenomenon governed by laws; a received signal; an overflowing of a threshold; a pathological state; a passive experience; or an autonomous process with which the ego or self must cope.

Emotion is: an emotion-action or emotion-mode of action that people perform in the situations they define. They love and they hate; they act joyfully and they act depressively; and so forth and so on. These actions and modes define, as they are defined by, the agent's situations; and the agent defines, as he or she is defined by, these situations, actions, and modes. Depending on the projects set by the agent, these correlative definitions of person, situation, emotion-action, and emotion-mode will be more or less consistent with those frequently or generally presented by others in the agent's community or culture; to one extent or another, they will correspond to, or be versions of, the social and natural opportunities and limitations that constitute what we ordinarily call external reality or the environment.

Emotions are enactments. Ideas, too, are enactments. One idea that people enact is that emotion is an entity that is passively experienced in some lawful fashion and observed as a happening in the theater of the mind. According to the rules of action language, this idea is inadmissible; for emotions are done, not had, and in most respects one may have access to them much as one may have access to any other action or mode of action, whether it be one's own or another's. That people so often think of emotion as passivity constitutes one of the special technical problems of clinical psychoanalysis and one of the linguistic problems of theoretical psychoanalysis. As a mode of thinking, however, it is entirely incompatible with the present goal of stating psychoanalytic propositions systematically in the terms of action language.

This conclusion has also been the working premise of my entire discussion of the emotions. It may, however, be presented as a conclusion in this sense, that I have taken up a variety of terms and propositions that presuppose a passive view of emotional experience and have shown that they are neither well founded empirically nor logically necessary or sound or else that they may be reconceptualized in the terms of action language with greater clarity and with no troubling loss of significance. In this sense, I am drawing the conclusion that my premise is worthwhile. This is the circularity of an interpretive discipline, and psychoanalysis is that kind of discipline.

Part V
Conclusion

Film in a Dream

1st dream
of my dream
Sharon—women in S. purse—I
catch her, try to warn you
Film — girl, 36 bullets
people^s1 — ♂? women —
2same woman there.
Gather around Sh. Talk to
her. — I'm scared
Cut c I leave theatre
wait for ♀S. to come out.
Something wrong. I knew they
wanted to hurt us. Go back
in, they see us. Woman tells
us to go in. I say no. I'm
afraid of being hurt. She(?)
makes announcement — all
laugh. Herded in with
others, Everyone has to

...ongue

...ysis

ON

...od at the center of psycho-
...ion effects huge increments
...uch puzzling or seemingly
...ymptoms, errors, repetitive
...onality that is inappropriate
...nd these increments have al-
...alyst's strategy of consistently
...one who unconsciously both
...ntelligible phenomena; who has
...from creating, arranging, and
...or another; and who then, in any
...less, "encounters" them passive-
...openings to be observed, suffered,
...e. Not that all of one's life is thus
unconscious[ly] ...ged, and disclaimed, but that psychoanalytic interpretation deals methodically and specifically
with the large part of one's life that is one's own action; for it is
through its vision of life as made rather than encountered that
psychoanalysis accomplishes so much alleviation of neurotic
forms of misery and dysfunction.

Certainly, the psychoanalytic interpreter takes account of
sheer happening or necessity, that is, those past and present
events in the coming about of which the person has played no
hand. It would be absurd not to do so. But the analyst's rendition of these events always centers on the considerable extent
to which they are personal actions. It is warranted to view happening or necessity in this light because it can only enter into
someone's world through his or her way of recognizing it and
giving it significance. In this respect the events in question are
as much created as encountered, and so the analysand's account of them must be a personal statement that is amenable
to interpretation.

In conducting this lengthy exploration of the two alternative systematic languages—metapsychology and action language—I have tried to show that action language has always been the native tongue of psychoanalysis, though neglected, unsystematized, and devalued. For psychoanalysis is an interpretive discipline, not a natural science, and its interpretations concern human beings engaged in actions in various modes, particularly in the unconscious, infantile psychosexual, aggressive, and defensive modes.

But Freud did not see things this way. He made his positivistically conceived metapsychology the official tongue of psychoanalysis. More than a clinical explorer of the depths of the unconscious, Freud was also a systematic theoretician trying to colonize the population of this underworld by formalizing his ideas of it in the terms of an essentially ready-made scientific language. It is well known that Freud, in advance of his specifically psychoanalytic investigations, had self-consciously committed himself to the project of establishing a mental science on the model of the natural sciences of the late nineteenth century. Consequently, he took the official view that establishing intelligibility through interpretation could only be the first part of the psychoanalyst's job, the second being the translation of mere or crude mental phenomena into the quasi-physicochemical and quasi-biological language of energy, force, mechanism, structure, function, and the like. As a result, the action language that is needed to establish intelligibility in the first place has remained the slighted and undeveloped tongue of psychoanalysis. It has remained the taken-for-granted part of the language used by analysands and analysts to develop and formulate interpretations—an ordinary and pre-systematic language that is rather like a necessary but personally unacknowledged servant.

As the official metalanguage of theoretical psychoanalysis, metapsychology has always received the lion's share of creative and critical attention, and so it has evolved into a complex set of rules governing the choice and use of terms and the framing and interrelating of propositions about human development and conflict. Many features and consequences of this set of rules lack clarity, consistency, and necessity or relevance; additionally, it has been shown that many of them are inadequate to do the theoretical jobs for which they have been designed. Nevertheless, this set of rules is relatively complete and definite, so much so that it provides a warrant for calling metapsychology a language and for the informed critic to sort out good metapsychology from bad and good metapsychologists from bad. Meanwhile, we have followed Freud in ignoring the possibility of developing a systematic action language for psychoanalysis—a metalanguage with rules of its own and, unlike metapsychology, with an intrinsic relation to the method of clinical psychoanalysis.[1]

It must be said that the development and application of any systematic language for psychoanalytic interpretation implies some kind of colonization. Metapsychology is only one such. Consequently, the question to be considered is the flag under which this colonization will be carried out, which is to say the regime that will create the most favorable conditions for enlightened and enlightening development.

As I have already gone over these and many other related considerations in some detail and more than once in the body of this book, I shall not rehearse them any further here. I brought up these few points here in order to prepare the way for one of my two final actions as the author of this book. (The other will be my concluding remarks.) It is to pull together the rules of action language that, in the preceding chapters, I have only taken up or implied in different places, in different contexts, and for different purposes. In some instances I shall remind the reader of the problems with which each rule is intended to deal by appending a brief discussion of it. Actually, I began this formal exposition of the rules in section 2 of chapter 1, where I took up the first and fundamental rule of action language and some of its corollaries; accordingly, I shall only abstract and slightly rearrange the material I presented there, and I urge the reader to review these earlier passages in the present connection.

2. The Rules of Action Language

(1) One shall regard every psychological process, event,

---

1. While it must be granted in this connection that the person as agent has been featured in the writings of the existential analysts, it is also true that these analysts have not conceived and executed their general project as the development of a systematic action language.

experience, response, or other item of behavior as an action, and one shall designate it by an active verb and, when appropriate and useful, by an adverb or an adverbial locution that states the mode of this action.

(1a) Substantive and adjectivally elaborated designations of personal actions are no longer admissible. When speaking of any action, one shall not refer to it as a mental process or entity that runs its own course in some kind of mental space, moves in some kind of direction within that space, or has its own quantity, force, influence, or aims.

(1b) One shall not speak of actions as psychological properties that people *possess* or *have*.

(1c) One shall use the linking verbs *to be* and *to become* cautiously, because, customarily, one uses these verbs to state or at least to imply the now disallowed nominative and adjectival conceptions of personal action.

(1d) One shall make systematic psychoanalytic statements only in the active voice, thereby confronting theoretical problems rather than, as is all too common in metapsychological discourse, glossing over them by resorting to the passive voice and other vague or indefinite locutions that serve the same or similar functions as the passive voice.

(1e) One may no longer resort to the notion of propulsive entities on the order of impulses or drives that must initiate, propel, sustain, and guide actions and that, upon being gratified or discharged, terminate these actions. Whereas *to wish* is to perform an action of a certain sort and thus is a notion that is compatible with action language, *a wish,* in the sense of an autonomous dynamic agency, is now an inadmissible conception.

(2) One may designate action in an indefinitely large number of ways; that is to say, there can be no one final and correct statement of the action in question. This rule holds even though in specific contexts certain designations of an action will be more fitting, durable, and useful than others for purposes of psychoanalytic interpretation and personal transformation.

(2a) One would be incorrect to assume that there is ever only one action to designate interpretively; for now one must view each action as a manifold of possibilities. Although one must, of course, presuppose that there is something to refer to as an action, one can refer to it in more than one way—

hence, the manifold of possibilities. Every reference to *an* action or *the* action should be understood in this way.

(2b) One may designate an action on different levels of generality or abstractness. In designating an action in terms of a higher-order conception of it, one will be treating it as *constitutive of* the higher-order action; in designating an action as superordinate to other, more particular actions, one will be treating it as *constituted by* them. No question should arise as to which is the "real" action (see also rule 5c).

(2c) One may designate an action from different points of view with respect to which there is no question of significantly different levels of generality or abstractness. For example, one may describe an action variously as wishing, desiring, yearning, hoping, dreaming, daydreaming, or looking forward to something eagerly or pleasurably.

(2d) An action may be designated in contradictory ways even though only one person is its agent. As Freud put it, what is gratifying to the id may be alarming to the ego—of the same person! Thus, one may speak of the person's performing an action conflictedly, though one may also say that the person is performing paradoxical actions under one common sense aspect (see also rule 5 and its corollaries).

(2e) Whenever one designates an action in a new way— one does so often in the course of psychoanalytic work—one creates a new action without canceling out the old.

(3) The idea of an action includes many items that customarily have been designated as alternatives to action; for custom has it that action simply refers to overt physical activity in or on the environment.

(3a) Thinking is an action or mode of action to be stated through the use of verbs (e.g., remembering, anticipating, fantasizing) and adverbs (e.g., carefully, obsessionally, primitively).

(3b) Emotion is an action or mode of action to be stated through the use of verbs (e.g., to love, to hate, to fear) and adverbs (e.g., lovingly, hatefully, fearfully).

(3c) To think consciously is to think in only one of its possible modes; a person may also think unconsciously or preconsciously. Freud's adjectival designation of mental qualities—conscious, preconscious, unconscious—gives way to adverbial designations.

(3d) To perform actions overtly but unconsciously or preconsciously is to perform them in a certain mode, just as it is to perform them consciously—or recklessly, incompetently, pridefully, etc.

(3e) Refraining from performing certain actions is an action, too. No matter whether one performs this refraining action unconsciously, preconsciously, or consciously, one is still doing something; far from being passive or doing nothing at all, one is abstaining, desisting, repudiating, delaying, waiting, or what have you. We have the active verbs for it, and we must use them regularly.

(3f) To designate refraining as an action is not to say that everything one does *not* do must likewise be designated an action; it would be absurd to say so. One must have grounds for speaking of the action of refraining.

(4) The idea of action includes conditional or would-be actions as well as actions that are in fact carried out. These are the actions that one would perform under other circumstances or at least one anticipates that one would. What metapsychologists call repressed impulses, implying thereby that the ego, motivated by anxiety or guilt, has defended against its being invaded by certain mental forces, we now designate conditional actions, that is, the things one continues to wish to do but refrains from doing. Should circumstances change—which now can only mean should the person's view of these circumstances change, whether or not this change is "objectively" warranted —he or she would then perform the action in question.

(4a) It is one of the fundamental propositions of psychoanalysis that unconsciously maintained conditional actions ("repressed impulses") are psychologically ("psychically") real. Much wishing, self-punishing, forgetting, and the like become understandable only upon one's defining the conditional actions that are especially problematic to the person in question.

(4b) One may, however, also restate conditional actions as actions performed. Consider, for example, the conditional action of verbally abusing the analyst in connection with negative transference: one may redesignate it as the complex action of wishing unconsciously to abuse the analyst verbally, refraining anxiously or guiltily from doing so, and perhaps taking care not to realize consciously that one has constructed that problematic situation and now is acting in its terms. Whether to speak in this connection of actions as conditional or performed is a choice one must make on the basis of the explanatory context in which one is working.

(5) Actions vary in complexity. Consequently, in designating those that are more complex, one may have to use a number of verbs and adverbs arranged in combinations of phrases, clauses, and sentences; for systematic purposes, brevity of formulation should not be given the highest priority. For example, making an apt analytic interpretation is a complex action that we may specify roughly as the analyst's remembering relevantly, anticipating judiciously, timing sensitively, and communicating interventions in terms judged to have the best chance of effecting personal transformation.

(5a) The complexity of actions often includes contradictory or paradoxical constituents such as loving and hating, cooperating and defying, or fleeing and fighting. Actions of this sort are, of course, of special interest to psychoanalysts, who usually refer to *conflict* in this respect; however, they tend to speak of conflict in the psychodynamic and substantive terms of metapsychology, that is, as forces, structures, or functions in opposition to one another, when they could be saying that the person is acting conflictedly.

(5b) It may be fitting in certain contexts to speak of several actions rather than of one complex action and to say of them that they are performed simultaneously and in a more or less coordinated or mutually contradictory fashion. At other times, it may be best to include all the referents under the designation of a complex action (e.g., resisting). When psychoanalysts speak of multiple function and multiple determination or overdetermination, they are speaking in other terms of the actions that I am here terming complex actions; in doing so, they are attempting to translate into metapsychological language what they regard as preconceptually "real" or "purely phenomenal" features of people's lives.

(5c) In no case may any one constituent action or only one of the group of simultaneous and contradictory actions be designated the "real" action, where real would be being used in the sense of the only genuine or significant meaning of that which is being referred to; for any action must be as real as any other (e.g., pretending is as real an action as behaving sincerely). This rule applies equally to metapsychological language and action language.

(6) Actions may be carried out over stretches of time of any length whatever. Especially, certain higher-order actions may extend indefinitely through the time of one's psychological existence. For example, a son's action of loving his mother may be said to have no time limit during his existence.

(6a) In order to be said to be engaged in an action, a person need not be performing it continuously in the sense of doing it every moment of the stretch of time in question. For example, a woman may be said to be embarking on a professional career without its being entailed that she is engaged in some constituent action of this higher-order action at any given moment (cf. Ryle 1949).

(6b) There need be no fixed moment marking either the initiation or the termination of an action; the moment in question will be established by the designation of the action of which it is a feature. When, for example, is an analysis terminated? Clearly, the answer to this and similar questions will depend on the criteria being applied or, in other terms, the vantage point from which the actions of analysand and analyst are being viewed (cf. Freud 1937a).

(7) Experience is an action or a set of actions in various modes. The term experience refers to the person's giving meaning to somatic and environmental happenings; it refers as well to other actions of the person, whether these be past, present, or anticipated as well as actual or conditional. Experience does not refer to unmediated mental phenomena that are "there in the mind" to be observed in their pure form through introspection. Thus, experience is the construction of personal or subjective situations.

(7a) The notion of psychic reality, so important in psychoanalytic interpretation, is embraced by the rule that the term experience refers to actions and modes of action.

(7b) The experience of self is an action or set of actions in various modes.

(7c) The experience of passivity is an action or a set of actions in a particular mode.

(7d) Emotional experience is an action or set of actions in various modes (see also rule 3b). As such, it is neither ineffable nor privileged, though the agent may define it crudely or keep it more or less secret from others and perhaps even from himself or herself. Emotion is not experienced in the sense of that which is undergone; emotion is enacted, that is, it is the making of a certain kind of experience.

(7e) Using metaphors is one way of performing the action of experiencing; it is not a way of talking about experience already undergone. There is no *it* that metaphors capture and so there is no way of testing the truth of a metaphoric construction of experience when one has only the metaphor to work with. Thus, it is self-contradictory to assert—it is so often asserted—that certain experiences can be expressed *only* metaphorically; for if the assertion is true, then there is no way of assessing the metaphor against its referent and so no basis for making the claim in the first place. Although it is often the case that metaphoric statements are all one works with or encounters, that is another matter altogether. It is also another matter when one uses metaphor deliberately as sheer literary adornment: then there is an *it* that one could just as well state nonmetaphorically and in all likelihood has in fact already done so. No doubt there are ambiguous and transitional cases in this regard, the study of which should shed further light on the possibilities and limitations of action language.

(7f) Psychoanalytic interpretation of subjective experience can, therefore, only be the interpretation of the analysand's interpretations; for it never deals directly with experience unmediated by some personal construction of it.

(8) Actions may be stated in terms of their reasons, that is, the personal meanings of doing them, what they are about, their point, the goals they imply, and the situations they imply. As with actions, these reasons may be stated on any level of generality or abstractness.

(8a) Actions do not have causes. Although causes of actions, in the sense of their necessary and sufficient conditions, may seem to be ascertainable, this is simply not the case; for within the action system these causes must always be mediated by the person's interpretations, constructions, or understanding of them; consequently, an infinite regress would be entailed by any effort to state the cause of a personal interpretation, in that that cause would also be mediated by personal interpretation, and so on ad infinitum.

(8b) The idea of causes has a place only in the behavioristic approach to people. In that approach mediation is ignored and behavior (not action) is what the independent observer or experimenter says it is, not what the agent says it is, and particularly not what the agent ultimately says it is in the course of his or her personal psychoanalysis.

(8c) The terms *motives* and *motivation,* when used in any other sense than reasons (as given above), are inadmissible in action language; for when they are used in other senses, these terms imply that actions must be propelled in order to be performed, that is, must have a force behind them or below them ("deeper" than they) before they can be initiated and carried through (see also rule 1c).

(8d) An action may have multiple reasons.

(8e) Multiple actions may share the same reason.

(8f) The ideas of action and subjective situation are correlative; that is to say, they co-define each other. Consequently, there can be only one action corresponding to a situation or, to allow for ambiguities, only similar actions in similar situations. To say this is not to reintroduce the casuality that was disallowed in rule 8a; it is just to make clear the logical implications of the concepts we are now using.

(8g) The designation of actions is also their interpretation or explanation; for if we work with reasons rather than causes, and if actions and their situations are correlative, then explanation (the answer to the question, "Why?") can only be designation of an action in other terms. These other terms should be better suited to the context of the question and its point than the terms called into question, in that to ask, "Why?" is to ask for another designation of an action. Consequently, the distinction between mere description and explanation no longer retains any force.

(9) One may not use inability words in connection with actions, for actions are not achievements; they are performances, doings. One may say of them only that they are or are not performed, and if performed, how they are performed (e.g., resolutely, incompetently, unconsciously). Thus, when people say that they cannot do an action or are unable to do it, they are referring to their not doing it, even though it may be inferrable that, unconsciously, they are refusing to do it while disclaiming their refusal by pleading inability.

(9a) A person may simply lack the muscular strength or special skills needed to perform certain actions, such as lifting a heavy weight or playing a Mozart sonata. But here we are in the realm of achievement where inability words are admissible and action and mode of action are not in question.

(9b) One designates refusal to perform an action as being an action of a certain sort; this action may be taken consciously, preconsciously, or unconsciously. "Won't" refers to an action of refusal that, logically, is distinct from the action one refuses to perform.

(10) Interpretively, the idea of the person serves only as a pointer. The person specifies the originator of the actions and modes of action in question and nothing more than that; it refers to John, Mary, you, or me. One interprets actions and their modes, not persons. Having dispensed with propulsive energies and psychodynamics, mental structures and functions, and spatial notions of the self, nothing is left for the term person but to be a pointer. No loss of content is entailed by this restricted use of the idea of the person; it is just that the content hitherto ascribed to the person, ego, or self is now taken up under the aspect of the person's actions and modes of action.

(10a) One must assume that some criteria of organismic and social identity are satisfied or, in other words, that there is sufficient organismic continuity and personal recognizability for it to make sense to refer to anyone at all—in fact, for it to make sense to speak of anyone's referring to something. Admittedly, there exists a great range of philosophical questions concerning just what these criteria are or should be, but I do not think I am required even to begin to answer them at this point in the argument.

(11) A language does not depend for its existence on words or words alone, though to a considerable extent our world is a world of words.

(11a) Psychoanalytic interpretation, while it traffics especially with words, may and does also take into account the great variety of "expressive movements" and other nonverbal communicative actions, and, in the psychosomatic border territory, it even takes into account the bodily changes that are concomitants of actions, particularly of the emotion-actions and their modes.

(12) As a set of rules for saying things, a language is not subject to tests of truth or falsity.

(12a) Neither metapsychology nor action language is true or false; in either case, it is always a question of whether one is following the rules consistently so as to be always constructing facts of the same kind and interrelating them in an orderly and enlightening fashion. In addition to consistency, one may assess the logical coherence and the contextual utility of the individual rules and of the language as a whole.

(12b) There is, however, a sense in which a system that is more consistently applicable, more coherent, and more useful than another is the truer one of the two or has more truth value. This sense may be ascribed to the fact the two languages in question here—metapsychology and action language—are technical languages or metalanguages that have been designed specifically for the psychoanalytic study of human beings. In this view of the matter, one could, I think, legitimately assert that action language is truer than metapsychology. And this is part of what I am asserting by calling action language the native tongue of psychoanalysis.

To illustrate briefly the simultaneous application of all these rules, though without trying to be all-inclusive about it, I shall discuss the admonition, "Look before you leap." Both looking and leaping are actions. Both terms subsume constituent actions: in the case of looking, the constituents include the thought-actions of surveying the possibilities, anticipating and weighing the consequences, and relying in this regard on one's remembering comparable instances in the past; in the case of leaping, the constituents include performances that amount to leaping in whatever specific sense that metaphor is intended (e.g., deciding, speaking, objecting). Someone else might, however, designate the action differently—for instance, as merely "holding up the works." Indeed, the looking may extend over a considerable stretch of time. At the same time, the interpreter may consider looking before leaping as a constituent of a higher-order action such as conducting oneself responsibly, avoiding dangers in the environment, or obsessively avoiding subjective danger situations by procrastinating and doubting. In this last respect, the interpreter might also designate it as unconsciously manipulating others in order both to protect and torture them; in which case he or she would be viewing it either as a complex action with paradoxical ("conflicting") constituents or as paradoxical actions being performed simultaneously by one and the same person. These last few statements give the reasons, not the causes, of looking before leaping.

In the end, the person might decide to refrain from leaping while continuing to wish to leap, perhaps unconsciously: then, the refraining from leaping would be an action, too, and it might be continued indefinitely; concurrently, the leaping would become a conditional or would-be action, one that the analyst would have to take into account in order to understand the analysand's subsequent actions and modes of action in the same or similar circumstances. Among other possibilities, refraining from leaping may be a refusal to leap—a "won't" that is the reason for the "don't," but in no case is refraining or refusing a "can't." Looking before leaping may describe a momentary or circumscribed specific action or a lifetime of complex action.

3. Concluding Remarks

(1) I have been prescriptive only about systematic discourse. Fundamentally, I have not concerned myself with the languages of analytic sessions and everyday life even though, as I have demonstrated throughout these essays, especially in connection with disclaimed actions and concepts of self and identity, my discussions do have significant implications for these appropriately informal languages; for there are different ways of being informal, and some ways may be better suited for dealing with certain issues than others. Because I have concerned myself chiefly with systematic discourse, I think I am safe from the charge of advocating the use of a language that will impoverish our existence. Any systematic language entails a limiting and reductive approach to the manifold possibilities of constituting (not "representing") phenomena. Thus, those who object to any such limiting and reduction are, in effect, objecting to any systematic thinking at all. They are challenging the idea of any such enterprise, not my particular enterprise, let alone the manner in which I have executed it. I would add this final consideration to my response to the charge of impoverishing existance: even for the clinical or everyday rela-

tionship, action language is often the most direct and richly evocative of those available to us; we do often use it and there is room for considerable development of this resource. In any case, it is always possible that thinking about thinking or developing language about language, with all its necessary circularity and inevitable pitfalls, will in and of itself increase the range of personal existence; for these projects are perhaps the most distinctively human actions of them all.

(2) A psychoanalyst surveying the contents of this book might justly conclude that my coverage of essential topics is incomplete. In particular, he or she might insist that I should have systematically covered the topics of psychopathology and the theory and technique of psychoanalysis before I claimed to have identified and developed further the native tongue of psychoanalysis. This critical reader might grant that I have frequently, even if briefly, dealt with just these topics: chapter 3 is, in one of its main aspects, a discussion of the theory of the psychoanalytic process; chapter 7 includes discussions of errors, compulsion, and conflict; chapter 11 deals specifically and at some length with resistance; and throughout the book there are numerous comments on symptoms, transference, and the problems and methods of clinical psychoanalysis, including the implications and consequences of the words through which interpretations are created. Nevertheless, he or she might still insist that all these discussions have been primarily in the service of developing theoretical points rather than having been parts of a full-scale and formal discussion of clinical analysis and psychopathology, and insist further that many of these discussions have remained in the abstract areas traditionally covered by metapsychological essays and have been consistently oriented toward those essays, especially those by Freud and Hartmann. The critical reader might also grant that it is conceivable that he or she might independently think through the implications and consequences of my discussions for these relatively neglected topics and still insist that it is my burden to show how *I* would do this thinking through of action language, how *I* would test my ideas in the clinical crucible.

To these charges I must plead guilty, though in my own defense I would say that I am guilty of a lesser offense than that charged and that there are important mitigating considerations to be taken into account. It is a lesser offense because I have consistently couched my discussions in terms that apply directly to psychoanalytic interpretation or could do so with only a little modification—far more so, in fact, than is usual in formal metapsychological essays.

The mitigating considerations are of two kinds: (a) so long as one retains the clinical method and situation as the context of theoretical endeavors, one's first task of importance is to identify and clarify problems in the existing theory, to ask new and strategically significant questions, to propose reconceptualizations that seem to help answer these questions, and to make explicit and organize the rules for using these concepts in formulating basic propositions—and this is just what I have undertaken to do in this book; (b) however magically one may think of time, even to the point of unconsciously stopping the clock or removing its hands, one must also sooner or later face the fact that time continues on its serial course, with the result that one can get only so much done during a particular stretch of time. Which is another way of saying that although I realize how much remains to be done in the future, I do not find in that realization a compelling argument against presenting at this point a piece of work that is certainly not lacking in scope and detail. I might also mention in this connection that I have already begun a number of projects to expand the scope and detail of action language in the way that is being urged. These are projects on the theory of the psychoanalytic process viewed as a life-historical investigation defined primarily in the terms of action and its modes; on further refining the idea of conflict; on free association; on "inhibitions, symptoms, and anxiety"; on transference; and on the technique of interpretation. Some of this material should appear in print in the near future; some will not appear for a long while. Perhaps in time it will all add up to a second volume on action language.

To put these remarks in yet another way: my writing this book is the kind of action that can have no definite end; for in Balint's (1952) felicitous phrase, it is a "new beginning" and so its future must be open-ended. Its conclusion can only be an interruption.

References

Abel, L. ed. 1967. *Moderns on Tragedy.* Greenwich, Conn.: Fawcett Premier Books.

Abraham, K. 1924. A short study of the development of the libido, viewed in the light of mental disorders. In *Selected papers on psychoanalysis.* New York: Basic Books, 1954.

Anscombe, G.E.M. 1956. Intention. In *Essays in philosophical psychology,* ed. D.F. Gustafson. Garden City, New York: Anchor Books, 1964.

――――. 1958. Pretending. In *Philosophy of mind,* ed. S. Hampshire. New York: Harper & Row.

Apflebaum, B. 1966. On ego psychology: a critique of the structural approach to psychoanalytic theory. *Int. J. Psychoanal.* 47: 451-75.

Applegarth, A. 1971. Comments on aspects of the theory of psychic energy. *J. Amer. Psychoanal. Ass.* 19: 379-416.

Aristotle. *Ethics.* trans. J.A.K. Thomson. Baltimore, Md.: Penguin Books, 1953.

Austin, J.L. 1946. Other minds. In *Philosophical papers,* ed. J.O. Urmson and G.J. Warnock. Oxford: Clarendon Press, 1961.

――――. 1956. A plea for excuses. In *Philosophical papers,* ed. J.O. Urmson and G.J. Warnock. Oxford: Clarendon Press, 1961.

――――. 1957-8. Pretending. In *Philosophical papers,* ed. J.O. Urmson and G.J. Warnock. Oxford: Clarendon Press, 1961.

Balint, M. 1952. *Primary love and psycho-analytic technique.* London: Tavistock Publications, 1966.

Basch, M. 1973. Psychoanalysis and theory formation. *Annual of Psychoanal:* 1: 39-52.

Berlin, I. 1969. A note on Vico's concept of knowledge. *New York Rev. of Books.* 12/8: 23-6.

Bibring, E. 1936. The development and problems of the theory of the instincts. *Int. J. Psychoanal.* 50: 293-308.

――――. 1953. The mechanism of depression. In *Affective disorders,* ed P. Greenacre. New York: Int. Univ. Press.

Binswanger, L. 1936. Freud's conception of man in the light of anthropology. In *Being-in-the-world,* L. Binswanger. New York: Harper Torchbooks.

――――. 1946. The existential analytic school of thought. In *Existence: a new dimension in psychiatry and psychology,* eds. R. May, E. Angel, and H.F. Ellenberger. New York: Basic Books, 1958.

――――. 1963. *Selected papers of Ludwig Binswanger.* New York: Harper, 1967.

Blos, P. 1962. *On adolescence: a psychoanalytic interpretation.* New York: The Free Press of Glencoe.

――――. 1967. The second individuation process of adolescence. *Psychoanalytic Study of the Child.* 22: 162-86.

Bradley, A.C. 1904. *Shakespearean tragedy*. New York: World Publ. Co. Meridian Books, 1955.

———. 1909. *Oxford lectures on poetry*. London: Macmillan, 1926.

Brand, M. ed. 1970. *The nature of human action*. Glenview, Ill.: Scott, Foresman.

Brentano, F. 1874. *Psychology from an empirical standpoint*, trans. A. Rancurello, D. Terrell, and L. McAlister. London: Routledge and Kegan Paul, 1973.

Breuer, J., and Freud, S. 1893-95. Studies on hysteria. Stand. ed., vol. 2, London: Hogarth Press.

Brierley, M. 1937. Affects in theory and practice. In *Trends in psychoanalysis*. London: Hogarth Press and The Institute of Psychoanalysis, 1951.

Brooks, C. 1939. *Modern poetry and the tradition*. Chapel Hill: Univ. of N. Carolina Press.

———. ed. 1955. *Tragic themes in western literature*. New Haven: Yale Univ. Press.

Buber, M. 1923. *I and thou*. 2nd ed. New York: The Scribner Library, 1958.

Butcher, S.H. 1907. *Aristotle's theory of poetry and fine arts*. 4th ed. New York: Dover, 1951.

Carr, E.H. 1961. *What is history?* New York: Vintage Books, 1967.

Casey, E. 1972. Freud's theory of reality. *Rev. Metaphys.* 25: 659-90.

Deutsch, H. 1944, 1945. *The psychology of women*, vols. 1 and 2. New York: Grune and Stratton.

Edelson, M. 1972. Language and dreams: the interpretation of dreams revisited. *Psychoanal. Study of the Child* 27: 203-82.

Eissler, K. 1953. The effect of the structure of the ego on psychoanalytic technique, *J. Amer. Psychoanal. Ass.* 1: 104-43.

Eissler, R.A. and Eissler, K.R. 1964. Heinz Hartmann: a biographical sketch. *Bull. Menninger Clin.* 28: 289-301.

Erikson, E. 1950. *Childhood and Society*. New York: Norton.

———. 1956. The problem of ego identity. *J. Amer. Psychoanal. Ass.* 4: 56-121.

Escalona, S.K. 1968. *The roots of individuality: normal patterns of development in infancy*. Chicago: Aldine Press.

Fairbairn, W.R.D. 1952. *An object-relations theory of the personality*. New York: Basic Books, 1954.

Fenichel, O. 1941. *Problems of psychoanalytic technique*. Albany, New York: Psychoanalytic Quarterly, Inc.

———. 1945. *The psychoanalytic theory of neurosis*. New York: Norton.

Fingarette, H. 1963. *The self in transformation*. New York: Basic Books.

Francis, J.J. 1970. Panel on "Protest and Revolution." *Int. J. Psychoanal.* 51: 211-18.

Freud, A. 1936. *The ego and the mechanisms of defense*. New York: Int. Univ. Press, 1946.

———. 1958. Adolescence. *Psychoanal. Study of the Child* 13: 255-78.

Freud, S. 1905a. Fragment of an analysis of a case of hysteria. Stand. ed., vol. 7. London: Hogarth Press.

———. 1905b. Three essays on the theory of sexuality. Stand. ed., vol. 7. London: Hogarth Press.

———. 1905c. Psychopathic characters on the stage. Stand. ed., vol. 7. London: Hogarth Press.

———. 1909a. Analysis of a phobia in a five-year-old boy. Stand. ed., vol. 10. London: Hogarth Press.

———. 1909b. Notes upon a case of obsessional neurosis. Stand. ed., vol. 10. London: Hogarth Press.

———. 1911. Psycho-analytic notes on an autobiographical account of a case of paranoia (dementia paranoides). Stand. ed., vol. 12. London: Hogarth Press.

———. 1912. The dynamics of transference. Stand. ed., vol. 12. London: Hogarth Press.

———. 1913a. On beginning the treatment: further recommendations on the technique of psycho-analysis, I. Stand. ed., vol. 12. London: Hogarth Press.

———. 1913b. Totem and taboo. Stand. ed., vol. 13. London: Hogarth Press.

———. 1914. Remembering, repeating and working-through: further recommendations on the technique of psycho-analysis, II. Stand. ed., vol. 12. London: Hogarth Press.

———. 1915a. Observations on transference love. Stand. ed., vol. 12. London: Hogarth Press.

———. 1915b. Instincts and their vicissitudes. Stand. ed., vol. 14. London: Hogarth Press.

———. 1915c. The unconscious. Stand. ed., vol. 14. London: Hogarth Press.

———. 1915d. Thoughts for the times on war and death. Stand. ed., vol. 14. London: Hogarth Press.

———. 1916a. Some character-types met with in psycho-analysis. Stand. ed., vol. 14. London: Hogarth Press.

———. 1916b. Introductory lectures on psycho-analysis: parts I-II. Stand. ed., vol. 15. London: Hogarth Press.

———. 1917a. Mourning and melancholia. Stand. ed., vol. 14. London: Hogarth Press.

———. 1917b. Introductory lectures on psychoanalysis: part III. Stand. ed., vol. 16. London: Hogarth Press.

———. 1917c. A difficulty in the path of psychoanalysis. Stand. ed., vol. 17. London: Hogarth Press.

———. 1920a. Beyond the pleasure principle. Stand. ed., vol. 18. London: Hogarth Press.

———. 1920b. The psychogenesis of a case of homosexuality in a woman. Stand. ed., vol. 18. London: Hogarth Press.

———. 1923a. The ego and the id. Stand. ed., vol. 19. London: Hogarth Press.

———. 1923b. The infantile genital organization. Stand. ed., vol. 19. London: Hogarth Press.

———. 1925a. Some additional notes on dream-interpretation as a whole. Stand. ed., vol. 19. London: Hogarth Press.

———. 1925b. Negation. Stand. ed., vol. 19. London: Hogarth Press.

———. 1925c. Some psychical consequences of the anatomical distinction between the sexes. Stand. ed., vol. 19. London: Hogarth Press.

————. 1926. Inhibitions, symptoms and anxiety. Stand. ed., vol. 20. London: Hogarth Press.

————. 1927. The future of an illusion. Stand. ed., vol. 21. London: Hogarth Press.

————. 1928. Dostoevsky and parricide. Stand. ed., vol. 21. London: Hogarth Press.

————. 1930. Civilization and its discontents. Stand. ed., vol. 21. London: Hogarth Press.

————. 1931. Female sexuality. Stand. ed., vol. 21. London: Hogarth Press.

————. 1933. New introductory lectures on psycho-analysis. Stand. ed., vol. 22. London: Hogarth Press.

————. 1937a. Analysis terminable and interminable. Stand. ed., vol. 23. London: Hogarth Press.

————. 1937b. Constructions in analysis. Stand. ed., vol. 23. London: Hogarth Press.

————. 1940. An outline of psycho-analysis. Stand. ed., vol. 23. London: Hogarth Press.

Frye, N. 1957. *Anatomy of criticism.* New York: Athaneum, 1967.

Gedo, J.E., and Goldberg, A. 1973. *Models of the mind: a psychoanalytic theory.* Chicago: Univ. of Chicago Press.

Gill, M.M. 1963. Topography and systems in psychoanalytic theory. *Psychological Issues,* Monograph No. 10.

Gillespie, R. 1971. Aggression and instinct theory. *Int. J. Psychoanal.* 52: 155-60.

Glover, E. 1966. Metapsychology or metaphysics: a psychoanalytic essay. *Psychoanal. Quart.* 35: 173-90.

Greenson, R.R. 1954. The struggle against identification. *J. Amer. Psychoanal. Ass.* 2: 200-17.

Grossman, W.I., and Simon, B. 1969. Anthropomorphism: motive, meaning, and causality in psychoanalytic theory. *Psychoanal. Study of the Child* 24: 78-114.

Guntrip, H. 1967. The concept of psychodynamic science. *Int. J. Psychoanal.* 48: 32-43.

————. 1968. *Schizoid phenomena, object relations and the self.* London: Hogarth Press.

Habermas, J. 1971. *Knowledge and human interests.* Boston: Beacon Press.

Hampshire, S. 1959. *Thought and action.* New York: Viking Press.

————. 1962. Disposition and memory. *Int. J. Psychoanal.* 43: 59-68.

Hartmann, H. 1927. Understanding and explanation. In *Essays on ego psychology.* New York: Int. Univ. Press, 1964.

————. 1939a. Psychoanalysis and the concept of health. In *Essays on ego psychology.* New York: Int. Univ. Press, 1964.

————. 1939b. *Ego psychology and the problems of adaptation.* New York: Int. Univ. Press, 1958.

————. 1947. On rational and irrational action. In *Essays on ego psychology.* New York: Int. Univ. Press, 1964.

————. 1950. Comments on the psychoanalytic theory of the ego. In *Essays on ego psychology.* New York: Int. Univ. Press, 1964.

————. 1951. Technical implications of ego psychology. In *Essays on ego psychology*. New York: Int. Univ. Press, 1964.

————. 1952. The mutual influences in the development of ego and id. In *Essays on ego psychology*. New York: Int. Univ. Press, 1964.

————. 1955. On the theory of sublimation. In *Essays on ego psychology*. New York: Int. Univ. Press, 1964.

————. 1956. Notes on the reality principle. In *Essays on ego psychology*. New York: Int. Univ. Press, 1964.

————. 1959. Psychoanalysis as a scientific theory. In *Essays on ego psychology*. New York: Int. Univ. Press, 1964.

————. 1960. *Psychoanalysis and moral values*. New York: Int. Univ. Press.

————. 1964. *Essays on ego psychology, selected problems in psychoanalytic theory*. New York: Int. Univ. Press.

———— and Kris, E. 1945. The genetic approach in psychoanalysis. *Psychoanal. Study of the Child* 1: 11-30.

————, ————, and Loewenstein, R.M. 1946. Comments on the formation of psychic structure. *Psychoanal. Study of the Child* 2: 11-18.

————. 1947. Notes on the theory of aggression. *Psychoanal. Study of the Child* 3/4: 9-36.

————. 1964. Papers on psychoanalytic psychology. *Psychological Issues*, Monograph No. 14.

Hartmann, H., and Loewenstein, R.M. 1962. Notes on the superego. *Psychoanal. Study of the Child* 17: 42-81.

Hayman, A. 1969. What do we mean by "id"? *J. Amer. Psychoanal. Ass.* 17: 353-80.

Holt, R.R. 1965. A review of some of Freud's biological assumptions and their influence on his theories. In *Psychoanalysis and current biological thought*, ed. N.S. Greenfield and W.C. Lewis. Madison: Univ. of Wisconsin Press.

————. 1967. Beyond vitalism and mechanism; Freud's concept of psychic energy. In *Science and psychoanalysis*, vol. 11, ed. J.H. Masserman. New York: Grune and Stratton.

————. 1972. Freud's mechanistic and humanistic images of man. In *Psychoanalysis and contemporary science*, vol. I, ed. R.R. Holt and E. Peterfreund. New York: Macmillan.

Home, H.J. 1966. The concept of mind. *Int. J. Psychoanal.* 47: 43-9.

Horney, K. 1924. On the genesis of the castration-complex in women. *Int. J. Psychoanal.* 5: 50-65.

————. 1926. The flight from womanhood: the masculinity complex in women as viewed by men and by women. *Int. J. Psychoanal.* 7: 324-39.

————. 1932. The dread of women. *Int. J. Psychoanal.* 13: 348-61.

————. 1933. The denial of the vagina. *Int. J. Psychoanal.* 14: 57-70.

Jackson, S. 1967. Subjective experience and the concept of energy. *Perspectives in biology and medicine* 10: 602-26.

Jacobson, E. 1964. *The self and the object world*. New York: Int. Univ. Press.

Jaspers, K. 1952. The tragic: awareness; basic characteristics; fundamental interpretations. In *Tragedy: modern essays in criticism*, ed. L. Michel and R.B. Sewall. Englewood Cliffs, N.J.: Prentice-Hall, 1963.

Jones, E. 1929. Fear, guilt, and hate. In *Papers on psychoanalysis*. 5th ed. Boston: Beacon Press, 1961.

Kaufman, W. 1968. *Tragedy and philosophy*. Garden City, New York: Doubleday.

Kenny, A. 1963. *Action, emotion and will*. New York: Humanities Press.

Klein, G.S. 1966a. The several grades of memory. In *Psychoanalysis—a general psychology*, eds. R.M. Loewenstein *et al.* New York: Int. Univ. Press.

———. 1966b. Unpublished paper presented to Western New England Psychoanalytic Society.

———. 1967. Peremptory ideation: structure and force in motivated ideas. In *Motives and thought: psychoanalytic essays in honor of David Rapaport*, ed. R.R. Holt. New York: Int. Univ. Press.

———. 1969. Freud's two theories of sexuality: perspectives to change in psychoanalytic theory. In *Clinical-cognitive psychology: models and integrations*, ed. L. Breger, New York: Prentice-Hall.

———. 1970. *Perception, motives, and personality*. New York: Knopf.

Klein, M. 1935. A contribution to the psychogenesis of manic-depressive states. *Contributions to psycho-analysis 1921-1945*. New York: McGraw-Hill, 1964.

Kohut, H. 1959. Introspection, empathy, and psychoanalysis. *J. Amer. Psychoanal. Ass.* 7: 459-83.

———. 1966. Forms and transformations of narcissism. *J. Amer. Psychoanal. Ass.* 14: 243-72.

———. 1971. *The analysis of the self: a systematic approach to the psychoanalytic treatment of narcissistic personality disorders*. Monograph Series of the Psychoanalytic Study of the Child, No. 4. New York: Int. Univ. Press.

Kreiger, M. 1960. *The tragic vision*. Chicago: Univ. of Chicago Phoenix Books, 1966.

Kris, E. 1937. Ego development and the comic: In *Psychoanalytic explorations in art*. New York: Int. Univ. Press, 1952.

———. 1952. *Psychoanalytic explorations in art*. New York: Int. Univ. Press.

———. 1956a. The personal myth: a problem in psychoanalytic technique. *J. Amer. Psychoanal. Ass.* 4: 653-81.

———. 1956b. The recovery of childhood memories in psychoanalysis. *Psychoanal. Study of the Child*. 11: 54-88.

Kuhn, T.S. 1970. *The structure of scientific revolutions*. 2d. ed. Chicago: Univ. of Chicago Press.

Laing, R.D. 1969a. *The divided self: a study of sanity and madness*. 2nd. ed. New York: Pantheon Books.

———. 1969b. *The self and others: further studies in sanity and madness*. 2nd. ed. New York: Pantheon Books.

Langer, S. 1967. *Mind: an essay on human feeling*, vol. 1. Baltimore: The Johns Hopkins Press.

Lauter, P., ed. 1964. *Theories of comedy*. Garden City, New York: Doubleday Anchor Books.

Leites, N. 1971. *The new ego*. New York: Science House.

Lesser, S.O. 1957. *Fiction and the unconscious*. Boston: Beacon Press.

Levin, D.C. 1969. The self: a contribution to its place in theory and technique. *Int. J. Psychoanal.* 50: 41-52.

————. 1970. Summary of introductory remarks by the author. In Discussion of 'the self: a contribution to its place in theory and technique'. *Int. J. Psychoanal.* 51: 175-81.

Lewin, B.D. 1952. Phobic symptoms and dream interpretation. *Psychoanal. Quart.* 21: 295-322.

————. 1971. Metaphor, mind, and manikin. *Psychoanal. Quart.* 50: 6-39.

Loewald, H.W. 1960. On the therapeutic action of psychoanalysis. *Int. J. Psychoanal.* 41: 16-33.

————. 1962. Internalization, separation, mourning and the superego. *Psychoanal. Quart.* 31: 483-504.

Loewenstein, R.M. 1951. The problem of interpretation. *Psychoanal. Quart.* 20: 1-14.

————. 1966. Heinz Hartmann: psychology of the ego. In *Psychoanalytic pioneers*, ed. F. Alexander *et al.* New York: Basic Books.

MacIntyre, A.C. 1958. *The unconscious: a conceptual analysis.* New York: Humanities Press.

Macmurray, J. 1957. *The self as agent.* London: Faber and Faber.

Mahler, M.S. 1968. *On human symbiosis and the vicissitudes of individuation*, vol. 1. *Infantile psychosis.* New York: Int. Univ. Press.

Melden, A.I. 1961. *Free action.* New York: Humanities Press.

Michel, L., and Sewall, R.B., eds. 1963. *Tragedy: modern essays in criticism.* Englewood Cliffs, N.J.: Prentice-Hall.

Myerson, P.G. 1963. Assimilation of unconscious material. *Int. J. Psychoanal.* 44: 317-27.

————. 1965. Modes of insight. *J. Amer. Psychoanal. Ass.* 13: 771-92.

Nietzsche, F. 1870. *The birth of tragedy.* Garden City, N.Y.: Doubleday Anchor Books, 1956.

Novey, S. 1968. *The second look: the reconstruction of personal history in psychiatry and psychoanalysis.* Baltimore: The Johns Hopkins Press.

Pears, D. 1969. *Ludwig Wittgenstein.* New York: Viking Press.

Prelinger, E. 1972. Does psychoanalysis have a future in American psychology? *Psychoanal. Quart.* 51: 90-103.

Rangell, L. 1965. The scope of Heinz Hartmann. *Int. J. Psychoanal.* 46: 5-30.

————. 1969. The intrapsychic process and its analysis—a recent line of thought and its current implications. *Int. J. Psychoanal.* 50: 65-77.

Rapaport, D. 1951. *Organization and pathology of thought.* New York: Columbia Univ. Press.

————. 1953. Some metapsychological considerations concerning activity and passivity. In *The collected papers of David Rapaport*, ed. M.M. Gill. New York: Basic Books, 1967.

————. 1959. The structure of psychoanalytic theory: a systematizing attempt. *Psychological issues*, Monograph No. 6. New York: Int. Univ. Press.

————. 1967. *The collected papers of David Rapaport*, ed. M.M. Gill. New York: Basic Books.

———— and Gill, M.M. 1959. The points of view and assumptions of metapsychology. *Int. J. Psychoanal.* 40: 153-62.

Reich, W. 1933. *Character-analysis.* New York: Orgone Institute Press, 1949.

Rescher, N. 1970. On the characterization of actions. In *The nature of human action.* ed. M. Brand. Glenview, Ill.: Scott, Foresman, 1970.

Ricoeur, P. 1970. *Freud and philosophy: an essay in interpretation.* New Haven: Yale Univ. Press.

Rycroft, C. 1966. Introduction: causes and meaning. In *Psychoanalysis observed.* London: Constable.

_____. 1968. *A critical dictionary of psychoanalysis.* New York: Basic Books.

Ryle, G. 1949. *The concept of mind.* New York: Barnes and Noble, 1965.

Sandler, J., and Joffe, W.G. 1969. Towards a basic psycho-analytic model. *Int. J. Psychoanal.* 50: 79-90.

Sartre, J.P. 1943, *Existential psychoanalysis.* New York: Philosophical Library, 1953.

Schafer, R. 1959. Generative empathy in the treatment situation. *Psychoanal. Quart.* 28: 342-73.

_____. 1960. The loving and beloved superego in Freud's structural theory. *Psychoanal. Study of the Child* 15: 163-88.

_____. 1964. The clinical analysis of affects. *J. Amer. Psychoanal. Ass.* 12: 275-99.

_____. 1967a. Ego autonomy and the return of repression. *Int. J. Psychiat.* 3: 515-18.

_____. 1967b. Ideals, the ego ideal, and the ideal self. In *Motives and thought: psychoanalytic essays in honor of David Rapaport,* ed. R.R. Holt. *Psychological Issues,* Monograph 18/19: 129-74. New York: Int. Univ. Press.

_____. 1968a. The mechanisms of defense. *Int. J. Psychoanal.* 49: 49-62.

_____. 1968b. *Aspects of Internalization.* New York: Int. Univ. Press.

_____. 1968c. On the theoretical and technical conceptualization of activity and passivity. *Psychoanal. Quart.* 37: 173-98.

_____. 1970a. The psychoanalytic vision of reality. *Int. J. Psychoanal.* 51: 279-97.

_____. 1970b. An overview of Heinz Hartmann's contributions to psychoanalysis. *Int. J. Psychoanal.* 51: 425-46.

_____. 1970c. Requirements for a critique of the theory of cartharsis. *J. Consult. Clin. Psychol.* 35: 13-7.

_____. 1972a. Review: *Perception, motives, and personality* by G.S. Klein. *Psychoanal. Quart.* 41: 265-8.

_____. 1972b. Internalization: process or fantasy? *Psychoanal. Study of the Child* 27: 411-36.

_____. 1973a. Action: its place in psychoanalytic interpretation and theory. *Annual of Psychoanal.* 1: 159-96.

_____. 1973b. The concepts of self and identity and the experience of separation-individuation in adolescence. *Psychoanal. Quart.* 42: 42-59.

_____. 1973c. The idea of resistance. *Int. J. Psychoanal.* 54: 259-85.

_____. 1974a. Problems in Freud's psychology of women. *J. Amer. Psychoanal. Ass.* 22: 459-85.

_____. 1974b. On the theory of the psychoanalytic process. Paper read at the December 1974 meetings of the American Psychoanalytic Association.

———. 1975a. Psychoanalysis without psychodynamics. *Int. J. Psychoanal.* 56: 41-55.

———. 1975b. Emotion in the language of action. In *Psychological Issues*, Monograph No. 36. New York: Int. Univ. Press.

Scheler, M. 1954. On the tragic. In *Tragedy: modern essays in criticism*, eds. L. Michel and R.B. Sewall. Englewood Cliffs, N.J.: Prentice-Hall, 1963.

Sewall, R.B. 1959. *The vision of tragedy*. New Haven: Yale Univ. Press.

Simon, B. 1973. Plato and Freud: the mind in conflict and the mind in dialogue. *Psychoanal. Quart.* 42: 91-122.

Spiegel, L.A. 1958. Comments on the psychoanalytic psychology of adolescence. *Psychoanal. Study of the Child* 13: 296-308.

———. 1959. The self, the sense of self, and perception. *Psychoanal. Study of the Child* 14: 81-109.

Stone, L. 1961. *The psychoanalytic situation*. New York: Int. Univ. Press.

Unamuno, M. de. 1921. The man of flesh and bone. In *Tragedy: modern essays in criticism*, eds. L. Michel and R.B. Sewall. Englewood Cliffs, N.J.: Prentice-Hall, 1963.

Waelder, R. 1930. The principle of multiple function. *Psychoanal. Quart.* 15: (1936) 45-62.

Watts, H.H. 1955. Myth and drama. In *Tragedy: modern essays in criticism*, eds. L. Michel and R.B. Sewall. Englewood Cliffs, N.J.: Prentice-Hall, 1963.

Webster's new collegiate dictionary. 2nd ed. 1953. Springfield, Mass.: G & S. Merriam.

Williams, B.A.O. 1956. Personal identity and individuation. In *Essays in philosophical psychology*, ed. D.F. Gustafson. Garden City, New York: Anchor Books, 1964.

Winnicott, D.W. 1958. *Collected papers: through pediatrics to psychoanalysis*. New York: Basic Books.

———. 1965. *The maturational process and the facilitating environment: studies in the theory of emotional development*. New York: Int. Univ. Press.

Wittgenstein, L. 1934-1935. *The blue and brown books*. New York: Harper Torchbooks, 1965.

———. 1945-1949. *Philosophical investigations*. 3rd ed. New York: Macmillan.

Wollheim R. 1974. *Freud: a collection of critical essays*. Garden City, N.Y.: Doubleday Anchor Press.

Index

Index

24 Visions of Reality Inherent in psychoanalytic thought & practice

      — hopefulness

27-31 1. Comic Vision — implication of Timelessness; cyclic

        Conflict betw. defending old & Transformation

   2. Romantic vision — life as quest.
       Idealization

   3. Tragic — linear Time; internal split; "tragic Knot"
        aims at momentous aspects; values Total involvement

   4. ironic — readiness To seak out contradictions, ambiguities,
        paradoxes
      aims at detachment, perspective

  psychoanalysis as study of human action   [speech-act]
     intro; 127, 128

  Disclaimed Action
     1. slip of Tongue
     2. Mind
133   "mind is something we do"
     3. Conflict

137 Refraining actions :

  "Thought is silenced speech"

139- Action